Praise for
The Faith Club

"Three mothers' engaging account of their interfaith dialogue. . . . The three charming narrators transform potentially dry theological discourses into personal, intimate heart-to-hearts. . . . An invitation to discussion that's hard to turn down—and a natural for book groups."
—*Kirkus*

"The world needs this book."

—*Library Journal*

"This book is the real thing: three tough, strong women take on each other's religious differences. Achieving a true sisterhood in faith that crosses the religious traditions, these sassy moms will knock you out."
—Asma Gull Hasan, author of *Why I Am a Muslim* and
American Muslims: The New Generation

"Millions of Americans crave a way to have interfaith conversation, but have no idea where to begin. This book is a great place to start. *The Faith Club* is unfailingly honest, always engaging, and even suspenseful. The authors have set a path that many more will want to follow. I raced to the end to see how it all turned out. Hurrah!"
—Bruce Feiler, author of *Walking the Bible* and
Where God Was Born

"I've enjoyed *The Faith Club* immensely. It's an extraordinary—maybe even unique—discussion of religions and their comparabilities. All three of you deserve congratulations and thanks for providing a path to enlightenment and reconciliation."

—Governor Mario Cuomo

"Idliby, Oliver, and Warner come across as intelligent, articulate, and caring people, but they also speak in ways that most of us would never dare. What they have done is truly courageous, confronting each other with the greatest respect about the things that each holds dearest . . . you can't help but get wrapped up in their personal stories."

—Sally Quinn, *On Faith*

"Violent conflict, painful contradiction, and heated controversy make up the headlines on religion today. But a deeper story is unfolding as well: Three contemporary women—Jew, Christian, and Muslim—search together across the divides of prejudice and fear. Their honesty becomes a path to connection; their courage leads into the ranges of the heart opened by their own religions. Working together, they each arrive where alone they could not go. Read this important book."

—Dr. William F. Vendley, Secretary General, World Conference of Religions for Peace

"I loved *The Faith Club* because it provides hope for mothers of all backgrounds that it is indeed possible to create dialogue among us in a post-9/11 world. The book is a brilliant blueprint for creating peace among diverse people everywhere. And if there's one thing about *The Faith Club* I have faith in, it's that it will catch fire among women's groups and book clubs across America."

—Donna Dees-Thomases, author of *Looking for a Few Good Moms* and founder of the Million Mom March

"A must-read. A major contribution to interfaith understanding that encourages dialogue, discussion, and debate to take us beyond ignorance, stereotypes, and misunderstanding and to a mutual understanding and respect so critical in these times."

—John L. Esposito, PhD, University Professor, Georgetown University, and author of *What Everyone Needs to Know about Islam*

"People who read their book are struck by how tough it is, how direct, how it sticks its chin out at the nasty conflicts that divide the three Abrahamic faiths. . . . At points, *The Faith Club* reads like a brutally honest, if bloodless, *Fight Club*."

—Gary Stern, *The* (Gannett) *Journal News*

"The women voice opinions and thoughts we all have or are exposed to but would never consider safe to speak about in a 'P.C.' climate. In so doing, they demonstrate that it is precisely in speaking the unspeakable with an attitude of humility and listening in an undefended posture that a way forward can be found."

—The Right Reverend Catherine S. Roskam,
Bishop Suffragan of the Episcopal Diocese of New York

The Faith Club

A Muslim, a Christian, a Jew—
Three Women Search for Understanding

Ranya Idliby
Suzanne Oliver
Priscilla Warner

FREE PRESS
New York   London   Toronto   Sydney

*f*P

FREE PRESS
A Division of Simon & Schuster, Inc.
1230 Avenue of the Americas
New York, NY 10020

First Free Press trade paperback edition June 2007

FREE PRESS and colophon are trademarks of Simon & Schuster, Inc.

For information about special discounts for bulk purchases,
please contact Simon & Schuster Special Sales:
1-800-456-6798 or business@simonandschuster.com

Designed by Davina Mock

Manufactured in the United States of America
15   17   19   20   18   16

The Library of Congress has catalogued the hardcover edition as follows:
Idliby, Ranya.
The faith club: a Muslim, Christian, Jew—three women search for understanding /
Ranya Idliby, Suzanne Oliver, Priscilla Warner.
p. cm.
Includes bibliographical references.
1. Idliby, Ranya. 2. Oliver, Suzanne. 3. Warner, Priscilla. 4. Religions—Relations.
5. Judaism—Relations—Christianity. 6. Christianity and other religions—Judaism.
7. Judaism—Relations—Islam. 8. Islam—Relations—Judaism. 9. Islam—
Relations—Christianity. 10. Christianity and other religions—Islam.
I. Oliver, Suzanne. II. Warner, Priscilla. III. Title.
BL410 .I35   2006
201'.5—dc22   2006045408

ISBN-13: 978-0-7432-9047-0
ISBN-10:   0-7432-9047-X
ISBN-13: 978-0-7432-9048-7 (Pbk)
ISBN-10:   0-7432-9048-8 (Pbk)

For Leia and Taymor
and all Abraham's children

Burdens are the foundations of ease
and bitter things the forerunners of pleasure.
—JELALLUDDIN RUMI

For Anne, Thomas, and Theodore,
with gratitude for my sister Kristin

Judge not, and you will not be judged;
condemn not, and you will not be condemned;
forgive, and you will be forgiven;
give, and it will be given to you;
good measure, pressed down, shaken together,
running over, will be put into your lap.
For the measure you give will be the measure you get back.
—LUKE 6:37

For Jimmy, Max, and Jack

When two people relate to each other
authentically and humanly,
God is the electricity that surges between them.
—MARTIN BUBER

Contents

Preface   1

CHAPTER ONE   In the Beginning   3

CHAPTER TWO   A Muslim, a Christian, and a Jew
Walk into a Room . . .   9

CHAPTER THREE   The Abrahamic Family Feud   26

CHAPTER FOUR   The Crucifixion Crisis   37

CHAPTER FIVE   Stop Stereotyping Me!   54

CHAPTER SIX   Could You Convert?   81

CHAPTER SEVEN   Oh, Where Are You, God?   96

CHAPTER EIGHT   Ranya's Madrassah   109

CHAPTER NINE   The Promised Land   123

CHAPTER TEN   Prayer   145

CHAPTER ELEVEN   Rituals   158

CHAPTER TWELVE   Intimations of Mortality   180

CHAPTER THIRTEEN   Conversations with a Priest,
an Imam, and a Rabbi   200

CHAPTER FOURTEEN   A Day of Atonement   218

CHAPTER FIFTEEN   Happy Holidays   241

Contents

CHAPTER SIXTEEN Facing Our Communities 248

CHAPTER SEVENTEEN Awakenings 257

CHAPTER EIGHTEEN Faltering Faith 272

CHAPTER NINETEEN From Here to Eternity 283

Bibliography 295

Acknowledgments 299

Reading Group Guide 305

How to Start a Faith Club 345

The Faith Club

Preface

Meet the Faith Club. We're three mothers from three faiths—Islam, Christianity, and Judaism—who got together to write a picture book for our children that would highlight the connections between our religions. But no sooner had we started talking about our beliefs and how to explain them to our children than our differences led to misunderstandings. Our project nearly fell apart.

We realized that before we could talk about what united us we had to confront what divided us in matters of faith, God, and religion. We had to reveal our own worst fears, prejudices, and stereotypes.

So we made a commitment to meet regularly. We talked in our living rooms over cups of jasmine tea and bars of dark chocolate. No question was deemed inappropriate, no matter how rude or politically incorrect. We taped our conversations and kept journals as we discussed everything from jihad to Jesus, heaven to holy texts. Somewhere along the way, our moments of conflict, frustration, and anger gave way to new understanding and great respect.

Now we invite you into our Faith Club to eavesdrop on our conversations. Come into our living rooms and share our life-altering experience. Perhaps when you're finished, you will want to have a faith club of your own.

CHAPTER ONE

In the Beginning

Ranya:

The phone rang on the morning of September 11th. It was my husband, screaming for me to turn on the TV. With sheer horror, I watched as the second plane hit the World Trade Center.

"Please don't let this be connected to Islam," I thought desperately.

As the city began to mourn, churches and temples opened their doors for worship and emotional support. I longed for a mosque, or a Muslim religious leader, an imam, who could help support my family during this horrific time. I needed a spiritual community, a safe haven where we could seek comfort.

Back then, I knew of no alternative Muslim voice that could represent the silent majority of Muslims, no nearby place where we could congregate. I did not feel comfortable at the mosque in our neighborhood, where women prayed separately from men. I wanted to feel respected. I longed to enter a mosque on an equal footing with Muslim men, to be treated as an equal, as I know I am in the eyes of God.

Tensions rose, and as some Muslims, or those mistaken for Muslims, were attacked or rounded up for questioning, I began to feel self-conscious about our Muslim identity. I was concerned and fearful for the security of my children as American Muslims. I avoided calling my son by his Muslim name, addressing him in public only by his nicknames, Ty and Timmy. When my grandmother came to visit, I asked her not to speak Arabic in public. And when my parents were in New York, they were approached by a stranger who advised them not to speak Arabic on the street. A well-meaning friend, trying to make me feel better (and warning me not to "take it the wrong way"), told me that my family and I "don't look Muslim." This, she thought, might protect us from discrimination. What were Muslims supposed to look like, I wondered?

My husband and I were challenged on both fronts, by Muslims abroad who questioned the very possibility of a future for our children as American Muslims of Arab descent, and on the home front, by the stereotypes and prejudices that were heightened by the attacks of 9/11. On street corners, people joked about Muslim martyrs "racing to heaven to meet their brown-eyed virgins," a supposed reference to the Quran, but something I had never heard before. While we took heart from our president's visit to the mosque in Washington, D.C., we were also aware of the voices within his own administration who felt he had gone too far and who maintained that, at its core, Islam was a militant and dangerous religion. I wondered who was representing my faith.

Although my husband and I had at first chosen to spare our children the details of the attacks, we soon found out that our kindergarten-age daughter, who was the only Muslim in her class, was learning a great deal from friends at school. We explained to her that evil men who were Arab and called themselves Muslim had performed an evil deed. Since her only experience of the Arab world overseas had involved her grandparents, she anxiously asked if her grandmother knew these men or was involved in any way.

Soon thereafter, my daughter came home from school and asked me a simple question: "Do we celebrate Hanukah or Christmas?" Her friends at school wanted to know. I wasn't sure how to respond. I worried that the reality of 9/11 had made it unworkable for my children to be both Muslim and American. Would their sense of belonging be compromised? Would they as Americans feel burdened by their religion and heritage? So far I'd tried to raise my children with moral character and pride in their Muslim heritage despite the fact that we did not practice many specific religious rituals or worship at a mosque. We do celebrate a commercial kind of Christmas. But we're Muslims. We believe Jesus was a prophet, not the son of God. How could I give my daughter an intelligent, clear answer that she could confidently deliver to other kindergarteners? Was there such an answer? As a concerned parent I created a challenge for myself: If I was unable to give my children good reasons why they should remain Muslims, other than out of pure ancestral loyalty, I would not ask them to remain true to Islam, a religion that had come to seem to me to be more of a burden than a privilege in America.

A student at heart, I started researching Islam looking for possible answers for my concerns. Soon, I stumbled upon the story of Muhammad's night flight journey and ascension to heaven, essentially an interfaith vision in which Muhammad rides a magical winged horse ridden before him by Jesus, Moses, and other biblical prophets. As he ascends a jeweled staircase to the threshold of the kingdom of God, Muhammad is welcomed by various prophets as a fellow brother and prophet. Along with Jesus and Moses, he stands at the Temple Mount in Jerusalem for communal prayers.

My heart raced with excitement as I read all this. I was dumbfounded. Why weren't Muslims telling the world this story? It was the perfect way to share the beauty and true voice within Islam when so many, including many Muslims, were so desperately looking for answers. The terror of September 11th turned my alienation and frustration into anger at those who had invoked Islam to justify such heinous crimes. I felt an urgent need to do something. I could no longer be apathetic; I could no longer resign myself to just accepting the prevailing image of Islam, if only for the sake of my children. Wouldn't it be wonderful, I thought, to find a Christian and Jewish mother to write a children's book with me that would highlight the connections within Judaism, Christianity, and Islam.

Suzanne:

In the fall of 2001, I was an ex-Catholic, happily participating in a vibrant Episcopal church in New York City, when that cozy, homogeneous community was confronted in very different ways by Islam and

Judaism. First, terrorists calling themselves Muslims crashed into the World Trade Center killing our neighbors, colleagues, and one parishioner. Then, days later, our neo-gothic, beautifully adorned church closed for renovation, and our Sunday services were moved to a modern synagogue, which had offered to share space with us.

As the 9/11 bombing challenged our perceptions of Islam and Muslims, our church's relocation to a temple tested our relationship with Judaism and Jews. Many of our church members went elsewhere rather than attend Sunday services there. To some, the setting was off-putting, to others a barricade-protected temple felt like a dangerous place in the aftermath of 9/11.

At the time New York was a city on high alert. Everyone speculated about how and when the terrorists would strike again, but we didn't have enough information to make an informed judgment. Who were these people? And why did they hate us? My book club started selecting books on the Middle East, and as I began my reading, I thought of a woman I greeted each morning at the school bus stop. Our daughters were in the same kindergarten class. I didn't know her background. She looked like a stylish blend of Europe and the Middle East, and her name, Ranya Idliby, sounded Middle Eastern to me.

One morning as we waited for the bus together, I asked her where she was from, and she told me that her parents were Palestinian refugees and that she was born in Kuwait and had grown up in Dubai and in McLean, Virginia. I had never heard of Dubai, but I nodded my head anyway. After hearing about Ranya's family history and her experience studying Middle Eastern politics, I invited her to join my book group discussion. To my surprise, a Jewish member of my book club then declined to host the next meeting. But the book club went on without that hostess, and Ranya and I started to become friends.

As our children played together we shared conversations about Islam, and I became intrigued by the roots Ranya said our religions shared. One afternoon she mentioned to me her idea to bring together a Muslim, a Jewish, and a Christian mother to write a children's book of miracles, and I jumped at the chance. The intent of the book—to educate children about our common heritage—seemed a necessary and noble goal in the months after September 11th. So I told Ranya I'd love to be part of her trio and offered to find a Jewish woman to join us. A friend recommended Priscilla Warner for our project. She had two sons and experience writing children's books.

It was an awkward first call. "Hi, Priscilla. I'm calling because you're Jewish; you're a mother; and you write." But the idea of talking religion with a Palestinian Muslim and a Christian didn't frighten Priscilla, and we made a date to meet.

I walked into our first meeting, my stiff new notebook in hand, ready to share stories of religious inspiration. I was comfortable in my own religion, having made a difficult decision to leave the Catholic Church of my parents for the relative liberalism of the Episcopal Church. After twelve years in Catholic schools, I was finally going to get an interfaith education. That education, however, proved not to be as neatly packaged as I had anticipated. It came with the messiness and complications of the real lives and perspectives of three women with very different relationships to their religions.

Priscilla:

When Suzanne Oliver called me, she wasn't looking for just any children's book writer. She was looking specifically for a Jewish mother who wrote.

I had never really defined myself in those terms. I was a writer. And most definitely a mother. But a Jew? Religion wasn't my field of expertise. Deflecting pain with humor was. I'd joked all my life about being a "neurotic Jew."

I knew a fair amount about my religion, thanks mostly to my father, who came from a family of conservative Jews and exposed me to Judaism early in life. I knew the rituals and stories of my religion. I had attended a somber interfaith service at my suburban reform temple on

September 12, 2001, where my rabbi, along with other local clergy, tried to make sense of the unfathomable events of 9/11. The temple was overflowing that night as people spilled out onto the steps, down into the street, where policemen stood watch. (It occurred to me later that no imam had been present.)

I was comforted by the words of the moving service and the fact that so many people of different faiths had gathered together to support one another. But despite the fact that I prayed along with others to God that night, I wasn't sure whether I really believed God existed.

Where was God on September 11th? I wondered for weeks afterward. The horrifying images of the World Trade Center attacks played over and over in my head, and I had a persistent fear that New York City would be attacked again. This time, I worried that my husband, who worked in lower Manhattan, wouldn't be fortunate enough to survive. Would the next attack be a nuclear one? Although my family was alive and well, safe in the suburbs, the horror of 9/11 had hit close to home. Our son's basketball coach, a kind, compassionate father of four, had died that day and a close friend's husband had escaped the South Tower just minutes before it collapsed.

For thirty-five years, I'd suffered from severe panic attacks. And after the events of September 11th, I was thrown into one long, never-ending state of low-grade panic. But I tried to keep my fears to myself. I didn't want to scare my kids. I wanted them to know and love New York as I did. So a couple of weeks after the attacks, I started bringing them back into the city. They wanted to come, and I pretended to be calm. I tried to convince myself that New York was still alive and well as I talked to them.

"Look around you," I said to my children. "Look at all these people!" We were in the middle of Times Square. People of all shapes, sizes, colors, and ages were streaming past us. "We come from all over the world!" I said. "We're the best of America! Look what people can do here! They can do anything they want. They can be anyone they want to be. They can worship wherever they want, whenever they want. New York is the very best of what America stands for."

Although I fantasized about moving my family to a "safer" city, I was still smitten with New York, the city I loved too much to flee.

So when Suzanne Oliver called me, I was eager to collaborate on a children's book that would bring children hope. And bring me hope. I wanted to try to explain the inexplicable to my kids. And to myself. To allay the fears everyone had. The fears that were overwhelming me.

CHAPTER TWO

A Muslim, a Christian, and a Jew Walk into a Room . . .

Priscilla:

Ranya opened the door to her home for our first meeting, and I was immediately intrigued. There was so much to look at: beautiful artwork on the walls, sensual fabrics and furnishings. The space felt both familiar and exotic to me at the same time. Ranya and I both own lush, color photographs by the same photographer. The identical chandelier illuminates the main room of both our homes. I felt that was an unusual omen.

I had never met a Palestinian woman before, but have always had both Jewish and Christian friends. So I focused on Ranya in particular at that first meeting. Suzanne was less mysterious to me, and Ranya was, well, Palestinian. I'm not sure how I expected a Palestinian woman to look or act, but I was intrigued by Ranya as a person. She was beautiful, smart, sophisticated, and warm. She was confident, but refreshingly self-deprecating, one of my favorite traits in any person. I felt an immediate connection to her.

Ranya spoke eloquently about the unique position she was in as a Muslim mother in New York, particularly after the attacks on the World Trade Center. "My daughter's confused," Ranya explained. "She knows she's different from the Christian and Jewish children she's surrounded by, and I feel it's time to educate her and my son about what it means to be a Muslim in America today." This was a difficult challenge for Ranya since Islam now had violent and confusing connotations for most Americans.

I'd never interacted so intimately with a Muslim woman, I kept thinking as I listened to Ranya speak about her concerns. This was going to be an interesting meeting. The air felt charged. Partly because I didn't know these women and we were getting into personal issues, partly because I didn't know, as a Jew, what political direction a conversation with a Palestinian woman might take. But primarily the air was charged because I was in a room with two substantial, intelligent women who felt an urgent need to connect and produce something meaningful out of that connection.

I asked Ranya where her family was from, and she told me and Suzanne, in vivid detail, the story of her family's history in Palestine. I was riveted. Ranya talked with passion and sensitivity. I was hearing the story of a displaced Palestinian family, told to me not by an angry person with a political ax to grind, but by a loving mother with a family and a story to tell. It was as simple as that.

In retrospect, I guess I had been expecting a woman straight out of the evening news shots of anguished Palestinian mothers in refugee camps. A woman who would never sit down and talk to me, face to face, so calmly.

Ranya:

The morning of our first meeting, I lit a scented candle, fussed with the cushions on my couch and waited for Priscilla and Suzanne to arrive. I was not nervous about meeting a Jewish woman. Unlike Priscilla, who was meeting her first Palestinian woman, I had met many Jewish people representing an array of political opinions. Even before I'd moved to New York City ten years earlier, I'd had many

Jewish friends. Still, I knew it was possible that Priscilla and I could clash. Palestinians and Israelis were at war. And while I may suffer less than those in refugee camps, my identity is tied up in my family's displacement from our ancestral home half a century ago.

As soon as I met Priscilla, her eagerness to connect was evident, and, I hoped, an indicator of the warmth and generosity of her spirit. Priscilla was a reform Jew, and in my mind she represented the great Jewish liberal tradition of debate and free thought. As she confirmed later in our discussions, a large part of the Jewish theological tradition is based on the commentaries, which represent centuries of ongoing debate and interpretation of the Jewish Holy Books. The fact that I was able to talk so freely to Priscilla and Suzanne served as a sad reminder to me of the lack of debate in Islam today.

I had grown up hearing of a legendary time in history when the door was closed on Islamic theological debate (*Ijthihad*). So as Priscilla explained the evolution of the reform, conservative, and orthodox branches of Judaism in America, it occurred to me that Islam needed a parallel experience. America is a country that was built on the principle of freedom of worship, and in America today Islam needs an American journey.

When I shared my family story with Priscilla, although I felt self-conscious of such instant intimacy and a little awkward about sharing my family's sense of loss and victimhood, I felt that I was in the presence of someone open to meaningful dialogue. While Priscilla accepted my story at face value, she told me later that some of her friends were skeptical.

Suzanne:

From the time I discovered Ranya was Muslim, I was intrigued. I wanted to understand the basis of her faith and how she reconciled her modern, Westernized life with what was widely viewed as an unenlightened religion of the developing world. My knowledge of Islam was meager. I knew Muslims followed the teaching of an Arab called

Muhammad, that they worshiped in mosques, that they had a holy book called the Quran, and that they were obliged to make a pilgrimage to Mecca once in their lifetime.

I had visited mosques in Istanbul, and I had heard the enchanting Arabic calls to prayer of the muezzin throughout Turkey and Morocco. But I held an image of Islam as a violent religion controlled by men to promote the continued hegemony of men, a religion of mistreated women, polygamy, and an "eye for an eye" justice system. All of these images fit with stereotypes popularized in books I'd read, like Jean Sasson's *Princess*, and were supported by reports in the American media at various times—stories about women being stoned, about the 9/11 attackers being inspired by the Quran, about the death sentence placed on author Salman Rushdie by the Iranian Ayatollah Khomeini.

During my own travels in Muslim countries, I had seen women treated as second-class citizens. They covered their heads with scarves or even their entire bodies in shapeless cloaks. In Istanbul, I was shooed out of the courtyard of a mosque while I could see men prostrating themselves in prayer inside. One man quickly emerged and waved me out of the mosque's gates. I was not allowed to look.

I had left the Catholic church to become an Episcopalian, in part because Catholics don't allow women to become priests, so I was curious to learn how Ranya could reconcile her modern life with Islam. After all, she did not wear a head scarf. She drank alcohol. And she wasn't fighting a jihad against the West, at least as far as I could tell.

In retrospect, Ranya was on a jihad—a word I later learned to mean an inner struggle. She was struggling to define her Muslim faith. And she was struggling to have this faith recognized in the West.

Priscilla:

The first question the three of us asked each other at our initial meeting was "What is your religious background?" Mine, I explained to Ranya and Suzanne, was an eclectic one.

A Muslim, a Christian, and a Jew Walk into a Room

I grew up in Providence, Rhode Island, a diverse city with a sizeable Jewish population. My father was from a small town in Massachusetts, and my mother grew up in Hollywood, California. Although they were both Jewish, they came from very different backgrounds. In their sunny California house, my mother claims that her family served spaghetti as a traditional Passover meal. My father's conservative Jewish upbringing meant that his seders lasted hours while everyone digested the matzoh balls my grandmother had slaved over for days.

When I was seven, my grandfather died, and my father recited Kaddish, a memorial prayer, twice a day for an entire year, in his father's memory. At Narragansett Beach, where we rented a cottage that summer, he did this with a tiny group of men who were also in mourning. Clearly influenced by this experience, he enrolled me and my siblings in a Hebrew day school when I was in third grade. I spent four years there studying Hebrew, Torah, and Jewish history all morning and secular subjects like math and history in the afternoon.

I remember the Hebrew day school as an exotic, insular experience, where I began to think the earth was primarily populated by Jews. Boys talked endlessly about Sandy Koufax and girls claimed Paul Newman was 100 percent Jewish. I was afraid of the principal, a stern rabbi in a black suit. The whole experience felt serious and no-nonsense. I was a good student, learned my prayers and began praying by myself at home.

When I was in seventh grade, my father abruptly pulled me out of the Hebrew day school and enrolled me in a Quaker girls' school. He never explained this sudden shift in my education. In retrospect, I suppose he sent me to what he felt was the best school in the area. While my father was proud to be a Jew, he was a Jew on his own terms. Sometimes he fasted on Yom Kippur; other years he didn't. On some Passovers he ate no bread; other years he started the day with an English muffin.

As a family, we still went to temple on important Jewish holidays. But at school I went to chapel every day and sang dozens of hymns along with my new blonde friends. There were other Jewish girls in my class, and we all went along with the program. The Quakers never

13

rammed religion down our throats; we were exposed to it as part of a curriculum that would help us become better human beings.

In December, we participated in Christmas Vespers, a musical assembly that included Christmas carols and prayers. I hesitated over the name "Jesus," but I sang, and appreciated the beauty of the songs.

Every Friday my entire school held a Quaker silent meeting. Designated students and teachers took turns sitting on "the facing bench" at the front of the room. And then everyone fell silent. Anyone could stand up to recite a poem or prayer or say whatever was on their minds. It felt enormously empowering to be able to speak about whatever subject moved us. I enjoyed going to a Quaker school. The religion stressed open-mindedness and felt liberating in contrast to my years at the Hebrew day school, which I remember as rigid and small-minded.

In college I socialized with both Christian and Jewish friends, but my world was less Jewish than ever, since I dated a WASP from Boston. I was the only Jew in the room on many occasions with him. That made me particularly uncomfortable once when an older man visiting from the South asked everyone in our little group to reveal their religions.

Growing up Jewish meant growing up with an attachment to Israel. My family's attachment was not especially strong or pro-Zionist. But I do remember my father boasting of the bravery of the Israeli soldiers during the Six Day War. I took a trip to Israel with my family when I was twelve, and I recounted that trip to Ranya and Suzanne. My grandmother organized our itinerary, and we visited cousins of hers in a kibbutz near Galilee. "That's probably quite close to where my family is from," Ranya told me.

I'd walked the ancient streets of Jerusalem, floated in the waters of the Dead Sea, and peered into the entrances of the caves where the Dead Sea scrolls were discovered. Our trip reinforced my connection as a Jew to Israel, a connection that had been stressed at the Hebrew day school. But when I went on to a Quaker school and adolescent concerns took over my life, Judaism and Israel took a back seat. As I grew older and began to learn about the politics of the Middle East, I became uncomfortable with Israel's policies on the West Bank. This was not something I discussed with my friends or family. But when I was in my twenties, out working on my own, and the United Jewish Appeal tracked me down to make a fund-raising call, I told them that I was not comfortable sending money to Israel as long as the government was building settlements in what was formerly Jordan. I thought that was an unnecessarily provocative act.

I mentioned this anecdote to Ranya and Suzanne. I suppose I was putting my cards out on the table for Ranya to see, letting her know I was an "enlightened Jew," a Jew who was open-minded to the issue of Palestinians' rights. Maybe I was indeed a bit more open to learning about Ranya's family history and political opinions than another Jewish woman might have been. That was for Ranya to decide. I did, however, stand on the sidewalk outside her apartment building after our first meeting and rave to Suzanne about Ranya, the project, and the ease with which we all seemed to communicate.

Ranya:

Early on, I shared with Priscilla and Suzanne that, when I was a self-conscious, insecure teenager, the worst question you could ask me was, "Where are you from?" Now, as a mother, I tell the story of where I'm from with the hope that my personal journey, with what small insights it reveals, will help my American children feel pride in their heritage in these troubled times.

I am a Muslim woman of Palestinian heritage, and no matter where I have lived I have always been an outcast. I have struggled to develop my own personal identity in the shadow of whatever stereotype others have attributed to a Muslim Palestinian woman. This struggle has affected many aspects of my life, from my choice of a major at university (political science) to my enormous appreciation of the security and comfort that becoming an American citizen has afforded me.

I was born in Kuwait, where Palestinians were not granted citizenship at birth. My parents had lived briefly in Jordan, as refugees fleeing Palestine, and that fact allowed me to inherit their Jordanian citizenship. Rumor had it that because we were Palestinian, our passports were encoded so that Jordanian officials could distinguish us from native Jordanians. Thus, from the beginning, I felt officially documented as an outsider.

I grew up in the oil-prosperous emirate of Kuwait in the 1970s, where my father started his career after earning two degrees in the United States. Although my father was financially successful from an early age, there were elements in Kuwaiti society who resented the success of those they believed were opportunistic refugees. Non-Kuwaiti nationals, especially those considered most threatening to the status quo, such as the Palestinians, were given the derogatory title of "Abu al-Pantalon," a term that meant, literally "Those of the Pants." It was an unspoken rule that only Kuwaitis could wear traditional white robes and head scarves. Everyone else was immediately identifiable as a noncitizen and had little hope of ever gaining citizenship, except for a lucky few who won it as a gift through royal decree.

My father rose above any attempts to marginalize him, and he constantly reminded his family that we lived in Kuwait because of economic necessity. He spoke often of our family's history, and much of my identity grew out of a sense of what my family had lost and what I had never had. My father placed a large premium on our heritage. He told and retold the story of our family's life in Palestine with a great sense of pride and empowerment in response to those who sought to make us feel inadequate or secondary in a hierarchical society. There were clearly a host of lessons we were supposed to learn from our family's experiences.

Our family name, Tabari, was derived from Tiberias, the area of Palestine surrounding the Sea of Galilee. It was there that, as governors under the Ottoman Empire, my family members were substantial landowners. My father spoke of a rarified childhood; he and his five siblings were dubbed "the children of the nylon," when nylon replaced silk stockings as a rare luxury in the intra-war period of Palestine's history.

His family lived in a large home, which now houses an Israeli sewing school. His father, a medical doctor, owned the area's first motorcar, a 1933 Ford. His mother, a renowned beauty from Jerusalem, donned a bathing suit and swam in Lake Tiberias, where Jesus of Nazareth walked on water. She was also an astute businesswoman. She spoke five languages and was in the process of developing plans for hotels and resort villas around Lake Tiberias when she was forced to leave Palestine.

After World War I, Palestine was ruled as a British mandate. Then, after World War II, the international community decided to set aside part of Palestine for the Jewish people. So in 1948, when it was evident that the world was ready to recognize a Jewish state of Israel in a partitioned Palestine, the British began their withdrawal from areas such as Tiberias. My father's family and his Muslim and Christian neighbors felt sabotaged by the UN partition plan, which made Tiberias and other Palestinian villages a part of Israel. The land was appropriated by the Jewish National Fund and set aside for Jews from around the world who wanted to invoke their so-called "right of return." That period of time, when so many Palestinians lost their property, is known throughout the Middle East as the Nakba (Catastrophe.) It is described in the book *The Transformation of Palestine* by Ibrahim Abu Lughod and more recently by Israeli historian Benny Morris in his book *The Birth of the Palestinian Refugee Problem Revisited.*

My grandfather belonged to a local Palestinian committee organized by the men of the area as part of an effort to protect their families and homes. When it became clear that war would break out, he got into his car and drove north to try to obtain arms. (Under British mandate laws, Palestinians had not been allowed to own or carry arms.) While my grandfather was gone, the house next to his was being used as a shelter for these fighting men. My grandmother offered them food and provisions. But when that house was bombed, a Jewish woman who was my grandmother's friend before the war and had since joined the Ha-gannah, a Jewish paramilitary organization, warned my grandmother that she and her family were not safe. My grandmother became concerned enough to call General McGregor, an English Army officer and Britain's representative for Tiberias, seeking his advice. He expressed extreme concern for her safety and that of her children should they remain in their house. He strongly recommended that they all leave and graciously offered them transportation and protection.

My grandmother, without much thought or planning, loaded her five children into the back of a Saladin, an armored military vehicle. The children lay on top of a pair of Persian carpets, the only belongings they took with them. These rugs remain today our most treasured family possessions and cherished symbols of our heritage.

Ironically, General McGregor's protection of my grandmother and the honor he bestowed upon my family through her special treatment effectively meant that she could never return home again. Thinking they would be gone a short time, she and thousands of other Palestinians left their keys under their doormats when they fled the chaos and danger of war. Little did they know they would never be allowed to retrieve their keys or reclaim their homes. In 1948, the UN estimated the number of displaced Palestinians to be around 750,000. Today these refugees and their descendants are believed to number four million worldwide.

When my grandfather drove back from Syria in search of his family, soldiers stopped his car on the road and discovered a cache of weapons in his trunk. They dragged him in front of a firing squad, and, just as he was about to be killed, a Palestinian Jew pushed his way out of the crowd and pleaded with the Israeli soldiers to spare my grandfather's life.

My grandfather, Dr. Tabari, was a physician who treated Jews, Christians, and Muslims alike, and when this Palestinian Jew spoke out on his behalf, and related that he himself had been treated with dignity and skill by Dr. Tabari, the soldiers spared my grandfather's life.

The fact that my grandfather treated Jews, Christians, and Muslims equally was admirable but not miraculous. My parents talk often of a time in Palestine when people of the three faiths coexisted peacefully, when, in an often-told family anecdote, my grandmother drove down to Tel Aviv to buy her wedding dress from the finest Jewish seamstresses.

But all that changed in 1948.

My father's family left behind everything they owned when they became refugees in Jordan. Distraught and financially ruined, my grandfather managed to secure a full, three-year scholarship for my father at a boarding school in Lebanon. When my father turned sixteen, his father had saved enough money to buy him and his brother two one-way tickets to America, where they joined a cousin in Chicago.

My father had to falsify his age in order to get his first job working the night shift on the Chicago docks. His brother, his cousin, and he shared one coat in the bitter Chicago winter. Whoever got up first each morning had the warmer day. For ten years, my father attended college during the day and worked the night shift as a dock porter. He earned degrees in math and civil engineering from the University of Illinois. The hardships he and his brother endured as teenagers instilled in him an almost Protestant work ethic that he then passed on to his children.

While he was away, his mother died in Jordan. Tragically, my father and his brother weren't told because no one could afford to buy them plane tickets to return for the funeral. When my father finally returned to the Middle East, his own father did not immediately recognize him. He had left a boy and come home a twenty-six-year-old man.

When my father suffered a heart attack years later, at the age of forty, he attributed this, and his mother's early death, to the anguish and hardship they had suffered after they left their home in Palestine.

My father and mother, who is also a Palestinian refugee, have instilled in me a sense of pride in my past and a commitment to my heritage. To deny this identity would be nothing short of betrayal of my family. In fact, I told Suzanne and Priscilla, I have always thought it cowardly when Palestinians identify themselves only in terms of their adopted citizenship. I have been determined to set a defiant example as a proud Palestinian. My role model is my thoroughly liberated Muslim Palestinian grandmother, whose mantle I inherited.

Suzanne:

"My background sounds so dull in comparison," I laughed, giving Ranya and Priscilla a self-conscious smile. "It was ordinary, safe, and Midwestern, like Wonder Bread and Hallmark Cards."

When I was growing up in Kansas City, I never missed a Sunday mass or even masses on the holy days of obligation that don't necessarily fall on Sundays. It was never an option in my family. We went to church together every weekend. As my four siblings and I grew older and got involved with sports or jobs that kept us busy on Sunday mornings, our mass attendance was still monitored by our parents. And, with three Catholic churches within an easy drive, there was always a mass going on somewhere, sometime between five o'clock on Saturday afternoon and seven o'clock Sunday evening.

Prayer was part of our life at home, too. We said grace before dinner, and we knelt by our beds for nighttime prayers. In my bedroom I had a plastic statue of the holy family (Jesus, Mary, and Joseph) on whose base were the words, "The family that prays together stays together." Inside the base was a rosary. One long summer, I told Ranya and Priscilla, my parents asked the three oldest children to take turns reading a chapter of the Bible aloud each night after dinner. As I listened to my eight-year-old brother sound out words like "Sadducees," my attention tuned to the sounds of the freeze tag game next door. I would have given my new AM/FM radio to jump out of my seat and join the fun.

I spent twelve years at Catholic schools and went to an overabundance of religious services. From sixth through eighth grade, I had to attend mass once a week with my class, once with the whole school and once again with my family on Sundays. My memories of the school services are of sore knees and the smell of vomit sprinkled with anti-septic powder then left to age until the service was over. I also got a re-curring pain in my ankle as I stood on the side of my shoe so that I wouldn't appear taller than all the boys. A few of the sermons caught my attention. I remember one of the priests telling us about saints who suffered stigmata. Saint Francis of Assisi's hands and feet bled in ex-actly the same places that Jesus had bled, he told us. And we learned about people in modern life who had similar bleeding experiences. We wondered, "Would this ever happen to us? How would we play volley-ball?"

At school, I went to confession once a month. "Bless me, Father, for I have sinned," I would say through the screen dividing the sections of the confessional booth. "It has been one month since my last confes-sion. In that time I have been mean to my brothers and sister, disobeyed my parents, and taken Twinkies out of the freezer without permission." For that, I would say three Hail Marys then have a clean, white soul again. How lucky to die right after confession, I thought. I would go straight to heaven.

In spite of twelve years in parochial schools, I didn't have much of a theological understanding of Christianity. The last substantive Christ-ian religion class I could remember was in sixth grade when we memo-rized Jesus' beatitudes. ("Blessed are the poor in spirit, for theirs is the kingdom of heaven . . .") To fulfill my religion credits, I took two Eastern religion classes, one in high school and one in college. But now it strikes me as odd that Islam was not included in either. I was exposed to Bud-dhism, Taoism, and Confucianism. In humanities courses, I learned Greek and Roman mythology. But Islam entered my life peripherally. It came through travel, through books, and through war.

Though I attended church infrequently during college, I still con-sidered myself Catholic. On a tour of St. Peter's Basilica in Rome I was brought to tears by the tombs of so many courageous Christian martyrs who had died for their faith. And I wept before Michelangelo's *Pietà*. For me, the sculpture of Mary holding a crucified Jesus symbolized the tragedy of humanity's betrayal of Christ, both at his crucifixion and every day when we failed to live according to his teaching. I thanked God for the gift of being raised a Catholic and resolved to be a better one.

Alas, the thrill of being twenty-something in New York City got in the way. Not until I had children did I begin to focus on my spiritual life in a significant way. At that time my husband and I made the switch from Catholicism to the less rigid Episcopal Church.

Ranya:

I explained to Priscilla and Suzanne that although I have sometimes been cautious about speaking up as a Muslim American woman, I was given the tools to do so by my parents. As dispossessed refugees, my mother and father were firm believers in the merits of education as a necessary tool for survival. They worked hard to send me and my siblings to the best schools they could find. In spite of their personal loss they were optimists at heart who nurtured in us the value of independent thinking and encouraged us to believe in our potential as men and women committed to a better future.

In Kuwait and Dubai, where they found the public schools lacking in curriculum and qualified teachers, my parents opted to send me to the privately run French Lycée in Kuwait and The English School in Dubai. This meant that I was often one of very few Muslims, if not the only Muslim, in my class.

At the Lycée, I learned my ABCs in French and wrote letters to "Cher Papa Noel," or "Dear Father Christmas," during the month of December. When we lived in Dubai, from the time I was seven until age sixteen, I sang "Silent Night" and "Noel" at school Christmas concerts and I "danced" the color purple in my school's musical production of *Joseph and His Amazing Technicolor Dreamcoat.*

In those days, religion was not a required part of the school curriculum, and whatever I learned about Islam was strictly through the customs and traditions of my family, especially my maternal grandparents, who were our neighbors. We didn't attend a mosque, but we practiced Islam at home through prayer, charity, and traditions.

During Ramadan, the holiest month in the Islamic calendar, my parents and grandparents fasted from sunrise to sunset. I remember standing with my brother in my grandparents' garden, waiting for the sound of the cannon, which signaled the end of the day's fast. During this month, we exercise discipline and attempt to cleanse mind, body, and soul of vices and bad thoughts. When I attempted to fast, however, I was told I was too young, that my growing body needed nourishment. Instead, my grandmother advised me to participate in the spirit of the month by meeting different challenges. I was urged to control my temper or to give a thirsty person a glass of water before taking care of my own thirst. This, I was told, was a sure way to get to heaven.

The highlight of the month was always Eid, the celebration marking the end of Ramadan. We received gifts and allowances and dressed from head to toe in new clothing for the occasion. I had a particular fondness for new shoes, which I was careful to keep close to my bedside, impatient for morning to arrive.

Islam and the traditions I was exposed to became an integral part of my life. Today I always carry a Quran in my purse and sometimes wear a verse from the Quran around my neck. I pray, but not necessarily five times a day as more traditional Muslims do. I am reluctant to throw out leftover bread without kissing it and asking for God's forgiveness, a custom reminding Muslims that many people in our world remain hungry. And I still surprise myself when I go through our apartment, making sure that no shoes remain with their soles facing up toward God in a sign of disrespect.

When I was in college at Georgetown University, and it was time to pick a major, international politics was a natural, even a necessary choice. I needed scholarly tools and historical perspective to help me understand my own family's experience. The Middle East was a volcano waiting to erupt, full of people with claims and counterclaims, people who laid their absolute truths on everything from how a woman should or should not cover her hair to those who invoked the Old Testament promise of Palestine to the Jews to justify Israel's policies. During my high school years there had been an American hostage crisis in revolutionary Iran and a civil war in Lebanon during which Palestinians were massacred at the Sabra and Shatila refugee camps by Lebanese Christians under the watchful eyes of the Israelis. I felt I needed to study political history and international relations so that I could move beyond these tragic headlines and formulate my own opinions about the motivations, policies, and people behind them.

At Georgetown's School of Foreign Service, our curriculum required courses in American government, Western civilization and philosophies, and comparative theology. I was smitten with the American dream, the founding fathers, and the democratic principles of the American government. These were more than just historical and political facts to me. They addressed my sense of homelessness and insecurity. I described to Priscilla and Suzanne my pride when, in my twenties, I was first able to return to America from abroad and stand in the U.S. Customs line under "citizen" instead of "alien."

I was an American protected by law and awarded inalienable rights. Then came the attacks of 9/11, and I felt vulnerable and insecure again.

Priscilla:

A few days after my initial meeting with Suzanne and Ranya, I was still high from the experience, and I told a Jewish friend about it. I even shared Ranya's history. "It was incredible what her family had to go through in Palestine!" I told Tobi.

"You know," my friend said, looking somewhat skeptical, "I'm not so sure you've got your facts right."

"What do you mean?" I asked.

"Well, don't be so sure that your friend's family had to leave Palestine," she said.

"But they did! She told me exactly what happened! Her grandfather . . ."

"I just wouldn't necessarily believe that you got the whole story," Tobi repeated. "People weren't kicked off their lands. A lot of Palestinians chose to leave." My friend Tobi is fairly religious, not orthodox, but a strong supporter of Israel, and opinionated about the Middle East and, truth be told, everything else in the world.

I was a bit disheartened. And confused.

"But why would she make that up?" I asked.

"I'm not saying she made anything up," Tobi said. "But you're not hearing all sides of the story. Read the book *One Palestine Complete* by Tom Segev. That'll give you an idea of what really went on."

I was sorry I'd shared my story with Tobi. I didn't really want to read political science books about the Middle East. I wanted my learning experience to be a private, personal one. I wanted to talk and listen to Ranya. To have a dialogue with a person of another faith. Would that be possible? I decided I wouldn't even mention Ranya to another friend of mine who knows the Middle East quite intimately. He might muddy the waters even further for me. My friend Chaim is an Israeli whose parents moved to Jerusalem from Iraq in the 1920s. Chaim and I have had many political discussions about the Middle East. With violence breaking out every day in Israel and the occupied territories, such conversations had been unavoidable. And Chaim, like Tobi, has been opinionated and vocal. "You know who should really be playing a role in all this?" he'd asked me on more than one occasion. "Jordan! They should give the Palestinians a big chunk of Jordan. Why should tiny Israel have to give up such a large portion of our land?" Discussions about Middle East politics with friends have made my head spin over the years. But now I had Ranya to talk to. And Suzanne. For the time being, I thought I would just stick to that.

CHAPTER THREE

The Abrahamic Family Feud

Priscilla:

As I drove into New York for my second meeting with Ranya and Suzanne, it was fear, not faith, that had the upper hand in my life. A familiar sense of panic I'd known for years began seeping back into my body as I worried about where the next terrorist attack would occur. Would they set off a dirty bomb in Grand Central Terminal? My husband rode commuter trains and subways for a total of three hours every day. The idea of him trapped underground haunted me.

I started driving my car into the city instead of taking the train. I felt safe in a car, my own private space capsule. I justified my fear of public transportation to friends by saying that it was easier to drive. I had good luck finding parking meters. I didn't tell them that I was trying to play the odds, sure that one parent in the New York subway system was enough to tempt fate. Two parents would be way too risky.

I felt like a fraud. Although I had fallen in love with New York years ago, I now thought maybe I wasn't cut out to be a true New Yorker. Who was I kidding? Maybe I didn't have the courage. Unlike my husband, who appeared to go about his business calmly, I could easily picture people plotting to wipe New York off the map.

Had I become a cowering suburban wife and mother? Did my fears define me? That certainly seemed to be the case. My husband felt the need to start attending Friday night services at our synagogue after September 11th. He constantly urged me to go, but I declined. I could have easily participated; I knew all the prayers and rituals from my early Hebrew day school experience. But I still resisted. I didn't think it would help me to worship in a group of people who I thought felt something

26

I didn't feel. Truth be told, I was lost spiritually. I wasn't sure if I believed in God anymore.

Yet here I was sucking it up and driving into the city to meet my new acquaintances, Suzanne and Ranya, to talk about God. I wasn't finding solace in my own religious community; but somehow I was drawn to Ranya, a Muslim woman I barely knew.

I rolled down my windows as I passed over the Third Avenue bridge. Just in case someone had placed a bomb underneath that bridge. Just in case the bridge exploded and my car was thrown into the East River. In retrospect I was clearly in search of something as I lurched my way into Manhattan.

As soon as I walked into Ranya's apartment I felt better, calmer in the sanctuary of her home, sinking into the same spot on her spacious gray couch that I had left behind just a week ago. I was eager to share the details of my meeting with Jeffrey Sirkman, the rabbi at our temple, whom I had consulted during the past week as I had searched for an Old Testament story to retell for our children's book.

Jeffrey is a terrific person—warm, caring, and easy to talk to. He has a sharp mind, and his enthusiasm makes the Torah come alive to adults and children. He has a large fan club of congregants of all ages.

I described to Suzanne and Ranya how excited I was about the project we'd started together and how I'd shared my enthusiasm with Jeffrey. I'd explained Ranya's predicament as a Muslim woman in New York who wanted to help her children understand their religion in a city wary of Muslims and a world wracked with religious conflict. Ranya wanted to connect the three great monotheistic religions of the world, I told Jeffrey. "Great idea," he said. "And much needed."

"Why is it that people can use religion to whip up so much hatred?" I asked my rabbi. We talked about ultraconservative religious leaders of all faiths who were spewing hateful rhetoric all over the globe.

"You want people to use their sacred texts to make the world a better place," explained Jeffrey. "But that text can become a weapon in the wrong hands. You know what they say, 'Even the devil can quote scripture.'"

I explained to Jeffrey that I wanted to choose a religious story to share, something that included a message of tolerance. "You know," said Jeffrey, shaking his head, "I never liked that word 'tolerance.' It's too passive. Think about it. To tolerate someone? That doesn't sound very positive. It's not a call to engage and understand someone else. I like the phrase 'mutual appreciation.' That can lead to an understanding that no one faith has a monopoly on the truth."

In Jeffrey's cozy, book-packed office, I couldn't jot down notes fast enough. Everything Jeffrey said made sense to me. "The first story that springs to mind for you to tell is the binding of Isaac." He shook his head. "But I don't know."

I knew that Jeffrey was referring to the passage in which Abraham is called by God to sacrifice his son Isaac. "But that's such a scary story," I told my rabbi. "And a negative one. Didn't Abraham have a son, Ishmael, with his servant, Hagar?" Jeffrey nodded. "And Sarah, who was jealous, sent the two of them away," I continued. "Isn't that where all the trouble started with the Muslims and the Jews? When Hagar and Ishmael were banished?"

Jeffrey didn't comment on my interpretation of Ishmael's fate. He was on to the next idea. "I've got a great story for you to tell children!" he exclaimed. "Moses and the Burning Bush! Now that's a terrific story!"

Ranya:

Banished! I was truly taken aback. I've never heard Muslims refer to themselves as banished! As a Muslim, I never thought that the binding of Isaac was a negative story. My problem with the story is that I believe that God ordered Abraham to sacrifice a different son, Ishmael, and not Isaac. How ironic that others interpret the story of Ishmael so negatively, while Muslims highlight and celebrate these connections. Nor do we harbor any ancient biblical ill will, I told Priscilla and Suzanne. Sarah and Isaac, or "Ishaac" as he is known in Islam, continue to be popular names in the Muslim world. Muslims even refer to Jews as "Oulad Al Am," which literally means cousins. Come to think of it, I think we are all originally Jews.

In spite of Priscilla's doubts, I was determined to share with her the Muslim perspective—that we have meaningful ties to one another. I had the perfect tool, the story of Isra' and Mi'raj, also known as Muhammad's night flight and ascension.

Although I was vaguely familiar with the story from my childhood, when I read it as an adult, I finally understood its meaning: Muhammad's need to emphasize Islam's positive connection to Judaism and Christianity. He affirms those prophets who came before him, while fulfilling his role as the promised prophet to Ishmael's descendants.

I picked up my cup of jasmine green tea and began to read to Priscilla and Suzanne my version of the story of Muhammad's ascension to heaven.

One night, when Muhammad was having difficulty sleeping, he went to visit the Ka'aba, Mecca's holy shrine, where he knelt down to pray to God and soon fell asleep. Suddenly he was shaken out of his slumber by the angel Gabriel, who appeared before him bearing a golden goblet and leading a dazzling white, winged horse. "Drink," said Gabriel as he held the cup to Muhammad's lips. Muhammad drank from the goblet and was filled with wisdom and faith.

Gabriel bid Muhammad to mount the fantastic horse, which was named Baraq. He told Muhammad the horse had been ridden to the heavens by Abraham, Moses, and Jesus before him. Muhammad climbed onto Baraq's back, and in only a few strides they flew all the way to Jerusalem, where they descended on the Temple Mount. Muhammad tied Baraq to the hitching post used by the prophets before him. A ladder of silver and gold embedded with pearls appeared before them, and Muhammad and Gabriel climbed the ladder into the heavens.

In the first heaven Muhammad was welcomed by Adam, the

first man God placed on earth. Gabriel then led Muhammad into the higher heavens, where he was greeted as a righteous man, a fellow brother, and a prophet by Jesus, John the Baptist, Moses, and finally Abraham. At last Gabriel took Muhammad even higher until they reached the lote tree, the boundary of the throne of God. The sweet-smelling tree, whose leaves were as big as elephant ears, marked the limit of human knowledge. At the foot of the tree Muhammad saw two milky white rivers with vessels of gold and silver floating in them. Along the banks of these rivers stood tents whose silken fabrics sparkled with iridescent pearls, shining sapphires, and other glimmering stones. Enchanting green birds flew overhead. Muhammad bent down to taste the river water, and on his tongue it was sweeter than honey. He looked up to see seventy thousand angels at prayer.

As the story continues, Muhammad is given the command of daily prayers. Moses acts as an advocate for mankind, urging Muhammad to go back to God and seek a reduction from the numerous prayers originally prescribed to a more manageable number, which turns out to be five. The story ends with Moses, Jesus, and Muhammad communally praying alongside each other by the Temple Mount in Jerusalem. Today, these five prayers still begin and end with a salutation of peace to the entire Abrahamic family (Jews, Christians, and Muslims) and Muhammad's predecessors in prophecy.

PRISCILLA: *So Muslims all over the world begin and end their prayers wishing peace for Jews and Christians? We're actually in your prayers?*

RANYA: *Absolutely. In fact, it's not coincidental that Muhammad ascended from Jerusalem's Temple Mount.*

PRISCILLA: *What do you mean?*

Ranya:

The location of Muhammad's night flight journey reaffirms the significance of Jerusalem as a holy site to Islam as well as Judaism and Christianity. It is the spot where the world's 1.6 billion Muslims believe that humanity will someday assemble and rise to heaven to be judged. Indeed the Dome of the Rock in Jerusalem, a stately mosque with a distinctive golden dome, was built by Muslims on that specific site to commemorate the Prophet's ascension and to celebrate Islam's connections to its extended Abrahamic family. The Dome of the Rock is the site upon which King David is believed to have built the first Jewish temple, which was destroyed by the Romans and neglected as a dump under Christian Hellenistic rule. Sadly, some Jews and Christians have sought to bring down the Dome of the Rock, either to rebuild the Jewish temple that would fulfill the prophecy of the coming of the messiah or to deny Muslims any claims to the Holy City.

Muslims, I explained, believe Muhammad to be the last of a series of twenty-five messengers and prophets, starting with Adam and including Moses and Jesus, who were sent by God to guide people to the right path. Muhammad was born in 570 and died in 632. Muslims believe that Judaism, Christianity, and Islam, which means peaceful surrender to the will of God, are three forms of one religion, which was the religion of the prophet Abraham.

> PRISCILLA: *Isn't that blasphemy, Ranya, to say that Islam is just a different version of Judaism and Christianity?*
> RANYA: *No. Not to me. Muslims are required to believe in the Gospels and the Torah. Your God is the Muslim God, too.*

Suzanne:

Muslims believe in the Gospels and the Torah? Our religions were closer than I had ever thought. It was thrilling! Thrilling and simultaneously unnerving because the Muslim view of events was not always the same as the Christian one.

As Ranya read her story of Muhammad's night flight, I was startled by her suggestion that Jesus had flown on the winged horse Baraq. I flinched, thinking, Jesus didn't ride on any winged horse. He traveled in his sandals or at best by donkey! But I didn't say anything; the story seemed like a fairy tale whose appropriation of Jesus was harmless.

Other differences, however, felt more threatening. Clearly the Muslim version of the Gospels was not the same as mine. As Ranya explained, "Muslims believe that Jesus is the prophet closest to God in spirit because of his virgin birth."

"You believe in the virgin birth?" I asked.

"Yes, but we still believe Jesus was a mortal man, not the son of God."

So if Jesus was just a prophet, what was Muhammad, I wondered?

"Tell me more about Muhammad," I said to Ranya. "What was his mission?"

"He was a reformer," Ranya replied. "He came to fix what had gone wrong in Judaism and Christianity."

"Wrong?" As I heard this I felt reflexively defensive. Sure, Christianity's had its share of problems. But were they bad enough to require God to summon another prophet? Hadn't God played his trump card with Jesus?

"Muhammad stood up to the idol worshipers who filled the Ka'aba, Mecca's holy shrine. He told everyone that there was only one God, the God of Abraham and his sons Isaac and Ishmael." Ranya paused. "And he stood for justice. Muhammad told people to take care of the weak and poor. He spoke up for women and orphans, and he fought to abolish slavery."

This sounded admirable.

"Of course not everyone liked hearing that," Ranya continued. "And early on Muhammad's enemies attacked him with sticks and stones. But he didn't fight back. He prayed to God saying, 'Guide these people in the right path for they do not know what they do.'"

"They know not what they do?" Those words sounded awfully familiar.

I thought of the Gospels, in which Jesus championed the sick, the outcasts, and the poor. He threw the money changers out of the temple. And as he was being crucified, he is quoted in the New Testament saying, "Forgive them Father, they know not what they do." Muhammad's words sounded like imitations of Jesus' own.

Was Muhammad a fraud?

"Did Muhammad know any Christians?" I asked. "Was he familiar with the Bible?"

He had met a Christian monk, Ranya explained, who is said to have recognized early signs in him as the promised final prophet. He had also met Jews and Christians on his many trips to the Holy Land with his merchant uncle. And after the angel Gabriel first visited Muhammad, a Christian cousin of his wife's confirmed Muhammad's prophetic experience.

I was immediately dubious of the authority of this Christian cousin. But I did not want to offend Ranya. Maybe we'd better change the subject, I thought. And, luckily, our conversation veered in another direction.

Priscilla turned back to Ranya's story of Muhammad's night flight. "We don't have anything quite as magical as winged horses in the Old Testament," she said. And she and I began to tell Ranya the Bible stories we'd learned as children. As we talked, Ranya smiled excitedly, jumped up, and went to her children's rooms. She returned with her arms full of small, brightly colored paperback books and spread them on the table before us.

"I can't believe you read these books!" Priscilla exclaimed as we looked over the titles: *Adam and Eve, Jonah and the Whale, Noah's Ark, The Ten Commandments.*

"Look!" Ranya said, holding up a bright blue paperback. "Here's the story of Moses and the manna God sent down from the sky to feed the Israelites starving in the desert!"

"Manna? Muslims know the story of manna?" Priscilla was delighted. I smiled along with her. We had all grown up on the same Old Testament writings!

We examined the books for ourselves. Sometimes there was a twist, but these were the same ancient stories of God, creation, morality, and faith that we had studied in our own religious traditions. Priscilla and I were astonished. Clearly, we had a lot to learn.

Priscilla:

I loved seeing Ranya's picture books. They certainly illustrated the connection between Christians, Muslims, and Jews, and contradicted what I'd been hearing lately in the news media, about the madrassahs of the Middle East, mysterious places where Muslim children memorized the Quran and their adult teachers preached jihad, or holy war. I wondered whether Muslim children across the globe were learning the comforting, familiar Bible stories Suzanne, Ranya, and I had grown up hearing.

I was surprised and thrilled to see Moses show up in Ranya's living room, to learn that he lived in her children's bedrooms, in the form of the little picture books they read at night. My rabbi had given me an interesting perspective on the story of Moses, which I shared with Ranya and Suzanne.

Rabbi Sirkman had urged me to share the story of how Yahweh, "the God of Abraham, Isaac, and Jacob," spoke to Moses at the site of the small, miraculous Burning Bush. "Take off your shoes!" God commanded Moses, because he was on holy ground. He then directed Moses to travel to Egypt to confront the Pharaoh and free the Israelites.

Jeffrey had suggested I write about the Burning Bush because he saw in Moses' reaction to being called to serve God a human hesitation as Moses asked God, "Why me? Why should I be the person to deliver this message?" He was afraid of the challenge God presented to him. But he ultimately rose to that challenge. And that's what we all have to do in life, my rabbi explained to me—answer the call of God and accept whatever challenges we face.

Suzanne:

After our meeting that day, I began my search for a New Testament miracle that would captivate children and help illustrate the connections between Judaism, Christianity, and Islam. Once I opened the Bible and started reading the Gospels, I found it difficult to stop. The life of Jesus was so familiar to me, but reading the Bible I sensed the excitement of being there at the time. The things that Jesus is reported to have done are so remarkable. He embraced those who were shunned—the blind, the lepers, and the lame. He calmed storms. He fed thousands on two fish and five loaves of bread. He brought his friend Lazarus back to life. And, by God, he rose from the dead himself. Which one of these miraculous stories should I tell?

As I read, I couldn't help but compare these miracles of healing and service to some of the miracles I knew from the Old Testament: the slaying of Egypt's first-born sons, the Red Sea swallowing the soldiers of Egypt, and the tumbling of the walls of Jericho followed by the Jews' slaughter of the residents of that city. The New Testament message of peace, love, and resurrection, I felt, added a necessary and even a more holy dimension to the Old Testament's history of the battles, trials, and survival of the Jewish people and their relationship with God.

I wasn't sure how the good news of the New Testament compared to the message of the Quran. But I felt pretty confident that Jesus' pacifism stood in contrast to Muhammad's role as a warrior and that Jesus' message of forgiveness was the opposite of Islam's practices of retribution. Unlike Muhammad and the prophets of the Old Testament, Jesus had no flaws. As he fasted in the desert, the devil tempted him with food, wealth, and power, yet Jesus easily resisted. He lived a peaceful life devoted to preaching about a loving and merciful God. He was not interested in writing rules or amassing earthly wealth or power. When he was asked by the temple leaders to name the most important of the Ten Commandments, he answered, "First love God with all your heart, soul, mind, and strength, then love your neighbor as yourself."

One Bible story in particular played into my image of Islam. According to the Gospel of John the high priests once brought an adultress to Jesus and asked if she should be stoned according to the law of Moses. Jesus said to them, "Let the one who has committed no sin throw the first stone." One by one the woman's accusers departed. The difference between this Christian ideal and what I understood was a Muslim practice of stoning female adulterers buttressed my view at the time that Christianity was a superior religion.

As I paged through the Bible, I wondered what miracle of Jesus could compete with Moses' rod that morphed into a snake or with Muhammad's flying horse. At last I chose the miracle of Pentecost, when the Holy Spirit visited Jesus' twelve apostles in the form of raging wind and tongues of fire. Through this miracle, God called the apostles to go out to many nations and spread the good news of Jesus' life, death, and resurrection. Speak up, God said. Ironically, it was the same thing he had said to Moses.

Pentecost had drama. There was just one problem. The event took place after Jesus' crucifixion. Jesus was dead, and I had to explain how he had died. While I didn't necessarily want to write about Jesus' death, it seemed to me that it was unavoidable. So, I began reading and writing about the crucifixion. Never did I anticipate what my choice would mean for our project.

CHAPTER FOUR

The Crucifixion Crisis

PRISCILLA: *You know, Suzanne, this is kind of upsetting to me, this stuff about the Jews killing Christ.*
SUZANNE: *Jews killing Christ? I never said that!*

Priscilla:

I walked into Ranya's apartment the following week interested to hear what Suzanne had written. She'd told us her subject was Pentecost, but I had no idea what the word meant. I was aware of the broad themes of Jesus' life. I knew he'd performed miracles. I knew he was a righteous man, and I knew he was a Jew. On my one trip to Israel, I'd actually visited the room in Jerusalem where the Last Supper was supposed to have taken place. The Last Supper, I knew, was a Passover seder.

But how had a man who started out as a Jew become such a stranger to me?

Growing up, I'd attended a couple of services with Christian friends, but I'd never talked to them about Jesus, and while polite enough to read prayers at their services, I could never bring myself to say "Jesus Christ Our Lord." I'd never read the New Testament. I'd seen hundreds of images of Jesus on the cross, but, frankly, they made me uncomfortable.

Suzanne handed out copies of her latest writing to me and Ranya and when she read the short description she'd woven together about Jesus' life, she had my full attention. Then she began reading an abridged version of the crucifixion. When she got to the part about Jesus and the wicked men who killed Christ, she *really* had my full attention. I started to squirm on Ranya's couch.

There was no way around it. Writing about the fury and the events

37

that led a crowd of men to nail a human being to a crucifix was a gory, disturbing story. This was a far cry from the gauzy, artistic renderings of a beatific Jesus I'd seen, a man in a loincloth who, oh yes, just happened to be hanging from a cross.

I squirmed a bit more. Then I felt a rush of adrenaline. Suzanne was calmly reading about this disturbing event, and a few words jumped out at me: "wicked hands" and "Israel."

"You know," I said, interrupting Suzanne. "This is kind of upsetting to me."

Suzanne glanced up from her papers. She had finished reading about the crucifixion. I don't think that was ever the main thrust of her story. And it was a story she'd heard hundreds of times, I'm sure. She was on to Pentecost, whatever that was, or the events leading up to it. She looked at me, puzzled.

"I just . . ." I struggled for words. "Could you read that part to me again?"

"What part?" Suzanne asked.

"The part about the Jews being the wicked men who killed Christ."

Suzanne shuffled through her pages. "Jews as wicked men? I never said that."

"I, well, I thought I heard something."

"I was very careful," Suzanne said.

"I thought I heard you mention the wicked men who killed Christ and something about them being Jews." I glanced at Ranya, whose expression I couldn't read.

"I know I never said that." Suzanne read again to me about the events leading to Christ's crucifixion.

"Right there!" I interrupted her. "You talk about men of Israel being the wicked hands that killed Jesus."

I paused. "Maybe I'm a little sensitive. Or I don't have all the facts, but this is setting off some kind of an alarm in me, something very primal about Jews as Christ killers. That's what people have called us Jews for centuries. Christ killers."

"I've never heard that term before," Suzanne said.

"Christ killers? Jews as Christ killers?" I was beginning to feel a bit crazy now. "I'm not making this up . . ."

"I'm not saying you're making anything up," Suzanne said. "I'm just saying that I've never heard that term before. And I was very careful to avoid saying the Jews alone had killed Jesus."

"Yes," I said. "But you do talk about the hypocrisy of the Jewish leaders. And the Jews were the people who stood there and watched Jesus die on the cross! That's the point! Christ was killed, and we've always been blamed for it." My blood pressure was beginning to rise; my voice was shaking.

I thought Suzanne looked annoyed. "I really don't see the problem. But, I could take another look at this."

At that moment, I wished I could have been more articulate. I wished that I was a theologian—a calm academic with a PhD, who could explain the thorniness of this issue in a rational and straightforward manner. I tried my best.

But I don't think my attempt was very successful. I was distracted; too busy wondering if I was an extremely paranoid Jew, or if, somehow, somewhere, I was right about something.

PRISCILLA: *I can't speak with great authority on this, but I'm telling you that I sense, somewhere deep in my bones, that I have heard the term "Christ killer" in relation to the Jews. I was never called that, but I know other Jews have been.*
SUZANNE: *I'm not disagreeing with you. I was just not aware of that.*
PRISCILLA: *Why can't you just remove the crucifixion from your story?*
SUZANNE: *I can't do that, Priscilla. I really believe that Pentecost is the best miracle for me to write about. And at the time, Jesus is risen from the dead. I have to explain it.*

Suzanne:

As I was reading the Gospels and some Gospel commentary before writing my crucifixion story, a mystery was solved for me. I learned that the Pharisees were the chief Jewish rabbis of the time. All my life I had heard about the Pharisees, yet didn't know who they were. Now the political tension between Jesus and the Jewish leaders became so obvious to me. When Jesus threw their money-making businesses out of the temple, he threatened their livelihood. And every time he pointed out their hypocrisy, he threatened their position.

When I wrote my first account of the crucifixion, I was wary of Priscilla taking offense. I used the term "Jewish people" instead of Jews because I noticed she did the same; perhaps she felt "Jews" was derogatory. I stressed Jesus' Jewishness. If I laid any blame for the death of Jesus (which I didn't feel I did), it was upon the Pharisees and the Roman governor Pontius Pilate. So I was taken by surprise when Priscilla felt personally affronted by my retelling of the crucifixion.

There we were side by side on Ranya's couch, and as I read I could sense Priscilla pulling farther and farther away from me. One minute I was reading, the next Priscilla was looking at me with profound disbelief. "You can't write this story. It just fuels the fires of anti-Semitism," she fumed. "Blaming Jews for Jesus' death has been a driving force of anti-Semitism for centuries. How can you not know that?"

"But Priscilla," I fumbled, "that's a tiny minority of Christians. Sensible people today don't hold Jews responsible for Jesus' death two thousand years ago."

Priscilla persisted. It seemed to me that Priscilla thought the very telling of the crucifixion was insensitive to the anti-Semitic concerns of the Jewish people. "Why write about this?" she asked. "It stirs up so much trouble!" I couldn't believe that she was trying to take away from me the most essential story of Christianity for an insult that she perceived but that I never intended.

Fortunately, Ranya jumped in as peacekeeper. She declared that certainly I had meant no harm by choosing to include the crucifixion in my Pentecost story.

"It has never crossed my mind to hold Jewish people responsible for Jesus' death, Priscilla. Nor has anyone ever expressed that view to me personally," I explained to her. "In every church I've attended on Palm Sunday the story of Jesus' passion is read aloud with priests and laypeople taking various parts. Those of us in the pews are always the crowd. So when Pilate asks us what we would like him to do with Jesus, we cry aloud, 'Crucify Him! Crucify Him!'

"This has always been a powerful moment to me," I confided. "I'm wearing the sandals of the people on the street that day, and I can feel how easily one might go along with the bloodthirsty crowd. To me, the crowd is humanity. There were sympathizers of Christ, enemies of Christ, and probably lots of people who didn't care one way or the other. As I speak, I don't think about Jews killing Jesus. So many in the story, including Jesus, were Jews! I think of the times in my own life when I have not followed Jesus, when I have turned my back and cried, metaphorically, 'Crucify Him!' "

"Well, many Christians don't realize that Christ was a Jew," Priscilla remarked.

"But does what a minority of anti-Semites think take away my ability to tell a story so important to Christianity?" I asked.

"No," Priscilla admitted. "Those are two separate issues."

I left Ranya's apartment that day feeling that I was being punished unfairly. Nevertheless, I sat down to edit my writing and review the phrases that Priscilla had found offensive. These appeared when the disciple Peter addressed the "men of Israel" after Jesus' resurrection, saying "wicked hands among you have crucified and slain Jesus, whom God has raised up." Peter then exhorted the "house of Israel" to repent of their sins and be baptized as followers of Jesus.

As I played up the political tension in my story and removed some of the lines spoken by Peter, I realized that Priscilla and I processed the phrase "house of Israel" entirely differently. I thought of the Jews who heard those words or read them later and stepped forward to be baptized. She thought of the ones who remained Jews and suffered from the blame of Jesus' death for centuries.

Once my changes were complete, I felt confident that the Jewish people were no longer so easily implicated in Jesus' death.

Priscilla:

I returned home upset and confused after my meeting at Ranya's house, so I picked up the phone and called my friend Lu for a reality check. Lu is a Catholic woman and the director of the religious education program at a local parish, so she was a natural person for me to seek out.

"Do you have a minute?" I asked when she answered the phone. "I have a weird question for you. Have you ever heard the term Christ killer?"

After a moment of silence, Lu said, very slowly, "Yes."

"You have? Phew! I'm not crazy!" I quickly recounted for Lu my experience with Suzanne that afternoon. "She said she had never heard the term Christ killer!" I reported. And then Lu and I got into a long, serious discussion about the life of Jesus Christ.

"I just don't understand why Suzanne chose to write about *the* hot-button issue between Jews and Christians," I complained. "Why choose to concentrate on the most controversial moment in the life of Jesus?"

"There are a lot of other things to write about," Lu told me. "Some wonderful things, actually. Particularly if you're writing about miracles. There's the story of the five loaves and two fishes, the wedding at Cana, when Jesus turned water into wine."

"Hold on a minute! Tell me that story," I said, eager to hear about Jesus and the wonderful things he did with his life before "wicked hands" nailed him to a cross.

So, for a half an hour I stood in my kitchen and listened to stories about Jesus, completely engrossed. "That's so cool," I'd say. Or, "I had no idea." Or, "I've never heard that story. Tell me more."

And then I got to thinking. If Lu had heard the term "Christ killer" before and was so sensitive to the issue, how could Suzanne be so insensitive? Or so ignorant? Was she covering up something? Was she uncomfortable around Jews? After all, I didn't really know Suzanne. I'd just met her through this project. I didn't know her politics; I didn't know her friends. Did I even know her values?

That Sunday morning, my husband attended a lecture at our temple while I carpooled to a basketball game. I'd filled Jimmy in on our "crucifixion crisis."

"You should have come with me today!" he announced when I returned home. "A fabulous history professor spoke for an hour about the crucifixion of Christ and how that one event became the root of anti-Semitism all over the world. He called a certain interpretation of the crucifixion 'the politics of contempt.'"

"Meaning?" I pulled out paper and a pen to jot down notes.

"The New Testament was written more than thirty years after the crucifixion, and its authors had political as well as religious purposes," my husband explained. "Enlightened Christians today understand this, but for centuries the Jews have been blamed because of Matthew's writing."

"Did this professor mention Christ killers?" I was obsessed.

"Not specifically. But he said that perception is more important than reality, and for centuries the perception has been that the Jews were responsible for the death of Jesus."

So I was right. "I've got to talk to this man," I said, getting up from the table.

"I'm sure he's gone by now," my husband reported.

The temple is three blocks from my home. I ran there and arrived breathless. But the professor was gone. In a twist of fate, I found out that he was the cousin of a good friend of mine, and he was now at her house. I ran over there quickly and introduced myself to him. "I know this is a little rude," I said, "but do you think I could talk to you for just a minute? I missed your lecture, and I'm working on a project . . ."

43

The poor man was about to leave for a long drive home, but he agreed to talk briefly. So we sat on a window seat, and I quickly explained our book and our "crucifixion crisis" to him.

"Read *Constantine's Sword*," the professor told me. "And the book of Matthew, chapter 27."

In my later research, I learned that according to Matthew's gospel, the Roman governor Pontius Pilate turned to the Jews and asked, "Whom do you want me to release, Barabbas or Jesus?" The Jews called for the release of Barabbas and the execution of Jesus. And then Pilate washed his hands of the whole matter, saying, "I am innocent of the blood of this just person." And the people answered, "His blood be upon us and our children."

As the history professor explained, "Many scholars of all faiths agree that what actually took place was not the way it was depicted in the New Testament. The Jews and Romans were both afraid of Jesus, but for different reasons. The Romans feared his political power, and the Jews feared his religious views. But, most importantly, the Romans would never have given the Jews such power over this decision, given them the option to authorize the death of Jesus."

I quickly related the story of how Suzanne had denied ever hearing the term "Christ killer." I expressed disbelief, given all that he'd said about the subject, that an informed Christian woman in this day and age could profess such ignorance.

But the professor was not surprised. He gave Suzanne the benefit of the doubt.

"I think it's probable that your friend raised this issue naively," he told me. And then he stood up to leave. I'd taken up more of his time than I'd intended. I followed him to the door and thanked him.

As I walked home, I felt slightly more educated but still very confused.

PRISCILLA: *Ranya, every single person I spoke to over the weekend, Jew and non-Jew, had heard the term "Christ killer."*

RANYA: *That doesn't surprise me.*

PRISCILLA: *But Suzanne hadn't heard it. And she made me feel nuts, or certainly paranoid. If she can't understand why I had a problem, I don't see how I can continue to work on this project.*

Ranya:

Priscilla arrived at my door for our next meeting clearly agitated. She had come early to talk to me alone. Up until now Priscilla had been so warm and open to dialogue. I'd thought of her as a nonconfrontational person, someone who sought to connect with people. She was interested in debate, but she also seemed able to see all sides. Or try to.

But today Priscilla was totally fired up, ready to take a stand and hold onto that position fiercely, come what may. Everything about her—her stance, her facial expressions and gestures—had assumed a certain gravity. This seemed to be a defining moment for her.

As Priscilla spoke, her words tumbled out quickly. She'd thought about her conversation with Suzanne all week, she told me. She'd consulted other people—a Catholic friend, a history professor—and now she felt, more than ever, that the issue of anti-Semitism arising from insensitive portrayals of the crucifixion was real, and one that had been hotly debated for centuries. "I'm not the only one who feels this way!" she was able to tell me now. Maybe that's what gave her the strength to say what she said to me and what she was planning to say to Suzanne.

Priscilla was planning to quit our project if she felt that Suzanne had not taken into account her sensitivities while rewriting her crucifixion chapter. "I need to know that Suzanne found my concerns valid," she said. I was dismayed. Priscilla had clearly debated this issue internally, but was not open to debate now.

"Maybe it's me," she said. "Maybe I *am* too sensitive. But if that's the case, then I'll just back off. I don't see how I can stay on. I wish you guys luck, and I think this is a terrific project. Maybe I'm just not the right person for it."

I listened to Priscilla, but when she told me that she had indeed drafted a letter of resignation to Suzanne and me, I told her that I thought she should keep an open mind. "Let's see what changes Suzanne has made," I suggested. I knew Suzanne was thoughtful and insightful, and I felt she would respond to Priscilla's concerns with sensitivity. We had, after all, ended our last meeting with the clear message that Priscilla was upset.

I realized that the role of mediator in this whole controversy was going to fall to me. How ironic, I thought. This was something I never expected. I had anticipated that other conflicts might arise in the course of this project, but the issue of the crucifixion was something I had never considered a hot topic.

My role as a mediator was such a Muslim one, I realized. After all, Muhammad called on his followers to respect both Christians and Jews, whom he called "people of the book." He affirmed the two faiths, and at the moment, that was my role in our threesome. I needed to tell both Priscilla and Suzanne that their feelings were valid.

I had heard the term "Christ killer" once before in my life. Years ago, in college, I had a Catholic friend who was in love with a Jewish boy, but she felt that she could never bring him home to meet her parents because as religious people they had grown up with the idea that the Jews were the people responsible for the death of Jesus.

I understood both sides of our debate, and I needed to contain Priscilla somehow, so that Suzanne wouldn't feel that we'd doubled up on her. I needed to make Suzanne feel safe if any progress was to be made.

The doorbell rang, and I went to greet Suzanne, who gave me a bright smile. I rolled my eyes and said, "We might not have a project here."

Priscilla:

I was a little nervous at the prospect of seeing Suzanne again, but when she walked in the door of Ranya's apartment, she seemed relaxed.

Had I demonized this lovely woman?

My husband has often remarked on my "hair-trigger" temper, my ability to fly off the handle if something or someone upsets me. Although I'd been ranting and raving about prejudice and bigotry over the last week, when Suzanne walked in the door I wondered if I hadn't overreacted, if my "hair trigger" had played a role in our "crucifixion crisis."

I kept my letter of resignation hidden under my pile of papers, and Ranya made what might have been an awkward situation, at least momentarily, quite comfortable. Suzanne, for her part, seemed relaxed. She smiled as she sat down next to me on the couch, and we dispensed with the small talk that usually opened our meetings, getting right down to business at Ranya's suggestion.

Suzanne reported that she'd reworked her chapter and was very happy with the results. I kept my mouth shut as she read aloud to us, and somehow I was able to hear what she was reading as though I was hearing it for the first time.

Her story of Jesus was colorful and engaging. I listened closely, especially when she began to describe the crucifixion. As hard as I listened, no words jumped out at me. Nothing sounded inflammatory. Before I knew it, her story was over. And nothing had happened. No alarms went off, despite the fact that Suzanne was basically retelling the same story she'd told the last time.

"Well," I said after a moment of slightly awkward silence, "that sounds fine. Thank you." Suzanne smiled, and put her papers down.

And that was that. I don't know if the fact that a history professor had given Suzanne the benefit of the doubt persuaded me to keep an open mind during this meeting. I don't know if I was just sick and tired of debating the issue of "Christ killers." Maybe Suzanne had made small but significant changes. Maybe all of the above were true.

Or maybe I had overreacted in the first place.

Was that possible?

SUZANNE: *Priscilla, do you think it was reasonable for you to take what I wrote about the crucifixion so personally?*
PRISCILLA: *No, it was visceral and emotional.*
SUZANNE: *So what was your reaction based on?*
PRISCILLA: *I think all Jews are sensitive to anti-Semitism, because of the Holocaust. You can't underestimate what that means to Jews.*
RANYA: *I don't think people do underestimate its meaning.*
PRISCILLA: *It happened once, and if it happened once it could happen again.*
SUZANNE: *Do you really think that?*
PRISCILLA: *No. The world is a different place. But fear is not rational. It's emotional.*

Suzanne:

I had been doing a little homework on anti-Semitism over the past week in an attempt to understand Priscilla's sensitivity to my crucifixion story. I had spent time online and made a trip to Barnes & Noble to buy *The Complete Idiot's Guide to Understanding Judaism* (along with *The Complete Idiot's Guide to Understanding Islam*). I figured I had to start somewhere.

As I explored the issue of anti-Semitism, I learned that throughout European history, Jews had been discriminated against, expelled from various regions, and their assets confiscated with the consent of governments. They were segregated, taxed, prevented from owning land or engaging in traditional crafts, and excluded from universities and academies. Hatred toward them had been whipped up through fabrications like one about Jews baking their matzoh with the blood of Christian children.

I was alarmed to read that even now there are some who believe the lies printed in the Zionist protocols, a document produced by an anti-Jewish movement in France at the turn of the twentieth century. As I read about how the crucifixion story had been used to stir up anti-Semitism, I began to understand the extent of the prejudice that Jews had lived with for centuries. How had it actually touched Priscilla in her own life? And why did Priscilla assume I was on that bandwagon?

> PRISCILLA: *Even the name of the Easter service you described to me—the Passion Play—sounds like the Jews are bloodthirsty. Like they're calling out for Jesus to be nailed to the cross.*
> SUZANNE: *Priscilla, the Passion Play is not about you at all! It's not about the Jews!*
> PRISCILLA: *But when you call out "Crucify him!" you're playing the part of the bad guys, and P.S., the bad guys were Jews!*

Priscilla:

"Jews have tried for centuries not to rock the boat," I tried to explain. "After the crucifixion, Christians created what they thought was a better religion, a religion that became hugely popular, leaving Jews in the dust. Jesus came along, and we didn't jump on the bandwagon, which, in the long run, has made our lives as Jews much more difficult."

When I returned home after our meeting, I identified a few other factors that had contributed to my reaction. I realized that some primal fears and discomfort had been stirred up in me as a result of Suzanne's writing and our discussions.

I remembered, for the first time in years, how my mother, never a particularly religious Jew, had yelled at a babysitter when she caught her preaching to us about how we should accept baby Jesus as our savior. As a child I felt excluded and isolated when I overheard the Christian kids in our neighborhood talk about how Jesus loved them. I'm sure the fact that I dated a Christian boy for so long, and lived in his truly "High Episcopalian" world, also contributed to my self-consciousness as a Jew.

I thought back to my days at the Hebrew Day School as well. Surely, I came away from that educational experience during my formative years strongly influenced by the notion that Jews needed to band together. Isolated from the outside world, I must have gotten the message that we needed to be wary of "others" who might be inhospitable to our faith.

My father's attitudes also contributed to my wariness. He had often felt like an outsider, in boarding school, in the Navy, in certain financial institutions in New England. On Christmas Day the year before he died, he made a pronouncement, half in jest, while Jimmy and I were spending a quiet day in the country with him, driving on unusually empty roads. I remarked how relaxing Christmas was for Jews. No presents to wrap, no tree to trim, no food to cook. "Christmas is a good day to relax," my father agreed. "For two days out of the year, Christmas and Easter, Jews should just leave the goyim [non-Jews] alone. It's better that way." I grew up in the company of Christians, but I had a sense of when I could participate and when I should just fly under the radar.

My youngest son once described the same sense of discomfort about being a Jew in a Christian country. When he was seven or eight, he took notice of all the Christmas lights in our neighborhood. "Why does everyone have to have such bright lights?" he asked me, slightly annoyed. "They're everywhere! It's not fair! We don't get to have lights, or trees, or presents."

Before our next meeting, I had a disturbing conversation with a woman at my health club that made me once again feel like an outsider. This woman asked what I'd been writing about lately. Amid the weight machines and busy health club members, I told her about our book project and that launched us into a discussion about extremist religious groups. This woman and I were soon talking about evangelical Christians and why they support Israel so strongly.

"You know," she told me, "they're waiting until Judgment Day." This woman was Christian. She was related to someone with strong evangelical beliefs. "They want the state of Israel to exist because that's where they expect the messiah will come again. But you know," she continued ominously, "once the messiah comes, they believe that all Jews will convert or perish. That's what the religious right isn't saying when they talk about keeping Israel safe. One day they expect there will be no Jews left."

I had never heard anyone explain to me exactly what the evangelicals believed about Jews, the messiah, and the end of the world, which even had a name: The Rapture. The story disturbed me. It didn't sound "good for the Jews," as my father might have said.

SUZANNE: *I still wonder what influences in your Jewish background affected your reaction to my retelling of the crucifixion.*
PRISCILLA: *I think I'm just wired to be sensitive to any situation in which a Jew feels excluded from the majority. Maybe that's hard to grasp because, as a Christian, you're the majority and so rarely feel persecution. And by the way, why do you have such a problem with me having a problem?*
SUZANNE: *I don't. I'm just curious about what's behind it.*
PRISCILLA: *I feel like I have to justify my feelings to you, Suzanne.*
SUZANNE: *I am not asking you to justify your feelings. They happened. They're valid. I would just like to understand why Jesus made you so uncomfortable.*
PRISCILLA: *I don't know . . . every time I see him up on a cross, suffering and bloody, I avert my eyes. When I checked into a hotel room in Italy once and there was a crucifix over the bed, I took it down.*
SUZANNE: *You did?*

Priscilla: *Yes. I didn't want a dead man who meant nothing to me hanging over my head. It's disturbing!*

Ranya: *Jesus meant nothing to you, Priscilla? I doubt that. He must have meant something if you went to the trouble of taking down that cross!*

Priscilla:

When Suzanne pressed me once again on what in my background made me react to her retelling of the crucifixion, I finally exploded. "We're outnumbered!" I cried out. "That's the point I've been trying to make all this time! It's very hard to be a minority!" I looked directly at Suzanne. "I envy you the luxury of knowing that millions and millions of people, the majority of the world you live in, agree with you on the very fundamental beliefs that govern most of your decisions."

I recounted a trip I took to Rome years ago. I remember walking into St. Peter's Basilica for the first time and being completely overwhelmed as I stood beneath Bernini's magnificent, lavishly conceived golden altar. I'd never felt so Jewish in my life, I told Suzanne and Ranya. For the very first time I felt, viscerally, the awesome power of the Catholic Church, especially when I reflected on the visit we'd just paid to the Jewish ghetto in Venice, where modest synagogues had been hidden behind heavy wooden shutters. We Jews are so outnumbered, I realized. We're such a small tribe, in comparison to the enormously powerful, wealthy religion of Catholicism. No wonder Jews feel so sensitive to anti-Semitism. We could be crushed and overpowered so easily. When we visited the Vatican Museum later, I was again overwhelmed. The church had amassed so much in worldly goods. For Jews there is nowhere on earth like the Vatican.

And there never will be. In the weeks following our crucifixion crisis, I started realizing that maybe I'd better get used to that fact. And that maybe Jesus was someone I needed to understand better. So I began letting him into my life a bit.

I was channel surfing in our den at home one evening when I came across a program on the last days of Jesus. It was a slightly cheesy reenactment, but I was really into it. Jesus was on my mind now. After all Suzanne and I had been through, I was curious to see how the crucifixion would be handled. I was mesmerized, hanging on every word.

But then my son walked into the room and got upset, confused as to why I was watching a show about Jesus. "Why are you watching that? Turn it off!" he said. Somehow I think he felt that same fear I had experienced as a child that studying Jesus carefully was some kind of no-no for a Jew. I tried to explain to him that Jesus was a Jew and a very good man, full of wonderful qualities that everyone can learn from.

My son left the room, but I did not turn off the special. I allowed myself to watch it and continued to be mesmerized. These specials ran every so often. I'd noticed them in the background all my life. But now I watched carefully to see how this version of events compared with what Suzanne had written for our book.

Jesus stood for everything righteous, I realized. His mere presence on earth was incredibly powerful. The kindness and goodness that emanated from him were Christian in the best sense of the word. At our next meeting, I told Suzanne and Ranya about the program.

"I'm on a first-name basis with Jesus now," I said. It was a joke. But I meant it. Jesus no longer scared me. I no longer felt like a bad Jew for finding his words and deeds fascinating to hear and something to learn from.

Ranya:

Unlike Priscilla, I've never felt threatened by Jesus. Muslims are taught that he was one of the most important prophets, immaculately conceived by the Virgin Mary. But clearly Priscilla had different feelings about Jesus, and they weren't good ones. I couldn't believe it when she told us that she had once taken down the crucifix she'd discovered in a hotel room.

I think Priscilla responded as she did to Suzanne's story because, as a Jew, Priscilla is basically hardwired to stay alert to anti-Semitism. She knows that Christian texts have been used against the Jewish people for centuries. Whether or not the person sitting across from her buys into the Jewish blame doesn't matter. Priscilla has some sort of primal fear that they might. As a result, she is constantly vigilant. I can understand how Suzanne, on the other hand, felt entitled to tell her uncensored story of Jesus' life and death without fear of being labeled an anti-Semite. I know this feeling well. I fear being labeled an anti-Semite whenever I am critical of Israel.

CHAPTER FIVE

Stop Stereotyping Me!

Ranya:

I was relieved that we had survived the crucifixion crisis even if I had felt a little sidelined, if not outright banished. I wondered if Suzanne and Priscilla were more interested in each other's religions than in exploring their connections to Islam. In spite of my creeping doubts, I recognized a growing attachment on my part to our meetings. I needed us to continue meeting and talking.

If initially I had reached out to them out of despair, anger, and concern for my children, lately Priscilla and Suzanne were fulfilling a more personal, selfish need. They had become my spiritual anchors, rescuing me from my spiritual isolation and frustration. My ongoing search for an imam and mosque continued to leave me stranded and empty handed. At times I felt lonely, fearful that such an imam or mosque may not actually exist. As a result, our meetings effectively became my mosque, church, and temple, headquartered right here in my living room. My surrogate spiritual community.

Our dialogue challenged me to examine many of my unresolved issues and fears, some long buried. As we made a commitment to continue to meet, explore, and reveal increasingly personal thoughts we certainly did not suffer from a shortage of questions or material. Life organically and generously provided us with a rich, abundant reservoir. Aging parents, curious children, skeptical friends, cocktail parties, book clubs, and even holiday cards inspired our conversations and revelations.

We were breaking an unspoken social rule. We were talking about God and religion at a time when the stakes were high, when turmoil and confusion were the order of the day. We were harried, busy mothers, but at our meetings we found ourselves released from time, suspended from the reality of the outside world. No matter how harrowing or challenging our conversations became, we found ourselves addicted, unable to imagine not pursuing the dialogue that had us coming back for more, week after week.

Our relationship was turning into something sacred, something we began to call our "Faith Club."

We signed no official pact, but we lived by a certain code: honesty was the first rule of the Faith Club, and with that tenet as a foundation, no topic was off limits.

Suzanne:

Ranya, Priscilla, and I had started out months earlier talking about what *Jews* believe, what *Christians* believe and what *Muslims* believe. We were like soldiers galloping forth from our camps carrying the standards of our people. We'd presented those standards to each other and examined them to see if they bore any of the same markings as our own. But now it was time to take off our uniforms and begin talking about the real people underneath. In other words, us.

So we made a commitment to each other to examine our own beliefs and prejudices and discuss them frankly. We would no longer hide behind Moses, Jesus, and Muhammad.

I was hesitant to make the leap from a children's book project to an interfaith dialogue. By nature, I am fairly reserved. And already the crucifixion crisis had stirred up more disagreement and anxiety than I was comfortable with. I feared that as we explored our differences, the connections we had made thus far would frizzle and break in the heat. When my husband and a few friends sensed my reluctance, they encouraged me to drop the project. But I couldn't let go. I felt that if Priscilla, Ranya, and I could stick together, we would learn a great deal. I was certain I would come out wiser in the end.

So that summer I borrowed a laptop and took it with me to New Hampshire, where we spend the months of July and August. Ranya, Priscilla, and I had assigned ourselves a summer writing project, "What religious stereotypes did we carry of one another?"

As I contemplated what to write, I was still thinking about Priscilla's anti-Semitic alarm. Did she need it to protect herself from someone like me? Was I an anti-Semite? Not in action. But sometimes, I realized as I thought back over the past year, I had harbored negative feelings about Jews, feelings I was not proud to share.

I remembered the time in the fall of 2001 when our church renovation meant that our Sunday services were relocated to a hospitable Jewish synagogue nearby. Honestly, I never got used to my children proudly crying out as we passed Seventy-sixth Street and Park Avenue, "Mommy! There's our temple!" At first I hushed them. "Why, Mom?" they asked. I couldn't tell them the truth. I couldn't say, "People will think we're Jewish." I was embarrassed to discover that I had that thought. And certainly that was not the message I wanted to give my children. So I let them cry out. But every time they did, it was a wake-up call to me. Why was I uncomfortable being mistaken for a Jew?

Could I possibly make this revelation to Priscilla? I hesitated. That summer the laptop sat open on the desk in my bedroom. Daily its keyboard dared me to type the words that would reveal my temple experience. I played tennis and kayaked. I hiked. I swam. But I always returned to that screen. Finally, that laptop became my confessional. I couldn't have made this revelation face to face with Priscilla back then. But I could on paper. I was making an offering to her. I was admitting my guilt. I was agreeing that perhaps she was right to be defensive about her Jewish identity. I hoped Priscilla would accept my guilt and forgive me.

But I was unsure of how she would respond. She'd almost quit over the crucifixion crisis, and that slight was accidental. This was the real thing.

When we gathered in my living room that fall, I sat nervously with three copies of my temple confession on my lap. I was prepared to share it. However, it quickly became clear that this wasn't the time to talk about anti-Semitism. Priscilla had just gotten disturbing news about her mother. She was upset and needed to talk. I felt traitorous as I searched for the words to comfort her, all the while holding the scarlet letter of my prejudice on my lap.

Priscilla:

Suzanne, Ranya, and I had agreed to examine our lives and go deeper in our discussions with each other. Ironically and unfortunately, I now had plenty to talk about. And agonize over.

My seventy-four-year-old mother, who had lived her life as a colorful, outspoken artist, had suffered two small strokes. Signs of dementia were evident, and doctors had determined that she could no longer live alone.

I had just returned from delivering that news to her, and I was exhausted, sad, and depleted as I arrived late to our meeting and related the details of my trip to Ranya and Suzanne.

I'd sat with my mother on her living room couch delivering difficult news quietly. I told my mother that we would have to find nursing care for her, that she could no longer drive or sleep alone in her house. "Do you want to talk more about this?" I asked her gently. She shook her head, no. Giant tears rolled down her cheeks, but she remained silent, never one to confront her feelings head on.

My mother never told any of the doctors who examined her that she had a sister in California who suffered from Alzheimer's disease, who'd been institutionalized years earlier. But she did tell me that I would be murdering her if I put her in a nursing home. The doctors had informed me that my mother had vascular dementia and possible Alzheimer's. I'm not sure exactly what they told her.

"What are you going to do?" Suzanne asked me.

"I have no idea." I shook my head sadly.

But my news was not all bad. I'd found an amazing woman to take care of my mother, I told Suzanne and Ranya. An enormously kind, highly competent woman named Betty had just moved in with her. The situation was stable.

But I was exhausted. I could see that my mother was becoming a much different person. Chunks of her old self were falling off like pieces of an iceberg. Cancer, as I experienced it with my father, was a valiant, oftentimes courageous battle. Dementia appeared to be a slow, steady, messy state of affairs.

"I guess I'll have plenty to write about," I said, mustering a sad smile.

Suzanne thought for a moment. She looked as if she had something to share, and then offered me some tea. And sympathy.

We talked about a couple of newspaper articles that had caught our attention since our last meeting and some books we had read. But I was distracted, and I had to leave early for a doctor's appointment in the neighborhood.

As I rose to gather my things, Suzanne stood up. "Here," she said. "I wrote something that I didn't get a chance to read to you today."

I put the envelope she handed to me into my satchel and headed out the door.

Ranya:

I stayed behind after Priscilla left that afternoon and helped Suzanne clear the dining table. As Priscilla rushed out the door I saw Suzanne give her a copy of the work she had prepared, then Suzanne came back into the kitchen and handed me my own. I was about to put it away to read later in the quiet of my home. "No," implored Suzanne. "Read it now. I want to know what you think."

I skimmed through Suzanne's writing until my eyes fixated with shock at the segment where Suzanne had revealed her deepest, perhaps even most subconscious, prejudice. Not only had she completely exposed herself, but she did it in the context of Judaism and temple. I knew that people could be labeled anti-Semitic for comments that were much less personal, such as criticism of Zionism and the Israeli state. In my own experience, even my insistence on being recognized as a Palestinian has made me feel suspect, in some Jewish circles, as an anti-Semite.

I read and reread that segment of Suzanne's writing a few times just to make sure that I had it right. I then looked up at her and asked, "Does Priscilla have the same document?"

"Yes."

"Do you think she'll ever talk to you again?"

"It's not that bad, is it?" Suzanne winced.

I paused. "It's my experience that it's very easy to be accused of anti-Semitism."

Priscilla:

I left Suzanne's envelope in my tote bag for a few days. Finally, when I had a quiet moment, I sat down and read her confession about hushing her children outside of the temple. I thought it was awfully brave of Suzanne to put herself out there. She was so honest about her feelings, feelings that other non-Jews might have hidden from me and others.

I was surprised at Suzanne's candor and honesty, but I was not shocked at the notion that she was uncomfortable being mistaken for a Jew. To be honest, our crucifixion crisis still lingered in my mind. I did not feel that Suzanne was an anti-Semite, but I did wonder just how much real, everyday exposure she'd had to Jews on a personal level. Did she have any Jewish friends? Her writing made me feel that she probably did not. But that fact did not surprise me. I grew up in a community in which Jews and Christians were often segregated.

It's not that I see every non-Jew as a potential anti-Semite, but I did grow up hearing stories of discrimination. I knew the derogatory slang terms for Jews that some of my friends (on rare occasions) had been called. One friend in particular had been driven home by his best friend's father who, upon pulling into his driveway, said, "Get out of the car, you little kike."

The city I grew up in was Christian for the most part, and segregated in many ways, at least socially. Jews belonged to clubs they had set up after some of the well-established Christian clubs had denied them access. My Jewish friends at the Quaker school sometimes joked that there were so many of us in our particular class because the school was building a new wing and raising money the year we were all admitted. Providence had for many years been dominated by a group of wealthy Protestants. It was a big deal when my parents were invited to join a "Waspy" club in town.

I could joke about anti-Semitism with my Jewish friends, but I also knew, deep down, the seriousness of the charge. Quite recently, my husband, who had a job in the media business, had been the target of a disturbing anonymous telephone call demanding to know if he was a Jew. I knew anti-Semitism existed all over the world, but I did not truly believe that it existed in my little world with Ranya and Suzanne.

To be honest, however, I did wonder if I would be Suzanne's first real "Jewish friend." And then I switched gears and wondered if the distance I'd felt sometimes with Suzanne was based on something else. Had I labeled her as "the reserved WASP" of our trio early on in our relationship while Ranya and I were more the fiery, emotional types? Were the differences I had with Suzanne due to personal qualities and characteristics, or to our religious faith, or both? Had I overreacted to her profession of the deep comfort that she felt from Jesus? I often felt a bit like a "neurotic Jew" with Suzanne. I tended to be more emotional and explosive. Suzanne was remarkably calm, composed, and seemed self-assured, a quality I admired but felt I did not possess—a quality that intimidated me.

> SUZANNE: *Priscilla, do you think of me as someone who follows her religion blindly?*
> PRISCILLA: *Like a sheep? No! I don't think that at all!*
> SUZANNE: *Do you feel I'm not as intelligent as you are because I don't have the same doubts you have?*
> PRISCILLA: *No!*
> SUZANNE: *But you've talked about the "rigidity" of my beliefs!*
> PRISCILLA: *I envy you for that belief!*
> SUZANNE: *I think you're boxing me into the image you have of a naive, Southern believer, someone with a smug attitude of superiority about her religion. And I don't think that's me.*

Suzanne:

A week had passed and Priscilla had not mentioned a word about my temple writing. Then she sent me an email.

It was not, as I'd feared, about my confession. It was about something I'd written ages ago. I breathed a sigh of relief, but then read on.

"I think you've raised some interesting points," Priscilla wrote. "But could you elaborate a bit more about the rigidity of your Christian beliefs?"

Rigidity? I was furious. With one word Priscilla had unintentionally revealed what I had suspected she thought of me and my faith.

I called Ranya and read her the email. "I can't believe she sent me this!"

"I'm sure she didn't mean to offend you. Why don't we get together, and you can ask Priscilla what she meant," Ranya offered. "How about Sunday evening at my place?"

When I called Priscilla to suggest a weekend meeting, our conversation was polite, but curt. I was eager to confront her, and she might have picked up on my mood. But still there was no mention of my temple writing.

On Sunday evening we assembled at Ranya's apartment. It was the middle of November, and the sky was darkening. Across the street the stained-glass windows of St. Jean-Baptiste were beginning to glow in red, blue, and yellow. Diverting us from the cozy living room couches where we usually sat, Ranya led the way to the dining room table, where she had a tape recorder ready at her place. This evening's meeting was all business.

"Would you like cake?" Ranya asked as we settled in. "It was Sami's birthday yesterday, and I have a great chocolate cake from Amy's Bread."

"You know I can't say no to chocolate," laughed Priscilla as she reached for a glistening, dark slice of cake.

Ranya made tea, while Priscilla and I discussed the traffic on the Hutchinson River Parkway. Then, as soon as Ranya sat down, I let out the steam that had been percolating inside me all weekend.

"Priscilla, I'm getting the impression that you think of me as someone who follows her religion blindly," I began. Priscilla barely had a chance to speak before I was at her again. All of my suppressed emotion bubbled to the surface as I attacked Priscilla for what I believed was her prejudice against churchgoing Christians.

Ranya tried to join the argument, but Priscilla shut her down, saying, "We're not talking about you right now! We are at a salient point in the Judeo-Christian conflict."

"But I feel excluded from the Judeo-Christian tradition. Why isn't it the Judeo-Christian-Muslim tradition?" Ranya persisted.

"Let's talk about that later," Priscilla and I answered. Then we turned back toward each other to continue our argument.

"Sure," Ranya mumbled in resignation. Her feelings were hurt, but she held back and allowed us to get deeper into our confrontation.

Priscilla:

I felt guilty for a moment that I was not addressing Ranya. Once again she was being "banished." But I had ground to cover with Suzanne. She'd called this meeting. And she'd called me on the carpet. Now I was going to give her a taste of her own medicine. Cake or no cake, this was no ordinary tea party we were having. I'd brought my copy of Suzanne's temple confession with me.

Suzanne sat directly opposite me with her notebook opened to a list of questions.

But I didn't need notes. I spoke from the heart.

Suzanne had accused me, based on an email I'd sent her, of labeling her Christian beliefs rigid.

"I don't think you're a blind follower," I told her. We'd had our confrontation over the crucifixion, but I would truly never have characterized Suzanne as naive or easily led. Nor would I call her smug, or arrogant in her beliefs.

But she'd written a confession that was extremely incriminating. And now I was ready to turn the tables and confront her.

"I have something to bring up with you," I said. My voice shook a bit. Suzanne was upset because I'd called her rigid? She'd confessed to something far more serious!

And now I had her right where I wanted her. Down on paper.

"Remember that journal entry you wrote?" I asked.

Suzanne's face revealed nothing.

I leaned across the table and looked straight into her eyes.

PRISCILLA: *You know, Suzanne, I read what you wrote last week. That was very brave of you to admit your discomfort. But you didn't explain exactly what you felt when you passed the temple with your children, and they called out, "There's our temple, Mommy!"*

SUZANNE: *I'm not sure I knew exactly what I felt.*

PRISCILLA: *Do you now?*

SUZANNE: *I think I didn't want to be identified as being the stereotype of a Jew.*

PRISCILLA: *There you go! So, what is the stereotype?*

SUZANNE: *Well . . .*

PRISCILLA: *What would be so bad about being mistaken for a Jew? Were you embarrassed? Did you not want to be a Jew?*

SUZANNE: *I'm not sure.*

PRISCILLA: *If my children said "There's our church!" I would say "No, honey, we're not Christians, we're Jews." But you felt something beyond that. What was it?*

SUZANNE: *I don't know how to express it.*

PRISCILLA: *Relax, Suzanne. I don't think you're anti-Semitic. But if I'm going to be honest, then you have to be honest. Right here and right now.*

Suzanne:

I was horrified when Priscilla called me on my temple moment. I thought it was enough that I had confessed my experience. But she needed more. She wanted to know why I felt that way—just like I wanted to know why she had reacted so emotionally to my crucifixion story. I wasn't sure I could articulate the answer. My face flushed. I hemmed and hawed, buying time.

"She wouldn't want to be a Muslim either," Ranya interjected.

But Priscilla wouldn't let me off the hook. "So, what's the stereotype, Suzanne?" she coaxed.

"You know I have Jewish friends, too, Priscilla," I said in a feeble attempt to defend myself.

"Some of my best friends are Jewish. Ha-ha," Priscilla teased. "So what's the stereotype?"

"All right," I sighed. "I guess it's someone who is pushy. And, well, someone who cares very much about money. And then there's the Woody Allen neuroticism."

"Suzanne, two out of three of those things justified the Holocaust. So I rest my case!" Priscilla said somewhat triumphantly.

"What case?" I asked her.

"I rest my case as to why Jews carry the Holocaust around with them. Why we are sometimes accused of being obsessed with it. Because even enlightened, intelligent, kind Christian people such as you can sit here at a table and verbalize the stereotype of a Jew as a pushy person who is obsessed with money."

"That stereotype is multiplied by one hundred for a Muslim today," Ranya remarked.

Priscilla cut her off. "Okay, but we are not talking about you right now, Ranya." Then she turned back to me. "Maybe you can understand now, Suzanne. You paused before you said those words. But they are very stereotypical words that you used, and they are the same words Hitler used. Pushy, aggressive, consumed with money. It all goes back to the money changers in the temple."

"Maybe this illustrates a difference between Christianity and Judaism," I speculated. "In Christianity, there is a prejudice against wealth and materialism. Jesus said that it is easier for a camel to get through the eye of a needle than for a rich man to get into heaven. There is another passage in which a wealthy man who follows all the commandments asks Jesus what else he can do. Jesus tells him, 'Leave all your goods behind and follow me.'"

"Well, corrupt CEOs like Ken Lay must have missed those sermons," Priscilla said sarcastically. "Listen, I can't quote scripture off the top of my head. Maybe Christians did have more guidance on the subject of materialism in the New Testament. But I can assure you that nowhere in the Torah does it say accumulate as much money as you can, and screw your investors! I was raised by my parents to be very generous to those less fortunate than we were. I have always led a charitable life and have taught my children to do the same. You know, whenever there's a scandal on Wall Street, we Jews say, please God, don't let it be a Jew! We're paranoid about the stereotype of Jews obsessed with accumulating money."

"Do you think that stereotype is a vestige of the Jewish struggle against persecution?" I wondered. "Wealth and education are two ways to ensure survival when you're being persecuted."

"Could be," Priscilla said with a shrug. "I know a woman whose parents were both Holocaust survivors. She said it was assumed in her family that she would go to college and get an advanced degree. Her father, who lost everything, told her that nobody would ever be able to take her education away from her."

"Just because I know those stereotypes doesn't make me an anti-Semite," I asserted.

"The fact that you know they exist doesn't make you bad," Priscilla replied. "But, you were embarrassed to say them."

Of course I was embarrassed. I flushed beet red as I talked about Jews being obsessed with money. But I realized I had to address Priscilla's question, just like I asked her to address mine. We were trying to understand each other, and sometimes the truth hurt. It was painful for the person saying it, and it hurt the person receiving it.

Priscilla wasn't finished yet. Next she asked me about those "Jewish friends" I mentioned. "Who are they?"

I knew lots of Jewish people, I told Priscilla. I live in New York after all.

But then I thought back in time. Did I know any Jews as a child? I grew up in a neighborhood with three or four orthodox families on the block, I remembered. But we weren't exactly friends. On Friday evenings in the summer, my friends and I would ride our bikes in front of their houses to peer in the living room windows at the black-coated men bowing and praying. As a child, I swam, played softball, and took ballet classes at the Jewish Community Center, but I don't remember having any Jewish friends there either. For the most part, we stuck with the Catholics who used the facility, too, I admitted finally to Priscilla.

When I worked at *Forbes* magazine, I became good friends with a Jewish woman, and I learned about being Jewish through our friendship. When this friend's mother died, we talked about how Jews view the afterlife. My husband and I went to her wedding and danced (or tried to dance) to Jewish music. But I went to work for another magazine, and my friend moved to the suburbs. We exchange holiday cards, but I hadn't talked to her in a couple of years.

So why didn't I have any close Jewish friends? In part because people, including me, gravitate toward others like ourselves. They're easier to understand. I moved from Kansas City to New York and married another Catholic Midwesterner. Priscilla married an East Coast Jew. Ranya found a Muslim Arab American. The other reason I don't have many close Jewish friends is because I don't have to. There are so many Christians to choose from. As Priscilla keeps telling me (in a way that makes me feel uncomfortable), I'm in the majority. I'm not forced to accommodate myself to the culture, religion, or even friendships of minorities.

Priscilla:

Suzanne and I had survived an amazing confrontation, and I was exhausted. Ranya, however, was still wide awake. And ready to talk. The least I could do was listen. It was her turn now, after all.

> RANYA: *I know, Priscilla, that you are not interested in my view. But I feel like I am fighting stereotypes every day. A mother hosting my daughter on a playdate asked if Leia had any dietary restrictions. Another acquaintance recently asked to see my sister's wedding pictures. She thought she would be wearing ethnic regalia. But, in fact, even my grandmother wore a white dress to her wedding.*

PRISCILLA: *Really?*

RANYA: *When I meet someone new I often feel I have to immediately sound smart and educated. That is one of the reasons I was a student forever.*

PRISCILLA: *Is that the stereotype? That Islamic women are not educated?*

RANYA: *Yes. That they don't go to school. That they don't know the worth of money, they buy one hundred of the same dress in the same color. They are repressed by their husbands, covered up, and controlled.*

PRISCILLA: *But that is such a stereotype. You're nothing like that!*

RANYA: *Yes, but sometimes I wonder, Priscilla, whether you admire me for who I am or because I defy some type of stereotype you might have.*

PRISCILLA: *Whoa! So you're saying that I stereotype Muslim women?*

Ranya:

Priscilla and Suzanne had been heatedly engaged for more than an hour. At last they turned their attention to me.

"I don't think Suzanne would like to be a Muslim woman either. Would you, Suzanne?" I asked.

"No. Especially after 9/11 it would be very uncomfortable," Suzanne admitted.

Priscilla wasn't so sure, however, that the life of a Muslim was influenced by stereotyping before then. "I think that before 9/11, Islam wasn't on the radar screen of most Americans," she said. "No offense, Ranya, but you're flattering yourself to think that there was a stereotype of a Muslim."

That was the last straw for me. Talk about being banished! I had been sitting there, patiently struggling to make my voice heard, as Suzanne and Priscilla went at it in their so-called "salient moment" of the Judeo-Christian tradition. Forget Judeo-Christian-Muslim tradition, I thought to myself. I could not even get my stereotypes recognized! Adding insult to injury, I'd recently heard that some churches in the United States had, in the past, justified slavery by calling it "Ishmael's curse." Some people believed that Africans were the descendants of Ishmael and that, as the illegitimate branch of the monotheistic family, discrimination against them was justified by the Bible.

"There were no Muslim stereotypes? You're kidding!" I exclaimed in exasperation. "What about the hijackings in the eighties? Pan Am/Lockerbie? We're living the eighties all over again now! This is what my college years were like. When Americans think of Islam, they think of terrorism, fanatics, abused women, spoiled rich Arabs, a religion of the sword, spread by the sword."

But Priscilla defended her observation. "When those planes hit the World Trade Center, the thought of Islam did not cross my mind."

"It did mine," Suzanne said.

"I think that prior to 9/11 people didn't think much about Muslims," Priscilla persisted.

"No? What about the images of fat oil sheikhs with camels and harems spending lots of money?" I asked her incredulously.

But Priscilla was nonplussed. "I think you are hypersensitive to your own stereotype. Some would say you are a self-hating Muslim. People sometimes accuse me of being a self-hating Jew because if you are at all critical of the stereotype of your own religion, you're accused of being self-hating."

"I strongly disagree," I said. "To be critical of a stereotype or aware of it is not to be self-hating."

How could I not be aware of the Muslim and Arab stereotypes? Even news commentators compared Arab political maneuvering to the "bargaining that takes place in the winding streets and souks of the marketplaces of the Middle East." No matter where we go or who we become, we are still carpet sellers, out to swindle innocent non-Muslims.

"Most people don't associate Islam with positive scientific or cultural world contributions like Europe's Renaissance," I continued.

"What do you mean?" Priscilla asked.

"Well, it was the Muslims who translated and preserved the Greek classics. Europe was reintroduced to these texts by Muslims. Muslims were great mathematicians. Few people know that algebra comes from an Arabic word—*aljabar*," I told Suzanne and Priscilla.

"And the maps and boats that were used to discover America were Muslim," I continued.

"Let me get this straight," Priscilla said. "Christopher Columbus used the inventions of the Islamic community to discover America?"

"Absolutely," I replied. "Ferdinand and Isabella used the know-how of centuries of Muslims, the inventors who had been there well before them."

I think Muslims and Arabs are now the only groups in our society about whom other people think they can make racial slurs and jokes without being labeled racists. Every other minority or ethnic group has its stereotypes, but people have a sense of political correctness about these groups and tend to edit or contain their stereotypes, whether in the movies, in books or even in the news commentaries. But you can find that stereotype of Muslims everywhere now—that they are aggressive, violent, abusive of women—and people don't feel any shame about holding or expressing it. Even well-meaning, nice people continue to say to me, "But you don't look Muslim!" Most of the time we Muslims simply laugh it off. It is harder, though, when your children are involved.

One day my daughter and I took a taxi to her pediatrician's office. When the American driver, a rarity in Manhattan, overheard us talking about her medical appointment, he mentioned that he might want to see a doctor himself for the sciatic back pain he had been suffering. As I told him that I had experienced such discomfort myself, he turned around and said, "I've heard so many people complain of similar pain that I say it must be those Muslims that are giving it to us."

At that moment, we arrived at our destination. I hastily paid the driver and scooted my daughter out of the cab, unwilling to engage this man in further conversation. I preferred to maintain my silence rather than share any personal information with him. I felt the urge to disengage, not to have to represent the entire religion of Islam in the back of a taxicab.

But this time, I had my daughter to contend with.

"You should have said something, Mommy," Leia said as we walked into her doctor's office.

When I told Suzanne and Priscilla this story, I explained the futility of educating every person on the street. It's something my American Muslim friends and I agree on. Better not to say anything. My daughter would have. But maybe that's because she's more confident in her American identity than I am.

After 9/11 I had another particularly awkward encounter when I must confess I did not act as confidently or courageously as my daughter might have liked. This incident took place with a stranger while I was vacationing in Europe, and I now related it to Suzanne and Priscilla.

My family and I had been invited by my in-laws to spend two weeks in a resort hotel in the south of France. Still recovering from the attacks of September 11th, I found myself surrendering to the warmth and serenity of the Mediterranean as I lay on a raft a little offshore from the hotel. An American woman, a stranger, joined me on the raft, and, as often happens to fellow citizens in foreign lands, we felt an instinct to bond and converse. As this woman and I shared our feelings about how nice it was to get away from the tension in the U.S., I was caught off guard by the last comment she made to me.

She was talking about the challenges of hunting down terrorists in the United States. "How can we possibly win this war?" she asked. "How can we identify these people? The problem," she continued, "is that these Arab-Muslims are everywhere! In Michigan, where I come from, they're living right among us! They're in our neighborhoods and cities."

As the absurd image of an Arab-American Muslim fifth column materialized in my mind, I failed to find the courage to identify myself. I didn't want to be an outsider. My desire to be as American as she was overrode my outrage at her insensitivity. So I stayed on vacation. I didn't point out that this woman had spent the last half hour with an Arab-American Muslim and didn't even know it. Forget "among us," I might have said. "We're everywhere you look!" But I said nothing. Instead I dived off the raft into the warm waters of the Mediterranean, as if to wash away the heaviness of the complications of my heritage, and swam back to shore.

> SUZANNE: *Remember when I invited you to join our book club discussion on the Middle East, Ranya?*
> RANYA: *Yes.*
> SUZANNE: *I never told you that the Jewish woman who was scheduled to host that evening bowed out after she heard you were coming.*
> RANYA: *You've got to be kidding!*

Suzanne:

Unfortunately, I wasn't kidding. And I told Ranya the story I'd kept from her for more than a year.

Right after I'd invited Ranya to the book group discussion, I had bumped into the woman who was supposed to host the next meeting. She was Jewish, though I didn't think about that as I excitedly told her about Ranya, her family, and her education in Middle East studies. As the would-be hostess listened to me, I noticed her expression stiffen. "Oh," she replied, then turned to hustle her children through the crowded doorway of the Episcopal preschool our children attended.

A few days later, she emailed to say that she could no longer host the meeting. I offered to reschedule the date, but she wasn't interested. Finally, I asked if she was declining to host because I had invited Ranya.

I assured her that Ranya was thoughtful and open-minded, that she had qualifications beyond her family story. "No," the woman said. "I think I will pass." She thought that if Ranya said something offensive to her, she would be in a difficult position as the hostess. I could understand that this friend didn't want to spend an evening arguing about Israel with a Palestinian guest in her home. Still, I was startled to hear that she assumed Ranya was likely to say something offensive.

RANYA: *Why didn't you tell me that before?*
SUZANNE: *I didn't want to make you feel uncomfortable.*
RANYA: *Can you imagine if you replaced Palestinian Muslim with African American or Asian? I dislike the stereotypes so much. That's why I want to be empowered. This is what this project is about for me. Not about me belonging, but me saying I am proud of who I am, and I refuse to be plugged into a stereotype. You could call me a coward for not speaking up on the raft. For not saying anything. What would a Jew have done in similar situations? Trust me, they would not have been silent. And now I want my voice to be heard.*
PRISCILLA: *Okay. Speak up!*
RANYA: *As a Muslim, Priscilla, we feel that we are the victims now.*
PRISCILLA: *Okay. I will give it to you. You can be a victim.*

Ranya:

Priscilla seemed to me to pass the mantle of victimhood so reluctantly that I didn't believe she meant what she said.

Suzanne was suspicious of our victim status, too. "People may have difficulty thinking about Muslims as victims because now there are so many aggressors using the name of your religion," she said.

It had been a long evening listening to Suzanne and Priscilla hash it out. Now that I was getting the opportunity to address some of my concerns, I sensed how difficult my audience was going to be. I had wanted to talk to Priscilla about more explosive issues, about Israel. But I was not encouraged by the fact that she was even having a hard time recognizing that stereotypes of Muslims and Arabs existed! I clearly still had a lot of ground to cover. We would need another day and a few more difficult discussions before Priscilla and Suzanne could sincerely and genuinely understand and validate my Muslim feelings and point of view.

Muslims feel that, in the West, Islam has been seen as an inherently violent religion that was unapologetically spread through the sword. Westerners seem to believe that Islam is inferior as a religion when they compare it to the message of Jesus Christ. Some in the West consider the modern-day violence committed in the name of Islam to be a modern manifestation of that religion and consider its prophet a false prophet with dubious, questionable morality; some consider him an epileptic and dismiss his visions; others consider him a madman. Some Westerners consider Islam's holy scriptures to be plagiarized versions of Christian and Jewish texts and consider Muslims barbaric, uncivilized, extreme, and unenlightened.

Every minority or ethnic group has at one point or another suffered from being stereotyped, but these days most people tend to view stereotypes as stereotypes and have a sense that they are not true. I think Islam is the exception to this rule: in the West most people have only one image of Islam—they carry a stereotype of Islam as a violent, radical, and regressive religion.

This stereotype unfortunately assumed explosive dimensions after the publication in Denmark of twelve cartoons of the prophet Muhammad commissioned by a newspaper editor "as a test of whether Muslim fundamentalists had begun affecting the freedom of expression in Denmark." The problem with that test is the assumption that the cartoons are offensive only to fundamentalists. This is not true: the majority of Muslims found the cartoons defamatory, inflammatory, blasphemous, and unnecessarily provocative in the stereotyping of their prophet, who is deeply respected and revered as a man of peace. In reality, the newspaper editor was not testing whether free speech was at risk, but rather whether Denmark, like the rest of the Muslim and non-Muslim world, was vulnerable to violence carried out in the name of Islam by extremists and radicals. This is particularly distressing when you consider that eleven ambassadors from Muslim countries, including Turkey, Bosnia, Iran, Egypt, and Indonesia, wrote to the Danish prime minister requesting a meeting to discuss the issue soon after the cartoons' publication, but were refused. When the proper channels of diplomacy and conflict resolution are closed, perfect conditions are created for extremists on both sides—European Islamaphobes and militant Muslims—to add fuel to their own fires. The conflict is framed and manipulated by those Europeans who are threatened, fearful, and prejudiced against their growing indigenous Muslim minorities, as a war of irreconcilable values between two sides: the liberal, enlightened, Christian West against the regressive, radical Muslim East. The controversy has become a rallying call for some Europeans, who have used it as a symbol for what they describe as the Muslim threat to Western civilization and "our way of life." And it has given militant Muslims, who frame it as one more perceived injustice suffered at the hands of Western imperialist anti-Muslim policies, an excuse for violence.

Had the issue been managed more rationally and less emotionally, it might have remained just a peripheral example of one editor's exercise in free expression, about which Muslims would have been free to express their objections. A less emotional, more confident European response would have acknowledged that, while freedom of speech is an absolute right, incitement of hatred and demonizing of others should be shunned. Just as death threats and violence are never acceptable and are truly un-Islamic, a worthy goal for both the Muslim and the non-Muslim world is to consider unacceptable all incidents of anti-Semitism, anti-Christianity, anti-Islam, or anti-minority sentiments. The majority of Muslims condemn the violence, and Europeans should refuse to be intimidated by it. Nonetheless, genuine European empathy for offended

Muslims and respect for their feelings are lacking. Clearly, a few stereotypes will have to be shed before people can even begin to imagine talking about a shared Judeo-Christian-Muslim tradition.

I understood and empathized, however, with the fact that although Suzanne and Priscilla both came from different traditions, they still had a hard time understanding how Muslims feel that they have been victims of unapologetic stereotyping. In fact, I told them that if I had been an American whose only exposure to Islam had been through the headline news, I would probably feel the same way. Suzanne felt that way primarily because the violence committed in the name of Islam had been the most enduring image of Islam available to her and to others. Priscilla, as a Jew, may have a hard time recognizing Muslims as victims because she may have felt threatened that this recognition would challenge her ownership of the Holocaust and ultimately the right of Israel to exist as a Jewish state.

I think Priscilla was reluctant to give me the title of victim because she felt that the Holocaust dwarfed all else and that I somehow was challenging her ownership of the experience and its very validity. She may have felt that as a Muslim I was not recognizing the magnitude of the Holocaust. It was going to take time before we would have a true heart-to-heart so that she could genuinely accept the victimhood of the Palestinians without feeling that I was taking anything away from the suffering of the Jews when I speak about the suffering of the Palestinians and Muslims.

But just because our suffering is not of the magnitude of the Holocaust doesn't mean that Palestinians, Muslims, and Christians aren't suffering, dying, starving, and homeless. I'm not denying the Holocaust by any means—and would never do so—but I think that upon the founding of Israel, the Zionists claimed the high ground, and up until today, it's been hard for Palestinians to be heard and thought of as victims.

SUZANNE: *So what is your stereotype of Christians, Priscilla?*
PRISCILLA: *You really want to know?*

SUZANNE: *Sure. Because I don't think I'm going to be personally affected by it.*

PRISCILLA: *Because you're in the majority. What do you care?*

SUZANNE: *No. It's because I feel personally I am not the stereotype. So I'm wondering if you felt the same distance when I expressed my stereotype of Jews.*

PRISCILLA: *I take it more personally as a Jew.*

RANYA: *Maybe part of the reason you're not affected, Suzanne, is that the overriding culture we are in is Christian. The whole world operates according to a Christian calendar. We learn about Christianity through osmosis. But what do Christians learn about us?*

SUZANNE: *I agree. But why are you holding it against me?*

PRISCILLA: *Ranya and I understand each other. We have a kinship because we are minorities. Right?*

SUZANNE: *I don't know. Explain the kinship you have, the things that you feel that I don't that make you different.*

PRISCILLA: *I think that it's like a schoolyard where there are social outcasts, and then there is the popular crowd. The Christians are the popular crowd, and you are one of them.*

Priscilla:

We'd been talking for more than two hours now. I reached for another piece of chocolate cake, the best I'd ever had. I wondered if Suzanne, Ranya, and I were getting close to the end of our conversation. The drive back to the suburbs would take me almost an hour at this time. Would my chocolate buzz keep me up for a while?

Suzanne jolted me out of my reveries on chocolate. "Priscilla," she asked, "do you feel like you can't connect with me because I am part of a majority?"

Hadn't Suzanne gotten the point? Majority rules! They don't have to worry about how I feel, excluded or not. When would Suzanne figure this out? "You wouldn't understand," I said dismissively.

"How do you know that?" Suzanne shot back.

I listened and thought about it. "You're right," I said. "That's discrimination on my part."

"I have felt very much like an outsider," Suzanne said. Her face flushed. She was adamant about this. "I came from Kansas City to New York City. I went to a relatively unknown college in Texas and then in New York competed for jobs with people whose families had gone to Yale or Harvard for generations. I can feel like an outsider, too. In college I was on a full-tuition scholarship amid lots of oil-rich Texans with shiny BMWs and boxes of gold jewelry."

Suzanne paused, took a deep breath and forged on. I didn't say a word. Her usual confident persona was shifting before my eyes. She was peeling off a layer of herself and revealing doubts and insecurities I never thought she had. Her WASP reserve was cracking.

"Those people didn't have to work for a dime," she said, "while I waited tables and earned extra money editing English papers for two Middle Eastern students. And, by the way, my parents were of the first generation in their families to go to college."

"My parents were the first, too," I said.

"But you came from a Jewish background that values education and grew up surrounded by first-class Ivy League schools." Suzanne wasn't about to concede or back down from her point. "My father told me that it didn't matter where I went to college, that it wouldn't affect me in the long run."

I was moved by Suzanne's description of her feelings as a newcomer to New York. So moved, in fact, that this was a turning point for me. I could never, in a million years, have pictured Suzanne as an outsider, feeling insecure, feeling inferior to others. She always seemed so confident, both in her religion and her personal attitude.

How many months had I spent with Suzanne? And now, in just a couple of moments, after hours of conversation, she had spoken just a few words that changed all my preconceptions of her.

All my stereotypes.

"I never thought of you as an outsider," I told Suzanne now.

"Well, I was. Or I am sometimes," she said. "Just because I'm Christian doesn't mean that I can't connect with your feelings as a minority."

SUZANNE: *So what's the rest of the Christian stereotype for you?*

PRISCILLA: *There are some shrill, smug, close-minded zealots of your faith who think they have a lock on morality with their "Christian values." And then, of course, there's an old saying that you'd better eat something before you go to a Christian wedding, because there'll be nothing to eat there except cucumber sandwiches. Just lots to drink.*

SUZANNE: *That's not so bad.*

PRISCILLA: *You know, when I see my boys being unkind, I tell them to be nice. If they ask why, I say, because it's the Christian thing to do. I know that's ironic. I interchange that with "it's a mitzvah," which is Hebrew for a good deed. I used the phrase "a Christian thing to do" before I began to understand how good Jesus was. Now when you say Jesus is about love, I get it. I think of Christianity as a good religion. I think of Christians as good people, but we don't need the propaganda.*

Suzanne:

I winced when Priscilla said propaganda. I knew what she meant. You can't travel far in America without some message about Jesus assaulting you. He's not only in churches. He's on bumper stickers, billboards, and pamphlets. Most of the propaganda is benign. You can easily say "No, thank you" to the newsletters offered in the subway stations by the Jehovah's Witnesses. But sometimes the message is a real turnoff.

Recently I had passed a billboard outside Emporia, Kansas, when I'd been visiting my family. In big bold letters, the sign read: "Accept

Jesus Christ and Be Saved or Regret It Forever." I cringed when I read it. It's that kind of proselytizing that makes me self-conscious about talking about Jesus. Its message reinforces an image of Christians as judgmental and arrogant missionaries. I'm not that kind of Christian, and I don't want to be labeled that way.

Priscilla:

Suzanne had pleaded her case. She'd distanced herself from the Christians whose motives I had questioned. "Do you really think that I'm one of them?" she asked me.

And, truthfully, I answered "No."

I elaborated. "In fact," I said, "you're right, Suzanne. I've been stereotyping you."

Blinded by my own fears of being stereotyped, I'd never been able to see that I was lumping Suzanne together with a bunch of unenlightened bigots—people who blamed Jews for the death of Christ.

It had been a long night. A long couple of months, actually. Tempers had flared over the crucifixion, Suzanne had bravely confessed her discomfort with being mistaken for a Jew. She'd described the stereotype of a Jew in words that I had never, ever heard a Christian person say out loud.

She'd been brave. And I told her that months later, after some time had passed, wounds had healed, and we'd begun speaking about the things that united us rather than the things that divided us.

CHAPTER SIX
Could You Convert?

SUZANNE: *Have you been to the mosque on Ninety-sixth Street, Ranya?*

RANYA: *I was married there. But it's too conservative for me. I'm afraid I'll be judged by whether I cover my hair, what I wear and how I pray. You're lucky, Suzanne. I don't have a neighborhood place to worship like you do.*

SUZANNE: *If you're uncomfortable in a mosque, Ranya, why not try a church or a temple?*

Ranya:

For months, I'd been longing for a mosque and an imam who could promote and sustain our family's understanding of the Muslim faith and God. I wanted a mosque in which my American family would not feel foreign, a mosque that was not dominated by first-generation immigrant men who had left their families behind in either their home countries or their homes in New York. I needed a mosque not only for myself but for my four-year-old son, who had begun asking incessant questions about life and death. I was filled with sadness as I saw my son struggle to overcome his fears and come to terms with his own and his loved ones' mortality. Those questions were challenging me to reexamine my own unresolved faith issues. I craved, for him, a setting similar to a Sunday school or Hebrew school, where his religious education could be taken care of without me having to wrestle with the answers to his questions alone.

"I feel like I'm suffering from a severe case of temple and church envy," I half-jokingly confessed to Suzanne and Priscilla.

This feeling has ebbed and flowed throughout my life, even in my days as a college student when I was envious of my Catholic roommate's connection with the Jesuit priests at Georgetown and the luxury of spiritual healing and support she could receive at chapel every Sunday evening.

"Did your family worship at mosques when you were growing up in the Middle East?" Priscilla wondered.

"No. We never did," I replied. "And I recently asked my parents why that was the case."

My father's explanation for not belonging to a mosque seemed to me to be as valid today in our contemporary Muslim experience in America as it had been for my parents in the Arabian Gulf. At the core is the issue of dislocation. Had my father continued his life in Tiberias, he probably would have frequented the local mosque, whose imam would have married him and eventually his children. There would have been continuity—the local community worshiped at the same mosque from generation to generation. In fact, my maternal grandmother recently shared with me memories of her father making his weekly Friday excursion from Ramleh to Jerusalem to perform the special Friday prayers in the holiest of cities at Al-Aqsa mosque. But as immigrants in Kuwait, even the mosques seemed foreign and outside the comfort of our native social and cultural landscape.

My father's challenge to find his family a house of worship is paralleled today in the experience of our Muslim family in New York City. We have lived in New York for ten years, yet never been affiliated with a mosque. It is difficult to find a mosque whose imam and congregation have a similar understanding of Islam to mine and my family's.

While churches and temples seem to dot Manhattan's landscape, mosques are much harder to find. Until 2003, I knew of only one mosque in New York City, the Ninety-sixth Street Mosque. The majority of Muslims who worship there, however, appear to be new immigrants who still are closer culturally to their home countries than they are to America. I feared that, because their concerns, opinions, and prejudice might reflect their lives and experiences as new immigrants, my American family would stick out like sore thumbs.

One of the problems with Islam in America is that it has become a voice for the disaffected. Witness prison conversions. Sometimes, as a Muslim, I cringe at the process by which it seems you can commit a crime, enter prison, and become a member of the Nation of Islam! In the African American experience the Muslim voice can be an angry one, laden with issues of slavery. Or in the case of recent immigrants, that voice can be filled with the alienation and resentment that comes from losing a home, country, or culture, or having them threatened. Sometimes Islam's voice in immigrants' lives reflects a political or social agenda that is inspired by the home country. Before 9/11 I could still distance my family from that version of Islam and educate my children about their Muslim heritage at home. But after 9/11 I felt that we could no longer afford to be complacent. My husband and I had to find that alternative Muslim voice—an American, maternal voice.

Suzanne:

Ranya's religious "homelessness" had become a recurring theme in our conversations, and I wanted to help. I didn't have the time or expertise to scout New York's mosques. But I did have our Episcopal church to offer. Though Ranya didn't believe Jesus was the Son of God, she did believe he was a holy prophet. Maybe she could overlook the distinction for the benefit of participating in a religious community.

I didn't want to appear imperialist, forcing the "immigrant" to adopt the religion of the new country. But I wanted to offer it. I believe that one's spirituality needs to be nourished in order to thrive. Community, study, acts of charity, and meditation all strengthen our faith. And our children need a moral and spiritual education that is not offered in secular schools. If Ranya wasn't finding those tools in her own tradition,

I was offering—though not at all pushing—mine. I wondered if my church might be sort of a foster home for her and her children. Ranya wouldn't be the first non-Christian at St. James'. An elderly Jewish man came to our services every Sunday wearing his yarmulke.

So, after one of our meetings I called Ranya and invited her and her family to Easter service at our church followed by brunch at our home. "Please don't feel any pressure," I said. "I won't be offended if you tell me that you would rather not go. But, if you think you might enjoy it, we would love to have you."

After speaking to her husband, Ranya accepted our invitation. She quizzed me on the proper church attire for her family and offered to bring a side dish for our brunch. I decided I would make my traditional Easter dish, coulibiac, a brioche dough surrounding layers of crepes, salmon mousse, saffron rice and hard-boiled eggs. I ordered a chocolate Easter cake and bought bejeweled egg-shaped candles for the table. I wanted our Easter party to be a success.

Ranya:

When Suzanne invited my family to join hers for an Easter service at their church, followed by a family brunch, I was delighted but a little anxious. Suzanne herself prefaced the invitation by saying, "If you don't feel comfortable, don't feel you have to." Although I had visited many historic churches, attended an outdoor mass as part of my graduation from Georgetown, and even sneaked into our neighboring church to get a close-up view of the beautiful stained glass windows that our apartment is lucky enough to face, this was the first time our family was officially invited to participate in a holiday service that was fundamental to the Christian tradition.

When I first shared the invitation with Sami, I was surprised at his reaction. He is the more secular of the two of us. Not only did he express concern that the children might come away confused, especially since they had never worshiped at a mosque, but he teasingly joked about my imminent conversion. I, on the other hand, was ready to take my developing ecumenical belief one step further. I had become aware that the more I learned about the common beliefs that link our three faith traditions, the more my belief in God was strengthened. I explained that I hoped our visit to the Olivers' church would render meaning to rituals we already participated in culturally but not spiritually. As a child I had colored Easter eggs and participated in egg hunts. And now my own children received Easter baskets every year.

We agreed to meet at St. James' Church at nine in the morning. Conscious of the early start, I prepared a chickpea dish with sesame paste, garlic, and pine nuts the night before. As I garnished the bowl with olive oil and parsley, I felt the beginning of a sore throat. I laid out the children's clothes and went to bed hoping to recover after a good night's rest. The following morning I was so sick and achy, I could hardly move. The thought of missing the service or not showing up was out of the question for me. I was determined to make it, come what may. I felt that Suzanne had reached out graciously and wholeheartedly by including us in her family's Easter. She had recognized my angst and longing to be part of a spiritual community, and the frustration I have felt at times when as a family we have missed out on the communal celebration of certain colorful Muslim traditions and holidays. So Suzanne had invited us to share hers. Appreciating her generous gesture, I popped two Advil pills, and we made our way to church.

Once I entered Suzanne's church and the service began, I forgot how sick I was. My deepest reserves of energy were easily summoned by the powerfully transcendent music. The sense of occasion the music conjured up gave me a new appreciation of the beauty of the details in the church's gilded altarpiece and architecture. I realized that I could be moved as much in church as when I listen to recitations of the Quran. I was brought to tears as I observed the generations gathered together to worship in the pews around me. Father and son, mother and daughter: one in the image of the other, both in the image of God, all personifying the miracle and continuity of life. The rituals, the sense of occasion and music humbled me in my humanity in the presence of God.

Suzanne:

At church Easter morning my family slid into a pew, and minutes later, the Idliby family joined us. Then the horns, organ, and drums began playing the triumphant music of Easter, and the congregation began to sing. I was filled with the joy of the occasion and thrilled to be sharing the beautiful experience with Ranya and her family.

But once the music stopped and the prayers started, I began to notice a self-consciousness I hadn't anticipated. I knew Ranya's Muslim view of Jesus was that he was a great prophet, not to be confused with the One God. In fact, Muslims and Jews question whether the Christian worship of the trinity (God the Father, Jesus the Son, and the Holy Spirit) can even be called monotheism. So, as I sat in church with Ranya and Sami, it was as if I was hearing our service through a filter of Islam, and each time we said, "Jesus Christ our Lord," I felt a twinge of discomfort. This is not appealing to them, I thought.

As Holy Communion approached, our prayers were filled with phrases like sacrifice, body and blood, and Lamb of God. I had heard these terms for decades, and they had never made me blush. But now they did. After spending so much time with Ranya and Priscilla focusing on the "one God" that connected us all, I was faced with an aspect of God that divided us—the divinity of Jesus and the purpose of his death. We were celebrating the sacrifice of someone—someone we believed to be both God and human—whose death helped to purchase everlasting life for us. I recognized how completely wild the concept sounded. I also recognized how difficult it would be for someone to join our community without believing it. St. James' couldn't be Ranya's religious foster home. Every gathering she attended there would begin with a prayer that concluded with the words, "Through Jesus Christ our Lord."

Feeling increasingly uncomfortable, I found myself looking forward to the service's conclusion when we would head home to a brunch of coulibiac, salad, and Ranya's Middle Eastern chickpeas. I was pretty sure that it would be easier for us to connect over chocolate rabbits and colored eggs than over the story of Jesus' resurrection.

Ranya:

As Suzanne's Easter service was nearing its end, I did not anticipate my sudden reversal of feelings. I had been so focused on the beauty of the service, enjoying the God that unites us, that I was caught off guard by my increasing self-consciousness. When people turned in their pews before communion to say "Peace be with you" and shake the hands of everyone around them, I began to feel like an imposter. I could not help wondering to myself if these parishioners would be as comfortable in their greetings to me and my family if they knew we were Muslims. Might they think we were lost souls that needed to be saved by accepting Jesus as the savior, or even renouncing Islam? Then came Holy Communion. It was at that point that my Muslim identity actively began to reassert itself. My Muslim understanding of Jesus as human made me feel apart from those who were lining up to take bread. The ritual of receiving bread, in my mind, is the strongest embodiment and symbolic enactment of the concept of the Holy Trinity and the Christian understanding of Jesus as divine, as God on earth.

As we emerged from the church, into the crisp spring air, a well-meaning gentleman began chatting with me, complimenting me on my lovely children. He introduced himself as a new parishioner who was feeling lonely and nostalgic for his grown-up children who were absent on this Easter Sunday. The ironic symbolism of the moment hit me. Here stood a Christian, reaching out to a Muslim whom he perceived to be a church insider, a fellow Christian. I did not disabuse him of this notion. Smiling politely, I left my Easter Sunday experience with plenty of food for thought to share with Suzanne and Priscilla at our next faith club meeting.

SUZANNE: *No one would have "outed you" at my church, Ranya. They just ask non-Christians not to step forward to receive communion.*

PRISCILLA: *That moment of communion is always awkward for Jews too, Ranya. I can remember sitting in my pew at many services, feeling extremely Jewish while my Christian friends lined up to take communion.*

RANYA: *Yes. That's when I felt my Muslim identity reassert itself.*

SUZANNE: *And probably when you realized you weren't about to convert. Have you ever thought of converting, Priscilla?*

PRISCILLA: *No. I think that Jews feel an obligation to be Jews. There are so few of us.*

SUZANNE: *And what does it mean for you to be Jewish?*

PRISCILLA: *It's like a tribal thing.*

RANYA: *I've heard that before, and I don't understand it.*

PRISCILLA: *There's an expression Jews use, laughingly, "M.O.T." It stands for Member of the Tribe.*

SUZANNE: *So it's a loyalty to ancestors?*

PRISCILLA: *Yes, and for me, it's primarily to my father. My mother was a Jew by birth, but she explored Buddhism and every kind of New Age therapy. My father was the one who insisted we go to temple. When I sit in temple now listening to the prayers and songs, I feel my father's presence in the very best way.*

Priscilla:

My father has always been the link to my beliefs and traditions as a Jew. After all, he was the one who urged me to go to temple in my youth and enrolled me in Hebrew day school. We celebrated Passover and the High Holidays at his mother's house when I was growing up.

And as I grew older, Jewish traditions and rituals were often ways in which I felt connected to my father.

My father always stressed the need for Jews to maintain their religious identity. He was a Jew on his own terms, which meant that he loved bacon but also spent time studying the Talmud. And he imparted bits of Jewish wisdom and traditions to his children as he did everything else in life—in unconventional ways.

During one of the most difficult periods of his life, when his business was going bankrupt, my father used to drive up to Boston to study the Talmud with a rabbi he greatly admired. He never shared too much about the conversations he had with this man, but I knew that my father was wrestling to do the right thing by his creditors, studying ancient texts in order to decide what his modern-day moral obligations were.

Should he, for example, pay Jimmy the chicken man, a poultry wholesaler who'd done business with my grandfather for decades, before he paid Kraft Foods, a huge, anonymous company with a staff of threatening lawyers? (My father told me years later that he chose Jimmy the chicken man.)

My father always found a way to connect with his children, even in painful times. And often he forged these connections with Yiddish stories his parents had told him.

I loved best what he called "The Paper Bag Story," which addressed the challenges people face in life, challenges he himself had faced.

"Imagine this," he used to say to us. "Take your problems, all of them, from the tiniest, annoying concerns to the most horrific, difficult challenges, and put all those problems into a brown paper bag." He'd pause. "Then imagine if everyone else in the world took all of their problems and put them into their own paper bags. Think of how many bags there would be, all piled up into one gigantic mountain of brown paper!" The image was vivid to me.

"If you were told that you could pick any bag of problems and take it home with you, do you think you'd want someone else's problems?"

my father would ask. "I don't think so. You'd be scampering like crazy to find your own bag in that mountain of brown paper."

Toward the end of his life, after his business had failed, his fortune was lost, and the pain of his terminal disease was so bad he'd begun taking morphine, I asked my father, "So, if you had it to do all over again, would you still want your own brown paper bag?"

My father didn't hesitate. "Absolutely," he said. "Yes."

And the fact that my father accepted the final challenge he'd been dealt gave me the courage later in life to think that I might be strong enough to face my own paper bag full of challenges.

"Sometimes being a proud Jew is one of those challenges," I told Suzanne and Ranya. "So many people have tried to wipe us off the planet. I know people who lost relatives in concentration camps. I know people who hid Jews. The Holocaust isn't something I think about every moment, but it is with me every day. And, partly because of that, I would never turn my back on my religion, on the Jews who came before me. For me there is no choice. I am a Jew."

PRISCILLA: *Don't you feel that kind of tribal connection to your faith, Ranya?*

RANYA: *Not at all, my tribe today is the American tribe. Islam allows anyone to become Muslim simply by saying the Shahada, or testimony of faith, "I believe there is only one God, and Muhammad is his prophet." It has nothing to do with a blood connection. People can come and go from Islam as they please. There is no tradition of baptism or confirmation. It's pretty much between you and God.*

SUZANNE: *What makes you stay in the Muslim faith when you've found it so difficult in America today?*

RANYA: *At church the other day, I realized that I have a very Muslim understanding of what God is.*

SUZANNE: *Tell us about it.*

RANYA: *The God I know through Islam recognizes Jesus, Moses, and the prophets before him.*

SUZANNE: *Christians recognize Jesus, Moses, and the prophets before him.*

RANYA: *My issue with Christianity is the concept of the Trinity. I saw a bumper sticker recently that said, "Jesus loves you. Jesus will save you." I feel that God will save me. That Jesus died for my sins, I can do without.*

Ranya:

Like other parents, my husband and I have devoted much energy and resources to securing for our children what we believe is in their best interest—the best education, medical attention, and cultural and social experiences—so that our children can realize their potential as adults. I hadn't thought much about their religious identity. To me, one's religion is primarily an accident of birth. Yet, after 9/11, I became concerned that our Muslim religion meant more than that. I felt that being Muslim and American might be more of a challenge than a privilege that my children were inheriting.

When I started researching Islam I really did not know whether I could find within it the answers that could sustain my faith in it. So I was thrilled when I discovered Islam's inherent affirmation of people of other faiths. I explained to Suzanne and Priscilla how, unlike some versions of Christianity, there is not an Islamic belief that people must convert to Islam in order to be saved by God. The Quran has a broad, universal definition of believers. Islam has no tradition of prerequisite rituals, such as baptism or bar mitzvahs, that officially make you a Muslim. It recognizes all believers as "Muslims," meaning those who have submitted to the will of God.

Those who believe, the Jews, the Christians, and the Sabeans, any who believe in God and the Last Day, and work righteousness shall have their reward with their Lord: on them shall be no fear, nor shall they grieve. (2:62)

SAY: *We believe in God and what is revealed to us; in that which was revealed to Abraham and Ishmael, to Isaac and Jacob and the tribes; and that which their Lord gave Moses and Jesus and the prophets. We discriminate against none of them. To him we submit. (3:84)*

Islam, I quickly learned, didn't see itself as a new religion but as a continuation of the Abrahamic faith tradition. Someone said that if Muhammad saw all the different religions that exist today, including Buddhism and Confucianism, he would say that they're all originally Islam. Even within the Quran I was able to find verses supporting this pluralistic, universal approach to God. According to the Quran, diversity in human faith traditions, cultures, and race is part of God's intended design.

Among his signs is the creation of the Heavens and the Earth, and the diversity of your tongues and colors. In that surely are signs for those who possess knowledge. (30:23)

Understanding Islam's connection to Judaism and Christianity stirred in me a renewed interest and commitment to the faith I had inherited from my parents and grandparents. The Quran was able to fulfill my need for a God who would not and could not leave a people behind, for it specifically confirms that all nations were sent prophets and apostles (35:24), that there is "no compulsion in religion"(10:100), and that by accepting Muhammad as a prophet you are confirming and affirming all those prophets that were sent before him.

In its best reading, Islam is egalitarian and accessible. It is a religion that tries to simplify, to do away with pomp and circumstance. That's why mosques are not ornate. They are usually geometric and austere. That works for me. It's less distracting. Another strength of Islam, and its weakness, is that you don't have to rely on an ordained clergy to interpret the Quran. You can pretty much read it and have your own personal understanding and relationship with God. This is especially true for Sunni or orthodox Islam, that has no religious hierarchy that acts as an intermediary to God.

The God that I was beginning to appreciate and recognize as the Muslim God, through my own reading and research of the Quran, had a distinctly universal, accessible, even modern sensibility. This appealed to me more than the Jewish God, who appeared to be available only through a connection to Judaism's Twelve Tribes, or to the Christian God, who seemed to offer salvation only through Jesus.

The question was would I be able to have this God supported and sustained outside my personal readings and through the formal religious support of a Muslim cleric or mosque?

As Priscilla, Suzanne, and I continued our discussions, we were not only talking about three different religions, but we were also talking about three personal and entirely different relationships with our own religions. At that time, I told Priscilla and Suzanne that it often felt like I had faith but no religion, that Priscilla had religion but no faith, and that Suzanne had both.

RANYA: *Why are you a Christian, Suzanne?*
SUZANNE: *Initially because I was born that way. But I stay in the faith because I am a follower of Jesus. He was a better role model than the prophets of the Old Testament and Muhammad. He was a perfect example of love, charity, and humility, unlike Moses and Muhammad who were both flawed men.*
RANYA: *Muslims believe Muhammad had a different calling than Jesus. He made no claims to be perfect. We are supposed to emulate him, but he doesn't proclaim God-like perfection. He was a leader of a complicated community. He was a husband, father, and statesman. And it is specifically Muhammad's accessible humanity, as opposed to Jesus' divinity, that makes him a role model. As a statesman, Muhammad had to tackle real issues, social and political problems, things Jesus never had to tackle. He made laws promoting social justice and human rights. As a military leader he*

*tried to develop codes of justice and ethics that would govern acts
of war.*

SUZANNE: *You're right. Jesus' role on earth was different from
that. He preached love and humility, and he turned the other
cheek right up until his death. If we all behaved that way, there
would be a lot more peace on earth. And that's one of the reasons I
think Christianity is the best religion.*

PRISCILLA: *Suzanne, did you just say that you thought Christianity was the best religion?*

SUZANNE: *I meant to say that it was the best religion for me.*

RANYA: *I can see why you admire Jesus so much, but I think that
Christianity today is only a better religion because it's had the
time to evolve. It has been the dominant religion in places where
there's free speech and civil liberties. That is a huge advantage, especially when you contrast it with Islam, which is predominantly
a religion of the developing world.*

Suzanne:

My confidence that Christianity was a superior religion to Judaism
and Islam was strengthened during our first months of meetings as I
listened to Priscilla and Ranya discuss their doubts and discomfort
about their faiths. Priscilla called herself a Jew, though she didn't
know if she believed in God. How strange, I thought. If I didn't believe in God I wouldn't walk around calling myself a Christian. Ranya
believed in something, but not the reactionary, political Islam that
many recognized as the only Islam.

I thought there must be something wrong with Judaism and Islam
if they weren't able to relieve Ranya's and Priscilla's anxieties. Christianity must be a better vehicle for connecting with God, I reasoned. I wondered whether Priscilla and Ranya would eventually come to that view.

At the same time, however, I felt self-conscious about my faith. At
times I felt that both Priscilla and Ranya characterized believers and

those who participated in the rituals of a community of faith as followers who were unable to think critically.

In my opinion, I had thought critically about my religion. I had been raised a Catholic, but had made the decision to switch to the Episcopal Church. That decision was not easily accepted by my parents. It took a few years before they would join us in our new church. Instead they would go to a Catholic service at our old parish, while my own family went to the Episcopal service at our new one. At last my mom came to a Sunday service at our church because she wanted to see my children sing in the choir. Since that time, my parents have joined us whenever they have visited.

So why did my husband and I convert? We were turned off by uninspiring Sunday sermons, by the Catholic Church's conservative positions on social issues, and by its rigidity. We had seen the rule-making culture and inflexibility of the church lead people, including my husband and me, to behave illogically in order to satisfy church rules. A prime example was our wedding.

My husband and I had wanted to get married in an eighteenth-century meetinghouse in a New Hampshire village. The Catholic priest, however, insisted that we marry in the Catholic Church. After all, both of us were Catholic. If one of us had not been Catholic, the rules would have allowed him to marry us in the meetinghouse. It seemed to us like typical Catholic reasoning.

Our solution was to get married twice. On the day of our wedding, I put on my white dress and got married at one o'clock in the Catholic Church in front of our families. Then we proceeded down to the meetinghouse, where a friend who was a Presbyterian minister married us before all the rest of our guests at three o'clock. Only a few people knew we had already made our vows and signed the marriage contract at the other end of Main Street.

The male dominance of the Catholic Church also bothered me. I believe women are as capable as men to serve as priests. In fact, I think they are better suited in some respects. I also believe that celibacy does not necessarily make a person more holy. (Witness the pedophilia among Catholic priests.) Humans need the love and touch of other humans. And a married priest is able to be empathetic to the family experiences of those in his or her congregation.

Finally, for all the people I know who call themselves Catholic, few follow all the Church's teachings on issues like birth control, abortion, homosexuality, and even mass attendance. I can't think of a Catholic I know in my generation who goes to church every Sunday. According to the Catholic Church, that's sinful. I came to wonder, what was the point of being loyal to a religion of my parents if I did so hypocritically?

My husband and I found the Episcopal Church less rigid in its doctrine. It allows women to become priests. You don't have to attend mass every Sunday. You don't have to believe that the bread and wine at communion actually become the body and blood of Jesus. And finally, each parish has its own representative democracy. We elect a vestry, which is able to hire and fire the parish's priests. That way we can ensure that our priests fit our congregation. In the Catholic Church, priests are assigned to each parish by the bishop. Church members have no say in the matter.

I felt very comfortable at our new Episcopal church. I thought I had found the best congregation and the best religion. In fact, I wondered whether Priscilla, who was lacking in faith, and Ranya, who lacked a religious community, would soon long for the spiritual comfort and enlightened doctrine of the Episcopal Church, too.

CHAPTER SEVEN
Oh, Where Are You, God?

Priscilla:

I was overwhelmed with sadness and worry when I walked into Suzanne's apartment one morning. My younger sister, who lives in California, had just been diagnosed with breast cancer. That was disturbing enough, but it was made more upsetting by the fact that she had been suffering for eight years with a rare lung disease. She'd taken high doses of steroids for those eight years, and between her illness and the steroids, her entire immune system was impaired. She had to contend with kidney problems, thyroid problems, circulatory problems, allergies, and high blood pressure at the same time that she received her cancer diagnosis.

My sister had just undergone a lumpectomy, and tests determined that cancer had spread to two lymph nodes. I had been crying on and off for days, which was unlike me. Anxiety and panic were my usual reactions to life stresses, but I felt so sad for my sister and all she'd had to endure and would be forced to endure in the future. I was having a hard time understanding and accepting the fact that my own life had been blessedly free of any severe health problems.

"Where are you, God?" I kept wondering. "Are you going to take care of my sister? Do you have a plan I don't know about? Are you running this show? Is anyone running this show?"

"Why has my sister been given so many challenges?" I asked Suzanne as she brought me a glass of water and placed a tray of fruit, cheese, bread, and cookies on the coffee table between us. Ranya was running late, so we began our meeting without her.

"It's hard to accept that life is so unfair," Suzanne agreed. "I have a young cousin who just became a mother, and she is fighting cancer, too. It's heartbreaking."

"How do these struggles end?" I asked.

"I hope they end with God for most people."

"Jews don't have the promise of an afterlife," I said, teary-eyed.

Suzanne and I talked about how people live with cancer nowadays, often for years, but how much they suffer sometimes in the process. I revealed more about my sister's condition. Suzanne listened. And understood.

"Why does God allow pain and suffering to exist?" I wondered aloud.

Suzanne didn't have a glib answer. But she did venture an explanation. "This sounds a little simple, but I think if we didn't know illness, we wouldn't really feel the exhilaration of good health. And if we never cried, we wouldn't be able to recognize joy. In a way, the good only gains value when it is contrasted with the bad."

I felt numb. I was tired from the crying I'd done sporadically that morning on my drive into the city. "I have just decided to surrender to a higher power," I finally said. I'd spoken those same words to a couple of other people that week. Now I was trying them out again on Suzanne. I wasn't sure what I meant by a "higher power." But I knew I had to surrender. I could not control the outcome of my sister's illness.

I felt a bit better after my conversation with Suzanne. I had connected with her in a deep, personal way that I never had before. I'd been bruised by our "crucifixion crisis," but now I'd been healed by her generosity and compassion.

Suzanne had referred early on in our relationship to her sister's sudden death, and the pain it caused her and her family, but she had not gone into specifics. Now I felt comfortable bringing up the subject.

"How exactly did your sister die?" I asked quietly, wiping away tears.

Suzanne told me the details, and I thought it was generous of her to relive the pain of her sister's death in order to help me. Suzanne, Ranya, and I were becoming friends, I realized. Although we used our time together efficiently, focusing on our work at hand, life events sometimes intervened and came to the forefront of our conversations, as they did on this day.

Suzanne:

Priscilla's sadness that day reopened a tender wound for me. My only sister, Kristin, had been killed in a car accident four years earlier. My family was still recovering and probably always would be. "It was devastating," I told Priscilla. "But in my grief, I felt God more than at any other time in my life. Through this tragedy, Kristin gave me a price-less gift—faith in God."

The night my sister died, my brother called me from the hospital, with panic in his voice. One thousand miles away, I had a difficult time grasping the severity of Kristin's injuries. Eric put a nurse on the phone, who told me that my sister's condition was "code blue." Maybe I didn't watch enough *ER,* but I didn't know what "code blue" meant. "How serious is that?" I asked.

"Well, it's code blue," the nurse answered.

"I don't know what that means," I persisted. But the tone of her voice and her evasiveness told me what I didn't want to hear. "Do people recover from code blue?" I asked.

"Sometimes," she said.

A heart surgeon and two other doctors massaged my sister's heart, trying to get it to start again. But it was so badly bruised from the impact when she hit the dashboard that it would not pump again. "Because she is so young and healthy, we were hopeful. We called in the cardiac specialist and did absolutely everything we could. But it didn't work," the emergency room doctor told me later that night. Kristin was dead.

Half an hour later, as I lay in bed, I felt my sister passing through my room as if to say good-bye. It was like a trembling, but nothing really moved. I perceived it through a sense I can't even describe. But she was with me at that moment. And then I knew that some spiritual part of her had survived that crash. I prayed with all my heart that her spirit was on its way to God.

The conviction that Kristin's spirit had visited me didn't make her death any easier to handle. There were days of shock, during which I couldn't eat or think about anything else. I remember sitting under a tree in my parents' front yard two days after my sister was killed. My seven-month-old son Thomas was stretched across my lap. As I fed him a bottle, I marveled at his perfect skin, hair, and eyes. The moment seemed so cruel. How could I savor the beauty of my child and process the devastation of my sister's death at the same time? It was too much. "Now you have a guardian angel," I whispered to Thomas, and I cried for my sister, his godmother whom he would never know.

I was furious at God. At my parents' house, I lay in my childhood bed and smothered my screams with a pillow. A Catholic priest from my parents' parish came every day while I was there. He was big and kind. I took comfort in both attributes. Somehow it seemed he could prop us up. My family and I prayed with him in our living room. But as I prayed for the soul of my sister, the rage at the unfairness of such a short life took over. I screamed and cried. It was too cruel for her to die at age twenty-seven.

Yet, gradually, I began to recognize the grace of God in those around me. I saw the most extraordinary example of divine grace in my parents. In their grief, they were able to offer compassion and forgiveness to my sister's friend who had been driving the car that evening. I also felt God in the embrace of my husband, the courage of my brothers and the sincere hugs, handshakes, and good wishes of friends and family who reached out to us.

At Kristin's wake and funeral, God gave comfort to our family through hundreds of people. They came forward from a line that laced all the way around the church. Some people waited an hour or more to come inside during the wake. There were also flowers, letters, phone calls, and gifts. I believed it was the grace of God in all of these people that moved them to offer our souls comfort during the tragedy.

That awareness of God's presence and my need for comfort after Kristin's death led me to renew my search for a church home in New York. After trying several, my husband and I found and joined St. James' Church, where I enrolled in a grief group to help me sort through my sadness and anger following my sister's death.

Priscilla:

As I listened to Suzanne I felt that I was in the presence of someone with deep faith who had dealt with suffering and loss in a way that I couldn't. I was a bit envious of Suzanne's strong belief in God. I wished it would rub off on me. I wished I could believe that God would get me and my sister through the upcoming months that I knew would be so challenging.

When Ranya arrived, I filled her in on my sister's condition, and her eyes registered the concern and sympathy I needed. She asked about my sister's treatment and encouraged me to take care of myself as I tended to her.

"I don't know if I can handle this," I confessed, getting teary again.

And then I decided to share with Ranya and Suzanne the source of my biggest doubts and fears.

"I'm not someone who handles stress very well," I confessed. "I'm basically living in a state of low-grade panic. A state I've lived in all my life, essentially."

I grew up in an unconventional household, I explained. My mother was an artist who held dream analysis workshops in our basement every week, shunning PTA meetings for gatherings of like-minded free spirits. In his forties, my father was diagnosed as a "mild" (in his words) manic-depressive. And, over the years, certain members of his extended family suffered "nervous breakdowns," which were whispered about behind closed doors. They spent time in and out of mental institutions all their lives, and the constant awareness of this instilled in me a fear that I, too, would one day go crazy, suffer a "nervous breakdown," disintegrate into madness.

This theory of mine was given validity by the one secret I had largely kept to myself: the terrible, debilitating panic attacks I'd suffered from the time I was fifteen years old. These attacks came out of the blue. They started as a rush of adrenaline, a jolt of electricity that caused my whole body to shake. My heart galloped; my lungs tightened up so badly that I felt like my chest was being crushed. My throat closed, and I couldn't breathe. I gasped and gulped for air, like a fish on dry land. I thought I was dying. I felt nuts, sure that this had never happened to anyone else in their life, ever.

My first panic attack had taken place while I was working as a waitress at the Brown University Cafeteria in Providence. As I stood in my polyester uniform dishing out peas, surrounded by strangers and bathed in fluorescent lighting, I hyperventilated for the first time. I couldn't breathe. I couldn't work. I could barely stagger to the pay phone to call my parents and plead for a ride home. A doctor who made house calls examined me as I lay in my parents' bed, terrified, and told me I was "just a little bit nervous." He wrote out a prescription for Librium, a tranquilizer, and for the next thirty years I was left wondering what on earth was wrong with me.

I switched from Librium to Valium, but the panic attacks continued regardless of what I took, ate, thought, did, or felt. I had no idea what caused them. Maybe I was mentally ill. Certainly things were out of control in my body and my mind. I suffered panic attacks at night, alone in my room, behind the cash register at my father's supermarket, in restaurants, in college classes, at work in various ad agencies, in subways, buses and cars, even at the beach.

Despite my weak emotional constitution and looming panic attacks, I managed to build a good life for myself, with friends and boyfriends, academic and artistic successes. I met the love of my life and got married. I survived two pregnancies, despite several panic attacks, and gave birth to two wonderful, healthy sons. But I was a fraud. Nobody knew I was broken, that my body reared up and betrayed me on a regular basis.

"Maybe that's why I have such a hard time declaring myself a true believer in God," I told Suzanne and Ranya. "My body has always felt out of control, which has made my whole life feel out of control. If your own body is in chaos, it's hard to imagine a world of order, or a God who keeps things in order."

Suzanne and Ranya didn't look at God that way. They didn't see

God as keeping the world in order. "That's because you've never felt the kind of frantic chaos within your own body that I've felt," I told them. "You've never longed for that order."

After reading a medical pamphlet a friend gave me, I'd linked my own panic disorder to the fact that I had mitral valve prolapse, a common heart murmur. Sometimes a valve in my heart didn't completely shut. And often my body reacted with a "fight-or-flight" response. I'd also traced my panic to a near-death experience when I was sixteen months old and hospitalized with a dangerously high fever, convulsions, and an acute infection. A doctor happened to find me in serious distress, alone in my bed and unable to breathe. He performed an emergency tracheotomy on me right then and there.

No wonder I worried about dying, I told Suzanne and Ranya. No wonder I worried now that I would not be a source of strength for my sister.

"I wish I believed in God," I said out loud for the first time. Nobody in my family had ever talked about God. Not my father, my mother, my sister, or my brother. In twenty years of marriage, I'd had only one two-minute conversation with my husband about God.

Maybe, I realized as I spoke, all that was about to change. After the attacks of 9/11, I'd been afraid God didn't exist. Now, with my sister sick, I wished with all my heart that I could believe in God. Maybe Suzanne and Ranya would show me how.

RANYA: *For me, whenever I need affirmation of my faith, I look around . . . to the stars, the moon above . . .*
SUZANNE: *And that's where you find proof of God?*
RANYA: *I get goose bumps and tears when I hear recitations of that part of the Quran that says "And those who say nay or deny, ask them to look around them, do they not see God . . ." Islam seeks to provide evidence in the wonder of nature. It's not simply faith in your heart. The Islamic way is: Question, consider, think, reflect, and you should come out a believer.*

Ranya:

I was moved and saddened by Priscilla's and Suzanne's pain and in some ways could relate to both. Sometimes in my life, the presence of God has seemed impossible to deny, and at other times, I have felt doubt and alienation from a God defined and made available only through formal religion and its rituals. It is precisely the suffering and pain that so challenged Priscilla's sister that makes me so desperately want to believe that life is more than just a short visit in preparation for the unknown beyond.

I described to Priscilla and Suzanne how even as a child I longed and searched for some meaning to a life that was beyond the here and now. I remember sitting in the backseat of our family car staring upward at the starry night sky. I was only eight and was having more or less existentialist thoughts. I considered my hand, its five fingers, their shape and function, and wondered at God's divine hand in our human engineering. Was my hand, my body, my life part of some predetermined divine story? Were we all given the gift of life in order to face spiritual challenges and moral tests which upon our death might serve as our qualification for heaven? Or, God forbid, hell?

Or, I wondered, was my hand a random form, a chance, not so much part of God's will, but even—and this really scared me—an imagined reality? Was reality out there with the stars, or even in my dreams? Why did God make me who I am? And why am I alive?

As I have muddled my way through my confused spiritual state, my husband has often told me that I was too spiritual not to believe in God. When I have doubt, I try to remember those moments when the possibility of God, or at the very least a transcendent force, has been too difficult to deny. A few incidents that come to mind have to do with dreams that are difficult to explain without accepting the possibility of another realm or force that influences this earthly life.

I am not someone who spends any time inferring meanings from the details of my random dreams. Though aware that we all enter in and out of different sleep and dream cycles, it is a rare morning when I do recall my dreams. But the summer of my graduation from college, I was presented by my roommate's father with a graduation gift: a wristwatch that had the name of my university engraved on its inner dial, "Georgetown University." One morning I woke up distressed by a vividly disturbing dream. The glass case of my watch was cracked and the letters that spelled "Georgetown University" were seeping blood that, no matter what I did to wipe it away with my thumb, kept flowing. After sharing my dream with my mother, who was dismissive of it, I did not give it another thought until after my brother was involved in a fatal car accident later that same night. He and two passengers in his car were rushed to Georgetown University hospital, where one of his friends passed away.

Two other dreams that seem to me to be connected or inspired by another dimension involve my children. Soon after my first pregnancy was confirmed I unequivocally knew that I was having a girl, for I saw her as she would eventually look as a toddler, with big brown eyes and a mass of golden curls. Early in my second pregnancy I was greatly distressed because the survival of the pregnancy was in question. One morning I woke up asking my mother to complete for me the Quranic verse that I had been reciting in my dream: "Read in the name of God, in the name of God who has created mankind from alaq." The word "alaq" has different meanings, one of which is something that sticks or glues. My mother and I took that to mean that the baby would stay in my womb. And indeed I carried a beautiful full-term baby.

Some may dismiss these as merely interesting occurrences or at best romanticized experiences. I don't. I hang on to the idea of God because the alternative seems so futile. Ultimately, everything seems to go back to my childhood question: All this for what? Could our lives just be random specks in a random universe? Could galaxy upon galaxy with billions of stars, some orbiting, others spiraling, be random? I understand science's big bang theory, but that still does nothing to explain what transpired before the bang. I need to believe in a higher order that started that bang, not plain scientific randomness. In fact, the more that science unravels about the wonders of life (for instance, genetics) and the universe, the more I am in awe of it. To Muslims, the beauty and wonder of the universe and all that surrounds us offers proof of God. I like that idea.

If Suzanne's God is the God of passion and love, and Priscilla's God is a judicial God of mitzvahs (good deeds or acts), then my God is a poetic rationalist who appeals to my mind and heart. He asks me to consider the universe and its wonderment, to consider the scale of our human achievements in science or medicine, to marvel at our human intellect and its continuous progress, and then challenges me to deny his existence. Could all this be just a random occurrence, he asks me? If we are so impressed by our humanity, earth and its beauty, then surely we need to remain humble and mindful of that greater force that put it all together in the first place. Herein lies the temptation in my choices and every human choice. Do we choose to forfeit God's role and focus on the randomness of life and the inherent arrogance and cynicism that that bestows on our humanity? Or do we remain humble, mindful, and spiritual on this earthly journey, hopeful that though our individual lives represent an inequitable randomness of luck and good fortune, that in death we shall be compensated?

Priscilla:

Our meeting ended, but our conversations about the existence of God lingered in my mind. Suzanne had described the genesis of her faith so eloquently, and I loved the way Ranya found proof of God in the wonders of the universe. They both had so much faith in the existence of God and talked about it with so much grace.

I think I must have taken a piece of them with me on a long-scheduled trip I took shortly after that meeting. My husband had left days earlier for a business trip to Seattle, and my sons and I were to fly out there to meet him for a family vacation.

The war in Iraq had begun and security at JFK Airport in New York was extremely tight. We passed national guardsmen on patrol as we headed toward our gate and boarded our flight.

But once we were in the air, I began to feel a sense of relief. I was leaving behind me the possibility of another terrorist attack on New York City, the pressure of my mother's care, and my sister's frightening health crisis.

With my boys next to me, I sat by the window of the 757 as we headed toward the sunset. The air was turbulent, so our plane flew at an unusually low altitude. As we passed over a huge, unfamiliar body of water, I consulted a map in the back of the airline magazine to try to figure out where we were. We were flying over the Great Lakes, at sunset. I'd never seen the Great Lakes. They were enormous, flat, still, and silver as a mirror. Tiny waves lapped silently against the shores of Michigan. I stared out the window intently, and my eyes filled with tears.

"Why are you crying?" my younger son asked me.

"It's just so beautiful," I told him. I didn't tell him that I finally felt safe, leaving New York and the ruins of the Towers behind. I didn't tell him that I'd had to take a Klonopin in order to get on the plane. I didn't mention the female soldier I'd seen in the airport bathroom, washing her hands at the sink, her rifle close by.

I looked out the window and stared at the giant lakes below me, and started to think about the conversations I had shared with Ranya and Suzanne over the past months. If I was writing a book about the three great monotheistic religions, identifying myself as a Jew, shouldn't I be trusting in the one, all-powerful God of my people? I was talking the talk; shouldn't I be walking the walk? I used to believe God existed. Why not go back to that plan? What other explanation was there for the beauty beneath me? I was reminded of Ranya's words about the proof of God in the beauty of the universe.

My own constant obsessing and worrying wasn't going to do much, I realized sadly. It was making me appreciate my husband's embrace at the end of the day, when he walked in the door, home safe from work. But who was I kidding? I wasn't keeping the world safe. I was not all-powerful. I looked out the windows of the airplane over the Great Lakes and decided, as I had told Suzanne the week before, to try to surrender to a higher power.

Our plane landed safely in Seattle, and we spent a few days sightseeing, then drove along the beautiful, dramatic coastline to Vancouver. One rainy morning, I went alone to the Vancouver Museum of Art to see an exhibit of paintings by the great Canadian artist Emily Carr, who had spent most of her life in the forests of the Pacific Northwest. My own family had just taken hikes in those forests, and the quiet, magnificent terrain had soothed my troubled New York soul. Now Carr's vivid renditions of massive trees and mountains surrounded me as I walked alone through the galleries. On the wall of one room, a plaque described the era in which her work was completed, amid the chaos of two World Wars and the Great Depression. "The papers are full of horrible horrors," wrote Emily Carr. "And the earth is so lovely."

The earth is indeed lovely, I realized. Including New York City.

And so I decided to take a leap of faith. Life is, after all, a series of leaps of faith. Falling in love and believing that I will grow old with my husband is a leap. Losing a parent and believing I will recover is a leap. Giving birth to children and letting go as they grow, hoping they will lead safe, happy lives is a leap. Living in a world of chaos, believing good will prevail over evil, is a leap.

I'd felt a connection to God in that airplane, twenty thousand feet above the earth.

Maybe I could hold God's hand as I leaped.

CHAPTER EIGHT

Ranya's Madrassah

PRISCILLA: *Ranya, I know that you've said the Muslim God is a universal God, the same God as the Jewish God, the Christian God. But when I go out into the world I find that people don't really believe that . . . What do I say to people who cite suicide bombers as proof that Islam is a violent religion spread through war?*

RANYA: *Nowhere in the Quran does it say kill and you shall be rewarded. Dying in the name of religion is not unique to Islam. Christianity is full of examples of people who were martyred in the name of their religion. Some of those people, in fact, are considered saints. The Tamils in Sri Lanka blow themselves up for their cause. Buddhist monks burn themselves up in protest of war. But we all should recognize that when religion is used as a rationale for aggression, a tactic of war, or to justify a promise of land, then it is politicized religion. It becomes a human ideology that has nothing to do with Godly values. That doesn't excuse all this craziness, but it is not anything particular or exclusive to Islam.*

PRISCILLA: *And the word "jihad" is terrifying to most people. What exactly is jihad?*

RANYA: *Jihad has more than one meaning. The first is the idea of the inner struggle to be a better Muslim, considered to be the greater and more important jihad. The second meaning refers to the lesser jihad, which is the idea of holy war in defense of the faith, especially when mortal danger is perceived. But this "jihad against the infidels" demonstrated in the recent horrific terrorist attacks is not only crazy, but a terribly faulty reading of Islam. By Islam's definition, Christians and Jews are "people of the book" and therefore not infidels.*

PRISCILLA: *What about the religious schools, the madrassahs, that are teaching Holy War?*

RANYA: *There are madrassahs out there. But to understand the violence that is being preached there you have to look beyond the holy text. Most people would find it absurd to look at the roots of the Spanish Inquisition exclusively through references to the Bible. Most would agree that the persecution had a lot more to do with human power and ambition than the Christian message. And, by the way, few would condemn Judaism as an inherently aggressive and expansive territorial religion on the grounds that some have taken the Old Testament's promise of land to its militant conclusion.*

Priscilla:

I was getting to know Ranya well, and when people expressed their views on Muslim behavior to me, I began listening to them in a more critical way. I now recognized that there was such a thing as a moderate Muslim, so my instinct was to come to Islam's defense. But I didn't always have the language to do that.

At one cocktail party in particular I had a memorable conversation with a stranger, an intelligent Jewish man who was depressed at what he viewed as the religious indoctrination taking place in the madrassahs, the conservative religious schools in the Middle East. I told him that I didn't think jihad was encouraged in the scriptures. But then he started quoting Quranic verses. He told me that although early parts of the Quran do not prescribe jihad, later passages, which supercede them, urge the overthrow of infidels. I knew more about the Quran than I did before I met Ranya, but I didn't know enough to argue with him. So one afternoon as we sat in Suzanne's living room, I asked Ranya to tell Suzanne and me about jihad, the madrassahs, and martyrs.

"With violence taking place in the Middle East, these topics come up all the time," I said to Ranya. "I need you to give me the tools to respond to people who speak about your religion at cocktail parties and in everyday life. If we knew how to respond to the most vocal critics, then maybe Suzanne and I could be, in our own way, sort of ambassadors for Islam."

Ranya was patient as Suzanne and I ran through some of the negative images that were associated with Islam in the West.

"Is suicide accepted in Islam?" Suzanne asked.

"No. It's considered a sin, as I believe it is in Judaism and Christianity," Ranya answered.

"But what about suicide bombers? How do we respond when people cite their actions? What about the 9/11 attackers who believed that heaven and forty brown-eyed virgins awaited them after their suicides?" Suzanne continued.

"The whole matter of the virgins and suicide is ridiculous," Ranya stated. "I've been a Muslim my whole life, and I'd never heard about the virgins in heaven until after 9/11. Anyway, the translation used in that verse of the ancient Arabic is questioned by scholars who say that the term actually refers to a fruit, something like a grape, rather than a virgin. But this promise is only allegorical. It's poetic description, an image like rivers of milk and honey.

"But in my opinion, all this talk about virgins is irrelevant because it assumes that people are blowing themselves up solely for the virgins rather than political reasons, or even personal ones. And, by the way, what about the female suicide bombers? I don't think they're interested in the virgins."

Ranya had a point there. Was her voice rising? I felt guilty interrogating her like this, but if I was going to defend her religion, her Muslim God, I needed some facts.

Ranya:

It was not just Priscilla who needed facts. I needed them too. When people ask the question, "Is Islam contrary to the American way of life?" they are already projecting their view of Islam into the question—the Islam that says no drinking, no movies, no bikinis, no this, no that. If they didn't think they already knew the answer, they wouldn't be asking that question in the first place. Any religion can exist anywhere if it is about worship, as long as it doesn't teach people to harm others. This country guarantees freedom to worship.

It is not only outsiders who judge Islam that way. Other Muslims do too. This is because many Muslims these days don't have an understanding of their own religion. Much of what we have grown to accept as Islam, as I recently discovered, is in reality an historical aberration. The Wahabi Islam that has had such a strong influence on our most recent, persistent understanding of Islam is a reactionary brand of Islam that has striven to "purify" Islam by returning to the beliefs and practices of the first three decades of Muslim rulers! Followers of Wahabism, which began in Arabia in the eighteenth century, reject the entire body of Islamic theory, law, and theology that has been developed over the past fourteen hundred years of Islamic history, preferring to espouse a literal reading of the Quran based on the practices and laws of only the first three decades.

Asia, not being at the epicenter of this modern political Arabian Islam, has been able to maintain some of the historical Islamic tradition of plurality even while Wahabi Islam has gained prominence through the support of the oil-rich Saudi government, which came to power and survives through its alliance with the Wahabist leaders. In turn Saudi "oil" money has enabled the Wahabists to promote their brand of Islam through the financing of mosques and schools around the world, including a school in Washington, DC. And through their government support Wahabists have also been able to influence and control the image of Islam in the media.

Even Indonesia and Turkey, both secular democracies with a Muslim majority, have not completely escaped the influence of the Saudis who have funded mosques, schools, books, teachers, and imams who spread the Wahabi Saudi form of Islam in those countries. As a result,

Wahabi Islam has become to Muslims and non-Muslims alike the only recognizable form of Islam.

Few Muslims have picked up the Quran and read it for themselves, I explained to Suzanne and Priscilla. Much of their knowledge is either cultural or based on myth or hearsay. This is in spite of the fact that the first command Muhammad heard from God was, "Read in the name of God." And God's power gave Muhammad, an illiterate man, the ability to read.

I told Suzanne and Priscilla that I have always carried a Quran with me, clutching it as I gave birth to my children as a sign of submission to something that was so much greater than I.

"You held a Quran during childbirth? I didn't carry a prayer book," Priscilla said, turning to Suzanne. "Did you carry a Bible?" Suzanne answered that she had not.

"So you have always had a connection to the Quran," Priscilla asserted.

"Yes," I said. "But it wasn't until we began our conversations that I have become bold enough to open it and try to read and interpret on my own."

Recently, I related, I was having a conversation with Sami and my mother about Islam, and they challenged my idea that I could drink wine and still be a Muslim. "So I pulled my Quran off the shelf and read the passages regarding alcohol," I said.

"What did you find?" Suzanne asked.

"I didn't find anything prohibiting the consumption of wine," I replied. "The Quran says, don't approach prayer while you're drinking. It says that alcohol is the work of the devil, so avoid it. Well, I can see that. The devil brings temptation, and so does alcohol. It loosens you up and distorts your judgment. I can see that if I am drunk, I am not in my most Godly state. But the Quran doesn't forbid drinking. You may be a better Muslim if you avoid alcohol. But Islam is a journey. We have the concept of jihad, something that is a daily struggle. It is Islamic to think of your religion that way, something that you struggle with each day as you try to be better. So someone who abstains may be a better Muslim, but the judgment at the end of the day is God's."

> SUZANNE: *I passed the Ninety-sixth Street mosque this morning, Ranya, and the yard was filled with men praying. Where were the women? How can you be a Muslim when women are not treated equally?*
>
> RANYA: *It's a Muslim holiday, so the mosque was probably over-crowded. So some men had to pray out in the yard. But you're right, even inside the women would be segregated.*
>
> PRISCILLA: *You know, Orthodox Jewish synagogues separate men from women in prayer, too.*
>
> RANYA: *But in the most important mosque—the one in Mecca where people make their pilgrimage—there is no segregation. Listen, that criticism is there. It's sad that Islam is practiced today in a way that relegates women to a second-class position.*
>
> SUZANNE: *Why are men and women segregated?*
>
> RANYA: *The argument is that it is distracting if you are prostrating and there is an attractive woman in front of you. You may be distracted by her form, her body.*
>
> SUZANNE: *What about a woman being distracted by a man?*
>
> RANYA: *I agree. It is sexist.*
>
> SUZANNE: *How does it make you feel?*
>
> RANYA: *I don't like it. Still, I can see how sometimes a head covering can just be a sign of respect in the house of God. But I don't want it to be the one thing that defines a woman's membership in Islam.*

Suzanne:

"I can't justify the fact that most Muslim countries deny women equal rights," Ranya told Priscilla and me. "But that says more about the condition of these societies and their legal systems than about Islam. I don't think that is what Muhammad intended. If we look at his actions in the context of the time he lived in, he was revolutionary. He championed women's rights. He gave women marital rights and inheritance rights. A woman could divorce her husband if he did not satisfy her sexually! He put an end to the desert practice of killing female babies. I don't see him as a discriminator but as a liberator. But, once again, the words of the Quran got twisted."

"What about polygamy?" I asked. "How many wives does the Quran say a man can have?"

"The Quran, because it is written in such ancient and allegorical prose, could be interpreted to mean that a man can have four wives," Ranya answered. "But Muhammad was again revolutionary, because he reduced the common practice of polygamy at the time to four wives, and he stipulated that a man could marry four wives only if he was absolutely equal and fair in his treatment of all of them. And that's impossible. I would never allow that for my daughter. Ever."

"What about extreme abuse of women, like stoning?" Priscilla asked.

And then Ranya got upset. "Stoning? Hello? People who do that are insane! Even criminal! Ten girls died in a fire at their school in Saudi Arabia because the firemen wouldn't go in to save them. They were worried that the girls would be seen without their heads covered. Please! I have to speak out. This is going too far!"

"That is a heartbreaking story, extreme to be sure," I told Ranya. "But what about the more benign example of Muslim women wearing veils? Is that required?"

"Veiling came down in a verse in which the prophet was praying in a mosque somewhere, and he was distracted by a woman in a see-through dress," Ranya explained. "So Muhammad said 'Take your shawl and cover your bosom.' This shawl was just part of the traditional dress at the time."

"How do you feel about the images we see of women wearing

burqas that cover everything except their eyes? Are you embarrassed for your religion?" asked Priscilla.

"I don't see that as religious," Ranya replied. "The veil means different things in different settings. There is no such thing as one Muslim veil. Some veils are political, others are cultural, and some are just conservative expressions of piety. Women put it on for different reasons. In Afghanistan, the veil was enforced by a reactionary, brutal regime, the Taliban."

"What is going on in France?" Priscilla asked. "Where wearing veils in schools is so controversial?"

"In France immigrant Muslim girls have defended their right to wear a veil as a symbol or affirmation of pride in their identity, in the face of perceived discrimination or alienation from French culture," Ranya explained. "But in some Muslim countries the veil is simply tribal or traditional dress."

"Are you an exception, Ranya?" I asked.

"No! The majority of Muslim women are uncovered like I am. They have full lives and reject the very idea that their Muslim identity might be judged by some strictly on the basis of whether or not they wear a veil."

And now Ranya had reached her boiling point. "I believe that it is a woman's personal choice to put on a veil or not. I can respect that. But I find it insulting to have my relationship with God, or my authenticity as a Muslim, be judged by others on the basis of exterior wardrobe choices as opposed to my actions or beliefs. It is sad for me to see how much time is spent by some Muslims who choose to focus on veiling as a question of supreme importance. The Islamic civilization has made so many contributions to the world in terms of history, art, and culture. I can't believe we are now reduced to debating whether we should cover our noses, our heads, our breasts, our behinds . . . that's such an insult!"

Ranya had made her point passionately, and Priscilla and I steered the conversation into milder territory.

SUZANNE: *How does the Quran inspire you spiritually?*

RANYA: *It is very egalitarian and poetic. It strives to be an open book, accessible to all.*

SUZANNE: *Is it true that you can be a Muslim just by reciting the Shahada and then reading the Quran?*

RANYA: *Yes. I think the most important things are the five pillars of Islam. They are the Shahada, or testimony of faith, daily prayer, charity, fasting, and pilgrimage.*

Ranya:

Our discussion of Islam had taken place over the course of several meetings. Finally, at the end of a long conversation, Suzanne and Priscilla asked me if they could read the Quran on their own and understand it. "Yes," I said. "But it may not read as it should. It could sound very repetitious. The Quran is almost operatic. Its beauty brings tears to my eyes."

Excited by their interest, I pulled out a copy of Harold Bloom's book *Genius* and read aloud from it. "The Quran is a perfect poem in itself. For what is the Quran? It is anything but a closed book. Even if it is the seal of prophecy, as much as the Bible or Dante or even Shakespeare, the Quran is the book of life, as vital as any person whoever she or he is, since the God addresses all of us who will hear. It is a universal book, again, as open and generous as the greatest works of secular literature, as the master works of Shakespeare and Cervantes."

Then I read from the Quran, chapter 24, verse 35.

God is the Light of Heaven and Earth!
His light may be compared to a niche
in which there is a lamp; the lamp
is in a glass; the glass
is just as if it were a glittering star
kindled from a blessed olive tree,

(which is) neither Eastern nor Western,
whose oil will almost glow though fire
has never touched it. Light upon light,
God guides anyone He wishes to His light.
God composes parables for mankind;
God is aware of everything!

"It's really poetic," Priscilla marveled.

"I'll read you Bloom's interpretation," I said. "He writes: 'The niche may be the heart of Mohammad or any discerning heart: God guides to his light whom he will. That blessed olive tree, neither of the East nor the West, is everywhere and nowhere, wherever and whenever, a purified vision, a light.'"

"Ranya, that's you!" Suzanne and Priscilla cried in unison. "Neither East nor West!"

They were right. I did identify with that verse, which to me represented the truth of Islam. It is about universal faith that knows no geographic boundaries—a faith in which those who are religious are serene, reflective, and gracious of spirit. I found a definition of that Islam that I knew when I picked up the Quran later.

It is not righteousness that ye turn your faces to the East and the
West: but righteousness is he who believes in God and the Last Day
and the angels and the scripture and the prophets; he who, though
he loves it dearly gives away his wealth to the kinsfolk and to or-
phans and the needy and the wayfarer and to those who ask, and to
set slaves free; and observes proper worship, and pays the poor-due.
And those who keep their treaty when they make one, and the pa-
tient in tribulation and adversity and in times of stress. Such are
they who are sincere. Such are the God-fearing. (2:177)

But that is not the voice of Islam I hear now. I hear an angry voice, and it is not about religion. It is politics masquerading as religion.

Priscilla:

Soon after our discussions, I had a firsthand chance to meet another vibrant, modern, unveiled Muslim woman when Ranya's mother, Aida Tabari, came to New York for a visit, and Ranya invited me to meet her.

"My mother has brought you a special treat," Ranya informed me when she invited me to her apartment for lunch.

When Ranya, Suzanne, and I had shared the Bible stories we'd learned as children, Ranya had mentioned manna, the sweet bread sent down by God to the Jews starving in the desert. I was surprised to hear that she'd eaten manna as a child.

"It's a type of Persian candy," Ranya had explained. "Muslim children are told it comes from the heavens." Now Ranya had arranged for her mother to bring me some, straight from the Middle East.

As I walked into Ranya's apartment building, I wondered how I would get along with her mother. The first time I'd met Ranya, I had viewed her as a Palestinian. But now, after all of our heated, honest conversations, Ranya was my friend. I was still intrigued by her background, however, and our friendship still felt a bit exotic to me. And now I was meeting her mother, only the second Palestinian woman I'd ever met.

Aida Tabari was as warm and open-hearted as her daughter. I was ushered into Ranya's apartment by the two of them, and we never stopped talking. I felt instantly comfortable with Aida, as though we'd known each other for years. Ranya has often said that Arabs and Jews are like cousins, and, indeed, Ranya's mother felt to me like a visiting cousin. She has a beautiful, friendly face and a hearty, ready laugh. We all speak fast, so words were flying around Ranya's apartment.

The first thing Aida did was hand me my box of manna, a type of Turkish delight candy from Iran, in a beautifully colored box. I asked her to tell me what Ranya was like growing up, and Aida described her daughter lovingly, sharing with me some amusing anecdotes. She also told me the story of how she had met her husband, and when Aida Tabari described herself as a nineteen-year-old flirting with the man who turned out to be the love of her life, I heard a universal story.

It wasn't until months later, after some difficult conversations with Ranya, that I realized just how much I'd been changed by my meeting with her and her mother. I'd gained a new perspective. So when people I talked to grew angry with the Palestinians and laid blame or criticized them as one violent, angry mob, saying "they" think this or "they" do that, I wondered to myself: "How can you speak with such certainty about these people? Do you know any Palestinians? Have you ever met a Palestinian person? Have you ever broken bread with a Palestinian person?"

I'd now met two wonderful, lively, unique Muslim women. And I'd broken bread with them. Magical bread. Manna from heaven.

Suzanne:

My interfaith meetings with Ranya and Priscilla were slowly affecting my approach to religion. I noticed it in my Sunday school classroom. The changes were minor, but they represented an ecumenical approach to Christianity that I had not considered before.

When we did our lesson on Abraham, I talked about how Abraham was considered the father of Judaism, Christianity, and Islam.

"Jewish people don't believe in God," one six-year-old boy said.

"Of course they do," I answered. "They worship the same God we do. And the Muslims do too. We all share parts of the same religious tradition even though we worship in different ways and in different places." We talked about praying in churches, mosques, and temples. The children were familiar with temples because our parish had worshiped in a temple the previous year. But no one had been in a mosque before.

When we taught our class about Moses, I read the story Priscilla had written for our children's book and talked about how Moses and Jesus were both Jews.

I realized this was just scratching the surface of understanding, however. I wanted to know what things in particular about Muhammad and the Quran inspired Muslims. What tools did Islam offer Ranya in her quest to find God? What was it in the Hebrew Bible that spoke to Priscilla? As we continued to meet I asked them questions along these lines. Meanwhile, I made another trip to Barnes & Noble, spent an afternoon in the religion section, and left with an armful of books.

As I began reading about Islam's view of creation, I found things that appealed to me more than the Catholic doctrine I had learned in school. In the Quran, Eve does not trick Adam into eating the apple. Adam and Eve act together. More importantly, the transgression of Adam does not mark humanity with "original sin" as had been taught by Catholics when I was in school. The idea of original sin had troubled me from the time I came across it in a book I read to prepare to receive the sacrament of confirmation in grade school. Simply speaking, the doctrine of original sin teaches that all humans are marked by a stain at birth and only the grace of God can bring a person to a sinless state. Catholics used to rush their babies to the baptismal font lest they perish before baptism removed their original sin.

The teaching of the Catholic Church does not come down so hard on newborns any longer; however, the doctrine of original sin still exists. In fact, I had recently come across a reference to it in a project that my daughter had brought home from a religion class, and I was surprised by the strength of my reaction. Anne was a guest in the class, a nondenominational Bible class, and she brought home a construction paper booklet that she had made there. The book was meant to represent the Christian view of creation and salvation. The first page had a green construction paper background. On it, Anne had glued a picture she had drawn of Adam and Eve. The next page was red, and there was the tree of life with its apple. The third page was entirely black. There was no picture.

"What is this black page?" I asked Anne.

"It's sin," she answered.

"Whose sin?" I asked.

"The sin we're born with."

"You mean original sin?" My eyes widened.

"Yes," she nodded. My thoughts immediately went back to a picture from a childhood catechism book I had. The picture, which I had found so troubling, showed a child with a black blotch on his soul representing original sin.

"Tear that page out," I told Anne.

"Why?" she asked.

"Because I don't believe original sin exists. I believe that we start out marked by the love of God, not the sin of Adam. If Adam needed to be forgiven, God forgave him long ago."

Anne thought for a few seconds. "Yeah, I think you're right," she said as she ripped the black page out of her booklet and threw it in the garbage.

As I watched her, I was reminded that my view of Christianity was not the same as many others'. There were millions of Christians in America who focused on man's sinfulness and God's severe judgment rather than on God's love of humanity and his forgiveness—qualities that were demonstrated by Jesus' ministry, which extended to all. Those Christians, whose image of God seemed severe and exclusive to me, were gaining a larger voice in politics, education, and religion. I needed to be on guard for the sake of my children.

CHAPTER NINE

The Promised Land

SUZANNE: *Priscilla, how does the Jewish history of persecution affect your outlook on the world?*

PRISCILLA: *In my everyday life, not much. I'm not affected personally. But, to be honest, I do think Jews have an innate sense of the most fundamental persecution that Christians and Muslims just don't have. I know about the genocide in Armenia, the killing fields of Cambodia, the massacres in Rwanda, the Sudan, Bosnia. But, to be perfectly honest, there is nothing comparable in modern history to the slaughter of six million people.*

RANYA: *Do you think Jews suffer more discrimination than Muslims in America today?*

PRISCILLA: *Absolutely not. I think that after September 11th, people are terrified and confused about Islam. They are also, for the most part, completely ignorant. And so they are discriminating against Muslims. We read about Muslims locked up in jail for months, without any charges filed against them. I don't know how it will work out for Islam, but I don't think it's going to end up with six million Muslims being gassed in camps. You can't underestimate the enormity of the Holocaust.*

RANYA: *I don't think people do underestimate its enormity. But you have to transcend it sometimes, not make it the cornerstone of who you are.*

PRISCILLA: *But it is the cornerstone! Every Jew is told "Never forget." That's what we learn constantly in Hebrew school. "Never forget. It could happen again." I know it sounds crazy, but Jews are always waiting for that knock on the door, to be rounded up . . .*

Ranya:

I had been holding out, waiting to have what I knew would be a challenging conversation with Priscilla ever since she'd described her relationship to her Jewish God as being "in her blood." When she'd talked about Jews calling themselves "M.O.T.s," or Members of the Tribe, I'd instinctively felt excluded. I wanted to tell her that. And I wanted to explore her relationship with her God in the context of the Holy Land.

I wavered for a while—could I push the envelope and have the conversation I'd been tiptoeing around for months? Should I explore issues I knew would be provocative, engage in a conversation that might threaten the friendship we'd begun to cherish? I could be leading us both into dangerous territory.

On a cold winter morning, Priscilla arrived at my apartment bearing a gift, a tin of hot chocolate that she described as "highly addictive." We might need some drugs, I thought as I prepared three mugs full of the dense chocolate drink in my kitchen. I knew that the conversation we were about to engage in would be challenging.

The three of us sat around my dining table chatting for a few moments and then called our meeting to order, getting down to business. I had been the one to convene this meeting because of my angst and impatience over certain issues I felt had to be addressed. We were meeting just about every other week, and whenever someone had a particular subject she wanted to discuss, she was free to call a meeting and set the agenda for that meeting.

By then, Suzanne, Priscilla, and I had reached a point in our conversations in which things could get quite heated. "Playing by street rules" or "taking off the gloves" were some of the euphemisms we had used to describe our encounters lately. I, for one, no longer wondered what my voice would or should be. In fact, I was now ready to address my colleagues' questions, thoughts, and stereotypes, letting down my guard.

On some level I felt that Priscilla was still more preoccupied with the sparks that often emanated from her dialogues with Suzanne than with exploring our possible differences. Priscilla felt that she and I shared common ground, as members of minority religions in America, even comparing us to social outcasts in contrast to Suzanne's insider status. Though I didn't say it at the time, I did not feel the same sense of exclusion that she did. Though I have always been an outsider, I have worked hard to embrace the cultures in which I have lived and to make myself comfortable within them.

My growing friendship with Priscilla and her warm, empathetic ways made it difficult for me to differentiate our views and painful for me to dig deeper. So when Suzanne opened the door to a discussion about anti-Semitism at one of our meetings, I felt that I might finally have the opportunity to get my views heard. I had on many occasions felt frustrated, even angry, that criticism of the Israeli state, or disagreement with its founding principles, implied that you were by definition anti-Jewish and therefore anti-Semitic.

It reminded me of years ago, when I was in college, and my father would engage in numerous heated conversations over dinner with Jewish friends. He would try to explain the difference between being Jewish and being a Zionist. He would insist that he was not anti-Jewish, but that he was certainly anti-Zionist, since it was, after all, Zionism, with its goal of establishing a Jewish state in historical Palestine, where the Jews were a minority, that had personally cost him his land and life as he knew it as a boy.

Sometimes, the very idea of calling myself Palestinian makes me feel that by definition I'm suspect, as someone who is anti-Israeli, and as a result anti-Jewish. I have had people challenge me on the very idea of being Palestinian. Some have asked me, "But what does it mean to be Palestinian? There was no such state." "Are you not just Arab?" others have asked me. It is quite a burden when your national identity becomes an existential challenge, synonymous with anti-Semitism.

For months, I had to bide my time patiently as Priscilla and Suzanne engaged in what I felt was their bilateral monologue about the Jewish-Christian experience of anti-Semitism. I worked hard at hearing Priscilla through, gaining her trust, relating my empathy and understanding of her Jewish experience of the Holocaust. I let Priscilla and Suzanne set the agenda for our meetings as I explained and answered their most immediate concerns and pressing questions about Islam before I could finally turn the table around and press them on my own issues.

RANYA: *Priscilla, why is it so difficult to criticize anything relating to the Jews without being labeled anti-Semitic?*
PRISCILLA: *It's all about the Holocaust. Every Jew grows up thinking there but for the grace of God go I.*
SUZANNE: *Is there a fear of the Holocaust happening again?*
PRISCILLA: *Absolutely. If it happened once, it can happen again. It is your worst, worst fear. You never go to it. I don't really think it could happen. The world is a different place. But as I've said before, I'm describing an emotional fear, not a rational one.*
RANYA: *But that fear is playing itself out in a weird way in terms of the Jewish state. People can no longer express an opinion, even if in the long run that opinion is in the interest of the survival of the Israeli state, without being accused of anti-Semitism.*

Priscilla:

After Ranya served the hot chocolate I'd brought, she laid out her signature platter of delicious sandwiches. I could always count on her to keep me well fed. And, it turned out, I could also count on her to be a deep thinker, an honest, outspoken proponent for the Palestinian people, and someone who was going to push me, prod me, and cause me to think till my head hurt.

Ranya and I were on solid ground. Our friendship was still evolving. We talked often on the phone. We shared amusing anecdotes about our children, commiserated over stressful family dynamics. As a mother of older children, I had lived through the years of high fevers and sleepless nights. I often complimented Ranya on her mothering and assured her that these tough years would be replaced with, well, tough years with teenagers! We were friends.

But Israeli-Palestinian relations during the same period were strained, to say the least. News of the Intifada was in the papers almost daily. Disturbing, violent images were being transmitted all over the world. Blood was being shed on all sides. Suzanne, Ranya, and I couldn't help but talk about Israel. And when Ranya began her attempt to separate my thoughts about the Israeli-Palestinian conflict from my emotions about the Holocaust, I felt threatened.

The Holocaust is obviously something that Jews will never and should never forget. And the notion that Arabs have been trying to push the Jews into the ocean is something I had grown up hearing, at the Hebrew Day School, from my father's comments about the 1967 War, and lately, when Jews spoke among themselves, expressing concern about the survival of Israel. Up until the time I met Ranya, my stereotype of an Arab had been someone who was trying to annihilate the Jews all over again.

Maybe that's why Ranya surprised me so much when I met her and got to know her, I now realized. She didn't fit that stereotype. I thought back to what she had said to me once, when she chided me for praising her so lavishly at a meeting. She'd found me a bit condescending and questioned whether I liked her so much because of who she was or because she defied my stereotype of what a Muslim woman should be.

Ranya did defy my stereotype of an Arab woman, I now realized. She was so warm, loving, gracious, and understanding. We sometimes had different points of view on faith. We'd been careful, thoughtful, and considerate in our dealings with each other.

But Israel was in turmoil. And we would now have to address that fact. We'd have to talk about the tough issues, the things that might tear our friendship apart. Ranya would try to make me see things through her eyes. And I would have to imagine myself in her shoes, to listen. And think.

SUZANNE: *Priscilla, do you really believe Palestinians are victims?*
PRISCILLA: *Absolutely.*
RANYA: *But you laughed a while back and said "Okay, Ranya, I'll give it to you . . . you can be a victim!" I wonder if that wasn't just a flippant response, because, after all, Jews have the Holocaust as justification for that claim, while Muslims don't. Maybe you don't think we have a legitimate claim of persecution.*
PRISCILLA: *To be perfectly honest, I think that's what Palestinians and Jews have in common. I think that we are both victims.*
RANYA: *But then that leads me to the next thought . . . I haven't wanted our conversations to become political, but you need to recognize that Israel is a Jewish state, so the issue is a Jewish issue. It is not the Israeli-Palestinian conflict but the Jewish-Palestinian conflict.*

Priscilla:

I hadn't felt this tense in a meeting with Suzanne and Ranya since we'd had our big stereotype discussion, where the drama, I now realized, had been largely between me and Suzanne. Ranya, it seemed, had saved her provocative questions for a later date. And that date was now. Ranya had called this meeting and set the agenda. She clearly had something on her mind, something she'd wanted to address with me for some time. At least that was the sense I got. Her body language signaled that to me. She leaned forward in her chair, pointed at me for emphasis, shook her head adamantly when she disagreed with me, raised her voice when she thought I needed to listen to something especially important.

Sitting at Ranya's dining room table, my eyes took in the beautiful photographs that covered the walls of her home, the elegant white orchid plant that sat on a nearby coffee table. I was in familiar surroundings but unfamiliar territory. I was being challenged. By a Palestinian woman. By my friend. Which was she? Could she be both?

I felt a bit like a mouse being teased by a cat. Was Ranya setting a trap for me? Did I need to be careful? Wary? Honest? Defensive?

Where was Suzanne in all this? Had she known what our agenda would be? I couldn't read the expression on Suzanne's face, and she didn't say too much.

I was, after all, the only Jew in the room.

RANYA: *Priscilla, you're Jewish because you belong to a tribe, right?*

PRISCILLA: *Yes.*

RANYA: *So that means that you can't take your Jewishness away from you. It means that you have something in common with all Jews that sets you apart from anyone else living on that land, that Promised Land, which you believe God gave to the Jews.*

PRISCILLA: *But I don't call Israel "The Promised Land"!*

RANYA: *You may not call it the Promised Land. But my understanding is that Jews believe they have a covenant with God which gives them that land. And the settlers are using that religious claim to justify the building of settlements, the forcing of people off their land. So what I'm saying is that although you have already come out against the settlements, can you now recognize how elements of your own religion are being used to provide a rationale for taking land away from people?*

PRISCILLA: *But Ranya, you've got the wrong Jew here! I'm against the settlements! I always have been! I think the founding of Israel is one thing, and, because of the Holocaust, religion*

129

played a huge role then. But the survival of Israel is a different matter. Religion is causing so many problems now.

RANYA: *You might be getting yourself in trouble with that kind of talk, Priscilla. Israel is a Jewish state. That allows some people to say "I as a Jew have a relationship with God that allows me to force people out of their homes, off their land, that gives me an exclusive, biblical, Godly right."*

PRISCILLA: *But that's all interpretation. And it goes back to the question I have as to whether or not the Bible is a historical document. I would never say at the moment that Israelis can always claim the moral high ground. They've made mistakes. I cannot defend the way they've treated many people in the occupied territories. And there are Jews here and in Israel who agree with me.*

RANYA: *Yes, but you must understand that while the average American sees images of primarily militant, angry Muslims on TV and characterizes Islam as violent, the average Muslim sees equally violent images of angry Israeli settlers and Israeli soldiers and helicopters firing missiles onto cars, killing innocent Palestinian children. So what kind of image do you think they have of Jews? Or of American support of Israel?*

PRISCILLA: *So you're saying that in the Muslim world, Jews are considered violent, because the loudest voice of Judaism is an occupying, aggressive military voice?*

RANYA: *Absolutely! They don't know Priscilla over there!*

Ranya:

From the moment I met Priscilla she'd taken a position opposed to the settlements in the occupied territories. I knew that this was a significant stance for her to take. I had no idea what her friends thought, who she associated with socially, or if her friends were even politically inclined. I had no idea if she discussed Middle East politics with them. All I really cared about was the dialogue that the two of us had started with each other. And I felt that dialogue had thus far been a bit lopsided. I felt that I had taken a brave stand vis-à-vis my own religion. I had been critical of those Muslims who I felt distorted and manipulated holy text for their own political gain. Now I wanted Priscilla to do the same. I wanted her to go further than she'd ever thought of going, to examine and articulate how her religion was being used by some people to justify territorial claims.

When Priscilla first stated that Judaism was in her blood, that she felt a tribal connection to other Jews, I realized that she might be closer than she realized to her religion. If that were the case, if she truly was a Jew by birth, like it or not, I wanted to hear that the religion that coursed through her veins, that she could never disavow, provided claims to some who used their holy text to justify their actions.

If Priscilla and I were indeed friends, I needed her to be genuine. This was new territory for us. I didn't want to hurt Priscilla, but there were things I needed to say, things that I had been holding back for some time.

RANYA: *There is a perception that people are on the receiving end of Jewish aggression because Jews believe they are promised their land by God. So then it's not a very difficult leap to say "Allah is my God, and I am promised another promise." You mirror your enemy. Is Judaism wired to be violent? Is Islam?*

PRISCILLA: *This is so much to absorb. My head hurts from thinking so hard. Do you know how much thinking you have to do in order to question? Then you have to ask all the right questions. Then you have to reach your own conclusion. And then you have to take action. It's HUGE!*

RANYA: *Yes, but while you distance yourself from Israel by saying it has nothing to do with reform Judaism, I am able to say that I hate what is happening in the name of Islam. The connection between politics and religion is closer than you think. And just as I*

*need to address the idea that people are able to hijack Islam in
their name . . .*

PRISCILLA: *So settlers have hijacked Judaism for their own purposes?*

RANYA: *Absolutely.*

PRISCILLA: *So what are we supposed to do? Be the voices of mod-
eration for our religions?*

RANYA: *I must examine text and see how it can be used to support
certain behavior. And in your case, you should recognize that your
text has something in it that allows people to make claims on this
land to the exclusion of others.*

PRISCILLA: *But it's not the Jews' fault that our book says we are
promised land, and it's not your fault that the Quran says you can
have four wives.*

Suzanne:

I had never seen Ranya on the attack like she was that afternoon. I
trembled for Priscilla, who I think was as clueless as I was about
where Ranya was leading her. As Ranya baited Priscilla, I remembered
how I had thought it unfair when Priscilla had held me responsible
for centuries of Christian anti-Semitism. Now I saw Priscilla being
held responsible for the creation and actions of the state of Israel. Did
she bear any more responsibility as a Jew than we did as Americans
for the catastrophic treatment the Palestinians have endured as a result of the creation of Israel? After all, the United States government
funds a substantial portion of Israel's annual military budget. And
sixty years ago America had supported the creation of the Jewish
state. Already Priscilla had professed her disapproval of Israeli policy
in the settlements, casting blame upon American leaders, who, she
said, should have gotten both sides back to the negotiating table.
What more could Ranya want from her, I wondered.

Then I sat back to listen. Ranya clearly knew what she wanted. She repeated a line from the Jewish holy services that seemed to implicate Jews everywhere in the aggression of the Israelis. "At your temple you say 'Next year in Jerusalem,' don't you?" Now I began to see the relationship between a Jewish woman in suburban New York and the actions of the Israeli government. When Ranya paused I asked Priscilla, "Do they collect money for Israel at your temple?"

"A few times a year they pass the plate for Israel," she answered.

"And what do you do?" I asked.

Priscilla didn't give a direct answer, saying instead, "I try to give money to organizations that help Palestinians and Israelis equally. Last month I went to a dinner that raised money for medical, legal, and economic aid for Arabs and Jews in Israel."

"Are you often around big donors to Israel? Does it make you uncomfortable because of your own position about Israel?" I persisted.

Again she avoided the question. "I don't hang around the heavy hitters like you guys do in Manhattan!"

I had never thought before about the pressure an American Jew might feel to support Israel. It wouldn't be easy to pass that collection plate down the row without putting anything into it. Certainly you would draw attention to yourself. Those sitting nearby would wonder what your actions implied. Did you support Israel or not? Did you recognize that Jews were victims of worldwide anti-Semitism or did you not? Unfortunately, as Ranya knew, the religion of Judaism and the politics of Israel had become inextricably entwined. That created a burden for Priscilla that I knew would be difficult to shoulder.

RANYA: *As a concerned Muslim I am addressing how my text is being misused and as an enlightened woman of your faith, you must personally address this also. So what are you going to do?*
PRISCILLA: *What do you mean? Do you think I should stand up and be more vocal?*
RANYA: *I think you need to be a bit more vocal in this setting, in terms of your feelings. You are Jewish, right? And at your temple*

you say, "Next year in Jerusalem," right? Does that mean a
Jerusalem that is only Jewish?

PRISCILLA: *Not to me! I'm willing to share it.*

RANYA: *I don't mind you thinking you'll be in Jerusalem next*
year, but I want to be there, too!

PRISCILLA: *I think Jews should take a good, hard look in the mir-*
ror and ask themselves what the "Christian thing" to do is. But
there are voices of dissent in the Jewish religion today, as in all re-
ligions.

SUZANNE: *Are you a voice?*

PRISCILLA: *I'm not standing out in the middle of Times Square,*
but I do it in my own way when the subject arises.

Priscilla:

I returned home from our meeting at Ranya's exhausted and a bit
shell-shocked. I had been challenged by Ranya to step up to the plate
as a Jew and to question my religion as it relates to modern-day Israel.

What a challenge.

I had no one, for the time being, to talk to about this. Life at home
was always busy. Raising two teenagers and running our home took up
a lot of our energy, and dominated most of my conversations with
Jimmy. He and I did not discuss my meetings with Suzanne and Ranya
much at all. So I was on my own in all this. Why did I have to deal with
this painful problem? I wondered. I wasn't a peace negotiator. But I did
want peace with my dear friend Ranya.

I thought back to my very first conversation with my rabbi, as we re-
viewed the story of Moses and the Burning Bush. "Each and every one of
us is called by God," Jeffrey said back then. "All of us are asked to stand
up and be counted, to lead a life worthy of God's respect. Moses was
afraid of the challenge God presented to him. But he rose to that challenge. And that's what all the rest of us have to do in life—answer the call
of God, rise to the occasion, and accept whatever challenges we face."

I did not wish to embark on a crusade to convert others to my way of thinking about peace in the Middle East, or anything else, for that matter. However, I had grown to respect Suzanne and Ranya so much over the course of the last two years, that I felt it would be disrespectful to them for me to sit back passively and not continue questioning what it means to be a good Jew and a good person every single day of my life, in all areas of my life.

I've declared myself to be a Jew. A Jew who believes in God. This, in and of itself, was hugely significant for me. And something I would never have done so publicly if I hadn't met Suzanne and Ranya.

I began raising the subject with people a couple of weeks after my talk with Ranya, and here are some of the comments I heard from my Jewish friends and acquaintances:

"Why should the Jews have to give back land? Our American forefathers took land away from Native Americans and never gave it back!"

"There will never be peace in the Middle East."

"We never *took* land from the Palestinians! We were *given* that land!"

"What about the busloads of Israelis who've been blown to smithereens? Innocent civilians have been murdered in cold blood, simply because they got up in the morning and boarded a bus to go to school, or to work."

"The Arabs want to push us into the ocean!"

"They want to wipe us off the map!"

"They don't want Israel to exist!"

"Israelis have made a big mistake in their treatment of Palestinians. They, of all people, should hold themselves up to higher moral standards!"

"We have to support Israel! Jews need to have a country! It was the only place in the world that would accept them! America sent boatloads of starving Jews back to Europe!"

"What if something like the Holocaust happens again? Where will Jews go if there is no Israel?"

The Palestinian conflict is heartbreakingly complex. Recent newspaper and magazine articles have described a rise in anti-Semitism all over the world, speculating that the Israeli army's aggressive actions in the occupied territories and the violent images transmitted as a result of those actions have triggered all this hatred.

Will Israel still exist as a Jewish state in a few years? Should it? Should Ranya's family and others like them be allowed to return?

Jews need to take a good look in the mirror, I tell people. But I want to hide under the covers some days. Why can't I sit back and worry about Britney Spears's belly button, like millions of other Americans do? On some days, that sounds like a plan.

But I can't. I can't sit back.

Why? Because of the dialogue that I started with Ranya and Suzanne two years ago. That dialogue is never-ending. New angles keep popping up daily. Suzanne, Ranya, and I email each other articles and discuss ideas regularly, raising new issues, shedding light on old ones.

I have had many conversations with my Israeli friend Chaim, who is admittedly intrigued by my collaboration with a Palestinian. On days when a bus is blown up in Israel he is furious. We can barely speak. On other days, he tells me how his grandmother used to feed her children goats' milk provided by an Arab shepherd. "What greater trust is there than that?" Chaim asks me. And I am optimistic all over again.

I discovered a group of Israeli rabbis who call themselves Rabbis for Morality. They stage civil disobedience protests inspired by Dr. Martin Luther King, Jr. A group of people called Machsom Watch have organized and stationed themselves along the controversial "wall" between Israel and the territories. Their mission is to make sure Palestinians are treated with as much dignity as possible. I met a French Jew who told me that unlike American Jews, French Jews feel free to criticize the Israeli government's policies without fear of being labeled self-hating anti-Semites. They don't write Israel a blank check. They question. Like me.

I have a vivid memory of standing in my kitchen several years ago, early in the morning, watching Itzhak Rabin's funeral on television. I stood at my kitchen counter and tears poured down my face, catching my boys totally off guard. I explained to them that a very great man had died and that I was very sad. What I didn't tell them was that, unimaginably, another Jew had killed him. If this could happen, I had no idea what else on earth was possible. A Jew killing another Jew? This was terrifying new territory.

The words Rabin had spoken years earlier haunted me:

"We, the soldiers who have returned from battles stained with blood; we who have seen our relatives and friends killed before our eyes; we who have attended their funerals and cannot look in the eyes of their parents; we who have come from a land where parents bury their children; we who have fought against you, the Palestinians—we say to you today, in a loud and a clear voice: enough of blood and tears. Enough."

Rabin had earned the right, as an Israeli war hero, to utter those words. What rights and credibility did I have?

Still, I continued to speak up a bit about Israel, and Ranya and I continued speaking at our next meeting. Israel, after all, was not going to disappear off the map.

PRISCILLA: *You know, Ranya, some of the people I know are very skeptical when I tell them your family's story of leaving Palestine. One friend said to me, "Don't believe everything you hear. People weren't kicked off their land in 1948. They made choices."*

RANYA: *Your skeptical friend's position is devoid of any empathy for a people who have really suffered. Regardless of what she said, we're victims. Whether it's because we left on our own or we were kicked out, isn't the bottom line that there are a people out there who are, for a large part, refugees? I'm not a refugee, but I've been disconnected from my heritage. Here I am years later addressing issues of my children being Arab and Muslim in America. It's part of the Zionist mythology that Palestinians left their homes willingly.*

PRISCILLA: *Whoa! "Zionist mythology?" You know, Ranya, a while ago, that comment . . . I mean, I can't believe I can sit here now and just nod when you say that. We've come a long way.*

RANYA: *Priscilla, this a great example of how I feel that if I voice opinions that are critical of the Jewish state or critical of Zionism, then I'm going to be labeled anti-Semitic, even anti-Jewish, with a hidden agenda of pushing the Jews into the sea. All countries have their own defining experiences and historic moments that become part of the national mythology and landscape of that country.*

SUZANNE: *Think of the stories Americans tell of the Boston Tea Party, George Washington crossing the Delaware, Paul Revere and his ride. Or, here's a good analogy. Think of how we have portrayed Native Americans and our conquest of the West. They were dehumanized as heathen savages so that we could justify our treatment of them.*

Ranya:

It isn't easy for me to control my emotions when I am forced to confront those who, like Priscilla's friend, deny or downplay the tragically painful process of the dispossession of the Palestinian people. Priscilla had recounted her friend's reaction at our next meeting, and it angered me. "How would it feel for your friend to hear someone deny the Holocaust?" I asked Priscilla, hypothetically. "I have the same visceral reaction when I am confronted with what can only be called national myths concerning the facts and circumstances under which the creation of the state of Israel took place."

Priscilla decided a long time ago that she was against the expansion of the settlements in the occupied territories. She is a sensitive and empathetic woman, full of humanity and integrity. That is why I was able to reach out to her. I began to understand how she has experienced anti-Semitism on a cultural and social level in her life in America and how that touches her fear of the Holocaust.

"For the record," I told Suzanne and Priscilla, "I oppose the oppression of Jews wherever it exists as I oppose the oppression of Christians as, for example, it exists today in the Sudan." But then I continued. "It is not, however, anti-Semitic to oppose Israel's oppression of the Palestinian people who are both Muslim and Christian. Nor is it anti-Semitic for me to oppose Zionism. I am opposed to citizenship based on religion in any country, whether Jewish, Muslim, or Christian."

For most of my life, I have sublimated my feelings about what has happened in Palestine. But, as a result of this project, I have acknowledged them, and their reality is painful. Months after my provocative conversations with Priscilla, I felt physically sick as I came upon the Israeli Independence Day Parade while I tried to cross Fifth Avenue one beautiful spring Sunday. As I watched the floats go by, my heart raced and my stomach churned with emotion. "Does anyone here know what their day of celebration and pride means to me?" I wondered. "It is the Palestinians' Nakba [Catastrophe]."

The Israelis say that the Palestinians sold their land to Israel. This isn't true. The overwhelming majority of Palestinians fled in fear as war broke out. They believed that they would return when conditions calmed down. The Israeli army murdered Palestinians (for instance, during the Deir Yassin massacre) and used psychological warfare to frighten the Palestinians out of their homes. (This should not be so hard to believe since the state of Israel continues routinely to confiscate land, raze homes and even villages in the name of the security of the state of Israel.) Meron Benvenisti, the author of *Sacred Landscape: The Buried History of the Holy Land Since 1948*, explains how an Arab landscape, both physical and human, was transformed into an Israeli Jewish state. As a young man he accompanied his father, a distinguished geographer, who traveled through the Holy Land charting a Hebrew map that would replace the Arabic names of more than nine thousand natural features, villages, and ruins in what he now optimistically refers to as Eretz Israel/Palestine because of his belief that Israel/Palestine has enough historical and physical space to be shared by both people as a homeland.

Historically, although Palestine's boundaries were never constant, they always included the land between the Mediterranean Sea and the Jordan River. The earliest known inhabitants of Palestine were the same group as the Neanderthal inhabitants of Europe. By the third millennium B.C. most of the towns known in historical times had come into existence and most of Palestine was inhabited by herders and farmers. These inhabitants lived a rich, diverse history from one millennium to the other, even though they were conquered time and again, making Palestine a melting pot for diverse ethnic, cultural, and religious civilizations.

At the end of the second millennium B.C., when Moses led the Hebrew people out of Egypt, they lived as the subjects of a powerful kingdom established by the Philistines (Sea People) until 1000 B.C. when an independent Hebrew kingdom was established. In 950 B.C. this kingdom was broken up into two Hebrew states, which were eventually conquered in 720 B.C. by the Assyrians and the Babylonians. In 593 B.C. the Persians seized it, then Alexander the Great did the same in 333 B.C. In 142 B.C., after a Jewish revolt against Hellenism, a new Jewish state was set up, which lasted until 63 B.C., when Pompey conquered Palestine for Rome. It remained under Roman rule for almost 350 years, until Emperor Constantine converted to Christianity in A.D. 312, and Palestine became a center of Christian pilgrimage. In 640 it was conquered by Muslim Arabs. In 1516 it fell to Ottoman Muslim rule, under which it remained until the end of World War I.

During World War I a series of contradictory agreements and promises were made by the British to different parties regarding the status of Palestine, which set the seeds for future conflict. In 1915, the Arabs were promised independence in return for their revolt against the Ottoman sultan and for fighting alongside British Allied forces. Then the British entered an Anglo-French Agreement in 1916 that accepted the idea of Arab independence but divided the area into zones of permanent influence—with Iraq and Palestine going to the British and Syria and Lebanon to the French. In 1917, Lord Balfour made a promise to Chaim Weizmann, an astute Zionist statesman and greatly respected British scientist, which became known as the Balfour Declaration and promised to favor the establishment of a Jewish national home in Palestine, provided that it did not prejudice the civil and religious rights of the other inhabitants of the country.

The Balfour Declaration was threatening to Muslim and Christian Palestinians, who made up 88 percent of the population at the time yet were referred to as "other inhabitants." In 1920 at the San Remo conference of the League of Nations, Palestine became officially a British Mandate, or territory for the U.K. to administer. The mandate's terms incorporated the Balfour Declaration's promise of establishing a Jewish national home in Palestine. Initially, the mandate included both sides of the Jordan River, but in 1921 the emirate of Transjordan, east of the Jordan River in what is now Jordan, was officially separated from the mandate.

Palestinian leadership in 1948 was inexperienced, naive, and fractured. It did not understand that the final status of Palestine was not going to be determined by local realities and demographics but externally by the world's global powers. It underestimated the West's determination to support a Jewish homeland. Under the articles of the mandate, the British had supported waves of Jewish immigration from Europe. Between 1926 and 1932, the number of Jewish immigrants to Palestine averaged about 7,000 per year. This number reached 66,000 by 1935 as a result of Nazi persecution. By 1936, the Jewish population of Palestine had exploded to 28 percent of its total. In 1937, local riots and strikes broke out among the Palestinians, who felt threatened by the increased waves of Jewish immigration and settlements. The 1937 Peel Commission found that promises to Zionists and Arabs (Palestinians) were irreconcilable. It declared the mandate unworkable and recommended partition. In 1947 the British decided to wash their hands of the Palestine Problem and threw it in the lap of the UN, which eventually recommended Palestine's partition into two states. Although in retrospect it seems foolish for the Palestinians to have rejected partition, most viewed the newly immigrant European Jews as foreign implants allied with their colonial masters. Empowered by the reality that they still represented a clear Palestinian majority, they rejected the plan, which guaranteed the rights of one group of victims, the Jews, by creating another group of victims, the non-Jewish Palestinians.

One of the early slogans championed by the Zionist Israel Zangwill described historical Palestine as a "Land Without People for a People Without Land." According to Israeli author Tom Segev, at the time of the 1948 war, 750,000 Palestinian refugees were denied the right to return to their homes so that Israel could begin building a Jewish majority in its new state. Golda Meir, an Israeli folk hero, infamously said, "There is no such thing as the Palestinian people." Ben-Gurion said, "We cannot let them return. The old will die, and the young will forget."

Israel has continued to facilitate waves of Jewish immigration from around the world into the country so that now the state is 80 percent Jewish. These new residents immediately gain citizenship under Israel's so-called right of return. The policy seeks to bring the descendants of the twelve tribes of Judaism back to Israel. These immigrants immediately become Israeli citizens and enjoy more freedom and privileges than both the Israeli Arabs and the Palestinians living in the occupied territories. An Israeli state inquiry called the Orr Commission, investigating the reasons behind the October 2000 Arab-Israeli protests in which thirteen Arab Israelis died, concluded that the government treatment of the Arab sector was characterized by "discrimination, underfunding, prejudice, and neglect."

My family's dispossession leaves me with a heartache about a life that I never had, one that would have birthed me and buried me in our ancestral home around Lake Tiberias. If I am asked to recognize and accept Israel, then the very least my family deserves is a redemption of dignity. Palestinians like us need an awareness and affirmation of our loss to replace the blame, denial, and dehumanization of our experience. I need to feel that I can tell my story and get recognition for what was taken away from me, for what I have had to pay as retribution for the sins of others.

RANYA: *I will tell you a joke, Priscilla. Do you know that when things don't go well for a Palestinian, we often shrug and say, "If only we were one of the chosen people . . ."*

PRISCILLA: *You use those words so much. My husband and I never use them. I don't even know where "the chosen people" comes from.*

SUZANNE: *It's from the Old Testament. Moses led the "chosen people" out of Egypt and to the "promised land."*

PRISCILLA: *It is interesting how Jews did make the desert bloom. I remember going to a kibbutz forty years ago and being shown the technology coming in.*

RANYA: *That's part of the Zionist mythology once again. It's the view that it took the superior Jewish race to bring civilization to a land that was left dying in the hands of barbaric Muslims.*

PRISCILLA: *So the Israelis did not make the desert bloom? It was blooming just fine before they came along?*

RANYA: *I don't know if it was blooming. Certainly under British control it was the backwater of the world.*

PRISCILLA: *On the kibbutz I visited we watched people harvesting trout in a man-made pond.*

RANYA: *I think if the Jews did make the desert bloom, it's because they were bringing know-how and money. I don't think the British were spending much on irrigation and infrastructure. They had other priorities at the time.*

Priscilla:

Had Ranya gone radical on me? Or was she just comfortable enough in our friendship now to be honest with me? Was I being supersensitive? Or did she talk about Israel this passionately with everyone?

I left our last meeting confused, upset, and a bit intimidated by the "new, radical Ranya" I'd encountered.

Whenever the subject of Israel comes up between the two of us these days, I get tense. And in between our conversations, it gnaws at me. I feel torn between my "tribe" and its history, its tragic heritage of the Holocaust, its repeated suffering in the face of anti-Semitism and the suffering of millions of Palestinians.

But Ranya has asked me to consider the situation in Israel as a human tragedy of enormous proportions on all sides. My rabbi has taught me that it's my obligation as a Jew to rise to that challenge.

I love Ranya, but it's difficult to separate myself from the suffering of my "tribe." I don't want to be pried away from what is part of my heritage, the recognition of the tragedies other Jews suffered. Just as Ranya lives as a proud Palestinian, I want to live as a proud Jew.

Hmmm.

Am I proud to be Jewish today?

Yes.

Am I proud of every single one of the actions the Israeli government has ever taken?

No.

Do I feel there has been far too much suffering on both sides of this never-ending conflict? Yes.

I have to place the suffering of the Jews in a universal context. I have to acknowledge the Holocaust and deaths of so many Jews in our history and separate that from what is going on in Israel today.

This issue comes up again and again between me and Ranya. It doesn't threaten our friendship, but it does put pressure on me. I've looked for support within my own religious community, and it's hard to find. I've thought of going to my rabbi, but I'm hesitant to do that, concerned that he and I might disagree. And if I disagree with my rabbi, what does that mean? Will I still be a good Jew?

Alone at home, after our latest Faith Club meeting, I agonized over this. What should I do?

"Examine your text," Ranya had told me months ago.

I have a prayer book called *Gates of Repentance,* which our congregation uses for High Holiday services. I thought there might be something in there that could shed some light.

Some light? How about a lightning bolt?

The first page I turned to contained this passage, which our rabbi and congregation read responsively. I don't remember ever seeing it before:

> When will redemption come?
> When we master the violence that fills our world.
> When we look upon others as we would have them look upon us.
> When we grant to every person the rights we claim for ourselves.

I shared this passage with Ranya at our very next Faith Club meeting. I thanked her for urging me to examine my text. And Israel, for the time being, was talked about less. There was pain all around; Ranya and I never ignored horrible headlines, but we turned inward. We began talking, with Suzanne, about that which united us: love, faith, hope, and charity.

CHAPTER TEN
Prayer

PRISCILLA: *The good fortune I've experienced in my life has always haunted me. I was grateful for it, but I felt guilty about it.*
RANYA: *But you weren't living in a bubble. Things went wrong for you. You've had pain.*
PRISCILLA: *Yes, but compared to 9/11? That threw me completely. My son's basketball coach vanished from the planet that day. Poof! There was no order to things. I took 9/11 very person-*

ally. I thought "This could happen to me! Where the hell is God?"

RANYA: *So your belief in God is tied to how good things are for you?*

PRISCILLA: *Yes, to my well-being. It is very selfish.*

Priscilla:

We'd decided that prayer would be the subject of our next meeting. Immediately, I thought back to my first memories of praying on my own, privately, and I described to Suzanne and Ranya the prayers I frantically said to myself when I was a teenager. Back then, when I was experiencing daily panic attacks, no one knew how much I suffered. Except maybe God. I turned to prayer in desperation and fear. I'd lie in bed at night and recite the Shema, the prayer I'd learned at the Hebrew day school. "*Hear O Israel the Lord is our God, the Lord is One! And you shall love the Lord your God with all your heart, with all your soul and with all your might.*" Then I'd say my own ad hoc prayer to God, directly to him (I never could think of God as a woman; I suppose I wanted an omnipotent father). I'd ask God to protect me and keep me and my family safe. To keep me alive.

I was praying to a God someone had put there for me, the teachers at the Hebrew day school perhaps. I knew my body wasn't strong enough to survive on its own, and I needed to believe that someone had control over the universe. So I prayed to that someone I thought might be of help.

I kept a mental tally of the difficulties I'd faced (few) and the advantages and blessings I'd received (many). I figured that keeping this kind of tally would bring me good luck, or ingratiate me with God. If I appreciated the life I had, the way my blessings outweighed my difficulties, then life and the people I loved could not be cruelly snatched away from me—by anybody, including God. If I were constantly vigilant, aware of how high the stakes were, how much I would miss the blessings I'd been given, then maybe I could hold onto them.

So I said prayers of gratitude all my life. There wasn't much to complain about, much to ask of God, other than the most important thing of all: the health, safety, and well-being of those I loved. My praying was an insurance policy. And I supplemented it, in the finest tradition of Jewish mothers everywhere, with worrying. Was worrying a form of gratefulness? Or was it simply self-centered and neurotic?

Whatever the answer, I still hedged my bets.

I prayed, and I worried, for good luck and health. I prayed before airplane flights (and popped half a Klonopin). I prayed when I was happy and grateful. The fact that I'd managed to meet the right person, marry him, and have children was a miracle, after all my years of panic, I told people. Maybe all the prayer had paid off. Although my beloved father had died too young, at age sixty, of cancer, I'd been blessed. Maybe God had come through for me. My house was finally in order. And then two jets hit the World Trade Center on a spectacular fall day, and suddenly, terrifyingly, all bets were off.

PRISCILLA: *Who did believe in God after 9/11?*

SUZANNE: *I did.*

PRISCILLA: *You did?*

SUZANNE: *Sure. I saw God in all those people rushing down to help at the scene. People from all over the country wrote letters, gave money to relief funds and sent emergency supplies. Our family donated water and energy bars to the rescue workers, and my kids and I brought food to the neighborhood fire department, which lost eight firemen.*

PRISCILLA: *I heard about all those things at the time. And we gave money and supplies, too. But as time passed, and the enormity of the tragedy took over my thoughts, I was too terrified to see that goodness anymore. Or remember it. All I could see was a big, dark, evil hole of death. I thought God had vanished.*

Suzanne:

At last I had the courage to ask Priscilla to explain her faith to me. For Priscilla that meant talking about September 11, 2001 because her God, the God to whom she prayed for protection, had vanished that day. What kind of God had she prayed to? A God who was "in charge," she said. I didn't think of God that way. To me God was very clearly not in charge of day-to-day life on this planet except to the extent that we chose to act according to His will.

"Weren't you terrified there would be another strike on Manhattan?" Priscilla asked Ranya and me.

"I was nervous about another attack," I replied. "But it did not make me question my belief in God. I tied the disaster to human decisions and actions, not God's."

"But didn't you think the world was a bad place?" Priscilla persisted.

"No," I said. "It wasn't any different. The evil was just closer to home. All you have to do is read the international section of the paper. You can find worse horrors in Africa—civil wars, AIDS, genocide, poverty. And they happen every day."

Ranya spoke up. "I remember being in Europe when the earthquake hit Iran," she said. "All these relief workers flew in from all over the world to help. At the airport I saw lines of Chinese aid workers in their bright orange suits. They stood out to me at the time as a symbol of the good in the world."

Priscilla sighed. "I wish I'd known you two right after 9/11," she said. You might have helped me put that tragedy in a broader context of world suffering."

Ranya was sympathetic. "Its vastness was hard to process for a lot of people. The attack was so evil in its dimensions."

PRISCILLA: *I cannot believe that you two walk around Manhattan and never think . . .*

SUZANNE: *That we're going to get blown away?*
PRISCILLA: *I want some of what you guys are drinking!*

Suzanne:

I returned home from our meeting and wondered what Ranya and I were in fact drinking. Was it faith in God? Careless denial of danger? Or recognition of our own helplessness? I thought about Priscilla's God, a God who had vanished on 9/11 or at least been obscured by its smoke. Why had her faith disappeared during tragedy, while mine had been strengthened by the tragedy of my own sister's death?

Our different ideas of the nature of God were on my mind that night as I knelt by my daughter's bed for some quick nighttime prayers. But as soon as I began, Anne interrupted. She needed to talk about God that day, too.

"Mom, who made God?" she asked me.

"No one, Anne. God has always existed," I answered reflexively.

"But how can that be? Everything has a beginning."

"God was the power that made all those beginnings. He was there first," I said.

"Where is God?" she asked.

"I don't know exactly. He is here with us and everywhere outside of us. Sometimes I picture our whole universe resting in the palm of his hand."

"I don't get it."

"Unfortunately, it's not something that I can explain much better," I said, feeling her disappointment and remembering my own as a child when I challenged my father with the same questions. I can show Anne Jerusalem on a globe, but I can't point to a place other than my heart and hers and tell her, "God is here."

"It's so frustrating," she said, smiling through clenched teeth and bouncing on her bed in wiggly frustration. "I hate things that I can't understand. How do you know it's true?"

"If there were no God, I don't think we would be here."

At last I turned off the light, and as I left the room I imagined Anne chewing over my words as she fell asleep. Did they satisfy her any more than my own father's had satisfied me? I thought back to my childhood and wondered how my own faith had developed. Its seed, I realized, was planted by God and then nurtured by my parents. I grew up in a home where there was no doubt that all humans are loved by God and that Jesus is the savior whose death made it possible for us to be with God forever. As a child, I accepted that belief though concrete evidence was often hard to find. I was on the lookout for a burning bush, a vision or a voice in my head. But it never came. My classmates and I were told to pray and listen for a calling about whether God wanted us to be priests or, in my case, a nun. I prayed, but nobody called. On my First Communion and Confirmation I was prepared to feel a new, glowing faith inside me. I loved the new clothes and the attention. But I didn't feel anything else change.

There were certainly moments, however, when I was convinced that I felt the spirit of the divine. There was the time Jan Wilson's brother hit her in the eye with a rock-centered mud ball. She was in the hospital, and our priest told us that she had been blinded. We were urged to pray so that the doctors could help her regain her sight. We prayed. And a week or so later we heard in church that Jan Wilson could see again. The priests told us that our prayers had influenced a true miracle. Inspired by the power of prayer, I fingered the beads of the glass rosary my grandmother had bought me in Mexico as I recited the Lord's Prayer and dozens of Hail Marys. (My grandmother had told me that Mary had appeared to children in Mexico and promised world peace if enough people prayed the rosary.)

At home I imitated the rituals of the church. One Good Friday (the day Christians remember Jesus' crucifixion) I made a shrine in my bedroom with a sheet, a Bible, and a statue of Jesus. I invited my brothers and sister to a prayer service, but they didn't come. Then, I tried to be silent from noon to three in the afternoon in memory of the three hours Jesus was said to have hung on the cross. I failed. The temptation to talk was too great.

In fact, the temptations of life always seemed too great. I was never able to achieve the spiritual tasks I set for myself. I often pledged to give up sweets for Lent, but I wasn't usually successful. I would make deals with God, then neglect to hold up my end of the one-sided bargain. After one late night high school dance, I misplaced my grandmother's pearl necklace that I had been wearing. As I desperately searched our house for it, I promised God I would never drink a beer again if I found it. I found the necklace, but didn't fulfill the pledge.

By the time I was a freshman in college I had outgrown my attraction to the rituals of church. God hadn't appeared to me in a profound way, and I had learned I could break a promise to God without repercussion. If God was around, he wasn't all that active in my life. I stopped going to church except when I was at home with my parents.

A few years later, the music of Bach and my visit to the Vatican connected me with the church again. I was living in Vienna, Austria. My grandfather had just died, and I was looking for a place to pray when I found the spectacular gothic Maria am Gestade church in my neighborhood. Its services were concerts in disguise—the masses of Bach, Haydn, and Beethoven. To be surrounded by such beauty—aural and visual—all created in praise of God tuned me to a more subtle God, a God that could be found in beauty and art, not necessarily in a child's innocent search for a booming voice or ghostly vision but a God that was evident in the goodness and generous actions of humans, in works of charity and service, and in the courage of rescue workers.

Ranya:

Although I did not share Priscilla's specific anxieties about being an imminent target of terrorism in New York or her loss of God on 9/11, I could relate to her sense of the fragility of life and anxiety about death. I had thought about these issues for years.

When I was a child, my weighty questions about life and death were generally answered by my mother, who tried to use Islam to affirm my moral upbringing and equip me with the tools needed to live a meaningful and just life. I was told that all I had to do to be Muslim was recite the Shahada, the proclamation of faith, which is traditionally whispered into every newborn Muslim's ear. After meals we said, "Al Hamdu lil lah," a prayer of thanks to God. And, as a reminder that ultimate power rests in the hands of God, I was taught to end many determined statements with the phrase, "In Sha'a Allah," which means God willing. This does not mean that all is predetermined; rather that people should live life to the best of their ability while realizing that some things are beyond their control. Finally, before embarking on any important project, I prefixed my work with "Bis millah," or "In the name of God," a phrase I often scribbled on examination papers for good luck.

By the age of ten, I had decided that although I did not have the answers to all my "life" questions, at least I knew life. I was a full-fledged member, aware of my experiences, enjoying most of them, and waiting with anticipation for those I still had not tried—my first kiss, my first job, my first apartment. I was in love with life. I remember reading *Charlie and the Chocolate Factory* and rereading those passages describing the texture, taste, and delight of chocolate. I tried to re-create that pleasure by savoring my very own piece of chocolate, placing it in the back of my mouth, then feeling it melt ever so slowly.

Life was sweet. What choked me with fear was death. That vast unknown. That fear made me, as a preteen, worry about falling asleep and not waking up. Prayer helped allay my fears somewhat. I knew prayer did not provide a guarantee, but it allowed me to relinquish control, or, as Muslims say, "submit."

As I grew older, I carried a Quran in my purse as a sign of my submission and reminder of a more powerful, transcendent force. In the Islamic tradition God is believed to be the bearer of ninety-nine qualities, which we enumerate regularly as we pray (the compassionate, the knowledgeable, the wise, the merciful . . .). Knowing that God possesses these qualities makes it easier for me to become a better Muslim, to take that leap of faith and feel God's rich spiritual presence in all aspects of my life. In that spirit, a trip to the Museum of Natural History in New York and a stop at its magnificent planetarium, for example, places my egocentric, earthly life in its correct perspective next to the amazing things God has revealed to us all. This ability to peacefully surrender (Istaslim) to a spiritual realm vaster and not physically defined in an image, body, or form, makes the leap of faith easier for me to make. The surrender to God, the creator, the compassionate, the merciful, the wise . . . can enrich our human experience as we start seeing God in the beauty of a flower, or in the courage of a brave, heroic act.

Suzanne:

As I had listened to Ranya and Priscilla talk about their fears—Ranya's fear of death and Priscilla's fear that her good luck would change—I longed to give them some comfort. I wanted to share the joy I felt from Christianity, but I wasn't sure how. What was it that resonated within me that gave me that joy? I felt it afresh each Sunday at church, but what was going on there that lifted me up? And how could I share it without sounding pious?

The next day I sat down at my computer and wrote my own profession of faith, which I brought to our next meeting. It was for Priscilla, Ranya, Anne, and me. As I read it aloud to Ranya and Priscilla, though, I worried that I sounded Pollyannaish.

I believe in a benevolent creator who willed space into being and controlled the process by which humankind evolved. I think God created us out of his love and desire to have the company of thinking creatures like himself. I imagine us somehow bursting from his imagination, our universe resting in the palm of his hand. I believe that God loves every human on earth and that we all are capable of living on with God forever, though I don't know how. I'd love to think that I will be reunited with those I love who have died. Resting in the heavens with my sister, my husband, my children, and the rest of my family basking in the glow of God's love forever sounds pretty wonderful. But I think it is probably not as simple as that. Will I have my current identity? I don't know. Perhaps I will be part of a joyful cosmic consciousness. If God was able to imagine our world, he is surely able to imagine something glorious for the hereafter.

"That's beautifully expressed, Suzanne," Priscilla reassured me as I finished reading. "But I have to tell you that I was also really moved by what you said about 9/11 last week, about all the goodness that flowed to the site of the Towers. Obviously I'd known about the policemen and firemen, the heroes who gave their lives. But only now, inspired by your strong, steadfast faith, can I see that enormous goodness existed that day, and that goodness can coexist with evil.

"I've been thinking about our conversations all week," she continued. "And trying to find proof of the coexistence of good and evil in my everyday life. I've thought about suffering and pain. And joy. And I know that people who suffer can love and be loved and live full, meaningful lives. My sister is one of those people. Her health is so compromised, but she looks forward to every day. She loves her husband. She loves life. She loves finding a good, ripe peach at the market. My friend Richard, who's struggled with MS and cancer, is another example of strength for me. His attitude is amazing, his humor intact. My friend Margaret lost two children and then started an organization to help other parents with gravely ill children. She still knows true joy.

"The common denominator with all of these people is that they are loved," Priscilla concluded. "And I think that if you are lucky enough to give and receive love, then you can be happy in the face of suffering. I was talking to a friend about this and we decided that maybe heaven is just that . . . love. And that heaven exists on a day-to-day basis within people. When they give and receive love, that's a little slice of heaven."

As Priscilla said this, I understood that my faith really was rubbing off on her. Somehow, my outlook on life, which was inspired by my faith, had broken through even though I felt my own words had been inadequate. Yet, the faith she described was different from my own. And I wanted to explore the differences.

I was eager to press Priscilla on her continually evolving definition of God. When beset with her mother's and sister's health crises, Priscilla had often told me and Ranya that in order to cope she had decided "to surrender to a higher power." I wondered what she meant by that. "To what power are you surrendering?" I asked her at our next meeting.

"To God," Priscilla replied. She had been struggling for control over her life, and now she was resigning herself to the idea that she had little control. She called that resignation, or surrender, faith. But that did not sound like faith to me. So I decided to press her on that.

SUZANNE: *Priscilla, what exactly happened to you when you were flying over the Great Lakes?*

PRISCILLA: *We were flying into a purple, orange, and pink sunset—and the Great Lakes appeared, flat and shimmering, reflecting the sunset. The ride was smooth and my children were next to me and I felt this incredible moment of gratefulness. I thought that with all this beauty below me, there must be more good than there is evil in the world. And there is something that is bigger than I am. I had a conversion; it wasn't instant. It was the beginning of accepting that there was a higher order to things.*

SUZANNE: *Is there order?*

PRISCILLA: *Sometimes. But I'm not the one creating it. I don't have that power. My panic, my scurrying around like a gerbil in one of those plastic wheels, is silly in light of the astonishing beauty I saw beneath me that day. It is futile. It is a waste of energy that could be channeled into appreciating all the beauty in life.*

SUZANNE: *So, in a way, you were humbled.*

PRISCILLA: *Exactly. I was humbled.*

SUZANNE: *And how did that make you feel?*

PRISCILLA: *Relieved. I left my ego behind. I said, "I am not in control of the universe. Some other force is." The universe does carry on in its messy, gorgeous way. It's held together by something and whatever that force is, I choose to believe that it is goodness and love. And something as wonderful as goodness, love, and beauty must come from some incredible supernatural force. And that must be God.*

SUZANNE: *I think it is. And that love of God is greater than any suffering that gets dished out on earth. We may feel that love through other people, meditation, prayer or holy books, but ultimately it is God's love that enables us to transcend suffering.*

Priscilla:

Suzanne Oliver, I tell people, was the midwife to my faith.

From the day I first met Suzanne, her calm, steadfast religious faith (which I once called "rigidity!") made a strong impression on me. I'd met people who attended church and temple. I'd met people who I knew believed strongly in God and practiced their religion, well, religiously. But I'd never had such intimate, sustained contact with a person of strong religious conviction, and I'd certainly never talked about faith for so many long, engaging hours with either a Christian or a Muslim woman before I met Ranya and Suzanne.

Ranya's spirituality impressed me the moment I met her. She radiates kindness and goodness. I've found enormous support in her presence and comfort in her gentle, strong essence. While Suzanne was the person who committed herself to asking the probing questions and ultimately pulled my faith right out of me, Ranya was there to confirm that what I had experienced was universal, that my submission to God, my acceptance of my humility, was a deeply held Islamic conviction.

Suzanne and Ranya were both in the delivery room with me. And it was, I believe, their own strong spiritual faith and generosity, combined with the trust and respect I had gained for them over the years, that allowed me to make my most important leap of faith, to understand my connection to God.

Whoever thought that I'd be using words like *delivery room* and *midwife* to describe my faith? Doesn't that come dangerously close to . . . oh, let's just get this over with . . . BORN AGAIN???

Could I possibly have something in common with Pat Robertson and all those other evangelical people I channel surf through on Sunday mornings?

All these thoughts gave me great pause.

But the peacefulness I felt after talking to Suzanne and Ranya was remarkable. And complete. People noticed it. My friends commented on my serenity (although it didn't last forever, it still comes more often than it goes).

When I pray now, I thank God for the good times, the bad times, the boring times, the terrifying times, the easy times, the hard times, the pain and the joy . . .

"Wait a minute," I realized one day. "This all sounds very familiar."

I've known this all along, it turns out. I selected the following Thomas Wolfe quotation to appear under my photo in my high school yearbook:

"Knowledge is finding out something for oneself with pain, with joy, with exultancy, with labor, and with all the little ticking, breathing moments of our lives."

The ticking, breathing moments of my life have all come together for me now.

I wouldn't have been able to appreciate the way my son Max ferociously fights for rebounds on the basketball court if I hadn't sat in the stands above him for an entire season clutching two different asthma inhalers he might need as he struggled with a three-month illness that turned out to be mono.

I wouldn't appreciate the intense bear hugs my first baseman, Jack, gives me if I hadn't sat by helplessly while he hemorrhaged, vomiting up bowls full of blood in an emergency room after a "routine" tonsillectomy.

I wouldn't appreciate the powerful, enduring connection I have with my husband if he hadn't helped me nurse my beloved father through the last agonizing stages of the cancer that ravaged his body.

And I wouldn't have the faith I now have if I hadn't sat through the most difficult, intimate, challenging conversations of my life with Ranya and Suzanne.

CHAPTER ELEVEN

Rituals

RANYA: *The issue is how much control you believe you have over your life, Priscilla. Although life may cooperate sometimes, our control is only an illusion. I have a harder time accepting negative outcomes on everyday decisions—like the choice of fabric for a couch—because I can control that. But when the scale is so overwhelming I submit.*

PRISCILLA: *To what?*

RANYA: *To fate. Or is it God's will? It is just submission. That is what Islam means.*

PRISCILLA: *Is submission a form of humility?*

RANYA: *You have free choice . . . but you are small, you are humble, you've submitted. In the plane, over the Great Lakes, at that moment, your submitting is exactly what Islam is about.*

PRISCILLA: *Have you submitted?*

RANYA: *Well, yes. I've struggled with my submission. But this journey is leading me to reconsider my idea of God.*

Ranya:

Lately, I told Priscilla and Suzanne, I have found myself reluctant or unable to call the force I believe in God. To me, the concept of God has been co-opted by the outspoken Muslims who speak of a conditional God who approves of me only if I pray, wash, dress, and eat a certain way.

This is not the Islam my parents practice. Their Islam is nonjudgmental. It is a religion of equality, morality, and charity. But that other, small-minded interpretation of Islam is difficult to avoid. My mother told me recently of her experience at a charity she was involved in. As the women gathered for prayer, one of them told my mother that her prayers could not be accepted because she wore nail polish. Dumbfounded, my mother explained that nail polish could not have been regulated by the Prophet since nail polish did not exist in his time. This kind of thinking is part of what contributes to my difficulty in finding a mosque today.

SUZANNE: *If you're longing for a communal religious experience, Ranya, why not just put on a scarf and go to a mosque? Isn't prayer about you and God, not you and the person beside you? Or are you prejudiced against the people there?*

RANYA: *I don't like their idea that I am only a Muslim if I cover my head and act a certain way. I can accept a head covering as a sign of respect in the house of God. But I don't want it to be the thing that qualifies a woman for membership in Islam. I don't believe in a religion that says you have to wash a certain way, pray a certain way, receive a particular sacrament a certain way, or be baptized a certain way in order to get to heaven. I feel I can pray to God at home or anywhere, for that matter. What I am lacking is a community of like-minded Muslims.*

SUZANNE: *I don't think that rigid adherence to rules is true of all religions.*

RANYA: *It's true of some readings of all religions.*

Suzanne:

Frankly, I was getting frustrated hearing Ranya lament week after week about how she had no imam, no mosque, and no community that would welcome her and her ideas. Was she out looking, I wondered? Had she opened the phone book and checked under "M" for mosque? Certainly she wasn't the only educated American Muslim looking for a place to worship in New York City. I wondered if her inability to find a welcoming mosque stemmed from a prejudice that religious communities were inherently close-minded. Did she think mine was?

Her comments evoked a self-consciousness I sometimes feel as a person who "practices" my religion. When I hear people disparage Sunday churchgoers, I often feel uncomfortable. Did they think I was unquestioning because I was a churchgoer?

"You're lucky," Ranya said to me. "I don't have a neighborhood mosque like you have your church where I can worship with friends I know from work or school." Although Ranya may have been earnest in her need, I could not help but be reminded of past conversations in which friends had dismissed churchgoing as a big coffee hour. At those times, I hadn't come to the church's defense. I didn't have the language or the confidence to express why I found church attendance important. But now that I was exploring my faith and religious practice with Priscilla and Ranya, I was gaining the voice to express why I do what I do.

Why did my husband and I muster our kids on Sunday morning, scrub them, dress them, and hurry our family to church by nine-fifteen? It wasn't just for a cup of tepid coffee and gossip, or a chance to check out everybody's wardrobe. Why did I teach Sunday school? Why have we served on committees devoted to the spiritual, financial, charitable and, yes, social aspects of our church community? Perhaps Jesus put it best: *"For where two or three are gathered in my name, there am I in the midst of them."* (Matthew 18:20).

My husband and I find that our church community helps us provide our children a moral compass for life. It helps us renew and enhance our own faith through communal prayer and study. And it provides the opportunity to experience God's goodness through communal acts of charity and service. It keeps me grounded at the same time that it lifts me up.

But just because I go to church doesn't mean that religious ritual is the only way I gain access to God. I appeal to Him in prayer throughout each day. When I was young, prayer was recitation. It was apology for sins committed, gratitude for what I had received, and praise to a powerful God. As I have grown older, my prayer has become more contemplative. I reflect.

A speaker I heard at church recently said, "Every human sigh is a prayer." My prayers are often like that these days—a sigh and a wish—a wish for patience for myself, health for my family and friends, wisdom for our leaders, food, medicine, and peace for the world. The same speaker said that every prayer is a call to action. So, as I pray, I contemplate what I can do to help bring about whatever I am praying for. In that way, I believe, I am guided to do God's will. I ask God for something, and he asks me what I can do to make that happen.

Recently I was given a copy of a prayer that Mother Teresa reportedly distributed on her "business card."

The fruit of silence is prayer.
The fruit of prayer is faith.
The fruit of faith is love.
The fruit of love is service.
The fruit of service is peace.

I long to follow Mother Teresa's example and perform some transcendent, life-changing act of service. I mean real, selfless service when there is nothing in it for me but the act itself. But what action can I really take now? I have three young children at home demanding every minute of my attention. I can't jet off to India to work with lepers or spend a month in an AIDs clinic in Africa. At the moment, my calling is motherhood, and motherhood is my prayer. It's difficult to think of it that way all the time, given the quotidian life of a mother—the carpools, the cooking, the laundry, the shopping, the homework. But I have to remind myself that all of those labors are service to others and therefore service to God. Meanwhile, it is the most rewarding job I can imagine. What better way to end the day than lying next to a three-year-old saying bedtime prayers and hearing him say, "Thank you, God, for my mommy."

> SUZANNE: *There are churches you can go into and believe what you want to believe, temples you can go into and do what you want to do. And there are people getting spiritual energy out of the rituals they participate in.*
> RANYA: *I agree. I just think some people get caught up in the rituals.*
> SUZANNE: *But the fact that some people are like that shouldn't affect your own relationship with God.*
> RANYA: *I'm glad to see that you go to church and recognize that the rituals help to create a community, not that, for instance, one specific piece of bread and sip of wine will guarantee you a place in heaven. But I wonder how many Christians, Jews, and Muslims practice their faith in the same open-minded way?*

Ranya:

As Suzanne and I continued debating the merits of religious rituals, Priscilla finally spoke up. "Let it go, Ranya," she told me. "Don't worry about other people and how they practice their religions. Don't think about anything but your own personal beliefs."

But I couldn't. "I am suspicious of the moment that man takes hold of religion."

"It's okay to be suspicious of that," Suzanne said. "But I think, right now, that suspicion is blocking your own spiritual development because you fear you might become one of those people immersed in ritual and dogma. I found a good quote on ritual in one of Elaine Pagels's books. 'Ritual is not an empty form but a way to enjoin people of diverse backgrounds in a spiritual community that can generate power and renew spiritual energy.' "

"You need to tune out everything around you, Ranya," Priscilla suggested. "Put in some earplugs and sit in your room and decide what your religion is. Don't worry about what anybody else is saying or doing. People are screaming about religion at the top of their lungs. But the point of our discussions is for you to explore your own personal religion."

And so I went back to the computer. I didn't wear earplugs because I didn't want to tune out the rest of the world. I needed to find my place in it. I wrote down my thoughts and the following reflection:

I do not believe that God, who created us in so many different variations, can be of a limited, close-minded nature. How is that possible? If we as humans have the ability to broaden our reach, imagine how broad and embracing God's vision is. And if that is true, then why would He communicate with just one person? Or why should persons of a single religion get to heaven? I don't believe God discriminates in that way, and that has always been my difficulty with organized religion.

I am not denying that there are churches, temples, or mosques that have a liberal, questioning tradition and acceptance of other religions. But, let's face it, we don't have to look far to recognize that religion on the world stage is more of a divider than a unifier. If you doubt that, consider the Holy Land.

I am not opposed to religious rituals or the spiritual benefits of communal congregations. I am the one, after all, who had church and temple envy. I do feel, though, that rituals are often used to help set apart different religious communities. I do not believe that the majority of religious rituals, whether they are in temples, churches, or mosques, are practiced in a manner that promotes the equality, legitimacy, and validity of all religious traditions as paths to God. But God at the end of the day is One God equally accessible and available to all. I feel that a majority of those who adhere to formal religious practices have decided that their tradition holds the one true key to God. My faith is in an equal-opportunity God, and my religion derives from Muslim traditions that promote the worship of such a God.

Priscilla:

"Actually," I said to Ranya and Suzanne, "I feel that I've been able to practice important Jewish rituals in an open-minded way. After all, I did have a bar mitzvah for my son in my backyard! As a reform Jew, I had that choice."

My son Jack, I explained, had dropped out of Hebrew school when he was in third grade. A stern teacher's sharp voice and harsh demeanor "freaked him out." So I'd found a female cantor, a prayer leader rather than a rabbi, who could tutor him privately, teaching him how to read and study Torah.

We planned for Jack's bar mitzvah service to take place in a tent in our backyard. Some Jews would say that bar mitzvahs must be held in temples. But both Cantor Alcott and Rabbi Sirkman assured me and my husband that a reform bar mitzvah service can be conducted anywhere a Torah is present.

The ceremony was scheduled to take place during Succot, a harvest holiday when Jews build a succah, a simple wooden structure wrapped in branches, vines, and fruit, in their backyards. They dine and rest out there in order to remind themselves of the days when they wandered in the desert and God watched over them as they built their temporary huts under the stars.

Our tent for 150 people would be a giant succah, I decided. Two days before the big day, I took a walk with my dog and discovered that someone in my neighborhood had pruned beautiful grasses and pine trees. Returning with my car, I scooped up sharp-scented pine boughs and long, dried grasses. I dragged them into the tent and began transforming the space. After I added pots of chrysanthemums, and baskets of apples, oranges, and grapes, our succah was complete.

On the day of Jack's bar mitzvah the sun shone, and relatives arrived from as far away as California. I escorted my frail mother onto the bimah (the dais) to bless Jack with a prayer. Other relatives stood to recite blessings, and the congregation said a special prayer for healing in honor of my absent sister. Jack did a fantastic job reading from the Torah. I read a portion myself, in Hebrew, something I hadn't done in at least thirty years, and we all had a spectacular experience.

It was a momentous day for me, because I helped Jack and our family define Judaism for ourselves, on our own terms. And for the very first time, I spoke about God in public. God was present on the lawn of our home. Really present. Ranya and Suzanne were both out of town that weekend, so they couldn't attend. But thanks no doubt to my conversations with them about faith and my newfound desire to believe in God, I was able to believe these words that I spoke aloud, toasting my son:

> *Jack, I hope you will always remember that today we built not only a giant succah in our backyard, but a holy place as well, a temple, which proves that God, indeed, can always be found everywhere and anywhere you look throughout your life, right in your own backyard, wherever that may be.*
>
> *I love you, Jack. Mazel tov on your bar mitzvah!*

SUZANNE: *Ranya, I was trying to understand your prejudice against organized religion. And I thought I got some insight when I read the eulogy of a political figure assassinated in the Middle East.*

RANYA: *I didn't see the article.*

SUZANNE: *The person giving the eulogy was quoted as saying, "The hand which dared to shoot you will be cut off." I was taken aback. You would never hear anything like that at a Christian fu-*

*neral. To me, those kinds of statements make Islam sound vengeful
and authoritarian. So, I'm wondering, is your hesitancy to participate in religion a reaction to those elements of Islam?*

Suzanne:

It was bitter cold outside, fifteen degrees that winter day, and
Priscilla's gift to Ranya, rich hot cocoa we'd come to love, came in
handy. As I cradled a mug of it in my hands to warm them, I asked
Ranya about an article I had read recently. In it I saw the iron-fisted
side of Islam, which I believed did not appeal to Ranya. I suspected
that Ranya was distrustful of organized religion because the only organized Islam that had been available to her was judgmental and authoritarian.

"Muslims would say that your observations reveal an underlying
prejudice that Islam is violent," Ranya challenged.

"I absolutely disagree with you! I am just trying to understand you,
and I thought that this article might be a window into your own issues
with organized religion."

"That was politics speaking in that eulogy, not religion. As a Muslim, when I hear you extracting that eulogy as an example, I feel the
same thing that a lot of other Muslims feel, which is that in the Judeo-
Christian world there is a belief that Islam is at its heart a violent, uncivilized religion. The eulogist is threatening his political enemies in that
speech by saying, 'If you rebel against us we'll kill you.' That was not
about God. It was a political threat." Ranya was clearly upset. I felt my
cheeks flush.

"I'm not judging," I said, repeating my motive. "I am just trying to
understand the source of your position on religion."

"Ninety-nine percent of Muslims lead nonviolent lives. Yet the ones
who get the big hype are the violent, political Muslims!" Her voice rose
with emotion. "I think Muslims would tell you that they are held to a

different standard. People are quick to judge them as violent and close-minded."

"Unfortunately, that is the image portrayed in our media much of the time," I answered in my defense.

"And your interpretation of it is an example of how people use the most liberal of lenses to judge their own religions and a literal lens when they look at Islam!"

Priscilla came to my defense. "But the fact of the matter is that these words were spoken at a funeral service, Ranya. Isn't Suzanne allowed to say that she felt that that kind of rhetoric was inappropriate to use at a funeral?"

"Yes. I think it's inappropriate, too!" Ranya agreed. "Had Suzanne said, 'Wasn't it awful and un-Islamic for this political message to be delivered at a religious service?' then I'd understand because that's how I feel. These people used the forum of a burial for a political rally. But that's not what Suzanne said."

No, it is not what I said. And it is certainly not what Americans read in their newspapers either. Indeed, readers often have to take an extra step to put the news involving Islam into perspective. They have to read to the last paragraphs of many articles to find the view of mainstream Islam, if they can find it at all. And good luck finding an article about what's going right in Islam or finding an article about Islam in the 82 percent of the Muslim world that isn't Arab. With little experience or education in Islam and without any diversity in news reporting, most Americans don't recognize the diversity within Islam. We approach each eulogy, each threat, each attack as if it is typical of the more than 1 billion Muslims who populate our world. This error in interpretation is well explained in Carl Ernst's book *Following Muhammad: Rethinking Islam in the Contemporary World*, which I discovered when I went shopping in an online bookstore after this troubling conversation with Ranya.

Our discussion of rituals in Islam wasn't exhausted yet. At our next meeting, Priscilla pressed Ranya on the importance of performing daily prayer rituals.

> PRISCILLA: *I met a group of Muslim women in Westchester, Ranya, and I thought they might be your "posse." But when they told me that they pray five times a day I wasn't so sure they would appeal to you. But isn't daily prayer part of being Muslim?*
>
> RANYA: *I try to mention the name of God as much as I can, before any major endeavor, before a meal. Do I specifically take the time to do it five times a day with the prescribed prayers and the prescribed position? No, I haven't yet. But that doesn't mean that I am not Muslim.*
>
> PRISCILLA: *When this woman asked me whether you pray five times a day, I wondered why you don't?*

Ranya:

The question of whether one can be a Muslim without the performance of the required ritual of five daily prayers is a contentious issue. It is often perceived as too stringent a demand that speaks volumes about the "built-in" extremism of Islam. So it didn't surprise me when Priscilla raised the subject one afternoon as we three ate lunch. My first impulse was to ask her to consider that within Judaism and Christianity there are some who may fault other followers for not adhering to specific rituals and thereby question the authenticity of their faith.

"Do you do every Jewish ritual every day?" I asked her.

"No," she quickly admitted. "I don't do the mikvah, the ritual bath. I don't wear a wig or keep a kosher kitchen. Some people would insist that the Shema be said with a tallis on as soon as you wake up in the morning. But I say it when I feel like it, usually when I'm out walking my dog."

"So why should I have to follow every rule?" I asked.

"You have a point," Priscilla said. "Nobody, including my rabbi, questioned my faith when I held the bar mitzvah in my backyard. I was able to do that, outside of a synagogue, because I'm a reform Jew. I see what you mean now about an American journey for Islam. But I do wonder where daily prayer lies in the importance of being Muslim. That's something non-Muslims wonder about."

"That is only because people don't recognize that pluralistic possibilities and flexibility can exist within Islam as they do in Judaism and Christianity," I told her. "Muslims are denied this plurality both by those extreme, literal Muslims who claim exclusive rights and ownership of the religion and by those on the outside who validate such claims because they accept them as the authentic, true voice of Islam. No wonder then that I, as a Muslim, am called on to defend my religious qualifications by Muslims and non-Muslims alike."

"I've heard the call to prayer in Turkey and Morocco, and it can sound very beautiful and inspirational," Suzanne said.

"I really miss that," I answered, remembering how in most Muslim countries, the call to prayer is broadcast over loudspeakers from the minarets, five times a day. When done properly, it can be hauntingly beautiful. To visitors, though, it can be intimidating. An American mother once shared with me her memories of a trip to Dubai. When commenting on the call to prayer she said, "They are very religious over there, aren't they?" For Muslims, the call to prayer is not so much about degree of religiosity but rather a tradition that is likened to the ringing of church bells. The call in its contents is universal, for it is nothing more than the affirmation of God's greatness and a reminder for all to pray.

"You know, when I'm in a Muslim country and I hear that call to prayer, I always stop whatever I am doing and say a little prayer," I told Priscilla and Suzanne.

"But in America, you don't hear it. Maybe you should run a tape in your house, have a virtual mosque set up!" Priscilla encouraged, only partially joking.

"I have wanted to bring back tapes of Quranic recitations to play. Listen, life is busy and complicated in New York. I am making an effort," I explained.

"I didn't mean to push you on the subject. I just think that if you believe in God, you should thank God," Priscilla said.

"I try as much as I can to bring God into my life throughout the day. But, at the end of the day, I believe in a forgiving God, a benevolent God, not one who says 'Hey, you forgot that one prayer!'" I explained. "The other night I was lying in bed with my son and, as we do every night, we were saying a prayer of thanks. He said, 'Thank you God for the good food, nice house, lovely parents, and thank you God that I am not a nosepicker.' I believe that's prayer. I believe in a God with a sense of humor who doesn't mind if I incorporate him into my life naturally."

"So all along you were an Islamic believer? Why did we go on this journey?" Priscilla laughed.

"Because my religion is in a state of crisis. Because I don't have institutions to help me, and I've had to refine my religious views in order to speak with confidence. Now I know there is justification for my faith, and I can pass it on to my children. I knew there was more to say than, 'I am a Muslim because I was born that way.'"

"Congratulations, Ranya!" Priscilla smiled. "Mission accomplished!"

Am I disqualified from Islam because I do not pray five times a day, a prescribed ritual? I don't think so. One day I may choose to pray five times a day in a more orthodox way. Do I pray? Yes, I do. I held a Quran and prayed before I gave birth. I prayed when my daughter had eye surgery. I pray when I'm in bed, thanking God for one more blessed day with my family. I pray for the safe return of my husband when he is traveling. Every night before I go to bed, I go to Leia and Taymor's rooms and listen to their rhythmic breathing as they sleep, and I kiss them. I pray that I will be able to hold on to the memory of their beauty as children, to remember their smell and warmth, the squishiness and softness of their flesh. Then I thank God for giving me that memory. I pray that their personal journeys are blessed and fortunate, endowed with all the goodness and innocence that children believe must be their inalienable birthright.

I pray when my heart is overflowing with joy and pride. At the embrace of a child, or at their sincere, unconditional trust. I thank God for this gift, for moments of extreme happiness when my heart physically flutters as it soars, connected to a universal human memory of wellness and well-being. I pray that it all may endure. I pray that we should all be so lucky to experience it. For now and eternity. I pray when I realize the precariousness of such joy. I pray in fear, in panic, when I consider all that could go wrong. I pray as I submit. I recognize my humble role. My insignificance in the scheme of the universe. I pray for peace of mind, for strength and the spiritual courage that will enable me to remain dignified, no matter the challenge. I pray that my children are safe and well, that when I'm not hovering protectively over them, I have deferred to God's will. I pray that I am able to sustain the fortitude and faith that is required if and when God's will involves suffering.

I believe in one God, an all-embracing God, a God who is neither male nor female, nor human, a merciful and compassionate God. In submitting to God's will and living a Muslim life I am asked to apply the discipline and judgment that will allow me to make the correct choices. To serve God, I am asked to be fair and just, charitable, and humble. To protect the weak, the orphaned, and the disenfranchised. To live an accountable, responsible, and moral life. To live a kind, honorable, and peaceful life. I believe God does not distinguish between humans because of their race, color, or religious traditions. God sees beyond the different rituals and judges the valor of humans not on the merits of one tradition over the other but rather on our own actions and choices.

RANYA: *I think God's expectations of us are evident. I think all religions agree on that point, which is good. Good is good. It's not about being arrogant. It's not about saying, "I am closer to God than you are because of my rituals."*

Suzanne: *What about the value of using charity and good deeds*
to deepen one's relationship with God?
Ranya: *Sure, charity is good. There is a whole tradition of charity*
in Islam.

Suzanne:

I was beginning to see how Ranya lived a religious life inspired by the ideals of Islam without displaying any of its epaulets. She wore no headscarf, didn't go to mosque, didn't obey every rule. Yet she lived with humility and love, acted generously and prayed privately. This religious practice—so free of an institutional framework—was not only a new way for me to view Islam, but a new way for me to view religion as well.

It turned out Ranya wasn't the only religious iconoclast I admired. When I picked up the Bible and reread the book of Matthew, I was struck by how closely Ranya's cynicism about empty ritual, public prayer, and religious hypocrisy fit with Jesus' own.

> *Beware of practicing your piety before men in order to be seen by*
> *them; for then you will have no reward from your Father who is in*
> *heaven. Thus, when you give alms, sound no trumpet before you, as*
> *the hypocrites do in the synagogues and in the streets, that they may*
> *be praised by men. . . . And when you pray, you must not be like the*
> *hypocrites; for they love to stand and pray in the synagogues and at*
> *the street corners, that they may be seen by men. . . . But when you*
> *pray, go into your room and shut the door and pray to your Father*
> *who is in secret; and your Father who sees in secret will reward you.*
> *Matthew: 6:1–6*

As my understanding of prayer changed through our Faith Club conversations, the way I experienced prayer within my own tradition changed, too. At our tiny, rustic Episcopal church near our home in

New Hampshire, the antique Middle Eastern rug before the altar reminded me of Ranya. I loved visualizing it being constructed by Muslim hands, then taking a circuitous journey, eventually coming to rest in our church.

As our priest stood on the rug and raised the bread and wine I was reminded of the Muslim affirmation of Christians as "people of the book." And as we turned to wish our neighbors peace, I thought of Muslims and Jews doing the same thing as they prayed together.

We were all so connected, I was realizing. Our traditions built upon one another like bricks in a foundation, with each new brick being supported by the old. I used to teach a Bible lesson in Sunday school that was meant to differentiate the "new commandment" taught by Jesus from the Ten Commandments given to Moses. It was based upon a story in which the Pharisees tried to trap Jesus by asking him which of the Ten Commandments was the greatest. Jesus avoided the argument by answering, "The greatest of the commands is this: to love God with all your heart, soul, mind, and strength and to love your neighbor as yourself." I used to explain to the children that Jesus' commandment was a revolutionary departure from the "Thou Shalt Not"s of the Old Testament. Then Priscilla taught me the Jewish Shema, and I realized that Jesus was building upon that ancient Hebrew prayer.

So now when I remembered Jesus' command, I thought of Priscilla and other Jews reciting the Shema. And I remembered other ways Jesus' idea was expressed, as in the rule of the Jewish leader Hillel, "What is hateful to you, do not do to others," and I remembered Muhammad's declaration, "None of you is a believer until you love for your neighbor what you love for yourself."

We were all reciting the same truths. In Hebrew, in Arabic, in English, and in every language in the world.

PRISCILLA: *I used to tell my rabbi I didn't like mixing my spiritual life with my social life. I find it distracting to be in a place of worship with people I know from the supermarket or wherever. I*

*need privacy, particularly when I pray. But now I think that if
you're really worshiping, you can tune things out. You don't have
to be seen. You can sit in the back of the room.*

RANYA: *I think Islam would suit you, Priscilla, in the sense that
it's very much you and your God anywhere.*

Ranya:

I called my mother as I do every Sunday. I immediately heard the anxiety in her voice. My father had complained of a headache and since he is a heart patient, with diabetes and high blood pressure, my mother had insisted that they check it out. His medical exam had revealed that a percentage of the main artery in his neck was blocked. And now they were waiting for test results to ascertain the percentage.

That afternoon it was hard for me to think of anything else. Fear for my father's health consumed me. Not even my children could distract me and force me to move on. So I spent the rest of the day praying intermittently.

When I related this to Priscilla and Suzanne at our next meeting, Priscilla wanted to know how I prayed. Her question forced me to put into words something I have been doing ever since I can remember. It is very personal and difficult to share.

I often start by reciting a small verse from the Quran and an affirmation of the absolute oneness of God. I begin my prayer, as all Muslims do, with the phrase "In the name of God, the compassionate, the merciful," and then I recite Al-Fatihah or the Exordium, one of the most important chapters in the Quran.

> *Gratitude be to God, Lord of the Universe,*
> *The Compassionate, the Merciful,*
> *Sovereign of the Day of Judgment!*
> *You alone we worship, and to You alone we turn for help.*
> *Guide us to the straight path,*

The path of those whom You have blessed with Your bounties,
Not of those who have incurred Your wrath,
Nor of those who have gone astray.

I then try to open up my soul, to expose my deepest fears and vulnerabilities, to connect with a bigger, higher unknowable force, to appeal for wellness, hope, and all that is good. I try to communicate through my senses—mental, physical, and emotional—my supreme appreciation and thanks for the blessings I have enjoyed and with all humility plead for more. My prayer is essentially a form of meditation in which I singularly apply my limited human physical capacity to try to connect with that omnipresent universal unknown force: God. Through that connection I seek the well-being and serenity that can come from prayer.

I don't have to be in a mosque or even at home to pray. Sometimes the simple concentric patterns of raindrops that form on a New York sidewalk can transport me and connect me with the beauty and mystery that I associate with that transcendent force.

Priscilla:

Ranya's description of seeing God's work in the raindrops of New York City street puddles stuck with me for days. Her faith was so strong. And her prayer so simple, so accessible.

I began seeing raindrops everywhere. And saying little prayers often. "Maybe everyone on Lexington Avenue is praying today, at this very moment," I thought as I left Ranya's apartment after our meeting. And if, as Suzanne said a while ago, every human sigh is a prayer, I, with my history of hyperventilating all my life, have been praying up a storm for decades.

It's become easier for me to pray now. I don't have to say the Shema. I don't have to speak to God with a litany of blessings, fears, hopes, and pleas. My prayers don't have to be poetic. As I think of the way Ranya described herself offering her soul up to God, I am reminded of a yoga posture in which I lean way back, arching my back dramatically, opening my chest up to the sky. To God. At that moment I am fully exposed but fully empowered.

Freed from the burden of reciting formal prayer, I began to pray often—erratically and sporadically, instantaneously. In fact, I now realized that for the past few years I'd been praying every day, or at least every school day.

My son Max drives himself to school, but luckily I've still had the pleasure of taking Jack in the morning. And just about every time I've dropped my delightfully droll son off at school, I've watched his back as he trudged up the path to his daily grind and involuntarily said, "Thank you, God." I've lingered in my car in the parking lot, snooping on my son, and, I now realize, saying a prayer of gratitude. That little thank-you to God was real, unconscious, meaningful prayer. I know people whose children have had major and minor health problems, and I've never taken my children's well-being for granted. I've thanked God every day for that.

I'm very busy these days, and my prayers are very quick. I hope God knows how much I love my husband, how I never take for granted the kiss he bestows upon me every night when he returns home safely.

As I accompanied Jimmy to a service at our synagogue recently, I picked up the prayer book and flipped through it. On the first page, something caught my eye. Something I'd never noticed before. It was the traditional first Jewish prayer of the morning, in Hebrew. The English translation popped out at me. "I thank you, God, who lives always, and Who, as I awaken, has in mercy returned my soul to me; we can ever trust in you."

Wow. How simple was that? I could start my days with this prayer, I thought. Thank you, God, for returning my soul to my body after a long (or sometimes restless) night of sleep. Suzanne once remarked that Jews seemed to have a prayer for everything. And this was a prayer *about* everything. About the simplest thing. About something Jews, Christians, and Muslims could agree on. That God has given us a soul and that each new day is a gift for which to be grateful.

I went home that night and found my father's fifty-year-old prayer book, the Siddur Tifereth David. I had tucked it away on a shelf years ago. The binding is worn and the pages are loose. I turned to the first page and pictured my father, ever the colorful eccentric, living in his camper in the parking lot of the hospital where he was receiving radiation treatment for his cancer fifteen years earlier. I pictured him waking up every morning, his tumor causing him discomfort, his head full of worries, his heart heavy with concern for his mortality. I pictured him picking up this very prayer book, which I'd seen lying on the table next to his bed. I imagined him saying this prayer: *I give thanks unto thee, O King, who liveth and endureth, who hast mercifully restored my soul unto me; great is thy faithfulness.*

Ranya:

Priscilla, Suzanne, and I were slowly beginning to understand each other's faith and relationship with God. Our discussions about God and prayer were allowing me to think through and refine my relationship with God and religion. Within the Faith Club, I felt and appreciated a newfound confidence and security about my Muslim identity, which stood in severe contrast to my isolation as a Muslim in the outside world. I explained to Priscilla and Suzanne how vulnerable I felt as a Muslim in the eyes of other Muslims who asserted that it was their right to qualify or disqualify me as a member of the religion.

Not a moment too soon, my aunt called. She had just attended the Aspen Institute interfaith lecture series. When it was time for the guest imam to speak, after hearing impressive Jewish and Christian lecturers, she had held her breath for fear of who and what kind of imam would represent her religion.

But my aunt was in for the best and biggest surprise: The imam, Imam Feisal Abdul al Rauf, spoke with great eloquence and spiritual understanding. His wife Daisy Khan was there also, and, my aunt reported, amazingly enough, Daisy's head was uncovered!

That fact in itself grabbed my attention. I had never met an imam's wife, but I had assumed that, at the very least, a traditional head scarf would be an essential prerequisite for the job. My aunt told me that this fascinating couple lives in New York, and that Daisy heads the ASMA Society (American Society for Muslim Advancement), a group founded by Imam Feisal that is dedicated to creating an American Muslim identity from the multiplicity of ethnic identities and experiences of American Muslims. Their goal is to improve relations between American Muslims and the larger American society.

I quickly contacted the ASMA Society and was invited to an upcoming study group. The topic was "What Does It Mean to Be an American Muslim?"—perfect for my purposes. The meeting was to take place at St. Paul and St. Andrew Church on the West Side of Manhattan.

I had no idea what to expect. In spite of my aunt's initial impressions, as I sat in the taxi on my way to the meeting, I suddenly wondered whether I would be required to cover my hair. Worse yet, would my views cast me as outlandish and un-Islamic?

The first indication that all would be fine was that as I stepped out of the taxi, I saw four young Asian women head inside the church. They had bright red lipstick on, high heels, and loose flowing hair. In retrospect, I'm surprised at how sensitive I must have been subconsciously to the stereotype of what is appropriate Muslim attire, even though I know that my credentials as a true Muslim cannot be judged from my exterior. At the time, however, I was greatly relieved by these women's appearances.

As I entered the church, still with some trepidation, I could see a large sheet spread out on the floor inside one of the halls. The Asian girls who were ahead of me had already removed their high heels and matter-of-factly joined other men and women in the evening prayer. I could not believe my eyes. Such fuss is made these days in some Muslim circles about the separation of the sexes, especially in prayer.

I hung back as the others prayed, still hostage to the notion that I might not do things correctly or the idea that since I had not performed wadu, the ritual washing, I would be disqualified from participating. Daisy beckoned me to join them but still I refrained.

After the prayers, we settled into two discussion groups to address the topic of the day. Daisy was warm and serene. She asked people to speak about their beliefs and embraced all opinions.

My first impression of the women sitting around me was how young they were, all educated and professional, some wearing a headscarf, all sincere in their efforts to explore their faith and their new identities as Muslim Americans or Muslims in America. Most had no extended families here, having left them behind in lands as varied as Malaysia and Uzbekistan. The overriding connection between these diverse young Muslim people was that many were tired of trying to pave the way on their own and needed the same connection, a community in which they could congregate and associate with other Muslims.

Life in America since 9/11 seemed to be overwhelmingly lonely for these bright, young, mostly single professionals. They operated, like me, with a sense of deep isolation, loneliness, and despair. They were frustrated by their constant struggle against negative perceptions of their religion. And as they charted their lives away from their extended families, they felt a need for the comfort of a spiritual home. I had finally found a group of Muslims who were trying to articulate a clear, intelligent, reflective voice for American Muslims today, and I shared with them my excitement in having found them.

Daisy introduced the idea of a spiritual retreat as a way to connect with other Muslims during the potentially lonely, long fasting days of Ramadan. The festivities and traditions of the holiday are made more meaningful, she explained, when those around you are all fasting, too. In Muslim countries, everything changes during Ramadan, from the television programming, to work schedules, to the way people socialize, inviting guests to Iftar meals at their homes. The experience of Ramadan in the West can be very lonely, by comparison. So when Daisy proposed a day of spiritual retreat, when we could all get together and reflect and then break our fasts together as a community, I marked the date on my calendar.

CHAPTER TWELVE

Intimations of Mortality

RANYA: *My attachment to my children is so painful. Last night when I put my head down next to Taymor's, and I watched his chest rise and fall, his mouth parted with those full lips, I cried. One day I won't know him, and he won't know me. Sometimes I wonder if I really believe what I say I believe.*

SUZANNE: *About an afterlife?*

RANYA: *Yes. I have more of a fear of death at this age. I used to look at my hand dreamily as an eight-year-old. Now I look at my hand and imagine my skin rotting away! I try to visualize it in my tomb.*

PRISCILLA: *Ranya! Are you serious?*

RANYA: *Sort of.*

Ranya:

As a young woman I was in love with life, intoxicated by its beauty, its potential, its thrill. I was never one to sleep through a morning, too eager to experience yet another full day. How cruel, I thought, that we all must die. Had I been given the ability at birth to choose life, I would have declined. Not because I did not enjoy life but rather because I enjoyed it too much. How could I have children, I wondered? How would I ever be able to safeguard them, shield them, love them, become so attached to them and yet have to separate in death?

My fear of death had me, as a young woman, in my more cynical moments, question the need or reason to have children. However, the temptation to experience this life-giving miracle proved too great for me to resist, and through it I felt a strong connection to the divine.

As any expecting mother will attest, that moment she feels the first flutter of her baby's movement must be the eighth wonder of the world. The divine becomes no longer a possibility, but a reality, a miracle and force of life. I marveled at my full belly, relishing every hiccup, kick, and bump. And when I experienced overwhelming anxiety about the health of the baby, I was forced to submit. Now as I see my children grow in size and independence and I have to stretch ever further to remember the sound of their heartbeat echoing from my womb, I am awed and honored by my humble participation in the miracle of their creation. That final moment of delivery when the head miraculously emerged was my most intimate and physical experience of the divine. I felt a soaring elation, a weightlessness that defied gravity, that opened my soul and connected it to a collective universal ecstasy. As I reflect on that memory, I find myself wondering whether in death, as in the delivery of life, we should be so lucky as to have a parallel physical experience and connection to God.

When I was with my grandmother in hospital the day my grandfather died, I heard a nurse report his death as "Patient Expiration in Ward 22." How poignant, I thought. We all are born with our own personal expiration dates. When famous living artists or personalities are written about, their birth dates are followed by a hyphen and a blank space. That gap has always appealed to my darker sense of humor. It's a testament to the power of life and the human spirit that we are able to fare so well while not knowing our own expiration dates.

RANYA: *I often think of death when I'm at my happiest. And my fear is related to the question of what comes next. I'm afraid of the unknown.*

PRISCILLA: *As a Jew, I've never been promised anything but the unknown.*

RANYA: *Is there a soul? I want to hang onto the idea that there is one so badly.*

PRISCILLA: *Maybe Jack had it right, When he was about four, he used to worry about death every night. I bought him a wonderful*

*book based on the Tibetan Book of the Dead, and we would read
about an old man, a woodcutter, who died, went up to the heavens
and asked God for another life. He got to pick the life he wanted
next . . . the galaxy, the planet, the country, the parents. Jack took
great comfort in this story, and every night before he went to bed,
he used to say to me: "Mom, don't forget to ask for another life!"
He told the same thing to his father and brother. "Don't forget!"*

Suzanne:

"I know what you mean about wanting a soul to live on," I said to Ranya. "After my sister died, I was desperate to know whether some part of her had survived or whether the closeness that I felt to her was coming from my own imagination.

"I joined a grief group at church," I continued and related an experience that I had there.

One evening, I told the grief group about the short "conversations" I often had with my sister in my head. I wasn't sure if these conversations were "real," or if I was doing the talking for both of us. Was I just making everything up to make myself feel better?

As I related my doubt to the group, I began sobbing. At this point, there were no words that could reach me. I needed to cry. The grief counselor, a Baptist minister, rose from her seat and came to stand behind me, massaging my shoulders. This is exactly what my sister would have done and did do for me so often when she was alive. Kristin worked as a physical therapist's assistant while she was studying to become an engineer, and she gave terrific shoulder massages. I absolutely believe that at that moment she was communicating with me, comforting me through the hands of this minister.

When I finally stopped crying, I told the minister my thoughts. She listened with complete understanding, then told me that once she had massaged the feet of a man who was dying in the hospital. "I'd never massaged anyone's feet before," she explained. The next day the man died. Later, the minister met his sister, who reported that "I couldn't make it to the hospital the night before he died, but I prayed to God that someone would massage his feet. He loved to have that done."

This minister had no idea how much this man liked to have his feet massaged. And she had never stood up during a counseling session and given anyone a shoulder massage before. I believe that she is simply a person who is open to the spiritual world. As a result, that world could reach us through her.

When I was in sixth grade and my sister was in kindergarten, she and I walked home from school for lunch one day. But when we got home, we found all the doors locked. We stood in the garage and saw on the ceiling above us the only way into the house. It was a very narrow laundry chute that led straight up to the floor of my parents' bedroom closet. I was too big, but Kristin agreed to give it a try. She stood on my shoulders and barely squeezed herself through that chute. Once in the house, she came downstairs and opened the door for me. We ate our peanut butter sandwiches and hurried back to school together.

Through her death, my sister once again squeezed ahead of me into a dark place that I can't see from where I stand. She stood on my shoulders, popped the door open, and pulled herself through into something I can only imagine. This time she left me standing below her on the ground, at least until I die, when I am hopeful that she will be there to open the door for me again.

RANYA: *Priscilla, you've said that Jews don't have the promise of an afterlife, but could we really just die, and that's it? I know you talk about living on in our children, but does that really give meaning to the experience?*

PRISCILLA: *Sure.*

RANYA: *What is the meaning?*

PRISCILLA: *What do you want it to mean?*

RANYA: *I don't know.*

PRISCILLA: *That you were on the planet, that you were lovely and*

loving and that you had an effect on people who will remember
you. And certain of your qualities will go on to other people.

SUZANNE: *That's enough for you, Priscilla?*

PRISCILLA: *I think so. Isn't it for you? I don't understand what*
else there is.

SUZANNE: *Something after.*

PRISCILLA: *You mean life beyond this?*

SUZANNE: *Sure.*

PRISCILLA: *I think that is too much to ask for. Look at what exists*
on this planet. It is so wonderful, so rich. Heaven would be like
eating dessert after a seventy-million-course meal.

RANYA: *But you've had dessert at various points in your life. Some*
people have had really miserable lives. What about people who
were born with handicaps or worse? Why do they have to face up
to their challenges every day?

PRISCILLA: *I think that those people find their desserts along the*
way. My sister carries a bag of medicine around with her and
takes ten pills a day. Yet she has incredible joy in her life. Her
sparks of joy might be surrounded by some darkness, but they are
just as brilliant as other people's sparks.

Priscilla:

As I talked with Suzanne and Ranya about death and heaven, I remembered a prayer from the Yizkor service, a Jewish memorial service that takes place at different times of the year, particularly on the
High Holidays. There's a passage from the service that always brings
tears to my eyes:

> *We are like a breath; our days are as a passing shadow; we come*
> *and go like grass, which in the morning shoots up, renewed, and in*
> *the evening fades and withers.*
>
> *If some messenger were to come to us with the offer that death*

should be overthrown, but with the one inseparable condition that birth should also cease; if the existing generation were given the chance to live forever, but on the clear understanding that never again would there be a child, or a youth, or first love, never again new persons with new hopes, new ideas, new achievements; ourselves for always and never any others—could the answer be in doubt?

My father died two years before my second son was born. The words "Never again would there be a child" have special meaning for me, since my love for my children was the very thing that helped me survive my father's death. My oldest son is now a young man who has experienced "first love." My younger son was named after my father, and his presence is a symbol for me of life after death.

Over the next few days, I tried to remember if anything else had consoled me after the death of my father. And then I remembered a conversation I had with a distinguished reform rabbi the day after my father died. This rabbi, a friend of my in-laws, paid a condolence call to me and my brother at my apartment. We sat next to each other on a couch, and my brother and I asked outright, "So what's the story? Is there life after death? What are we taught to believe as Jews?"

The rabbi did not describe a candy-colored heaven awaiting us above the clouds. "We don't really know," he told us. "Jews don't really come down on this issue on one side or another."

"Typical," my brother and I decided. "Leave it to the Jews to debate this for the rest of eternity." Free, open debate among Jews is one of the strengths of the Jewish faith. Differences over interpretation come up again and again.

But the rabbi offered us a glimmer of hope. "If you look at life sort of scientifically," he said, "your father's life was a strong force. He was real flesh, blood, and energy."

My brother and I nodded our heads. Our father had lived a life shorter than we would have liked, but he had led a very colorful, dynamic, intense life, with a lot of ups and downs, but very few dull moments.

"So where does all that matter go?" the rabbi asked. "It doesn't just evaporate. It lives on as energy, as real matter."

Hmmm. My brother and I grasped at any hope of life after death. That's better than nothing, we decided. "We'll go with the theory of energy that never disappears, that lingers on in one form or another."

At my father's funeral. I asked the rabbi who officiated to read something I'd seen in a reform prayer book. I pulled it off the shelf after our meeting to read again.

> Birth is a beginning
> And death a destination
> And life is a journey
> From childhood to maturity
> And youth to age;
> From innocence to awareness
> And ignorance to knowing;
> From foolishness to discretion
>   And then, perhaps, to wisdom;
> From weakness to strength
> Or strength to weakness—
>   And, often, back again;
> From offense to forgiveness,
> From loneliness to love,
> From joy to gratitude,
> From pain to compassion,
> And grief to understanding—
>   From fear to faith;
> From defeat to defeat to defeat—
> Until, looking backward or ahead,
> We see that victory lies
> Not at some high place along the way,

But in having made the journey, stage by stage,
      A sacred pilgrimage.
Birth is a beginning
And death a destination.
And life is a journey,
A sacred pilgrimage—
To life everlasting.

Life everlasting? I wasn't sure just how to take that.

PRISCILLA: *Ranya, are you interested in making the hajj some-time in your life?*
RANYA: *Yes. My mother and grandmother have done it. It is the biggest congregation of humanity on earth. And when I think that all of these people are there singularly trying to connect with a big-ger presence than a human life—their beginning and their end—it brings tears to my eyes today.*
PRISCILLA: *Why is that? Why are you crying now, Ranya?*
RANYA: *I just . . . I felt this way at church with Suzanne, and I would probably feel it just as much at a temple . . . It just moves me.*
PRISCILLA: *What do you do at the hajj?*
RANYA: *It is so simple, yet powerful. Imagine two million pilgrims chanting together: "God, we answer your call. Our gratitude and thanks are to you. There is only one God, and no other partner." It gives me goose bumps. The chant connects the pilgrims to some-thing much bigger than themselves and symbolically prepares them for the end of their journey on earth—for death—when all humans will assemble to meet their creator.*

Ranya:

The image of millions of humans gathered at the hajj before God is a symbol to me of our human longing to connect with another dimension beyond our own. I have felt that longing myself, and I know that need is universal. It is also a reminder to remain ever humble as we face God. The pilgrims wear identical unsewn white sheets of fabric as a sign of their equality before God. No thread or color differentiates them. After their deaths, Muslims are buried in these sheets, king and beggar alike.

"That's how I plan to be buried," I said to Suzanne and Priscilla, "wrapped in the white sheet of my hajj and placed directly into the ground."

"So Muslims do not use coffins?" Priscilla asked me.

"No. The idea of being exposed, covered with dirt, leaves me fearful of how my body will decompose," I replied. Slightly claustrophobic, I'm full of angst about burial, even though rationally I know it is absurd, since I will be dead. "I wonder if my fears are connected to what my religion teacher at school described as the 'punishment of the grave,' where those who have lived good lives will feel their grave as spacious and roomy, and those who have lived sinful lives will feel the constraints and tightness of their graves as we all wait for that final day of judgment. I have considered cremation, but that does nothing to assuage my fears. Besides, I believe it's un-Islamic, and I find myself unwilling to defy Islamic burial traditions."

I suddenly remembered a conversation I had with my father as we sat together one day side by side on a beach overlooking the bay on Long Island. I had been thinking about death a lot that summer, a subject I'd never discussed with my father. But something made me turn to him and say, "I am really afraid of death. I am having really big panic attacks about it."

"How did your father respond?" Suzanne asked me.

"My father is not touchy-feely," I replied. "He believes that you get up and you go to work. That's the Germanic in him."

"Why did you bring up death at that moment?" Priscilla wondered.

"I don't know," I replied. "It was a beautiful day. I suppose I just needed to. And he was almost dismissive. He said, 'It just happens. You have to accept it. It is part of our life. You can't say 'I'm afraid of it.' It just is.'"

My living room was quiet. Priscilla thought for a moment. "I think my father would have said that," she said. "He would have said 'Everybody's death is in their own brown paper bag.'"

"I'm not sure that I would call my father religious," I said. "But he lived ethically, Priscilla, and fairly, as you say your father did." And then I realized something. Isn't that where God is? "I think that I feel God when I reflect on my father and his sense of fairness. He has that graciousness of spirit. I think that is a godly moment for me. I think that's my father in his purest form."

"Everybody carries God within them, and it comes out at different times," Priscilla said.

"I believe we all have something divine in us, that Godlike impulse," Suzanne agreed. "Although some people choose not to live by it."

RANYA: *I have been thinking about what you said about eternity existing in your children, Priscilla. I remember when I was pregnant with Taymor . . . I almost lost my son and I had to spend some time on bed rest. I had a photograph of my father as a little boy, and I kept saying "Please, God, give me a baby like this one." And I really do think now that Taymor is like my father. Their birthdays are a few days apart.*

PRISCILLA: *How are they similar?*

RANYA: *They are both hard on themselves and others. My father was hard on his children in the sense that he had high expectations. But he is very kind, too, in business endeavors as well as with his family. He had his first heart attack at age forty, and he has had a tough life, with all sorts of health problems. . . . But he still picks up a racket and plays tennis. I have never heard him complain in his life. I have never heard him say, "I am afraid." He is a diabetic now also. He has many issues on his plate, yet he still has optimism, love for life, energy. He wakes up as if the world is there for him forever.*

PRISCILLA: *That's a wonderful quality.*

SUZANNE: *Do you see elements of your father in your children, Priscilla?*

PRISCILLA: *Yes, although I worried that they wouldn't know my father, as I promised him they would.*

RANYA: *I think kids know these things in their fabric, in their spirit. I never met my paternal grandfather but I know stories about how egalitarian he was, about how he gave my grand-mother access to bank accounts, which was not done in those days. If that spirit carries through, it becomes part of the fabric of your family from generation to generation.*

PRISCILLA: *I see my father in my sons more and more as they grow older, in their smiles, their sense of humor, their gentle, es-sential kindness. . . . My sons accept everyone at face value. They find all kinds of different people fascinating. They know who they are.*

SUZANNE: *They don't measure themselves by who they are with.*

PRISCILLA: *No, and neither did my father. He was friends with all sorts of people and didn't care what kind of impression he made.*

Priscilla:

When he was fifty-nine years old and diagnosed with cancer, my fa-ther was told he was going to die by an oncologist who had the same last name as he did. We'd thought that was a good omen when the doctor first introduced himself. Turned out we were wrong, although the doctor was kind and thoughtful in the way he talked to my father about his disease.

"How exactly am I going to die?" my father asked this oncologist, who was at least twenty years his junior.

I was in the hospital room where my father had been recuperating from unsuccessful surgery for colon cancer when this conversation took place. I saw the momentary look of surprise on the young doctor's face, followed by a look of relief, then respect. It was not often, I suppose, that he'd been asked this question this directly by a patient, so soon after he'd delivered bad news, the terminal prognosis.

"I can't tell you exactly how you're going to die," Dr. L told my father. "The cancer could take several courses. But I can tell you one thing. If it's pain you're worried about, you needn't worry. We've gotten very good at managing pain. We have not yet found a cure, but you will not suffer pain."

My father nodded, said nothing. The doctor shook his hand and left the room.

I stood by his hospital bed, waiting for my father to speak.

"What do you think it will be like?" he asked me. "Do you think I'll be able to communicate with you after I die?"

Even I, used to my father's direct, slightly askew view of the world, was surprised now at his candor and courage. "Maybe," I said, after a moment, trying to sound natural, relaxed, upbeat even. "Maybe we should have a sign, some way of communicating. Maybe I could feel a tickle at the back of my neck or something," I replied.

My father smiled, said nothing. He was often quiet and moody, even before he got sick. But when he felt like opening up to you, speaking and showing emotion, it was as if every cloud in the sky suddenly parted and dazzling sunshine poured down on you. That's what happens with people who conserve their words and emotional energy. I wouldn't know. I'm constantly spilling my guts.

On my wedding day, when I was freaking out at the thought of the two hundred "strangers" assembling in my parents' backyard, where the ceremony would take place, I started to cry. "I'm marrying a stranger!" I wailed to my father. (I'd been living with Jimmy for a year and a half.) My father took me seriously. He brought me into my childhood bedroom, sat down with me on my bed and told me that I was marrying a wonderful man, that I was leaving my old family, who would always be there for me, but that I'd be making a new family with Jimmy. He said we would build a wonderful life together. And we did.

My father faced his illness courageously. He didn't talk about his death again, but one day, while visiting me in New York, he insisted on buying me a pair of cowboy boots at his favorite Western store.

"You're Jewish!" I often reminded my father. "What's with the cowboy boots?"

But my father did love wearing them. And on this particular day, I tried on several pairs of boots. "They're not colorful enough!" my father said each time. Finally I slipped on the most colorful boots in the store, rainbow-colored lizard skin boots. "Those are perfect!" my father exclaimed with delight. "Now I'll be able to see you from up there!"

We both understood that "up there" was wherever my father was headed.

Two years later, when I was afraid to leave my father's deathbed, but afraid to watch him actually die, I called Jimmy from a pay phone at the nursing home where my father was receiving hospice care. "I don't know what to do," I said haltingly, in between sobs. "I don't want to leave, but I don't want to stay, either." I had never wanted to watch my father actually die and leave the planet. That terrified me. It was not part of my plan. My mother and sister would be in the room with him if I left. I knew that.

My husband was ready with exactly the right words. "Do whatever you want to do." He paused. "But I know Max would really like to see you."

Jimmy and Max, who was days away from his second birthday, were back in New York, three hours away. I knew immediately, viscerally, that my father would want me to be with them, to continue building the life he knew I would build for myself.

So I left my father's deathbed.

He'd been in a coma for days, not eating or drinking. He'd probably suffered strokes, the hospice nurses told us. His beautiful Paul

Newman—blue eyes were covered in an odd, milky film. Strangely, he'd been able to be guided to a chair in his room, where he sat for hours on end, motionless and silent.

I walked over to my father and sat down on a chair next to him. I reached for his emaciated hand, which felt limp in my own. And I spoke to him as though he could hear me. I told him how much I loved him. I promised him that I would never forget him, that his grandchildren would never forget him. I told him I'd talk about him every day, so that they would know him. And I thanked him for loving me. I told him I would never have been able to have the wonderful relationship I had with Jimmy if I hadn't first learned how to love and be loved by him.

My father, who hadn't spoken or acknowledged anyone's presence for days, moaned loudly. And then he raised his arms, held them up toward me, reaching for me, calling out in a primal, unforgettable way.

He was trying to hug me. He was trying to tell me that he'd heard every word I'd said, understood it all.

And so I was able to leave his side and return to Jimmy and Max.

I gave my father a long hug and kissed him good-bye one last time. I told him I loved him, and then I left the room, sobbing only when I was out of earshot. Then I returned to New York and the new family he'd promised me I'd make.

Our family was completed two years later, when I gave birth to our second son. His middle name is Paul, my father's name. Nine years after that, our son Max was bar mitzvahed. There is a point in the bar mitzvah service called Dor Vador, or Generation to Generation, where three generations stand on the bimah and the Torah is passed down from grandparent to parent to the bar mitzvah boy or girl. My father was not there to stand on the bimah with Max, Jimmy, and Jimmy's father. But in a remarkably comforting coincidence, my father's Yahrzeit, which is the day in the Jewish calendar that commemorates the death of a loved one, the day the special kaddish prayer is said, fell on the Saturday of Max's bar mitzvah. The Jewish calendar does not correspond to our standard calendar. This was not something we had planned in advance.

But as I stood on the bimah celebrating my son's entry into Jewish adulthood, my father was there. And at the end of the moving service, his name was announced and we said the kaddish prayer in memory of my father.

Four years later, Max's brother Jack was bar mitzvahed, and, once again, in a miraculous coincidence, his entry into adulthood fell on the same day as my father's Yahrzeit, and my father was present at the bar mitzvah of the grandson he never met, as the congregation said kaddish for him on that important day.

> SUZANNE: *Priscilla, without the promise of an afterlife, what do you think makes people want to be good?*
> PRISCILLA: *I do believe that God is inside all of us.*
> SUZANNE: *And he is willing to let that part die, and that is fine?*
> PRISCILLA: *Hmmm. He goes on to the next. We are like flowers that bloom, fade, and go back into the earth again. Ashes to ashes, dust to dust.*

Suzanne:

I couldn't believe that God would create us and then allow us to perish. Life had to have more value than our struggles and accomplishments on earth.

I had recently received a letter from the unclaimed property division of the Missouri State Treasurer, I told Priscilla and Ranya. It was a notice of assets presumed abandoned by my sister, Kristin Loeffelholz, when she died six years earlier. If I signed the notice and sent a copy of my driver's license and Social Security card, I could claim the assets, which amounted to $11.18.

The letter was like a jab to an old wound. Besides, I had no idea where my Social Security card was, and I didn't want to take the time to search the boxes and file cabinets in our closet and storage locker. Even if I found it, I would have to take a trip to the copy shop and the notary public. That seemed like an awful lot of effort for $11.18, so I put the paper in a pile of things to do another day.

A few weeks later, my mother asked me if I had received the notice, and I told her that I had. Still, I did nothing about it. Another few months passed before I was standing with my mother in her kitchen, and she asked me, "Did you ever file that abandoned property claim?"

I was ashamed to say that it lay in a pile of papers in New York. "It seems like a lot of trouble for eleven dollars and eighteen cents," I said. Tears filled my mother's eyes, and her face wore an expression of betrayal. How could I have been so flippant? I hugged her and told her I was sorry. Yes, I would locate my Social Security card and complete the paperwork.

My reluctance to fill out the lost property claim wasn't only because $11.18 was no fortune. But the task forced me to contemplate the relationship between the life and death of my sister and this $11.18. It was such a trifling legacy in comparison to the value of her life. I wanted to ignore that obvious and degrading connection. But, I realized that in presenting my claim I was honoring the memory of my sister. That money represented an hour of work she did at the hospital. It represented a forgotten bank account, a place where she had signed her name and hoped to accumulate some financial security. It represented hopes and plans unfulfilled.

So, I turned my files inside out in an effort to find my Social Security card. At last I realized it must have disappeared when my wallet was stolen five years earlier. So, I applied for a replacement, and, when it came, I completed the claim form. It was a sad exercise. I cried as I stood in the Postex shop making photocopies of my driver's license and Social Security card. One image kept coming to my mind. It was Kristin at her wake. Her body lay in the coffin, and she was wearing my "going away" suit, the one I had worn as my husband and I had joyfully waved good-bye to our wedding guests and headed off for the Caribbean eight years earlier. I had passed the suit along to her, and it was the nicest thing that hung in her closet when she died. Most of her other clothes lay strewn across her bedroom floor, student-style. So my mother had given that suit to the undertaker. I don't know if she remembered the special occasion on which I had first worn it. Now I stood in the Postex thinking of the strange path that suit had taken, from wedding to funeral. Did the suit herald a new beginning for Kristin as it had for me?

Anne asked me recently what my sister would look like now. "What's happened to her body in the coffin?" she asked. It wasn't something I wanted to think about, but I told her that modern coffins were airtight so bodies were protected for a long time.

Then I added, "But once we're dead, Anne, our bodies are irrelevant. Our spirits go on to be with God, and we leave those bodies behind." They become abandoned assets, I thought to myself. Like a bank account or an old wedding suit, they remain on the earth long after we've departed.

Teddy, my three-year-old, has found great interest in death lately, too. At least once a week he asks me, "Mommy, when will we die?"

I smile at his assumption that death is something we will do together, like going to the doctor's office or hopping on a plane. He needs to believe that I will be there to hold his hand. I hope I am not. I hope I am long dead. But do I dare to hope that I would be waiting in heaven to hug him and hold his hand again after he dies?

Then I answer him, "Hopefully we won't die until we are very old and tired."

"I've never been dead before."

"No, Teddy, you haven't."

Or has he? I was reminded of an anecdote I've heard about a newborn baby and his preschool-aged sister. The sister kept asking the parents if she could be alone with her new baby brother. At last, the nervous parents consented, but left the door open a crack so that they could see and hear what was happening in the room. The sister leaned over the baby's bassinet and asked her tiny brother, "Nathan, tell me what God looks like. I forgot."

SUZANNE: *I think our ultimate purpose is to be with God and, for that reason, some part of us will live forever.*
PRISCILLA: *You don't believe God created you to do good things on earth?*
SUZANNE: *I absolutely believe that. But I also believe I have a chance to be with God in some kind of heavenly kingdom.*
PRISCILLA: *Can I come?*
SUZANNE: *Absolutely.*
PRISCILLA: *That kingdom would be the icing on the cake for me.*
RANYA: *Well, if there is a heaven, I think that you would find a lot of people disagreeing as to who gets to go there.*

Ranya:

On one particularly memorable afternoon, Suzanne and I went to an orientation meeting for our daughters' swim team at the Jewish Y. As the parents sat in one room, the children were shepherded to another where they did their homework. My daughter, Leia, and Suzanne's daughter, Anne, sat next to a boy who was filling out a form. He asked Leia how to spell the name Muhammad.

"Why do you want to spell that name?" my daughter asked, intrigued, she told me later, by the thought that this boy might be Muslim.

"My father's name is Muhammad," the boy replied.

My daughter knew that Muhammad was a Muslim name. (Her friendly little brother asked every taxi cab driver in Manhattan for their name and once exclaimed, "There are so many Muhammads!")

"Are you Muslim?" Leia asked this little boy.

"Yes," he replied.

"So am I," Leia said proudly.

"That's good," the boy said, "because only Muslims get to go to heaven. Jews and Christians burn in hell because they don't listen to God."

Leia and Anne were appalled at this boy's words, and when we all got into a taxi to return home, they related everything to us excitedly.

"He looked like a nice kid," Leia marveled. "Why did he say that?"

"What he said was mean," I told Leia. "He also doesn't know what he is talking about. Islam considers Christians and Jews to be people of the book, and that means that just like us, if they're good people during their lives, we believe they'll go to heaven."

Anne looked at her mother, and Suzanne asked her, "You don't believe what that boy said, do you?" Anne shook her head no. "In your heart, you know it's not right," Suzanne continued, and that was that. She and her daughter could both easily dismiss the comment as untrue. Their faith, I felt, gave them a confidence in their religion that I did not have yet. I still felt insecure about Islam as a religion and insecure about my daughter's Muslim identity. So I kept the conversation going.

"There are people in this world who feel they are better than the rest of us," I began. "Or that their religion is better than ours. All different kinds of people can feel this way—Muslims, Jews, or Christians. They think they have the true path and everyone else is wrong." Leia nodded. "But you know," I said, "all religion is about love and respect for God and other people."

PRISCILLA: *I sometimes feel judged and left out of the picture when the whole subject of heaven comes up.*
SUZANNE: *Why do you say that?*
PRISCILLA: *I think that little boy is not the only one who feels nonbelievers will burn in hell. Some Christians have a very exclusionary idea of what heaven is. That you have to be baptized in order to get there. That you have to have accepted Jesus Christ as your savior. They think the "pearly gates" are locked to Jews.*

Suzanne:

As Priscilla said this, I felt irritation at those who would judge her that way. "Accept Jesus Christ and Be Saved or Regret It Forever," the billboard had said.

I did not agree with Christians who represented Christianity as the only path to God. I had met some of them, and their air of certainty unsettled me. In their hands Jesus seemed to become a polarizing force rather than a unifying one. I could distance myself from them and from the subject of Jesus' role in human salvation by advocating the virtues of Jesus the man, rather than Jesus the savior. After all, Priscilla and Ranya had both come to admire Jesus the man; his good nature was something we could all three agree on.

I wasn't sure Jesus' savior role was that important to my conception of God, anyway. I related to Jesus as my brother and my teacher. He helped me understand the qualities of God. He was the conduit to something much greater. I realized I never addressed Jesus when I prayed. I directed my prayers straight to God, my creator and my judge. Jesus felt too human next to the vast power I imagined when I thought of God.

Besides, when I thought of Jesus, hundreds of images from the corny to the gory blocked my way. He was a long-haired, brown-eyed, and berobed man preaching on a hillside, riding a donkey, sharing a meal with friends, or even hanging on a cross. Perhaps Muhammad was on to something when he ordered believers not to create images of God. They become too distracting. Or perhaps I just hadn't done enough thinking about the meaning of Jesus and his role in my life.

CHAPTER THIRTEEN

Conversations with a Priest, an Imam, and a Rabbi

SUZANNE: *I've been struggling with my faith since our conversation last week.*

PRISCILLA: *Why?*

SUZANNE: *After all our discussions about death, heaven, Jesus, and salvation I'm not sure I agree with Christian theology on all these issues.*

RANYA: *It sounds like you want to redefine your faith in a more open-minded way.*

SUZANNE: *To define it period. I would not have been called to do that if I hadn't wanted to share the Good News with you two. I've gotten great joy from Christianity, but now I need to understand what parts of the Christian faith are most important to me.*

PRISCILLA: *You started off as a steadfast believer, Suzanne. You led me down this whole path, so please don't let me down now! You were the light at the end of my tunnel!*

SUZANNE: *My God hasn't changed. But maybe my doctrine has.*

Suzanne:

While preparing for our meeting I had sat uneasily at my dining room table with the Bible open before me. My faith was wavering, and I was looking for support. Could I find convincing arguments to share with Priscilla and Ranya for all those things I had formerly been so confident of—the existence of God, the divinity of Jesus, and an afterlife with God? It seemed that while my faith was rubbing off on them their doubt was affecting me.

As I paged through the New Testament, I stopped when I got to the Beatitudes. Here was scripture that spoke to me of true Christian values as Jesus represented them in his own life. It spoke of God's understanding of our human pain and struggle for goodness, and of God's promise of recompense. I copied the passage and brought it to our next Faith Club meeting.

"I'd like to read you some Gospel quotations," I told Priscilla and Ranya. "About how God loves us and how we should live our lives. They're from Jesus' Sermon on the Mount, which your friend Lu mentioned to you, Priscilla." And so I read:

> Blessed are the poor in spirit; for theirs is the kingdom of heaven.
> Blessed are they that mourn; for they shall be comforted.
> Blessed are the meek; for they shall inherit the earth.
> Blessed are they which do hunger and thirst after righteousness; for
> they shall be filled.
> Blessed are the merciful; for they shall obtain mercy.
> Blessed are the pure in heart; for they shall see God.
> Blessed are the peacemakers; for they shall be called the children of
> God.

"There's more, but you get the idea."

"That's beautiful," Priscilla said. "And so inclusive. It speaks to everyone, Christian and non-Christian. It reinforces everything I've come to believe, through your help, about the teachings of Jesus. He's a wonderful embodiment of both suffering and love in one person, who you believe is divine."

Then I came clean with the extent of my new doubt. "I'm not sure."

Priscilla's eyes grew wide and her voice rose in surprise. "You don't believe Jesus is divine? Oh, my God! Stop the presses!"

Stop the presses was right. Suddenly I found myself in a very fearful position in our trio. For two years I had talked to Priscilla and Ranya about Jesus. I had represented him as a role model, miracle worker, Son of God, and savior. My partners had listened and reflected. They had discarded the miracle worker, Son of God, and savior part. But they had accepted Jesus as an exceptional human example of love and suffering. This left me questioning the aspects of Jesus that they had tossed aside. I found myself altering my view of Jesus to accommodate theirs.

I knew that the miracles of Jesus wouldn't persuade my partners of Jesus' divinity. Months before I had mentioned big miracles like Jesus bringing his friend Lazarus back to life, and I could see that Ranya and Priscilla were skeptical. It was too far-fetched for our modern thinking. Where was the eyewitness, the proof that Lazarus's heart had actually stopped beating before Jesus beckoned him to sit up again? I realized that it wasn't miracles that led to belief in Jesus, but rather belief in Jesus that led to belief in his miracles.

Jesus wasn't my only problem. I had also been challenged about the concept of heaven. When Priscilla had asked me "Can I come, too?" my instinct was to answer, of course. But I knew some Christians would disagree. In my heart, I couldn't believe in a heaven that wasn't available to all good people.

The Beatitudes, which I had just shared with Ranya and Priscilla, seemed to offer recompense in heaven for all those who suffer, not just followers of Jesus. But some Christians believe a person has to be baptized to get into heaven. Was there room in Christianity for a more open-minded view?

My faith was in crisis. And the rising voice of the evangelical Christians, calling for people to accept Jesus' atonement for their sins, wasn't helping. I couldn't believe in a God who would condemn those who hadn't "accepted" him. To me, God's love was the unconditional love and empathy expressed in the Beatitudes.

Although the exclusionary version of Christianity wasn't mine, I wasn't sure what my own version was in the face of these new challenges to my faith. "I'm not sure what I believe anymore," I confided.

This challenge was more than I could handle on my own. So I made an appointment to see Craig Townsend, one of the priests at my church.

As my meeting approached, I prepared a list of my questions. They boiled down to three big ones.

1. Do I have to believe that Jesus is God in order to call myself Christian?
2. Is there an afterlife for humans with God?
3. What is the purpose of Jesus' death and resurrection?

Ranya was right. I had been changed by my Faith Club conversations. I was looking for validation of a tolerant Christianity, one that would allow Priscilla and Ranya a place in the kingdom of God (if it existed). To do that, I felt I needed to go to the early days of Christianity, a time before authoritarian teaching took hold. I wanted to know what Christians were thinking between the time of Jesus' death and the writing of the Nicene Creed three hundred years later. Was there more flexibility before Rome took control of the church?

Obviously, this was a huge field of study that I couldn't hope to master quickly. I began by reading Elaine Pagels's books *Beyond Belief: The Secret Gospel of Thomas* and *The Gnostic Gospels.* These books explore early Christian texts, including many lost gospels discovered in Egypt in 1945. As I began reading *Beyond Belief,* I learned that Pagels had two of the same problems that I had with the traditional Christian church. She disliked its tendency to authorize a single set of beliefs and also its conviction that only Christian belief offers access to God. While I was aware of these tendencies within Catholicism, I hadn't felt them so much at my current Episcopal church. In fact, Craig Townsend had given a talk after mass one day acknowledging the struggle of maintaining Christian faith while recognizing that other paths to God existed. This was the trouble I was now having.

Beyond Belief further undermined what I had previously held to be true. The followers of the apostle Thomas believed that the kingdom of God is already here on this earth, Pagels argued. They held that the key to entry into the kingdom is simply recognizing your affinity with God, which all people can do. "The Kingdom of God is on earth, you just don't see it," wrote the author of the gospel.

As Pagels compared the gospels, both inside and outside the Bible, she called into question the divinity of Jesus, saying that only John calls Jesus the Son of God. The other gospel authors simply use the term "Messiah," which means "of God," and could refer to a prophet.

Now I was in over my head. I did not have the theological background to judge Pagels's arguments. Fortunately, my meeting with Craig arrived in time for him to throw me a line and pull me out of the quagmire into which I had sunk. I gave him an overview of our project, then described my predicament.

"I'm having trouble maintaining my Christian faith as I've moved to a better understanding of Judaism and Islam," I said. I mentioned how I was challenged by Priscilla's doubt about an afterlife and Ranya's doubt about the divinity of Jesus. I saw how they each gained moral and spiritual tools from their traditions, and I was no longer certain my way was the best way.

When I asked Craig my three questions, he smiled. "You've hit the major issues, that's for sure." Then he said something that immediately reassured me. "The opposite of faith is not doubt, it's certainty. It's okay to have doubt, everyone does."

Craig also told me that my experience was typical of interfaith dialogues. The tendency is for each participant to compromise and maintain only what everyone can agree on. Indeed, I had found myself wanting to discard beliefs that wouldn't please Ranya and Priscilla. Now I had moved uncomfortably far in that direction, and I needed to examine which beliefs I could discard and which for me were sacred and absolute.

As Craig and I talked, I felt him tugging me back onto solid ground. Whether or not I called Jesus the Son of God, I realized, was not the central issue. "The trinity is our way of talking about God in relationship to himself," Craig explained. "Unfortunately, we are stuck using language for a concept that defies language."

Then Craig validated what I had come to believe: that humans had experienced God throughout time and within and without the Christian experience. "God has been trying to reach humans for ages in many different ways," he said. "With Jesus, He was probably saying, 'Okay, let's try this another way. Do you get it now?'"

"So what's the message of Jesus' dying and rising?" I asked.

"The message of the crucifixion is that God understands our suffering. He has empathy for our pain. In order to demonstrate that, God had to become human," Craig continued. "The resurrection shows us that death is not the end."

"So there is a heaven?"

"Maybe we are in it already," Craig said. "Maybe we are living with one foot in this world and one foot in the other, but because we are stuck in our bodies, in this space and time, we can't perceive it. The key is that our belief in eternal life enables us to live differently today. Heaven is not a reward for faith. But rather, our faith allows us to see that we're in God's kingdom already and that we should live according to his wishes." That was a beautiful concept with practical implications that appealed to me.

Craig gave me a reading list and offered to help me make my way through Saint Augustine's *Confessions*. I felt energized when I left his office. I didn't have all the answers yet, but I had found a tutor whose language and exploration of Christianity appealed to me. (One of the books on the list he had given me was *The Crusades Through Arab Eyes*.) I also felt reassured that I could now acknowledge that little voice in my head asking, "What if I'm wrong?" That voice was making me humble. It allowed me to explore other views, but it didn't mean I had to abandon my faith.

RANYA: *Today a woman rushed past me on the street and whispered to me passionately, "Jesus loves you!"*

SUZANNE: *Really? Did you answer her?*

RANYA: *No. But I did not dismiss her as a complete eccentric. I now can be more empathetic about the passion and love Jesus embodies and inspires in the lives of many Christians. I have a clearer understanding of his suffering and ultimate sacrifice for the redemption of humanity. He died for convictions, and I find that inspirational.*

SUZANNE: *I think of martyrs like St. Peter as people who died for their conviction in their faith. I guess I am too Christian to think of Jesus as a human with extraordinary conviction; I think of him as one with God.*

PRISCILLA: *Last I heard, you were questioning whether he was God.*

SUZANNE: *It's true. But I feel certain he is not entirely human, either.*

PRISCILLA: *So you believe he was the son of God?*

SUZANNE: *I'm reluctant to use the term "son" because I see how that opens Christians to the criticism of polytheism. But unfortunately I am stuck with language to describe the indescribable. I would rather say that Jesus is of one mind with God and was sent by God to this earth.*

Suzanne:

At our next meeting, when Ranya spoke of Jesus as a person of conviction, my response was without forethought—as if I had heard her say Abraham Lincoln was a great Brazilian president. It's as difficult for me to think of Jesus as simply an extraordinary human as to imagine Lincoln doing the tango in Rio. In my heart, I feel Jesus and God are of the same essence. Essence is difficult to put into words, but that's what I recognized that afternoon with Ranya and Priscilla. You could take away the phrases "son of God" and "eternal kingdom," but I still had faith—faith that God existed, that Jesus was somehow divine, and that there was a purpose to our lives. Even while doubt lurked unwelcomingly in my heart, it was not powerful enough to put out the light of my faith. Yes, I felt uncertain about some details. But those details were only a sideshow.

Not long after my meeting with Craig, I went to a concert by the men's singing group Chanticleer at the Metropolitan Museum of Art and had a marvelous experience that affirmed the awesome, personal nature of faith. We sat in the cavernous, skylighted hall housing the ancient Egyptian Temple of Dendur, a symbol of man's quest for God thousands of years ago. The sublimely soulful voices of the singers echoed that same ancient, enduring human longing to be with God that the temple's architects had expressed. In between songs, I read the English translation of one of the group's pieces, "Cor Meum Est Templum Sacrum" by Patricia Van Ness. The truthfulness of its poetry resonated within me. It expressed the mystery of faith as I had experienced it. The foundation of my faith is not based on any particular book or proven in any theological argument. I believe in God because of what I find when I look into my own heart.

My Heart Is a Holy Place

My heart is a holy place
Wiser and holier than I know it to be
Wiser than my lips can speak
A spring of mystery and grace.
You have created my heart
And have filled it with things of wonder.
You have sculpted it, shaped it with your hands
Touched it with your breath.
In its own season it reveals itself to me.
It shows me rivers of gold
Flowing in elegance
And hidden paths of infinite beauty.
You touch me with your stillness as I await its time.

You have made it a dwelling place of richness and intricacies
Of wisdom beyond my understanding
Of grace and mysteries, from your hands.

My own heart soared as I read this. I felt freed by the truth I found in Van Ness's words. They expressed what I had been experiencing, that the mystery of faith was accessible through my own heart even when my system of belief was shifting. As a human, I wanted a creed in which to place my trust, but as a child of God, I had faith even without the creed.

RANYA: *Imam Feisal performed the services at my cousin's wedding in St. Bart's last weekend. I followed him everywhere. We talked about daily prayer, about the Quran being the word of God and about the pillars of Islam. No topic was off limits.*

SUZANNE: *Ranya's found a religious authority she can respect!*

RANYA: *His wife was helpful, too. She said to me, "Yes, there are parts of the Quran that I may not understand. But I don't allow those parts to inhibit me from embracing the others. Only God knows the truth.*

PRISCILLA: *That's a good attitude for everything.*

SUZANNE: *It's spectacular that you could have this conversation with them. Could you have done it a year ago?*

RANYA: *No. I didn't have the knowledge then.*

SUZANNE: *But now you've been reading and interpreting on your own. What did they think of that?*

RANYA: *That's completely Muslim because there is no ultimate hierarchy.*

SUZANNE: *You are also more familiar with the Quran itself.*

RANYA: *It's true. I could even quote some verses to defend my positions!*

Ranya:

"I have finally found my imam!" I announced to Suzanne and Priscilla at the start of our next faith club meeting.

During my evening at the ASMA Society discussion group, I had finally connected with like-minded Muslims living in New York City. But it wasn't until the ASMA Society Ramadan spiritual retreat that I had found an imam who could help me complete the journey I had begun.

The evening, which was organized by Daisy Khan, was designed to begin with Friday prayers led by her husband Imam Feisal Abdul Rauf at Masjid al Noor in downtown Manhattan. This was to be followed by a discussion with the imam. Then at sunset, we were invited to pray the evening prayers and then break our fasts at a meal organized by Daisy and a group of volunteers.

One of the primary reasons I have not fasted for almost all my years in America is the loneliness of breaking one's fast alone. Memories of the special Ramadan meals my mother prepared are still fresh in my mind—the ritual of first having a glass of water, followed by a date as the Prophet is reported to have done, followed by a soup, and mezzahs, or appetizers placed in the middle of the table and meant to be shared by all. Although I realize that Ramadan is more than these table traditions, the thought of breaking my fast alone (my husband is usually still at work at sunset) and the lack of time to prepare the meals I remember from my childhood had discouraged me from fasting.

"That's why the Ramadan retreat Daisy proposed was so appealing to me," I said to my faith club partners. "And I was anxious to meet her husband, the imam I've heard so much about."

I made arrangements for my children so that I could take the afternoon and evening off, hopped in a taxi, and headed downtown.

The mosque was difficult to identify, located in a nondescript two-story townhouse without any exterior indications of being a mosque. I had to look closely for the small sign at the door to confirm that I was indeed at my intended destination. As I pushed the door, I hastily wrapped the scarf hanging around my neck to cover my hair.

The place was drab but bursting at the seams with both floors packed with attendees. I was frankly taken aback by the lack of space and the mess of unorganized shoes abandoned behind a screen so that their owners could join in prayer. Clearly, this mosque and Imam Feisal were popular and could have used a bigger space.

Though initially wary of my untidy surroundings, having crossed that threshold, I was surprised at how quickly I was captivated by the imam's call to prayer and Quranic recitations. At the end of our prayers we turned right and left and saluted each other with the words "Peace be with you." This was my first visit and prayer at a mosque, and at that precise moment I could not help but be transported to that moment in Suzanne's church when I heard the very same words. I marveled at this parallel experience.

After prayer we sat on the cushioned floor for discussion with the imam facing us. I mustered up the courage to ask one of the questions that had been on my mind since Priscilla, Suzanne, and I had first discussed the violence associated with Islam. "Who is considered an infidel?" I blurted out. Suzanne and Priscilla had asked me about the word "infidel," a term used by extremist Muslims to make enemies out of all non-Muslims. Imam Feisal calmly explained that there is no temporal justice, meaning that humans cannot be judged on earth by fellow humans on matters of faith. The only judge of faith is God.

After Daisy officially introduced me to Imam Feisal, he invited me to sit next to him at the Ramadan table. Self-conscious in my scarf, I nervously explained our Faith Club project to him, trying to sound intelligent and informed while seeking his endorsement amid the celebratory chaos that signaled the end of a day of spiritual discipline and retreat. But the imam was interested in what I had to say. I told him about my struggle to help my children develop confidence in their American Muslim identity and mentioned Leia's question: "Does the Easter Bunny visit Muslim children?"

The imam looked at me. "Well, does he?" he asked.

Nervous, but never one to hold back, I said, "Yes, he does."

Imam Feisal laughed and replied, "Aha, mothers can make anything happen."

"And that was the moment," I told Suzanne and Priscilla. "I knew at that instant that my search had ended. I had finally found my imam!"

But that was, fortunately, not my last moment with Imam Feisal. If at my first meeting with the imam I was nervous and insecure, by the time I met him again a few months later there was a marked difference. I was farther along in my journey and I knew enough about him to feel more comfortable about his receptiveness to free and open dialogue. I trusted his intellect and faith.

My second meeting with the imam took place at the island wedding of my cousin. This time around I was not fiddling with a headscarf, but with a sarong. The ceremony took place at sunset with the Caribbean sea as a backdrop. The natural beauty around us magnified the presence of God as a witness to the matrimony. The imam had prepared an exceptional ceremony. Taking Khadija, the prophet's first and only wife until her death, as an example, he asked the bride to emulate her, and take the lead in initiating and proposing marriage to her groom as part of the religious ceremony. This was the imam's way of endorsing what he believes is the true spirit of the Prophet's views and position with respect to women—as empowered and equal partners in marriages.

The morning of the ceremony I had decided that in my conversation with the imam and Daisy I would not hold back. The imam was discussing the tradition of "thikr" or "remembrance of God," which encourages Muslims to make the Quran a part of their lives through its recitation and reading.

"Yes," I replied. "But isn't it true that its believed divinity as the word of God has been used by some to prohibit and intimidate? I have personally felt insecure and intimidated to make it part of my journey. I was afraid to reflect and consider parts that did not make sense to me."

"It is precisely because it is the word of God that should make you read it more, not less," the imam answered confidently. "Besides," he added, "those parts you don't understand should not inhibit you from embracing the others. For at the end of the day only God knows the truth."

The more the imam talked the more I began to understand. For years religious rituals and religion preached as a set of rules had alienated me by claiming to define a singular road or path to God. My Faith Club journey had allowed me to refine and fine-tune the difference between religion and faith. Imagine my delight when the imam related a story about the Prophet, in which he was asked, "What does it take to be a Muslim?" The Prophet is said to have explained that it involved three steps: The first is to accept God, or to submit to the will of God (Islam). The second step is to accept the message of God and Muhammad, that there's an end to the world, a day of judgment, and to accept all the prophets before Muhammad (Iman). The third part of being a Muslim is to act as if God is always with you in your actions. If he is not with you, at least he can see you (Ihsan). If you have embraced these three steps, the imam explained, then you have faith as a Muslim. If you have faith, then you can use the rituals of Islam, the five pillars, as a way to experience and get closer to God. These five pillars are proclamation of faith, prayer, fasting, alms giving, and hajj—the pilgrimage to Mecca. But to engage in the five pillars without faith is nothing.

By providing me with this insight, the imam was beginning to teach me how to respect religion in its ritual form. I now realized that I could pray when and how I wanted, but that ritual prayer was also an important component of a higher level of faith and communion with God. Prayer and the recitation of the Quran in its original language as the word of God are rituals that allow Muslims to experience God symbolically, as a community of faithful. That is comparable to the symbolic Christian experience of God found in the taking of the Eucharist, which defines the Christian community.

The imam was able to liberate me from my suspicion of practiced rituals and discomfort with them. I was able to understand that religion can be a part of a more disciplined embrace of God and faith in him, and in humanity as a community. Religion is not just a series of rules used by some to qualify or disqualify others, but a tool that, used effectively, could service my faith, my spirituality, my belief. It can enhance, expand, and promote the proximity and presence of God in my earthly life.

I wished that the imam could inspire all of the Muslims around me in a similar way. The morning after the ceremony, my immediate family was rushing to get dressed for a brunch. But it had been such a cold spring in New York that, come what may, I knew that I could not even begin thinking about packing us up again and getting the children ready to go back home without running for a quick dip and celebrating the feeling of sand between my toes one last time. I ran out of the room, leaving the children behind with Sami, quickly enough to escape his protest. I ran down the hill surrounded by lush vegetation, in a hotel bathrobe with a bathing suit underneath. I turned into the corner, and there were the imam and Daisy taking their own walk, before the beginning of the festivities.

I was horrifically self-conscious as I stood with them in my bathrobe making polite conversation, until I saw a group of twenty-something wedding guests making their way back from the pool, with shorts, sarongs, and wet bathing suits. I noticed how they respectfully tried to walk by unnoticed. So instead of taking a plunge in the pool, I took a plunge with the imam. I made a point of officially introducing them to the imam and said, "See all these beautiful people? They're Muslims! They swim . . . they drink . . . Empower them! Give them their religion back!"

"I love your enthusiasm!" the imam laughed.

Priscilla:

Just as I feared, I told Ranya and Suzanne, my rabbi, Jeffrey Sirkman, is not on the fence about the fence in Israel. I found this out when he delivered a sermon and said just that, eloquently making his case to me and his congregation.

I had been reluctant to approach Jeffrey, to make an appointment to talk with him about the things Ranya and I had debated over the last year: the subject of Israel as a Jewish state, the two-state solution, and the rights of Palestinians who had left their homes just as Ranya's family had. Of course I knew that Jeffrey's enormous capacity to include all people in his prayers and heart would mean that he cared deeply about people suffering on all sides in the conflict, but I had been afraid to approach him and ask, "What about my friend Ranya's opinion? What about the call to action that she issued to me, to speak out on her behalf? What should I do? What should I think?"

I was afraid that I would feel torn even more on the topic of Israel, and, worse, that Jeffrey might say something that would make me feel apart from him. He is the spiritual leader with whom I connect most personally. He is my spiritual leader, at least in a formal Jewish context. When I die, he will be the one to lead prayers at my graveside. I like and respect him enormously. But could we differ on our thoughts about Israel? The answer, of course, is yes. We're Jews, after all. We've been debaters for centuries. In his sermon, my rabbi spoke eloquently about all sides in the conflict. He quoted many people who were all passionate, all different in their thoughts about the fence. And then he gave his own view.

Rabbi Sirkman suggested that the controversial fence in Israel could in fact be a bridge between Israel and the Palestinians. He agreed with the Supreme Court in Israel that, as it currently stands, many changes have to be made to the fence in order to better accommodate the needs of Palestinians who have legitimate concerns about their land boundaries and need to travel easily back and forth to Israel. Ultimately, Rabbi Sirkman hoped and prayed that the fence would reduce terrorist attacks and lower the tension on both sides so that economic and social interaction might eventually be facilitated meaningfully.

I walked home from the service and talked about Jeffrey's sermon with my husband. I respected everything that Jeffrey had said, but I wasn't sure where I stood on the fence. Now I come to the whole question of Israel as a Jew, but also as Ranya's friend. I have enormous respect for my heritage and the suffering of my people, for those who died because they were Jews, for the haven that Israel became to millions of Holocaust survivors.

But I am not an Israeli Jew, I told Jimmy. I don't have the same kind of passionate, personal convictions that my friend Chaim has. And, to be truthful, I don't have the same strong, visceral emotional attachment to the land of Israel that Jeffrey and other Jews have. Jeffrey was preparing to lead members of my congregation on a trip to Israel. God bless them all, I said. But I have never had a deep urge to go back to the land of Israel.

Did that make me a watered-down Jew? A secular Jew? A legitimate Jew? Was I Jewish enough?

I knew the rituals and prayers of my faith. During some Sabbaths and holidays I attended temple; during others I didn't.

I was a Jew by birth, a proud Jew. But also a Jew who questions. And now, when I engaged in political conversations, I was beginning to be more outspoken.

"You would have been proud of me," I said to Ranya at our next meeting. "I'm speaking out. Not in the middle of Times Square, but in the middle of suburban dinner parties."

Ranya laughed. And I described to her and Suzanne about how my perspective had changed. "I listen to how people talk about 'the Palestinians,'" I said. "And I hear their words with what you taught me echoing in my mind."

Ranya smiled. "When someone says to me, 'The Palestinians have done nothing to help themselves,'" I continued, "I try to explain some of the very real obstacles that stand in their way. I try not to lay blame, but just to lay out the facts as I know them."

Once, a woman asked me during an after-dinner political discussion, "Why are the Arabs so violent, always firing weapons into the air at every opportunity?"

"Don't you think that sounds a bit racist?' I answered, surprised at my own forthrightness.

I am not a historian, I tell people. I don't have hundreds of statistics to recite. Nor am I a politician with an agenda to promote. I'm just trying to live a morally responsible life that I can be proud of and that will live up to the standards that Suzanne, Ranya, and I have set for ourselves.

When people talk about Israel, sometimes I wonder: What would I feel if I actually stood on Israeli soil? Would I feel an intense attachment to the land? Would I feel this was indeed my ancestral home, a place I felt a connection to deep inside my soul?

Maybe, I told Ranya and Suzanne. But then, I realized immediately, so would many other people, of many other religions. Israel is not called the Holy Land for nothing.

"I don't always know where I fit in," I told my faith club friends. "I'm a Jew, but I'm an American Jew, a reform Jew. I practice my religion the way I want to, but for that reason, some Jews would question my authenticity." I took a deep breath. "And when it comes to the politics of the Holy Land, I don't feel like I'm on the Israeli side of the fence but I'm also not on the Palestinian side. I don't want to be on either side," I confessed. "Sometimes I'm so confused."

But my friends were not confused.

"You don't have to be on either side of the fence," Ranya said, reassuringly. "Once you can see things from both sides, you're on the side of compassion. And humanity."

Okay, I thought. I'm a Jew on the side of humanity.

And I believe that makes me an authentic Jew.

Suzanne:

Soon after Ranya met Imam Feisal, she invited Priscilla and me to a lecture he was giving at the Center for Religious Inquiry at St. Bartholomew's Church in Manhattan. Its Byzantine-inspired architecture set the perfect stage for the evening; if it weren't for the pews and the cross, we might have been in a grand mosque.

The imam started his lecture, which was in connection with his new book *What's Right with Islam,* with a plea for interfaith dialogue. "We clarify and deepen our belief through interfaith dialogue," he explained. And those words rang true to me. It was through my own discussions with a Muslim and a Jew that I was beginning to understand my Christian soul in a way I never had before. In talking with two people of other faiths, everything I believed had been called into question. Every assumption was up for examination and debate. I never would have plumbed my faith to the extent I had if I had not been in this conversation. In my attempt to understand Ranya's and Priscilla's faiths, I had begun to understand what was vital in my own.

Imam Feisal also put his finger on the biggest roadblock to interfaith dialogue—the current rise in extremism. That trend feeds prejudice and makes it difficult to transcend stereotypes in every religion. "But persevere," he said. "We can't defend every single thing someone has said in the name of our religion. But that shouldn't prevent us from going forward." I quickly scribbled some of his quotes in my notebook. After the lecture, I bought the imam's book, and we all three joined the line to get his autograph. He had described Islam so eloquently and exuded such warmth and humility that it was easy to understand why Ranya was drawn to him.

A few months later Ranya invited Priscilla and me to meet the imam once again. This time it was for an interfaith Ramadan break fast meal at Imam Feisal's home. We weren't sure what to expect as we walked in, took off our shoes, and joined the circle of people sitting on the floor. But we were quickly welcomed into the small group that included Muslims, Christians, Jews, and even a rabbi. Imam Feisal listened as many of the young people there described their experiences working in various interfaith organizations in New York.

Then, Ranya shared the dessert she had brought, elegantly wrapped chocolates that her mother had sent from Mecca where she had just participated in the hajj. Each displayed a picture of the sacred Kaaba, the destination of the hajj pilgrims. As we savored the chocolates, the conversation took an ironic turn toward fasting, and Imam Feisal awed us with his description of his own experience.

On the first day of a fast, he explained, his mind generally focuses on hunger pains and physical cravings. But with each successive day, as the body realizes that its needs won't be met, each function, including the heart and mind, slows down. One gains a new type of awareness, he said. All senses are heightened. The body becomes light. And in that state, one becomes more open to the spiritual world. "The soul seems to rise out of the body," he said, "hovering as it looks down at the earth."

The experience, as he described it, sounded transporting. It seemed as if the imam might levitate straight to heaven. It was clear, Priscilla and I agreed, that we were in the presence of someone with great spiritual strength.

CHAPTER FOURTEEN

A Day of Atonement

Priscilla:

Suzanne, Ranya, and I always parted ways during the summer as we headed off for family vacations. We resumed our meetings in September, once our kids were back in school. That fall, we decided to celebrate our reunion by meeting for lunch. For the first time ever, we dined out together in the real world, at a small French restaurant in Ranya's neighborhood.

As I walked in, I took in the pastries in the mahogany cases, the tile floor, mirrors, and black-tied waiters, and felt as if I were in Paris again, where I'd just been vacationing with my husband. Except there sat Suzanne and Ranya, dressed up for the occasion and looking as lively and energetic as every other New Yorker in the bustling place. And to my eyes, of course, more so! I hadn't realized how much I'd missed them over the summer.

Catching up with Suzanne and Ranya is not like catching up with my other friends. Sure, I have meaningful conversations with my friends about deep personal issues, but we never talk about God. We never talk about our faith. We never talk about religion. After discussing our summer activities, our kids and families, Suzanne, Ranya, and I got right back on track talking about our spiritual lives.

I told Suzanne and Ranya how my European trip was a true test of my recently acquired faith. I had defined my belief in God and gained enormous strength within the confines of our Faith Club, but then I had to take that faith out on the road with me. I hated leaving my kids on one continent and flying to another. I hated flying over water. But I'd done it, thanks to my born-again, newfound strength—and, I laughed, my Klonopin. We'd visited friends in Brussels, Venice, and Paris. "And Jesus, too!" I joked. "He followed me all over Europe!"

Indeed, Jesus hung in all of the churches we'd visited, front and center. I pulled out postcards I'd bought of a painting in Venice. "This was my favorite Jesus moment," I said. "Tintoretto's masterpiece, *La Crucifissione*. It's the best crucifixion painting I've ever seen!"

"What impressed you about it?" Ranya asked me. And I thought back to the moment a year earlier when she'd listened to my confession about taking a crucifix off the wall because "I didn't want to sleep under a dead man who meant nothing to me." How I had changed.

"It just put the whole crucifixion in context," I said now. I picked up a postcard. "Look at all these people! Jews, Romans, future Christians, disciples . . . bystanders." In this depiction of a complex historical event, dozens of people were milling around, some overcome with emotion, some watching dispassionately. Two other men were being hoisted onto crosses as well.

"It's not clear who the Christ killers are. No Jews are singled out. Nobody seems to be blamed!" I laughed. "I have no Jewish guilt!"

I filled my friends in on the rest of our trip. After our stay in Brussels and Venice, we met up with friends in Paris. Because of the war in Iraq, new security measures were in place everywhere we went. Europeans were critical of America's involvement in the war and American tourists were scarce.

I'd never been an enthusiastic traveler until I met my husband, who'd traveled all over the world. I depended on his calm competence while overseas. But he had to leave Paris before I did, to return to work. I stayed on with friends, and as I took a cab by myself to Charles De Gaulle Airport I grew anxious. The thought of flying overseas alone scared me. I worried about terrorists targeting my flight. I couldn't help reverting to my old pre-Faith Club ways.

Worrying replaced faith as I sat in the brightly lit American Airlines lounge. My eyes darted around the room, checking for potential terrorists. I hoped God had a boarding pass for this flight. Apparently I still didn't believe that God was everywhere. "I needed you guys with me!" I told Suzanne and Ranya. "And now that I'm back I think I need you again. To prop me up. My faith is not so strong. I'm new to this God stuff, remember?"

I stopped joking. My eyes got teary for an instant. I'd just been to a funeral in Rhode Island. A close friend's mother had died, and as I watched the casket leaving the church, I couldn't help thinking about my own mother's impending death. She was deteriorating steadily, I reported. Slowly but surely.

Things had started churning around in my head again; my courage seemed to have evaporated. Gone was the serene Madonna I'd laughingly called myself after all my talks with Suzanne and Ranya. Inner peace? How about inner turmoil? My kids' school year had begun, and my calendar was now crammed with activities and responsibilities. A routine check-up had revealed that I had high blood pressure. I'd watched a CNN special about nuclear weapons falling into the hands of terrorists, and I was worried again about a future attack on New York.

"I'm a bit of a mess," I confessed. "I don't know what it is exactly, but I'm shaky." I tried to smile. "I've missed our faith club meetings. That's where I've found my strength over the past two years, not in temple. Rosh Hashanah, the Jewish New Year, is this week, and then comes Yom Kippur. But I'm not really thrilled about going to services this year."

"Do you usually go?" Suzanne asked me.

"Yes," I answered. "I go every year, especially on Yom Kippur, the holiest day of the year for Jews. We fast and pray to atone for our sins of the previous year, hoping to be forgiven. We ask to be written into the book of life."

"What's that?" Suzanne asked.

"It's God's metaphorical book," I explained, "listing who shall live and who shall die in the coming year, who shall see ripe age and who shall not. We recite a whole litany of disturbing possibilities—hunger, thirst, beast, sword, earthquake—and pray that we will be spared all of them."

"That's interesting, because we have the same idea—except our book of life is comprehensive. It is a record of our life's complete positive and negative actions," Ranya said, "where one good deed far outweighs a bad one. This is the book that we will have to face on the Day of Judgment."

"I guess Yom Kippur is a day of judgment for us," I said.

"But are you simply asking for one more year of life on earth?" Suzanne asked.

"Yes," I replied. "That's why, growing up, I developed a fear that God is very judgmental. We have to go through this year after year."

"And the big reward is just another year of life?" she asked again.

"Yes," I said. "We go back every Yom Kippur to ask for more time. It's exhausting for people like me who have panic disorders!" I laughed.

But Suzanne looked serious for a moment. "Maybe we should come to services with you," she suggested.

My eyes lit up. And so did my mood. "Would you really come?"

"Absolutely," my friends replied.

"Wow," I said. I felt better. A little less shaky. And suddenly enthusiastic about the services I'd been attending for decades.

Yom Kippur now seemed like a cause for celebration. It has always been a time for intense, personal recollection of the year gone by, a recounting of the good and the bad, the bitter and the sweet. I'd spent many hours over the last three years discussing those bittersweet experiences with Suzanne and Ranya, who had become so much a part of my faith. It seemed natural, even necessary, to include them in this most meaningful, solemn holiday. I'd repent for my sins and celebrate my good fortune in meeting them.

And Ranya and Suzanne would finally visit me up in the suburbs. We'd tried to schedule a working session at my house before, but with everyone's busy schedules, it always ended up easier to meet in the city.

The restaurant cleared out, and we continued talking. Suzanne reached into her bag and pulled out a bar of Valrhona dark chocolate with slivers of hazelnuts. "You're picking up my bad habits," I said as I grabbed a square of chocolate for myself.

Suzanne:

That year the Jewish High Holy Days finally became more than annoying school holidays that required me to entertain my children. They became holy days. And a teaching opportunity. My kids were home from school on Rosh Hashanah, sitting around our kitchen table sucking at their Go-Gurts while I fulfilled my usual morning role as short-order cook. The whistle on my kettle began blowing just as Anne's, Thomas's, and Teddy's argument about the day's events reached a crescendo.

I turned my back on the pleas and complaints, pressed the plunger on my coffee press, and reminded myself why my kids weren't on their way to school already. "Do you guys know why you don't have school today?" I asked.

"It's Rosh Hashanah," Anne and Thomas said in unison.

"Do you know what Rosh Hashanah is?"

"The Jewish New Year," Anne quickly replied.

"You're right," I answered as I marveled at how easily my older children had answered my questions. They already lived religious diversity in their New York City lives. They wouldn't grow up with the same misconceptions that I had had when I moved here. Thankfully, Ranya and Priscilla had beaten those ideas out of me like women beating an old rug. As they whacked at me, my thoughts had been driven into a haze of emotion, alarm, and confusion. But they helped me discover underneath a beautiful carpet woven of faith and friendship.

I wanted my children to be better informed than I had been. "The Jewish calendar is different from ours," I said.

"Why?" Thomas asked.

"Our calendar is the one most of the world lives by," I answered, a conversation with Ranya and Priscilla echoing in my head. "You don't have to acknowledge us," they had said to me. "We live by your calendar. Our schedules are dictated by your holidays!"

My friends would be proud, I thought, as I continued to Thomas, "The Christian calendar is the Gregorian calendar, which was created by a Catholic Pope named Gregory. It is used all over the world now by Christians and non-Christians, but many non-Christians who already had their own calendars kept using those calendars in order to preserve their own traditions."

"Oh," said my kids with mild interest. Then they returned to the pressing topic of playdates. Later that day I noted a bit enviously all the dressed-up families heading to temple for Rosh Hashanah services. I was rushing around running errands while they were heading into the temple for a spiritual retreat. They were escaping the treadmill that I was stuck on. I felt excluded, like a Jew on Christmas. Except on Christmas Jews can relax because all the shops are closed.

As I passed a synagogue near my home I paused to read the inscription above the gates, which I had passed hundreds of times before without notice. "For the sacred memory of the one million Jewish children who died in the Holocaust," it read. On the temple wall below the engraving was a sculpture of children hastening toward the safe embrace of a bearded man dressed in what could have been Old Testament robes.

If I didn't know the building was a synagogue, I might have taken the man for Jesus. Who was it? God? Moses? To me, the sculpture suggested an eternal life in heaven for the Holocaust children who were so horrifically murdered. But when I called the synagogue later, I found that the man and the message were something different, something much more Jewish in comparison to my very Christian interpretation.

The man was Janusz Korczak, a Polish Jewish pediatrician and writer who was devoted to children. "He was the original Dr. Spock," explained the executive director of the synagogue. Korczak ran two orphanages, one Jewish and one Catholic, and wrote children's fiction. When Jews were sent to the ghetto in Warsaw, he was offered refuge with the Gentiles on the other side. But he refused, saying, "You do not leave a sick child in the night, and you do not leave children at a time like this."

For two years Korczak took care of the orphans in the ghetto, until the Germans ordered his orphanage evacuated. Korczak was forced to gather his two hundred children and lead them to the train that would bring them to Treblinka. Onlookers marveled at the dignity of the procession. Some of the children played violins along the way. At the station, Korczak was told that he did not have to accompany the children, but he wouldn't abandon them. He got on the train with them and later died in Treblinka. The sculpture on the temple celebrates that march of the orphans and the heroic actions of Korczak.

When I heard this heartbreaking story, I felt chilled. Korczak was surely a hero. But why memorialize children smiling on their way to destruction? It's depressing. Then I remembered the dedication to the children of the Holocaust. And the message became clear: Don't forget these children. I was reminded of Priscilla saying that in Hebrew day school she was told: Never forget. Never forget. I was beginning to see how the Jewish history of persecution affected the message of modern Judaism and the outlook of today's Jews. I saw it once again the following week as I prepared to join Priscilla for Yom Kippur services at her temple.

I had asked Priscilla to bring me a prayer book so that I could read the prayers and reflect on the meaning of the day beforehand. "It's a day of fasting and asking forgiveness," Priscilla had said.

"Will you fast?" I'd asked her.

"I don't know. I'm like my Dad. Sometimes I fast, and sometimes I start the day with an English muffin."

On the Friday before Yom Kippur, my family was finishing dinner as I looked out our dining room windows to see the sun setting over the west side of Manhattan. I finished my last bite of acorn squash and decided to fast until the breaking of the fast at Priscilla's in-laws' home the following evening. I wanted the complete Yom Kippur experience. After the dishes were washed and the rest of my family asleep, I picked up the prayer book from Priscilla's temple and sat down to read the services for Rosh Hashanah and Yom Kippur. As I read in the quiet, dark night, I felt I was sharing some of the sacred influences that had shaped Priscilla's soul. I heard her voice in the prayers. I recognized her fears, her courage, and her convictions. Without Priscilla, these prayers would have sounded like a foreign language to me. Knowing Priscilla, I heard her voice in each one.

She had described the Yom Kippur service as a time when Jews prayed to God for one more year of life. At the time it struck me as a rather grim religion if one's best hope was for one more year of life on earth rather than eternal life in heaven. But as I read, I began to understand the faith behind Priscilla's comment that she was not promised eternal life. There was an appealing humility in it. And it did not require contortions of theological reasoning. It was described in prayers of praise to God like this.

Man's origin is dust, and dust is his end.

Each of us is a shattered urn,

A grass that must wither,
A flower that will fade . . .
But You are our Sovereign, the everlasting God!

The meditation reminded me of Priscilla telling Ranya and me how she believed we were all like flowers that bloom and fade. Of course, the words were also reminiscent of Christianity's Ash Wednesday prayer, "Oh Man, remember that you are dust and unto dust you shall return." Yet, forty days after Ash Wednesday we celebrate the resurrection of Jesus and the belief that we might also rise to join him. Belief in that eternal kingdom is a giant leap of faith that is not required of the Jews. Then again, they don't necessarily have the solace offered by that belief, either.

The High Holiday prayers I read suggested that man should help to bring God's kingdom to earth by worshiping God, obeying his laws and living peaceful, charitable lives. (This message was reminiscent of the gospel of Thomas, who, like the other gospel writers, was probably a Jew.) Any suggestion of eternity for man was vague, as it is in the following prayer.

. . . Teach us O God,
To see that when we link ourselves to You, and strive to do Your will,
Our lives acquire eternal meaning and value.
And sustain in us the hope, for we dare not ask for more,
That the human spirit, created in Your image, is,
like you, eternal . . .

The prayer suggested that humans should not presume that we deserve eternal life. Rather, we should focus on being our best here and now. Wasn't this our truest aim? To do the most good we could while we lived on earth? To leave a legacy like Janusz Korczak?

It was getting late, but I was losing myself in the aspirations of the prayers, so I kept reading. I was enamored of their simplicity and tone.

I could be a Jew, I thought, until I came to the meditations that reminded me that I could not be. I didn't have a Jewish mother. I didn't have a verifiable connection to one of the twelve tribes. "We look into each other's faces, and we know who we are," read one prayer. Suddenly I wondered, will they look into my face tomorrow at temple and know I am not one of them? Will my green eyes, pale skin, and fair hair give me away?

I felt further removed when I came to a haunting section of prayers and meditations on Jews who had been martyred throughout the ages, "hungry, harried, persecuted souls, who never had a choice . . . who had come to take another look at the stark terror of their savage death. Whose eyes all ask the ancient question: Why?"

I knew I didn't have the same connection to those brutal deaths that Jewish people had. They read those words thinking, that could have been me. They are the survivors. As such, they feel an obligation to carry on and to honor the memory of those who perished by preserving the Jewish traditions that they died upholding. They also seemed to carry the responsibility of the belief that they had a unique, exclusive relationship with God. "Without Jews there is no Jewish God," they would read at temple the following day. "If we leave this world the light will go out in Your tent." I wondered if there was room for me in that tent.

The next morning was beautiful and sunny, so my husband and I took our three children to the Bronx Zoo. As we approached the parking lot, I said, "We have to be home by two o'clock."

"Why?" my children whined.

"Because I am going to the Jewish Yom Kippur service with Mrs. Warner and Mrs. Idliby."

"I thought Jewish people didn't believe in God," said Thomas.

"You know they believe in God," I chided. "We share most of our Old Testament stories with them. And with the Muslims, too."

"Well, I don't believe in God," he challenged.

It wasn't the first time I had heard this from my seven-year-old son. He had repeated it throughout the summer when I had said bedtime prayers in the boys' room. I had addressed his disbelief from different angles, but never successfully convinced him of God's existence. So this time, I let his sister do the talking.

"Then who made the universe?" Anne asked him.

"Nobody. It was created in the Big Bang," he answered matter-of-factly.

"Well, what was before that?" Anne persisted.

"Nothing."

"Why are we here, then?" Anne asked, following a line of reasoning that I had also used.

"I don't know. We're just here. But God's not. Show me where he is," Thomas reasoned.

"He's in heaven," piped three-year-old Teddy from the last row of the minivan.

"There is no heaven," Thomas said. "There's just space."

"Well, you've never seen Pluto, but you believe it's there," Anne challenged.

"I've seen pictures of it," answered Thomas.

Teddy, clearly confused by this conversation, asserted, "Mom, God is Jesus, and Jesus is God. Right?"

"Yes, Teddy," I assured him, noting how his Sunday school teaching had already entered his reasoning.

"You can talk to me about Jesus because he lived on earth. But don't talk to me about God. He's not real because nobody ever saw him," Thomas insisted.

"Okay, Thomas, then let's talk about Jesus, who you agree lived on earth. He told us that God existed," I said. "And do you know that one of his apostles had the nickname Doubting Thomas because he doubted, like you?"

"No," Thomas said.

"After Jesus rose from the dead, he visited some of his apostles. But Thomas wasn't with them," I began. "When those apostles told Thomas that they had seen Jesus, he didn't believe them. 'I won't believe it until

I can put my fingers in the nail holes in his palms and touch the sword wound in his side,' he told them. Then a few days later Jesus appeared to the apostles again, and this time Thomas was with them. He approached Thomas and asked him to touch his hands and his side. Thomas did, and then he believed. And Jesus said to him, 'Thomas you see, and you believe. Blessed are those who cannot see, yet still believe.'"

"So you're Doubting Thomas," Anne teased.

"That's not why I told the story, Anne," I said. I didn't want the moniker to be used to malign my son the way the author of the Gospel of John may have used it to discredit the followers of the apostle Thomas. "Jesus said that to acknowledge how difficult it is to have faith in what you cannot see."

Thomas didn't say anything else about God, but I hoped that he had gotten my message that his disbelief was okay. I was certain that he would develop his own faith in his own time. And I knew that the quest was difficult. He seemed to be thinking about what I had told him. Though he may have been wondering what it would be like to put your fingers into someone else's bloody flesh wound.

Religion behind us for the moment, we made our way through the children's zoo. Still, God was the camel that kept poking its nose under the tent that day. When it was time for lunch, we walked to the café. David asked me what I would like, and I said "I'm fasting," a little embarrassed at my zeal.

He nodded, but Anne asked, "Mom, why aren't you eating lunch?"

"I'm fasting today for Yom Kippur," I answered.

Anne looked at me with concern, but Thomas laughed aloud. "Mom's a Jew today!" he exclaimed. David and Anne laughed, and I smiled along with them. What a change, I thought. Three years earlier I had hushed Thomas when he cried out, "There's our temple!" Now I was fasting and getting ready to spend an afternoon of prayer in a synagogue. I laughed at the irony.

Ranya:

As Yom Kippur approached, I busied myself with what seemed by now my approach to all new religious experience. While Suzanne delved into the prayer books Priscilla had given us, I researched the connection that Yom Kippur might have to Islamic tradition. I could already infer some meaning from the name of this Jewish holiday. Yom Kippur sounded close to "Yom Kabbir," which in Arabic means The Big Day. And I soon discovered that many Islamic scholars believe the Muslim day of Ashura, the tenth day of the first month of the Islamic calendar, corresponds to Yom Kippur and stems from Muhammad's practice of observing the Yom Kippur fast along with the Jews of Medina. Other scholars connected Ashura to the Jewish Passover, Abraham's birthday, and even Noah's deliverance from the great flood. Regardless, I liked the idea that Ashura could be viewed as a way to celebrate Islam's shared heritage with the Jews.

Having sorted out those details, I turned to the perennial female question of "what to wear?" This was especially relevant because Priscilla teasingly promised to parade me on Yom Kippur as her "Muslim Palestinian friend." Priscilla's only advice was to dress modestly; it was after all a day of remembrance and atonement. I finally settled on a light blue suit. But minutes later I was out on the street doing some shopping and noticed that most of the dressed-up women, presumably headed to temple, were wearing somber colors. I called Suzanne to confirm our departure time and to spy on her choice of wardrobe. She confirmed my observation about the dark colors out on the street, but said she had also seen at least one woman in a camel suit. That settled it. I stayed in my light blue choice.

It's funny how nerves play themselves out. Here I was, a Palestinian Muslim going to her first temple service ("Why?" was my mother's curious response), and I was entirely focused on my outfit. When I finally met Suzanne in her lobby, she was clutching a beautiful bouquet of flowers and wearing a pretty beige suit. At three o'clock on the dot

Suzanne, still fasting, drove us to Priscilla's house, with me as copilot carrying the directions in my hands. Our faith club meetings were now taking place in the real world: first the French bistro, and now Priscilla's house and suburban Jewish synagogue.

As we pulled into Priscilla's driveway, I found myself looking forward to finally seeing her on her own turf. She had spoken of our common chandelier and I recognized it as soon as I walked into her house. What I had not anticipated was the whirlwind of creative energy, the layers of mementos, art, and photographs that spoke of a lifetime.

Priscilla had hoped that the Yom Kippur service would help me with my "death issues." We had yet to go to temple and I already had a new appreciation for Priscilla's sensibilities about life and death when I saw her home. Where I strove to impose order and to control the clutter that can accumulate in a small New York apartment, Priscilla's home bore testimony to the rich continuum of life. There was art everywhere, photographs and paintings that suggested stories of friendships, travels, and experiences beyond their brushstrokes and compositions. Jim even had a Japanese plastic food art collection that had a home in the kitchen, mingling happily with cookbooks and car keys.

Priscilla had referred to her mother as an artist, but Suzanne and I had never imagined just how impressive an artist she really was. Priscilla's basement was bursting with pieces of her mother's work, some haunting compositions with powerful images and messages. As we tried to take in this prolific body of work, Suzanne pulled one out. "Ranya!" she said, "this one's for you!" She had stumbled on a lithograph that said, "Children should be seen and not heard, not unlike the refugee from another shore."

Priscilla had hung a few of her own favorites of her mother's work upstairs in her home. But for the most part the art was not organized or catalogued in any formal way. Filling her basement, Priscilla's mother could still be as whole, lively, and as willful as she had been her entire life.

Suzanne and I continued to admire her mother's artwork, only to be startled by Priscilla's screaming, "Oh, my god! She ate the chocolate!" Priscilla's golden retriever looked up from the basement floor. Near her paw was the gold foil and paper packaging of one of Priscilla's dark chocolate candy bars.

To know Priscilla is to know about her relationship with chocolate. For Priscilla, chocolate is not to be mistaken with the drugstore Halloween variety. When I once offered her a mint-flavored chocolate bar that I favored, Priscilla dismissed it as having the wrong ratio of chocolate to mint. Over the previous three years I had not seen Priscilla without a chocolate bar on her physical person or without knowing one would be in her immediate future. If she didn't offer me some from her handbag, I could count on finding some sticking out of her coat pocket or tucked in a shopping bag. If all that failed, I didn't have to look beyond the backseat of her car. The point is, I was shocked that her dog had not discovered Priscilla's stash earlier.

"Bad girl! You ate the chocolate! Jimmy! Mickey ate the chocolate!" For a good minute or two, Priscilla berated the dog. Chocolate can kill a dog, so in the ensuing drama, Priscilla got on the phone with Poison Control and tried to calculate the ratio of dog weight to chocolate consumed. Suzanne and I watched the clock tick past the time that the Yom Kippur service was to begin. Finally Mickey was given the all clear, and fifty dollars later, the charge for her phone call, Priscilla was given the all clear, too. Suzanne, Priscilla, and I hurried out the door and made our way to temple.

The memorial service, Priscilla's favorite part of the service, had started, so we stood in the back of the room next to what appeared to be a memorial wall with niches inscribed with the dates of the deceased, and filled with piled stones. I had yet to ask Priscilla the significance of this Jewish tradition, and had not been aware of its existence in temple, but I loved the idea that those pebbles may have been piled on by friends and relatives who had known the deceased, as a way of symbolically confirming their memory. They were not headstones in a graveyard separate and apart, but occupied the same physical space as the living. The proximity and accessibility of that memory, combined with the emotions evoked by the beautiful imagery of the memorial service, soothed my own troubled soul, for that moment, at least.

Death seemed natural and acceptable. As natural as "the rising sun, and its going down," and as natural as "the blowing of the wind, of the opening of the buds, of the blueness of the sky, of the rustling of the leaves, and of the beginning of the year and its end," as the rabbi read in the service.

The second part of the Yom Kippur service was more about atonement, forgiveness, and peace. At this point the congregation was asked to forgive and forget all manner of angry disputes. Life, we were told, was too short to harbor ill will. Before the gates are closed, the rabbi pleaded, the congregation must repent. As I looked up to see the symbolic gates near the ark that held the Torahs in the middle of the temple hall, my eyes were drawn to the Israeli flag that was directly in my line of vision. The adjacent gates that were opened were slowly inching their way to closure. "Before the gates are closed," the rabbi kept saying, and I could not help but wonder whether atonement and forgiveness would ever be achieved between the Israelis and Palestinians, before it's too late, before the gates were closed. I felt sadness as I mourned the difference between the loftier ideals of our religions and the brutal reality of our human actions.

Priscilla:

I had been eager to share with Suzanne and Ranya my favorite Jewish service, the memorial service of Yom Kippur. "Jews do death well," I'd told them on more than one occasion.

"The music is so beautiful," I whispered to my friends as we entered the temple. "So mournful." The words of the memorial service were mournful, as well. I was proud to have my friends hear the eloquently written, comforting prayers that have never failed to move me: Suzanne and I both shared the experience of losing a loved one. Ranya and I shared our anxiety about death. I thought my two friends would find the service comforting and kept glancing at them as the rabbi read some of my favorite passages:

We remember with sorrow those who death has taken from our midst during the past year . . .

In the rising of the sun and in its going down, we remember them.

In the blowing of the wind and in the chill of winter we remember them.

In the opening of buds and in the rebirth of spring, we remember them.

In the blueness of the sky and in the warmth of summer, we remember them.

In the rustling of leaves and in the beauty of autumn, we remember them.

In the beginning of the year and when it ends, we remember them.

When we are weary and in need of strength, we remember them.

When we are lost and sick at heart, we remember them.

When we have joys we yearn to share, we remember them.

So long as we live, they too shall live, for they are now a part of us, as we remember them.

I hoped Suzanne and Ranya understood the connection between these words and the thoughts I'd tried to convey to them about the Jewish outlook on death. I always thought of my father when I heard these words and wondered if Suzanne was thinking about her sister. I was moved and hoped my friends were moved.

But as happy as I was to have Suzanne and Ranya beside me, I also felt self-conscious about bringing a Muslim woman to a Jewish holy service. I had invited a Palestinian Muslim woman into our holy sanctuary.

And not all the words I heard at temple this time were comforting. Certain phrases jumped out at me. I'd noticed these words before, but now they appeared with more intensity:

At this hour of memorial we recall with grief all Your children who have perished through the cruelty of the oppressor, victims of demonic hate.

"Relax," I told myself. "Those words could apply to both Israeli and Palestinian victims, not to mention other victims of violence all over the world."

And then the concluding service began, and we read the following:

We turn to You once more to cry out our longing and the longing of all men and women for a beginning of that wholeness we call peace. Ever and again, we now admit, we have turned our backs on You, and on our sisters and brothers: forsaking Your Law, denying Your truth, ignoring Your will, defacing your beauty.

The intelligence You have implanted within us we have applied to the arts of war; with the skill we have from You we make engines of terror and pain.

We have prayed for peace, even as we laughed at truth; for blessing, but did not care to do Your will; for mercy, and we have shown none to others. We have prayed for impossible things: peace without justice, forgiveness without restitution, love without sacrifice.

I looked over at Ranya again and again as these words pierced my consciousness. I couldn't read the expression on her face. "We talk an awful lot about peace in this service," I thought. I wondered what Israelis felt when they heard these words. I wondered, specifically, what the most hard-line settlers thought, whether they even read words like these in the course of their services. All this talk about peace, on the holiest day of our year. I wondered if Ranya found these prayers hypocritical.

But Ranya is a peaceful, beautiful spirit, with a big heart and enormous dignity. When the service was over and all the congregants wished those around them a happy new year, I kissed Suzanne and Ranya and asked them point blank what they thought of the service. Suzanne loved the cantor's voice and the prayers she'd studied the night before. And Ranya? She smiled and said, "It was quite beautiful. Really. And so much talk about peace!"

We left the temple and headed over to my in-laws' house for a traditional meal to break the Yom Kippur fast. I was very excited to introduce Suzanne and Ranya to my extended family and did so immediately. A few people knew I had been engaged in an interfaith dialogue with my two friends, and they tried to sort out our triangle as they were introduced. "Are you the Muslim?" they asked Ranya.

Ranya took this in stride. "Yes, she's the Muslim," I said. And we all laughed. We sat down to eat, and Ranya and Suzanne began to ask questions about the service they had just attended, about "The Gates" that were closing on Yom Kippur.

"Those are the Gates of Life," I told them. "We're at the threshold of our own mortality on Yom Kippur, praying for God to inscribe us in the Book of Life for one more year."

"They're the Gates of Repentance," Jimmy weighed in. "That's what our prayer book is called: The Gates of Repentance."

Ranya:

As we sat down to enjoy a traditional Yom Kippur meal of smoked fish, herring, and bagels, Priscilla's mother-in-law introduced us to an older gentleman who wore a blazer with an emblem of the Tennis Club of Israel. As Suzanne, Priscilla, and I described to him our interfaith effort, he looked at me and gave me what would seem to many a compliment of the highest order. He said that he was happy to be with such a moderate Muslim and that he wished he could clone me.

Again, as I had on other occasions in other religious and political discussions, I felt that this compliment may have revealed more about this man's underlying prejudice and assumptions than about my genuine assets. It unwittingly betrayed his perception of me as a unique or rare Muslim specimen. As a Muslim, I was an exception to the religious norm.

My fears were confirmed as our discussion moved to the latest violence in Chechnya. A cold had settled in my head, and I was feeling rather tired and frankly inarticulate. This gentleman continued to develop his arguments about the violence in Islam, finishing off with, "Not every Muslim is a terrorist, but every terrorist is a Muslim." (I later found out that that dictum was formulated by a Muslim journalist who was doing some serious soul-searching.)

I could almost touch Priscilla's mounting tension as she leaned over and whispered complaints about her stiffening neck. I recognized in Suzanne's straightened posture that she wanted to come to my defense. I was only too happy to let her. I sat back as Suzanne and Priscilla argued on my behalf and on behalf of Islam, giving it their best shots. Finally I stepped in and asked "Can you think of other religions which may have been used toward violent ends?"

Soon this man responded with his own political question for us: "Can you think of any state that has not determined its final borders without the use of force?" This question was supposed to explain Israel's natural and legitimate use of force in the final confirmation of its expanded territorial boundaries. The cynicism of the moment was only heightened by my memory of the time spent hearing all the talk of peace at temple just hours earlier. I had lately been reading about Palestinians who argue that the conflict between the Palestinians and the Israelis should no longer be about independent Palestinian statehood but about equal citizenship and demographics. I now proposed that Israel may have to consider this within its expanded territorial boundaries, where Palestinians would soon outnumber Jews. This idea brought our conversation to a close.

Priscilla:

I was nervous and very protective of Ranya when our conversation grew political. I knew that my mother-in-law's friend was a good man, a committed philanthropist, and a thoughtful, intelligent individual. But I still sat on the edge of my chair, worried that an argument would break out, that Ranya would be upset.

But Ranya handled the whole situation with her usual grace and intelligence, talking calmly and politely. I, on the other hand, grew more and more tense with every verbal exchange. I listened carefully to every word Ranya and this man spoke. And I could sense that Suzanne felt the same urge to protect our dear friend as I did.

Suzanne stepped into the conversation sensitively, and I began to hear some of the same words and phrases the three of us had used in our sheltered little faith group now coming out in the open. We had discussed the fact that fundamentalist groups were unrepresentative of religions on the whole over and over again. We stood side by side on the issues, and side by side at this table.

Our conversation came to an end, and I was exhausted. Suzanne and Ranya left to drive back to New York, and I didn't sleep well that night, maybe because I had fasted. Or maybe it was the fact that Suzanne, Ranya, and I, after countless private, intimate conversations, confrontations, and rapprochements, were finally exposing ourselves to the outside world, together, as a group. I'd talked about my relationship with them with a few friends, but now the three of us were beginning to leave the safe haven of our Faith Club. We'd ventured out into the world, where opinions could be harsh. Where we could be judged, criticized, questioned, and hurt.

At least the three of us had a very tight bond, I realized. Things could get tough once we left the comfort and safety of our "Faith Club." And our Faith Club was such a sacred place to me now.

As I reflected on this days later, however, I realized that my favorite moment with Ranya and Suzanne had taken place not in a house of worship, but in a chain drugstore in a small strip mall near my house.

There, on Yom Kippur, the holiest day of the Jewish year, Ranya and Suzanne became my friends. Not my coauthors, not "the Christian woman I'm writing with," or "my Muslim coauthor," but my buddies.

I was so happy they'd come to my home to meet my family. "I want you to see how huge my sons' basketball shoes are!" I'd told them. Suzanne and Ranya's children are still little people; mine are young men. With big feet.

They'd seen the shoes, they'd toured my house, we'd almost poisoned my beloved dog, and we'd attended Yom Kippur services. We'd left my in-laws' house, and they were headed home. Ranya had a sinus infection and wanted to stop at a drugstore to get some throat lozenges.

"I'm in heaven! I'm a drugstore junkie!" Ranya exclaimed as we walked into the enormous, brightly lit drug superstore. Manhattan drugstores are smaller due to rent costs. She ooohed and ahhed at the size of the place, the width of the aisles.

Suzanne and I accompanied her as she picked up her meds. Then we stood in line waiting to pay at the cash register.

"I am so glad you guys are here!" I said happily. I threw my arms around Ranya and gave her a big kiss on the cheek. "Thank you for coming!" I told her. "I'm having a great time," she said, laughing.

I turned to Suzanne. "And thank you for coming!" I said. I gave her a big hug and a kiss. My dear "Waspy, reserved friend." Suzanne beamed at my emotional outburst.

We were all so happy. We were all so on the same page, in the same place, at the same time. We were in this together. In this project together, but, more importantly, in this world together. At this time and place, in this moment.

We were friends.

"How was Yom Kippur?" my husband asked when I got home that evening.

"It was lovely," I said. "Some of it felt very familiar. There were prayers of praise and thanks to God that would fit easily in a Christian service. But the tone was different from the prayers we're used to. The emphasis was on the mightiness of God and the flaws of humanity. One prayer called humans broken urns, dust, and dreams soon forgotten."

"Sounds depressing," my husband said.

"Well, yes. But there is an appealing humility in it."

"How?"

"In the Jewish prayers I hear the voice of a child praising his parent and hoping to earn his love and forgiveness. However, the child's not sure if he deserves that love. So, if he gets it, he will be doubly grateful. On the other hand, Christians can sound like spoiled children. We start out assuming God loves us and will forgive us and that eternal life has already been won for us by the death of Jesus Christ. If I had to choose, I would prefer the first child. He's less arrogant."

"I see what you mean."

"It's like the Jewish approach to heaven. Many Jews don't presume there's eternal life. They believe God is eternal. But they are unsure about eternity for the rest of us."

"Sounds rational."

"I agree."

"So how can you maintain your own faith if you agree with the Jews?" my husband asked.

This was the rub. With my religious belief expanding to include Judaism and Islam, I was still struggling with what Christian truth to hold onto.

"I still believe in Christianity," I said. "I believe Jesus was someone extraordinary and extraordinarily connected to God. I have faith in the truth of his message of love and compassion. In my own way I strive to follow his example. I'd like to believe that Jesus rose from the dead, but I can't prove it. I recognize that I may be wrong. At the same time I recognize that what I know to be true—that we should worship God and live by the Golden Rule—is also preached by other religions.

"Who's to say that God isn't revealing himself in many ways to many people who fit their epiphanies into their own cultural experiences? How can I judge which is right? Might they all be different paths to the same end?"

"They might be," David agreed.

"I've started thinking about religion like college degrees. One person might earn a BA in literature while another earns one in history. They're equally educated, though differently educated. The real test is how they apply that knowledge in their lives."

CHAPTER FIFTEEN
Happy Holidays

Ranya:

My parents moved to McLean, Virginia, in 1982, the year I started college. That December I came home from school to discover a Christmas tree center stage in our living room. I was not sure what to make of it. As a child in Dubai, I had hung a Christmas stocking from my bedpost each year, and it was filled with Santa chocolates and other treats. We traditionally spent Christmas Eve with my parents' closest friends, a Palestinian Christian family whose tree we had always admired. But our McLean tree felt different. It was in *our* home, and it was in America, a country where I was part of a religious minority. In Dubai, as part of the Muslim majority I could unself-consciously embrace some Christmas traditions, but as a minority in the States I was unsure yet of the boundaries of what would feel acceptable to me and to others. So my mother's Christmas tree made me feel a little uncomfortable as she put it up year after year.

It's been more than twenty years since I first confronted that Christmas tree in my living room, but now that I can appreciate the interfaith strength of Islam, my mother's beautiful traditional Christmas tree with its crystal ornaments no longer seems a hollow decorative gesture. If Christmas is a holiday that celebrates the birth of Jesus, as a Muslim I see no religious contradiction in doing just that. Even the possibility of a menorah in my home doesn't seem so far-fetched. The Jewish-Muslim conflict is political and not religious.

At a lunch with my son's new kindergarten friend and his mother, Taymor asked in between pizza bites if we celebrate Rosh Hashanah. He had overheard his friend's mother talk about the preparations she was busy making. Without missing a beat, I launched into what has by now become my standard response: "As Muslims we have other holiday traditions, but there's no reason we cannot participate in some Jewish and Christian holiday traditions, since Muslims believe in Moses and Jesus and in the Torah and the Gospels." I then looked self-consciously at my new "mother" friend and wondered how "off the wall" I sounded to her. Still, my response seemed to go down well with Taymor.

A recent conversation I had had with an Israeli Arab friend helped me understand why my mother may not have been as inhibited as I when it came to our McLean Christmas tree. This friend of mine, a Muslim who now lives in New York, grew up in Nazareth, where there were nativity scenes everywhere at Christmastime. In the United States she is surprised by their absence and their replacement with colorful, wrapped gift boxes. At home at Christmas she often attended midnight mass in Bethlehem with Christian friends, just as Palestinian Christians sometimes joined Muslims in their Ramadan fast, especially when they knew they would be sharing an elaborate evening meal in a Muslim home. This is the way my mother grew up in Palestine as well, and it explains why I often heard her asking

Christian friends to light a candle for her in church during stressful times.

Even in Dubai, the culture is less self-conscious in embracing multiple religions than we are in the United States. When my family lived there we sent and received holiday cards that wished Merry Christmas and Happy Eid in the same breath. Yet when Sami and I decided to send our own family holiday card in the States, I was plagued with doubt about how the cards would be judged by others. I stuck to simple messages like Happy New Year.

My children are able to enjoy the interfaith approach to the holiday season with my family in Dubai on our annual trip in December, where shopping malls display elaborate Christmas decorations, and my children have an abundance of Santa laps to sit upon while sharing their wish lists. This past December one of my favorite images was of a local woman in traditional black cloak and veil holding her infant dressed in Santa regalia as they waited in line to visit Santa. Experiences like this have helped my children realize that participating culturally in some Christian rituals carries no contradiction to being a Muslim. My daughter has worried that Santa might not make it all the way from the North Pole to the desert, where there is an extreme shortage of chimneys, but we have been able to allay her fears. Yes, Santa visits Dubai, and my children are becoming comfortable with that plurality in their lives. I saw it again this past holiday season when I received a card my daughter had made at school. It was decorated with three holiday symbols: a menorah, a Christmas tree, and the Muslim crescent and star.

My children are beginning to understand that God for our family is the God of all humanity and that as Muslims we differ from the majority in some religious traditions but not in moral ways. They have added religious practices they've observed in America to our own traditions. When they pray before a meal or at bedtime, I see them press their hands together in the Christian way as opposed to two palms up in the traditional Muslim manner. When I remind them of that, they giggle.

Not long ago, on a long family car ride to Vermont, I saw my son drop his cookie, pick it up, kiss it, then raise it to the sky before eating it. This reminded me of a Muslim tradition I had not seen since I was a little girl. For a split second I thought that my son carried this Muslim tradition genetically. "Where did you learn that?" I asked him. And he told me that a Jewish friend taught him that if food gets dropped on the ground, it should be kissed, and then it's okay to eat.

I have slowly begun to tell my children about my Palestinian heritage and to share their grandparents' stories. Though we have not discussed the Palestinian-Jewish conflict, I have pointed out the beauty of the Al Aqsa dome in Jerusalem and spoken of the special role of Jerusalem as a holy city for the three religions. I have told my children that Jerusalem is part of what was once Palestine, a place where people of different religions lived together in peace.

Suzanne:

I was walking with my aunt in New Hampshire before Christmas when she said to me, "I saw a news program that said they are taking the Christ out of Christmas in New York City. Is that true?"

I made a quick review of my own experiences that December. Handel's *Messiah* was being sung all over town. Park Avenue had been closed to traffic for a carol sing. Building windows and lobbies were filled with Christmas trees. The angels blew their trumpets before the tree in Rockefeller Center, and Radio City's Christmas Spectacular still concluded with a live manger scene. I answered that Christmas was alive and well in New York City. "You're not going to find a crèche in the window of Saks Fifth Avenue," I said. "But it doesn't belong there anyway."

It was true that if you stood on Madison Avenue looking up and down the street you wouldn't get the religious message of Christmas. Retailers had stripped the Christ out of Christmas long ago. But rather than resent the commercialism, perhaps we could recognize it as a way to include others who might feel excluded from this national holiday. After all, it's no threat to a Christian's identity if a Jew, a Muslim, a Hindu, or an atheist decorates a tree, hangs stockings, has a visit from Santa Claus, or even celebrates the birth of Jesus.

I loved it when I visited Ranya's home in December and found a stuffed Santa Claus offering Christmas chocolates on a table near the front door. Inside her home a plaid reindeer, silver pinecones, and a bowl of sparkling ornaments added Christmas cheer to the living room. Ranya was not isolating herself or her family, and she wasn't blaming me or other Christians for not celebrating Eid. "In Dubai, we all say Merry Christmas to each other!" she laughed.

Here, however, we struggle with what to say. At least we do in New York City. When I first received holiday cards from Jewish friends, I was caught by surprise. What should I send in return? My card said "Merry Christmas." Would Jewish people be offended by it? I resented being forced to compromise my tradition for their benefit. So I stuck with Merry Christmas for a few years, out of stubbornness. But as I began sending cards to more Jewish friends, I changed my message to Joy to the World. The words offer universal, and innocuous, good cheer, yet they are also those spoken by the angel announcing Jesus' birth to the shepherds outside Bethlehem. On many cards I handwrote the words Merry Christmas.

As I struggled that winter with my Christmas card greeting, I asked Priscilla and Ranya their opinions. "I think you should write something wonderful about Jesus," Priscilla said enthusiastically.

"You know *I* wouldn't be offended," added Ranya. But what about the other non-Christians on my list? I'm torn between sharing the joy I feel at Christmas and being considered insensitive or too religious. I think people who live in cities that are less diverse don't have this dilemma because every card I get from outside the New York City area seems to have mangers, angels, crèches, or Bible quotes. I've considered printing two cards, one Christian and one secular, but somehow that seems dishonest.

That year I was running late with my cards. Luckily I had a good fall photo of Anne, Thomas, and Teddy sitting side by side on the edge of the fountain at Lincoln Center. I cut a green border for the photo and hurried to the printer. It was only four days until the holiday break began. In my haste, I reverted to my standby message: "Joy to the World!" But it fit. Those three smiling faces on the front of that card— a beautifully poised, nine-year-old girl with chestnut eyes, a mischievous seven-year-old athlete clutching a Hacky Sack, and a funny, blond three-year-old with a big grin—were my greatest joy in the world, and I wished my friends and family the treasure of such joy in their own lives.

Priscilla:

Christmas was still a ways off, but already our strip malls were bathed in twinkling lights. The supersized mall was packed with post-Thanksgiving shoppers, but I'd braved the crowds with my sons and we'd had a lovely outing. I was driving my minivan home, checking out our industrious neighbors' Christmas decorations.

My son Jack doesn't complain anymore about all the fuss Christians make about Christmas. He's a big boy now, well accustomed to the role Jews in America play at Christmas. He's flying under the radar quite nicely, thank you.

And I, of course, am quite comfortable with Jesus, my "new friend," as I sometimes refer to him in the confines of my Faith Club. Still, I had never really had a conversation about Jesus with my sons. Not a real conversation. Not a post--Faith Club conversation.

So I started one. The best time to talk to teenage boys is when they're trapped in your minivan. So, driving my Windstar past The Gap and McDonald's, I proceeded to talk to my children about the life of Jesus Christ.

They knew very little about Jesus. They knew that I'd been meeting regularly with Suzanne and Ranya, talking about religion, talking about faith. They knew that we'd been working on a children's book about Jesus, Muhammad, and Moses.

And they knew Christmas was Jesus' birthday, that people were eagerly anticipating it. So, as we passed houses already decorated with lit-up reindeer, Santas, angels, and snowmen, we talked about Jesus, the man who had started all this. Here are the kinds of questions my sons asked me, which I answered to the best of my ability:

"Who wanted to kill Jesus?"

"Why did they want to kill Jesus?"

"Why did Judas betray Jesus?"

"What did Jesus preach that made him so controversial?"

"What was the Last Supper?"

"Did Jesus really exist?"

In that car ride, my children learned what I had learned over the previous two years. They learned that the Gospels interpreted the crucifixion in different ways and that people have interpreted the life and meaning of Jesus very differently over the past twenty centuries. They asked simple, direct questions. They were totally engaged. My older son even put down his cell phone and stopped text messaging his girlfriend for a few minutes.

Now, I figured, they were up to speed. They'd learned some of what I'd learned over the last three years. And over the course of their lives, when they meet their own Suzannes and Ranyas, my two sons will have plenty to talk about.

CHAPTER SIXTEEN
Facing Our Communities

PRISCILLA: *I feel a little isolated sometimes when I talk to people who haven't been through this experience.*

RANYA: *With your husband, you're busy running a household, getting on with the job of being a wife and mother. By the time eight o'clock rolls around, I don't want to have these kinds of conversations.*

PRISCILLA: *This relationship is like a life raft for me.*

SUZANNE: *Maybe we've each built our own life raft, and now we've strung them together.*

Ranya:

A friend who moved his American Muslim family to Switzerland after 9/11 comes to New York on regular business trips. When he does, we always go out to dinner and try to catch up. One of his visits happened after I'd had a long week, and I was more than ready to savor the piping hot Chinese dumplings we'd just been served and to ease into my Friday evening mode. We shared news of our children, their latest anecdotes, challenges, and concerns. He then politely asked about my faith club. I explained to him briefly about my growth as a Muslim, and he dismissively responded, "But you are not a Muslim! Islam is a way of life. It is different than other religions because it regulates both the private and the public. It has a lot to say about everything." I let his comments go, unwilling to turn a pleasant dinner into a lecture.

Why, I wondered later, do Muslims accept that Islam is different from other faith traditions because it regulates both private and public affairs? Last I checked, the Catholic Church and others had quite a bit to say about abortion and birth control. And some Jewish traditions have a lot to say about the way marriage is consummated and how food is consumed or a kitchen maintained. Unfortunately, most Muslims' understanding of their religion is often more influenced by myth, cultural traditions, and hearsay than it is from their own reading of the Quran. The majority of Muslims would greatly appreciate and benefit from a more diverse and flexible approach to Islam but are not supported by formal institutions, mosques, or imams. So most end up being hostage to those louder, literalist voices barked at them from some minarets, despite the fact that the Quran says,

> *You shall not accept any information, unless you verify it yourself. I have given you the hearing, the eyesight, and the brain, and you are responsible for using them. (17:36)*

> *He [God] has sent down to you [Muhammad] this book which contains some verses that are categorical and basic to the book and others equivocal. But those who are twisted of mind look for verses equivocal seeking deviation and giving them interpretations of their own but none knows their meaning except God. (3: 7)*

Although sermons are conducted in all languages and the Quran is translated, Muslims are still required to recite Quranic verses in Arabic. Because more than a generation has now grown up with Wahabist-influenced imams short on enlightened literacy and long on literal recitations, they would rather focus on teaching their students rote recitation over open discussion in which the Quran is studied in its proper historical context.

Only a few weeks after that dinner with friends, I was challenged again. Nagging doubts about the validity of my claim to be a Muslim seeped back into my life. This time it was a kindergartner who set the agenda. Her mother told me that since her daughter had started school, she was fascinated with one of her new teachers, a Muslim woman who covered her hair and wore a headscarf. This teacher explained to her students that she covered her hair so that she would not be attractive to men other than her husband. My friend's daughter, who had been with my son at nursery school, wanted to know why Mrs. Idliby, who was also a Muslim, did not cover her hair.

I know I have my answer. I wonder if this teacher has hers. Perhaps, if God sent down the verse that explains that we were created of different tribes and creeds as a test for our humanity, there is room for testing our humanity within the same religion. Had this teacher represented her choice as just one of many options for Muslim women, or was she claiming it as the only true Muslim choice?

Suzanne:

I was delighted to discover that my church was hosting a lecture and discussion titled "Islam: Myths and Realities." I immediately marked the date on my calendar and invited Ranya and Priscilla to attend. I was curious to learn from the guest speaker, Dr. Azza Karam, a political scientist at the United Nations, former director of the World Conference of Religions for Peace and editor of *Transnational Political Islam: Religion, Ideology and Power.*

Though Priscilla was unable to attend the lecture, Ranya accepted my invitation, and on the scheduled evening I walked to church expecting to meet her outside the front door of St. James'. But, as I turned the corner at Seventy-second Street and Madison Avenue, I saw Ranya striding purposefully up the church steps and disappearing through the arches. Gone was the self-conscious Ranya who had nervously sneaked into her neighborhood church to examine the stained-glass windows years ago. Here was a woman confident of her place in a religious institution.

I hurried to catch up with Ranya, and we made our way together to the church meeting room, where a buffet of Middle Eastern food had been laid out. The dishes were institutional cousins of the delicious home-made fatayer (spinach pies), balila (chick peas), and maklouba (a meat and eggplant pilaf) Ranya had served me and Priscilla over the years.

By chance Ranya and I were seated at the table with Dr. Karam. Ranya and Dr. Karam quickly discovered that she knew Ranya's aunt through Religions for Peace. Aha, I thought. Here's a member of that liberal, Western Islamic community that Ranya has been craving. Craig Townsend, the priest who had helped me through my recent faith crisis, was the host at our table.

After everyone had gathered, Dr. Karam stepped to the front of the room and introduced herself. Then she began, "Tell me anything that pops into your head when you hear the word Islam." She turned toward the easel, snapped the top off her black marker and prepared to write down the words she heard.

"Anything," she encouraged her reticent audience.

Well, she didn't have to say it three times.

"Fundamentalism."

"Jihad."

"Beheading as a terror tactic."

"Oil."

"Polygamy."

Anti-Jewish, anti-Christian, anti-woman, and anti-alcohol quickly joined the list. Karam wrote without expression. Ranya wore a polite smile, while I felt embarrassed by what these phrases suggested about the views of my fellow parishioners. Yet I knew how recently my own understanding of Islam had been the same. Now, like me, these people had come to be educated. Karam's list was their jumping-off point.

Craig must have also grown sensitive to the stack of negative words on Karam's easel paper. "People of the Book," he called out. Then a few others added Muhammad, the Quran, the Five Pillars, and calligraphy.

Dr. Karam pointed to these last five items and said, "These are related to the religion of Islam." Then she gestured toward everything else on the long list and said, "These are not." She put the cap on her marker and proceeded to tell us quickly and eloquently about the life of Muhammad, the Quran, the essential beliefs of Islam, and the differences between political and religious Islam. It was a fairly complex primer. And, I was glad to discover, it was a primer I already knew.

As Dr. Karam joined us again at our table, we began talking about how Muslims judge their fellow believers. "I sometimes worry that other Muslims believe I am not Muslim enough," Ranya confided.

In response Craig offered Ranya some sympathetic words. "When I first joined this church a few parishioners complained to our rector, my boss, that I wasn't Christian enough," he said candidly. Indeed, I had heard at least one parishioner criticize Craig's approach to the Bible, which was more allegorical than literal. He looked for metaphor, symbolic meaning, and historical context. But I don't think Craig judged his critics, and he only shared this information with us now in order to assure Ranya that every religion has its doctrinaires who pass judgment on the worthiness of the rest of us to participate in the community. Those judgments, however, shouldn't drive us away.

Craig's revelation gave me confidence as I returned to my role as an educator of children at our church. I had worried about whether it was still appropriate for me to teach Christianity to first graders. How could I do it while remaining truthful to myself and my interest in furthering interfaith understanding? If parents understood my evolving theology would they yank their children from my class and whisper about my heretical views? Someone had so judged Craig. But the effort to undermine him had been unsuccessful. Craig was still here. I hoped that I could gain confidence from his experience and from the interest other parishioners had expressed in my project as I took my interfaith message into my church and my life.

Priscilla:

My relationship with Israel started with trees. At the Hebrew day school, along with my third grade class, I diligently collected coins and placed them in slots on a piece of cardboard with Hebrew writing until every slot was filled and a grownup mailed the money off to Israel. Shortly thereafter, I received an official certificate in the mail, telling me that trees had been planted in Israel in my name. When I went there with my family in sixth grade, I wondered where my trees were planted, but we never did track them down. I hope they're thriving.

Last week I read about a grove of olive trees that was not so lucky. The controversial "fence" in Israel had sliced through olive groves a Palestinian man had been tending for thirty-four years. As a result, an Israeli company on the other side of the barrier brought bulldozers in to uproot ancient olive trees, some of which had existed in the Holy Land for six hundred years.

Shortly after the olive trees were destroyed, Israeli tanks, responding to mortar fire in the northern Gaza Strip, accidentally killed seven Palestinian youths, aged eleven to seventeen, who were harvesting strawberries in a field nearby. The Palestinian Center for Human Rights said it had investigated the shooting and found that "all victims of the attack were children working on their agricultural land."

The other day, I spoke to Suzanne about what had turned terribly wrong in the olive groves and strawberry fields of the Holy Land. I'd spent a lot of time talking about Israel with Ranya, about the centuries-old conflict between Jews and Arabs, between her people and my people.

Now the subject resurfaced between Suzanne and me. I spoke to her of my confusion, disillusionment, and concern for Israel, and she had questions for me.

"What exactly is the connection between American Jews and Israel?" she asked.

Of course Suzanne knew the historical and biblical answer to that question. It was the emotional tie she felt she still didn't quite understand.

"It's all about the Holocaust," I said. "And the persecution of Jews for centuries." We were back where we'd started, years earlier, when I explained to Suzanne and Ranya that being Jewish was "all about the Holocaust."

"So it's a safe haven from persecution?" Suzanne pressed me.

"Do you know about the boat?" I asked her. "The St. Louis?" I had seen the story of this boat at the Holocaust Museum in Washington, DC. Suzanne had heard of the St. Louis and asked for details. "In 1939," I said, "when thousands of Jews were desperate to flee Nazi Germany, about nine hundred of them managed to board a boat in Hamburg. All passengers held landing certificates they presumed would allow them to enter Cuba, but they were refused entry. The ship then sailed to Miami, where it was not allowed to dock. The captain pleaded for help, but U.S. Coast Guard boats patrolled the waters to make sure that no one jumped overboard and swam to freedom. The United States turned starving, desperate Jews away, and then millions of Jews were annihilated."

I continued. "Jews from all over the world hear that story and they identify with it. They can imagine themselves standing on the bow of that boat, terrified, desperate, their families and homes in ruins. And they wonder who would take them in. What country would have them? What people would welcome them?" I paused. "And then they imagine the Holy Land, the Promised Land, the Land of Milk and Honey, and they feel . . . home. They see salvation on the horizon. Literally. They feel . . . safe."

"But Israel is hardly safe now," Suzanne pointed out.

"Exactly," I agreed. "And that's my problem with the Holy Land, with the Israel I naively thought would be planted with trees and tended by the Jews happily ever after." I shook my head. "All I can do is talk from my own experience, and my own story is that somehow, even after my years at the Hebrew Day School and my strong indoctrination into the Jewish faith through my father, I felt thirty-five years ago that occupying the West Bank and Gaza changed the magical story of the

Promised Land for me. My father was a big military history buff. I'm sure if he were alive, he would explain to me Israel's military rationale for holding onto that territory. But my father is not alive. And I think now, as I thought so many years ago, that Israel does not belong in the occupied territories."

I was close to tears. I had struggled for so long to come to terms with my feelings about Israel. For so many Jews it is black and white. Israel must exist. I agree that the Israel I dreamed about planting trees in and the Israel so many Jews dreamed about as a beacon for freedom should exist. But how? And under what circumstances? And with what kind of population?

"How do you see Israel?" Suzanne asked me.

"I'd like to see it the way Ranya described it to me," I replied. "The way her parents described it to her. I'd like to imagine it a land of milk and honey, a place where Christians, Jews, and Muslims live together in that one little sliver of holy land in peace, where Jerusalem is the holy city for all faiths. Where saplings are planted and ancient olive trees revered. Where children of all religions and backgrounds believe they have a future. Many people would call me a dreamer. But I don't want to live my life any other way. If I weren't an optimist, I would never have entered into my relationship with you and Ranya. So many other people would have seen the obstacles to real dialogue and stopped talking. But I need to live in a world where I believe good will prevail over evil, where people will eventually, somehow, put down their arms, and say 'Enough.'

"I can imagine other Jews shaking their heads when they hear this," I told Suzanne. "I can hear them saying 'She's so naive.' But I am not so naive. I know there are people out there right now plotting the annihilation of the Jews all over again. I know it was not all rosy and peaceful back when Ranya's parents lived in Palestine. I've read enough now to understand how deeply and tragically conflicts evolved between the Jews and the Arabs over time. But I need to have a dream, to believe that place can exist again. Imperfectly and improbably. And I believe that being a dreamer might in fact take more courage than being a cynic."

After this conversation, I continued to speak out.

I took a yoga class one day and a few people lingered afterwards, talking. A couple of them had just returned from a trip to Israel. "How was it?" I asked them. They raved about the beauty of the land, a place they felt a strong connection to as Jews.

"Israel's important to a lot of people," I said. "It's the Holy Land, after all, sacred to Jews, Muslims, and Christians." I could have stopped there. I was relaxed from my yoga practice, but well-trained by Ranya. "But then there's the issue of the Palestinians," I found myself saying. "I have a friend whose family lived there for seven hundred years. They had a very strong connection to that land also, but it ended in 1948."

My voice was rising. I was killing people's yoga buzz.

"It's a very complicated situation," I said as I folded up my mat. I didn't want to talk politics after our relaxing meditation, to possibly offend these perfectly nice people. But I left the room conflicted. I felt perhaps that I might have said more. Or that I might have said too much already. Either way, there is ultimately no way for me to escape talking honestly about Israel. Hadn't I learned, after all, to see the good alongside the bad, the bitter with the sweet? Could I hear people talk about how beautiful the land of Israel is without pointing out how difficult life is in the Palestinian refugee camps?

I will speak out when the time is right, I've decided. I no longer have a choice. I still speak as a Jew, but a Jew with a Palestinian friend.

CHAPTER SEVENTEEN
Awakenings

RANYA: *I think that just as people have book clubs, they should have faith clubs, exploring their belief systems. Sometimes it's better to talk about what may be offensive, or what seems to be offensive, or is assumed to be offensive, because in the end people are better off for it.*

PRISCILLA: *If you put your worst fears and prejudices and stereotypes out on the table—if you say "Here's what I always thought your religion was about," or "Is this what you believe?" or "This is what I'm afraid you think," and you work through those fears and thoughts honestly and openly, one by one, you come out on the other side spiritually alive and free.*

SUZANNE: *I would also say that when you're asked about your faith by people who have different beliefs, you're forced to examine your faith in a way you never did before. You reconsider your beliefs in a new context. You keep some, change some, and throw some out. And in the process, you take ownership of your religion.*

Ranya:

A friend once suggested to me that children should be required in school to study a religion that was not their own, a religion whose name they had randomly drawn out of a bowl filled with the names of all the religions practiced in the world. I would go a step further to suggest that we all attend services at different houses of worship, not just weddings and funerals, but ordinary services in which those of different faiths aren't expected to be present.

When I first met Suzanne and Priscilla, I told them I suffered from temple and church envy. Now that I have shared important religious services with them at temple and church, my envy has dissipated. In its place I feel an appreciation for the opportunity I've had to experience through Jewish and Christian services the universal truths that connect our humanity even while the plurality of religious traditions and nuances of our faith set us apart.

As a Muslim, I am called upon to believe that the diversity in human faith traditions is intended by God's design and not a random occurrence. The universality of God and his accessibility to all is emphasized in the Muslim understanding that all religions have sprung from the same divine source and that God's message was sent to all people and cultures of all nations (35:25). Different communities are united in their devotion to God, yet what sets them apart is their good work, not the merit of one faith tradition over another.

Had God pleased, He could have made you one community. But it is His wish to prove you by that which he has bestowed upon you— vie with each other in good. (5:48)

O Humankind WE (GOD) have created you male and female, and made you in communities and tribes, so that you may know one another. Surely the noblest amongst you in the sight of God is the most God fearing of you. God is All-knowing and All-Aware. (49:13)

I was relieved to find support in the Quran for this fundamental belief of mine. I suspect the possibility of such a universal God is available to all faith traditions. I was surprised and humbled to find affirmation through a sermon of Gandhi's, to which a friend introduced me.

This friend, a Christian-born mother married to a Jewish man, is bringing up her children within the Jewish faith, even though she and her husband did not feel the need for her to convert. She told me that even mundane daily experiences can become challenging interfaith moments. In those moments, she has found inspiration in a small book, so dear to her that she keeps it hidden in her personal dresser drawer. The book is *The Message of Jesus Christ,* a collection of Gandhi's writings about his own interfaith journey in search of the true light.

Once I started reading this book, I could not stop. Gandhi's legacy and ideas were greatly influenced by the message of Jesus in the Sermon on the Mount. I felt humbled by the idea that such a great man had also examined other faiths. I rejoiced at how easily I could follow and identify with his conclusions and observations. Gandhi believed in the equality of all great religions of the world. He saw all religions as being true but imperfect, "inasmuch as they are presented through human agency and bear the impress of the imperfections and frailties of human beings."

As Gandhi studied Judaism, Islam, Christianity, and Zoroastrianism, he found, to his grief, contradictory interpretations of some texts. He rejected what he called orthodox Christianity in part because of its insistence that only Christians belong to the true faith. Gandhi confidently asserted, "If I have read the Bible correctly, I know many men who have never heard the name of Jesus Christ or who have even rejected the official interpretation of Christianity, who would, probably, if Jesus came in our midst today in the flesh, be owned by him more than many of us." Gandhi was convinced that Jesus' message in the Sermon on the Mount was meant for all humanity. Jesus, Gandhi believed, belonged to the world, to all races and people who strove to bring their own lives into harmony with Jesus' divine virtues.

Gandhi believed that religion is a personal matter between each person and his maker and advised the Christian missionaries who sometimes preached too aggressively to demonstrate Christianity by taking a lesson from the rose. "A rose does not need to preach. It simply spreads its fragrance. The fragrance is its own sermon." In my mind, this advice could be given equally to people of all religions. As Gandhi explained, the most effective way of preaching the Gospel (or Quran or Torah) is to live it in one's own life and thus let our lives speak to us even as the rose needs no speech but simply spreads its perfume.

I steeped myself in Gandhi and idealism. It was not long, though, before reality encroached, and I found myself challenged again.

Suzanne:

Far from being harshly judged, as I'd feared, the "new me" was welcomed into my Episcopal Church community. When I asked the head of the children's education programs for an opportunity for Ranya, Priscilla, and me to bring our interfaith message to the children of our parish, my offer was warmly received. Indeed it felt as if we had come full circle as we stood before the children of St. James' to talk about Judaism, Christianity, and Islam. We were spreading the message that had inspired us two years earlier.

Our first audience was our toughest: the teenagers. The group, primarily boys, looked bored and sleepy. (What else did we expect on Sunday morning?) A few maintained eye contact with us. But most looked off into space, or, even worse, closed their eyes altogether. When we finished speaking, we anxiously looked around the room. "Any questions?" One boy tentatively raised his hand off his knee. "Yes?" I asked, enormously grateful for a sign that someone was awake.

"In order for each of you to believe in your religion, don't you have to believe that the other two are wrong?" he asked.

So much for the easy questions. Here was the idea that I had been struggling with for months. Was there such a thing as separate but equal in religion? How could we all be right when we disagreed on seemingly big issues? I didn't have the answer, and I told him so.

"I can only tell you what has been helpful to me as I have grappled with this," I said. "I've thought about the quotes of Jesus saying things like, 'No one comes to the Father except through me.' This is something Christians might use to suggest that Christianity is the only path to God. But, what else could Jesus be saying?"

The boy shrugged, so I continued. "He couldn't be saying that the only way to avoid hell is to be a Christian because the Church was not established in his time. However, he could be saying that if you reject Jesus' example of living a life of compassion for your fellow man, then you are rejecting God. Of course, a holy life of love and compassion can be lived by any human of any faith. When Jesus talks about who will be in paradise, it is those who fed the hungry, clothed the poor, housed the homeless. He says, 'Whenever you do this for the least of my brethren, you do it for me.' In other words, our behavior is transformed by our recognition that God is in our fellow man, not necessarily the belief that Jesus is God.

"I'm sure you all know good people who aren't Christian," I said, looking hopefully around the room. A few kids nodded, but no one jumped to give an example. I suppose I was just being an obtuse adult stating the obvious.

"Even the disciple Peter, the rock upon which Jesus said he would build his church, is quoted in Acts saying, 'Truly I perceive that God shows no partiality, but in every nation anyone who fears him and does what is right is acceptable to him.'

"So that leads me to believe that a good Jew, a good Christian, and a good Muslim are all just as pleasing to God," I said.

The boy nodded. That seemed to be enough of an explanation.

A few days later, a friend brought me to a reading of the eighteenth-century play *Nathan the Wise*, whose main character had a beautiful answer to a question similar to the one I had addressed at St. James'. In the play, Nathan, a Jew living in Jerusalem during the Crusades of the twelfth century, is asked by the Muslim sultan which of three religions—Judaism, Christianity, and Islam—is best.

Too wise to answer directly, Nathan replies with a story about a beautiful ring that made its wearer "agreeable to God and human beings." For years, the ring remained in one family and was passed to each generation's favorite son. But then an heir appeared who loved his three sons equally. At various times he promised the ring to each of his sons. So as he neared his death he was in a bind. As a solution, he ordered a jeweler to make two exact copies of the ring, and he distributed the three indistinguishable rings to his sons.

After the father died, the sons quarreled about whose ring was the original. When they appealed to a judge, the judge reminded the sons of their father's equal love for them and that the father wouldn't treat two of them unfairly for the pleasure of the third. Remembering that the ring should make its wearer "agreeable to God and human beings," the judge ruled, "Let each of you strive to show the power of his ring's stone. Come to the aid of this power in gentleness, with heartfelt tolerance, in charity, with sincerest submission to God. And should the powers of the stone express themselves in your children's children's children, then let them come again before this bench. At that time, a wiser man than I will sit before them and rule."

The play was more than two hundred years old, yet its message resonated with modern significance.

Ranya:

One winter morning, one of the mothers in Taymor's kindergarten class graciously hosted a coffee in order for all the mothers to get to know each other a bit better. As several women filled their plates with food around the dining room table, the hostess asked us to introduce ourselves with an eye to giving a little family history and a few personal details. Both working and stay-at-home moms began weaving their individual family stories. The fact that her son had French grandparents explained why one mother gave her son French lessons. The two groups compared schedule details, and several spoke of careers and experiences that had taken them to foreign lands.

As I listened to my fellow moms, I became slightly anxious. I began to wonder. Should I, as I had in the past, keep things vague with these new people? I could say, as I did when Leia started kindergarten three years earlier, that our family was originally from the Middle East. That would keep things innocuous enough and place the reins in my hands until I desired to reveal more.

Or, I wondered, should I affirm my identity and not worry about stereotypes, proclaiming a pride and security in my heritage? Could I hand over the reins? I decided I could.

"I am of Palestinian heritage, and my husband is originally from Syria," I said quickly. "And when I am not busy being a mom, I keep myself occupied working on an interfaith project that involves a Jewish, a Christian, and a Muslim mom. I am the Muslim mother."

There, it was done. No more mystery or intrigue.

Still, I had stirred up interest in a few mothers who eventually made their way over to me to ask follow-up questions. "But you're not really bringing up Taymor to be a Muslim, are you?" one woman asked. "You must be a secular household." "Oh!" another woman said. "You go to Dubai once a year? But that's not really a religious Muslim country, is it? You don't have to cover up, do you?" I was a Muslim curiosity.

This was when I realized how changed I truly was. Three years ago, I may have confirmed the unreligious nature of our home, and I would have explained our secular ways. I would have praised Dubai as a fun tourist destination with an open, liberal society that was far removed from any religion, and where yes, you certainly did not have to cover up and where you could even enjoy a few drinks. The mothers' questions suggested an Islam of extremists and extreme political positions, of oppressed and abused women, terrorists, beheadings, and more. Three years ago I would not have had the knowledge and confidence to disagree with their image of Islam. But now I did.

"Yes," I said. "I am bringing Taymor up to be a Muslim, and we are a Muslim household. But perhaps your idea of Islam is not my definition of Islam." I took a deep breath and continued. "And yes, Dubai is a Muslim country in the sense that its rulers are Muslim and the majority of its citizens are Muslims. But it also has a diverse cultural community that embraces and celebrates many faith traditions, from Christmas to the Hindu celebration of Diwali. And no, I don't cover up when I go there."

One mother responded with a question I'd heard over and over again. "Why don't we hear more about Muslims like you?" This question is a very important one that I've sometimes heard framed in a more challenging or accusative tone: "Why don't the liberal Muslims go out in the streets and protest the actions of the extremists?" The underlying assumption is that there is something inherently flawed or violent within Islam. Or perhaps that the assumed silence implicates all Muslims. As a Muslim you are guilty by association unless you are seen as the exception, because either you are a secularist and not quite a Muslim or you're an exception, a rare specimen. I don't claim to have the answers, but I do have some thoughts on the matter.

There *are* Muslim voices protesting the violence committed in the name of Islam. The problem is that these voices aren't as sensational and therefore are deemed not as newsworthy as the violent stories out there. When I got home from my meeting, I did a quick search on the Internet, which produced evidence of some true soul-searching in the Muslim world and anguish at the beheadings, violence, and terror being committed in the name of Islam. I found an Internet online petition by the Council of American-Islamic Relations, "Not in the Name of Islam," that gathered 600,000 signatures of individuals and organizations worldwide seeking to disassociate Islam from the violence of a few. There were also articles on imams and Muslim institutions that were condemning the violence. The list included imams from the Middle Eastern countries of Saudi Arabia, Egypt, and Lebanon.

Though many people may wish for more effective voices, as I do, let us not forget that in many of these countries religion is often at the service of the government and its rulers who use it as an instrument to promote their legitimacy. Under such conditions it is taboo to question and challenge the state, its institutions, and mosques. To do so is nothing short of revolution. Religion reflects the nature and quality of its society, state, and government. It can only be as enlightened as the human hands it finds itself in, and it can only be as flexible, embracing, and pluralistic as its institutions. For us to find such a context in the Muslim world we unfortunately have to go back centuries, although there is evidence of it today in countries like Indonesia and Turkey.

PRISCILLA: *I used to dismiss people like you, Suzanne, who seemed to have such simple, straightforward faith. All I ever heard was "Jesus, Jesus, Jesus." But now I appreciate the complexity of how every person arrives at his faith.*

SUZANNE: *My belief system has continued to evolve as we've talked. I've definitely been challenged by our conversations.*

RANYA: *I think I was a doubter when we started talking because I didn't have a refined vision of my religion until now.*

PRISCILLA: *My doubt was purely emotional. . . . Where the hell is God? I need God! It doesn't seem like God's around!*

RANYA: *And I think it was easy for you to cast Suzanne as the believer because she was the one most immersed in the rituals and practice of her religion.*

PRISCILLA: *But now I appreciate how Suzanne lives her religion every day of her life, how it allays her fears because it's in her very make-up, in her heart.*

SUZANNE: *What's in my heart now is a priceless gift that I received from the tragedy of my sister's death.*

PRISCILLA: *Well, you passed that gift along to me.*

Priscilla:

I now realize, as Ranya pointed out to me, that on September 11th, the whole world was praying to the same God, the God I feared had disappeared. The people one hundred floors up in the World Trade Center, their families, the firemen, the policemen, the politicians, the volunteers, the world leaders were all praying to the same God.

Whatever you call prayer, wherever you do it, we're all doing it for the same reasons, toward the same end—to feel a connection, to fill a void, to feel whole and strong and somehow in control, even if we are surrendering that control to a higher authority in order to feel in control.

My friend Herb, whose parents survived the Holocaust while almost all of their family perished, worked just blocks from the Trade Center. As the Towers burned on 9/11, and people streamed uptown, Herb ushered ash-covered strangers into his office, offering them water and comfort. And then he returned to the street, he recalled to me later, and as the Towers collapsed, Herb recited the Kaddish, the Jewish mourner's prayer. He did so involuntarily, on behalf of anyone who needed such a prayer, regardless of where they came from and what religion they practiced.

Ranya is my first Muslim friend, but I feel as though we've lived our lives waiting to meet each other. It feels preordained, as does my relationship with Suzanne. They have taught me how to disagree and still stay the course, how to speak passionately and still listen, and, more importantly, hear others.

When I met my husband, we were both living in Boston. "How do you feel about New York?" he asked me early in our relationship. "I feel sorry for people who have to live there," I answered. But six months later, madly in love, I left my job, my apartment, and my friends to move with him to Manhattan. And I grew to love it, everything about it. I don't think it's an accident that Suzanne, Ranya, and I met and formed our Faith Club in New York. People talk about how tough it is to live here, how tough New Yorkers are. But everyone who lives in New York, I maintain, is a dreamer of one kind or another. And Ranya, Suzanne, and I are no exception.

I still worry for New York, the city I love too much to flee. Images of September 11th still haunt me, but I am beginning to feel like I am no longer too weak or frightened to claim the mantle of a real New Yorker. I can stand on a New York street and watch the dazzling parade of people from all nations hurry past me, marveling at the fact that New York City truly represents the world. And I can live in this world, because I'm finding the faith to do so.

Sometimes this new faith comes over me for no obvious reason. And maybe that's the sign of true faith, a feeling that pops up anywhere, that follows you everywhere. Even to my local pizzeria, I told Ranya and Suzanne.

I'd been writing for several days, reviewing my spiritual life over the last three years, when I took a break to pick up some dinner for my family. But first I stopped at a bookstore and purchased two books I'd been wanting to read about religion and God.

I'm out of the closet, I realized as I paid for them. I've found my religion.

My religion.

I'm one of the people I always wanted to be. Or at least I'm on the way to becoming one of the people I've always wanted to be.

I've met priests, ministers, and rabbis who I assumed had this feeling: inner peace.

I believe in God, I decided as I crossed the street and entered Sal's Pizzeria.

I believe that God is the goodness that exists inside each and every human being, every animal, every flower, and every miracle of God's creation. I believe that God is a force that binds us together, showing up in the moments when people make unexpected, magical connections with one another. God challenges us, I believe, to become our best selves, even in the toughest of times, when beauty and goodness seem to be mysteriously elusive, overshadowed by excruciating pain and evil.

I thought about God as I stood in line, watching a man lift my three Sicilian pizza slices, oozing with cheese, out of their pan and into my takeout box. I smelled the rich red tomato sauce, felt the warmth escaping from the oven in a way I never had before.

And tears filled my eyes when I walked out the door, clutching my pizza box.

Could it be? Could I possibly have found inner peace?

Surely this can't last forever, I thought immediately. I'll have trials and sorrows and enormous crises. And my heart will jump out of my chest once again, in panic. Or I'll take to my bed, terrified, frightened, depressed, or whatever.

But it will all be part of a whole—fear, joy, frustration, confusion, elation, control, loss of control, panic, calm, exhaustion, and exhilaration.

I will do my very best to enjoy my life. And I will always thank God that I was called to walk into the door of Ranya Idliby's apartment on a Wednesday morning in September, the day I began to search for my faith, the day I began to give up my doubts and fears, fears that had paralyzed me and chased me around whatever house I lived in for years.

RANYA: *The three of us are not the only ones who've been affected by our conversations. I think maybe this whole Faith Club experience has been a journey for our children as well. Certainly it's affected Leia and Taymor.*

PRISCILLA: *Absolutely!*

RANYA: *We have the answers to so many questions now. We have them as Jewish, Christian, and Muslim mothers. If your children come to you now with questions you know what to say.*

PRISCILLA: *Hopefully! It's pretty amazing that our Faith Club started with your daughter coming to you confused about which holiday you celebrate and now we're at a point where she's standing in front of a room making a presentation to her class about Islam.*

SUZANNE: *It's been an incredible journey. We've come full circle.*

Ranya:

I'd struggled in the past, second-guessing how my fellow Americans perceived me as an "atypical Muslim" or as a "cultural Muslim" as opposed to a true Muslim, but now my conversations with Priscilla and Suzanne had liberated me. I felt free: free not to worry about what others thought of me, good or bad, Muslim or not Muslim enough, free to define myself.

I became more of a believer because of what our three faiths have in common. That's what attracts me to religion, I realized. That sense that we are all one. It's all one life, one journey, and we're all in it together. That's what as a mother I hope to be able to give my children. And it was not long before Leia and Taymor needed me to do just that.

When my husband and I had our parent-teacher conference concerning Leia in the spring of 2004, we were shown a picture she had drawn as part of a project that allowed the girls to express their deepest vulnerabilities. The teacher had begun the sentence, "It's okay to be . . ." and the students finished the sentence and drew an accompanying picture. Leia wrote, "It's okay to be Muslim when everyone around me is Christian and Jewish." She then drew herself apart from two other girls holding hands.

My husband and I were caught off-guard by Leia's feelings. She had never expressed this concern to us before. Although I had done my best to contain her outsider status and promote a unified, universal image of God at home, it was no longer the home that counted most but her second home—her school and peers—where she was looking to affirm herself.

Even though our family has not prayed at a mosque, I had introduced my children to certain Muslim customs and rituals. I placed miniature Qurans in Leia's and Taymor's rooms, and when Leia was having a difficult time standing up for herself with one of her peers, I put the Quran in her backpack as a reminder that she did not have to please those who were unkind. The Quran reminded her to be strong and true to herself. It reminded her of her uniqueness and of the love of her family and of God. It reminded her that God's will was the only force she should submit to.

But I felt that it was time for Leia to take that identity out of her backpack and affirm it before her classmates. And now I had enough confidence in my own Muslim faith to sit down with her and plan a presentation that she could give to her class. The presentation took the form of ten questions, which Leia asked her classmates as she stood before them one morning.

"What is the name of my religion?" she asked. "What does Islam mean?" she continued as she shared the traditional Muslim greeting of "Peace be upon you." "What is the name of God for Muslims?" she probed and then explained how "Allah" is the word for God in Arabic, just like Dios is God in Spanish. "Do Muslim girls have to wear scarves? Do Muslims believe in Moses and Jesus? Are all Muslims Arabs? Where do Muslims pray? Do we believe in the Torah? Do we believe in the Bible? Does the Easter bunny visit me? How many Muslims are there in America? How many Muslims are there in the world?"

The afternoon following Leia's presentation, I could see in her bright eyes a great sense of pride as she affirmed her heritage and explained her beliefs to her peers. She had ownership of her religion. And no Muslim or non-Muslim was going to strip her of her newly empowered Muslim voice.

It was not long before Taymor would challenge my newfound confidence in his own way. It happened on a recent Monday afternoon at the end of his first day at a popular after-school sports program. "Mom," Taymor implored, "why did you pick such a difficult name for me?"

With a raised eyebrow and fearing the worst, that perhaps his school friends had teased him or laughed at his name, I worked on calming my voice and maintaining a casual, even tone as I asked him why he thought he had a difficult name.

"Well, today at my new sports program, the coach could not pronounce it and I had to keep repeating it to him," my son said.

Having feared the worst, I was quite relieved. I enthusiastically dismissed this coach's verbal incompetence to Taymor. "Some people have a hard time remembering things or names they have not heard before. Your name is not more difficult than some of the names of other boys in your class," I said, and I rattled off a list of four to five variations of names and nicknames. I wholeheartedly expected Taymor to move on, but never underestimate the memory and the mind of a six-year-old.

A few days later, as we were stepping out of a taxi that had brought us home, Taymor grabbed his backpack and ever so casually asked, "Why didn't you name me Jack?"

Since our last conversation had served to relieve me of the fear that he was being teased about his name, this time around I saw the humor in it, and decided to test Taymor's conviction, "Do you really like the name Jack?" I asked. "Do you want to be called Jack Idliby from now on?"

I had taken a gamble, and without missing a beat Taymor mischievously looked me in the eyes and said, "Yes." He had called me on my gamble and defied me to continue.

As we walked into the building I took him up on the challenge as I playfully reintroduced Taymor to our doorman. "Irving, I would like you to meet Jack Idliby," I said.

"Yes," Taymor sheepishly followed, "call me Jack."

My husband and I shared a few giggles over the incident that evening after we had put the children to bed. Never did we imagine what the results of one more week of thinking would produce in our son.

As we sat around our kitchen table a week later, Taymor caught our family off guard. He had not referred to himself as Jack, nor had he lodged any new complaints about his name. So when he complained about being nervous at the thought of moving on to "Big Boy" grades at school, the last thing that came to my mind was his name. I thought that he was nervous about getting older and more responsible.

"Why are you nervous?" I encouraged him to share his fears.

"When you are a big boy at my school, you sometimes carry the flag at assembly, and they announce your name. How can I carry the flag when they say my name and everyone hears it's Taymor?"

Needless to say, I tried to maintain my composure as I asked, "Has anyone told you that you are not American?" Had Taymor really made a far-fetched association between his name, the flag, and his Americanism, or was this just another episode in which the simple discomfort about the foreignness of his name was playing itself out?

"I would rather be called Jack," he concluded.

At this point I was getting frustrated at his insistence and confused and worried about any underlying significance.

"Why Jack?" I pleaded.

"Oh, it doesn't have to be Jack. It can be Michael, or Peter, or John," he reassured me.

"Ahah!" exclaimed his sister, who shocked me with her perceptiveness. "You just want a *Christian* name!"

We all laughed as I shared with my family a story from my childhood that came back to me as a result of our conversation. I had not spoken a word of English up to the age of eight. When we moved to Dubai, the best available school was the English School. So my brother and I diligently learned our English in a three-month crash course. Whenever we were given forms by our new British teachers I was always puzzled when I came to the box that required I write my "Christian name." Did I have one? I was finally reassured by a teacher that my Christian name was simply my first name. It was not until years later that I understood the irony.

CHAPTER EIGHTEEN
Faltering Faith

SUZANNE: *Priscilla, I was moved and intellectually challenged by your ability to believe in a God without the expectation of heaven—to me they've always come hand in hand.*

PRISCILLA: *Well, it's taken me fifty years to deal with that!*

SUZANNE: *I know! But they've always come hand in hand for me. So it's moving to see your acceptance and ability to find joy in life and to be grateful for it and to savor it and say thank you, God. God is in this flower, in my sons, in all these amazing things, and whatever happens afterward, I'm grateful for what I have right now. That is such a mature and strong idea, so I thought it was huge and challenging.*

RANYA: *It's something my religion has inspired me to do as well . . . to find the beauty in the world around me . . .*

PRISCILLA: *It can be tough sometimes. Let me tell you. It can be tough.*

Priscilla:

I started faltering again. My faith, apparently, was not as strong as I'd hoped. At least my faith in myself was not so strong. And neither was my body.

I'd started taking blood pressure medicine and one of the side effects was heart palpitations. I suffered a massive panic attack one night in bed while I was reading. I'd had anxiety over the last few years, but never had it announced itself with such fury.

The next day, I tried to figure out just what had caused me to panic. Was I overworked? Was it the medication I was on? The chocolate I'd eaten? Or was it the fact that I was leaving to pick up my mother and bring her back for a week's visit at my home that was setting my nervous system on fire?

It was probably all of the above, I realized later. But mostly it was about my mother. The Gates of Life that we mentioned on Yom Kippur were beginning to close for my mother despite prayer, love, and pharmaceuticals.

I took a train up to my mother's house two days after my panic attack, arrived at the station, got into a taxi, and began to cry. The city I grew up in was still and gray. It was about to rain. I cried all the way to my mother's house, fearful of what I would find. I hadn't seen her in a while.

And I had recently had a sobering talk with my mother's caregiver, Betty, about my mother's deterioration. It was steady and sure. "You do what you need to do this next year," Betty urged me. She'd been saying that a lot lately. "I mean if you want to take a trip somewhere far, or do something special, do it now," Betty said. "Things could get rough, and I'll need to call on you more often."

So I was a bit nervous when my frail, white-haired mother opened the back door of her house, after I'd gotten out of the taxi and dried my tears. And she was a bit confused. "I'm . . . sorry you had to . . . to get off the train," she said to me, and then I became confused. Did she mean to say that she was sorry I had to take a taxi from the train, that she couldn't pick me up?

My mother began to pop some pills into her mouth, but I knew she didn't take any medicine in the afternoon and stopped her. "Those pills are for you to bring to New York with you," I said. "You're coming home with me tomorrow."

"I am?" my mother asked, confused. Her bag was packed. We'd had a dozen conversations about this plan over the past couple of weeks. But my mother had no understanding of the fact that she was coming to visit me.

I gently took the pills away from her, walked into the next room, and began to cry. Surrounded by massive quantities of her art and the hundreds of artifacts she'd collected over the years, I wept silently. My mother's house is like a tiny, crazily stuffed museum, a living, breathing testament to her ego and artistic passion, full of hundreds of pieces of her artwork, framed all over the walls, and stuff everywhere you look, from plastic parrots hanging overhead to shrines with tiny Buddhas, a collection of old bride and groom ornaments, Pee Wee Herman dolls, and rubber snakes.

I slept restlessly that night, trying to summon my newfound strength. The next day, I brought my mother down to New York for a visit.

And then my heart took off again. I had another bad panic attack. And then another. I called my doctor and he prescribed a twenty-four-hour heart monitor, which I wore all over town for a day. I prayed for my heart to slow down. I wondered what on earth the results of this test would show.

I doubted that it would show what I worried was the truth: My heart was breaking. My mother was dying. No matter what I did for her in the week she was a guest in my home, her condition seemed to deteriorate before my eyes. She had trouble dressing herself, bathing herself, even rising from a chair by herself. And, worst of all, she was unable to make art with me. She was no longer herself. The evidence of her decline took my breath away, literally.

I'd been making jewelry lately, and I was planning on making a necklace or two with my mother. I'd gathered together boxes of large semiprecious stones. "Just take these and arrange them any way you like," I told her. "I'll string them together for you."

But my mother, the woman who had created thousands of paintings, prints, and collages in her lifetime as an artist, was unable to set the stones side by side. "This is too hard," she said. "I can't do it. It's too complicated. I don't know what to put next to a green stone."

My heart broke over and over again. And it shuddered and flopped around in my chest as I realized how damaged my mother's brain had become.

On the sixth day of her visit, my son Max turned eighteen. And my mother couldn't retain that information. "Whose birthday is it?" she asked repeatedly. "Max is eighteen," I told her at least a dozen times. We drove to the bakery together, I left her in the car, and in the five minutes it took for me to return with the boxed cake, she'd forgotten again. "Whose birthday is it?" she asked.

Later, when I arrived at the restaurant where we'd planned to meet Max for a little birthday party, I was a wreck. Max rose from his chair, and I cried into his strong shoulders. "I had such a hard day," I told him. "My mother is not doing well."

"I know, Mom," Max said. He didn't let go of me. Usually his hugs are short and sweet. I cried a bit more and he held me in his pumped-up basketball player's arms. My son Jack looked up at me from the table with concern.

I dried my eyes and sat down opposite my mother. She had no idea that I was upset. She was in her own world.

The birthday dinner was a success. My mother smiled as the cake she'd been so confused about arrived ablaze with candles and Max blew them out. He cut slices for all, posed for pictures with every guest. He was in charge. He was a big boy.

Days later, when I reflected on this, I remembered how Max used to love to "drive" when he was two. I have a photo of him in our car on one of those "drives." Jimmy and I had rented a house in the country the summer my father was dying, and my parents lived with us. Jimmy used to get into the driver's seat of our car, in the driveway, and put Max on his lap. Max would grasp the wheel and turn it with delight. "I'm diving!" he would exclaim over and over again. "I'm diving! I'm diving!"

When I took my mother home after one of the most difficult weeks of my life, I watched as she stared out the train window at the beautiful marshlands of Connecticut. My mother was off in her own world for much of the trip. Soon, I realize sadly, she will leave me. I will have to let her go. The gates are closing. What can I do besides panic?

As we reached our destination, Max's words from sixteen years ago came back to me. "I'm diving!" I said to myself as I helped my mother off the train. "I'm diving!" I said when I returned home and wondered how I'd be able to survive after losing my mother.

For days, I went about my business, trying to keep my eyes focused on the road ahead of me. I looked in my rearview mirror and saw Suzanne and Ranya staring back at me. Their faith was so strong. Mine was so fragile. I looked forward to our next meeting.

I thanked God we were still meeting.

PRISCILLA: *I think faith is sometimes just the act of getting up in the morning, putting both feet on the floor, and standing up.*
RANYA: *Yes. And faith is not the domain of one group or another. It belongs to anyone who chooses to have it. It doesn't have to have a label or a name.*
SUZANNE: *And it doesn't have to be sanctioned by any authority.*
RANYA: *Ultimately it's a choice we make as individuals—to have faith.*

Suzanne:

I had embraced other religions. I had become a universalist. So why was I so scared? Because I suddenly didn't know where to find truth. If all religions were equal, how did I know what to believe when they disagreed? There was one big area of agreement: that we should love God with all our heart, soul, mind, and strength and love our neighbor as ourselves. I was fine with that. But what about the other stuff? Religion was easier to think about when I thought I had the right answers.

Now I was becoming cynical. I kept worrying about the possibility that God had been imagined by man as something to grasp as we faced our mortality. Along with this cynicism came fear: the heart-pounding fear that I used to experience before my sister's death had deepened my faith. At night in bed, I nervously prayed to God for a return to the comfort I had found in my faith before I had started talking to Ranya and Priscilla.

My new interest in defining my religion had led me to begin a two-year course on faith that our priest, Craig, was teaching at my church. One of our first assignments was to read Ben Rice's novella *Pobby and Dingan*, whose story is an intriguing metaphor of faith and its effect on a community. The narrator, Ashmol Williams, has a sister who tells him one morning that she thinks that her best friends, Pobby and Dingan, are dead. Her father left them at his opal mine the previous night, and they never came home. Ashmol is dismissive, and for good reason: Pobby and Dingan are imaginary. Yet, after their disappearance his sister becomes severely ill, perhaps because of her broken heart over the loss of her friends.

Desperate to save his sister's life, Ashmol rallies the town on a search for Pobby and Dingan. "How will I know them?" he asks his sister. She gives him some relevant details. Pobby has a passion for Violet Crumble chocolate bars, and Dingan wears an opal in her belly button. After many unsuccessful attempts to deliver the invisible friends to his sister, Ashmol finally sneaks out into the night and climbs down into his father's mine, where he discovers a place in which the ceiling has collapsed. In a panic, he clears away the rubble and underneath finds an opal and a candy wrapper, proof of the disaster that befell his sister's invisible friends.

The story was lovely, but unsatisfying. "It's frustrating as a metaphor for faith because we don't get anything as real as opals and chocolate bar wrappers in real life," I said to Craig during the class. "I know we can debate how tangible the proof has to be. But personally, I'd love something I can touch, a candy bar wrapper or an opal I can hold onto."

Having said that, I knew it was too much to ask for, and I continued to feel uneasy about my faith. Then, a few mornings later, I woke from a dream that gave me as much reassurance about the existence of God's eternal kingdom as I think it is possible to find in this life. In the dream I sat at a long table playing cards with family and friends. My grandfather, whom I had adored, was there. He was a loving man of strong faith, good humor, and pancake-making prowess who died when I was in college. But now, in my dream, he beckoned me from the game table. "Suzy," he said, calling me by my childhood nickname. "I want to give you something."

I joined him at another table on top of which stood a wooden case. He opened the steel latch on the case and revealed a collection of jewelry—silver bracelets shimmering with blue jewels and silver necklaces bearing milky pink stones. The array was simple but dazzling. "Are you familiar with antique jewelry?" my grandfather asked me.

"Yes," I said.

"You see they are engraved." And he pointed to beautiful silver monogrammed charms that hung from a few of the pieces.

I reached out to lift an opal pendant from the velvet-lined box. "Is it real?" I asked.

"Yes," he answered softly. "It's real. It's all real." His words seemed the most important words I had ever heard. I hugged my grandfather in gratitude, feeling his bones and heft the way he felt before the cancer started eating away at his body. "Thank you, Grandpa," I whispered.

I was wrapped in my grandfather's loving embrace one moment, and the next moment I was waking up disoriented in the top bunk of my sons' beds. (I'd been displaced when both of them had squeezed into our bed the night before.) My cheeks were damp with tears, and I felt them in disbelief. I lay with my eyes closed, savoring every aspect of the dream. As I continued to wake, I touched the tears again to reassure myself that they belonged to this side of reality. As I felt the dampness between my thumb and forefinger, I realized that I had received a gift, miraculous and tangible, wet and salty.

I got out of bed but kept my mind focused on my dream until I had written down as much as I could remember. Then I found my husband at the dining room table with his nose over the Saturday newspaper. "I just had the most incredible experience," I began. As I retold my dream, its awesome effect lingered upon me. "I know that a cynical person would say that I created the dream out of bits and pieces that have been on my mind," I said to my husband. "But I really feel like I've been visited."

Later that day I called my mother, whose father had been in my dream, and described my experience to her. By that time I had put meaning to my vision. "I think the signatures authenticating the jewelry are like the names of the Bible authors providing proof of their experiences. And I think Grandpa's coming to me and saying 'It's real' means God's eternal kingdom is real." Then I described to my mother how I had been praying for something that would enable me to return to the calmness of my old faith. I had wanted something tangible, like Dingan's opal or Pobby's candy bar wrapper, but never expected to receive it.

My mother listened thoughtfully. "You're not going to believe this," she said.

"What?"

"The only piece of jewelry my father ever gave me is an opal necklace on a silver chain," my mom said. "Do you remember it?"

I pictured the milky stone striated with shimmers of gold, pink and green as it lay on my mother's freckled neck. Suddenly that stone represented so much. "Yes, I know the necklace," I answered.

"My dad bought a whole opal, then had it split and made into two necklaces. He gave one to me and one to my sister."

"Oh, my gosh. Now I am getting goose bumps," I said.

"It's a beautiful necklace," my mom continued. "And I think you should have it."

"I would treasure it," I said, gratefully looking forward to holding the opal in my fingers as I had in my dream.

Ranya:

On a trip to France, I saw how difficult it could be to speak up with my new voice about Islam. It was at a lazy summer lunch that my fellow Muslim companions could barely control their skepticism and outrage at my "Muslim Uncle Tom" ways. There, doubt and discomfort seeped back into my life.

We sat around a table on a balcony perched above rugged cliffs jutting out of the Mediterranean. It felt like we were suspended out into the middle of the sea with the infinite horizons of water and sky merging into one. Crisp white linen covered our table, where olives, feta cheese, country bread, and a basket of crudités were arranged as beautifully as in a still life painting. The serenity of the sunny moment only served to accentuate the about-face the conversation took as a gentleman closer in manner and form to his Oxford days than to his native Syrian roots asserted to me, "American policy in the Middle East has nothing to do with its declared intentions and values. Americans preach one way and act in another. All they're interested in at the end of the day is oil. There is no consideration for the suffering of the Palestinians and the concerns of the Muslim world."

I put down my bread as I saw my vision of a peaceful lunch evaporating in the noonday sun. "You may be right. But some would argue that morality should not be the engine of foreign policy in the first place," I answered, weary of the habit Arabs and Muslims have of blaming everything on America. "Perhaps Arabs and Muslims bear some responsibility. Perhaps they should be more critical of their own states and regimes, which have made them vulnerable to such foreign policy in the first place."

"What do you mean?" my lunch companion scoffed. "You cannot be saying that these puny, weak states stand a chance next to the power of the mighty U.S.?"

"What I'm saying is that these regimes have not fulfilled their social contract with their own people. They are more concerned with their own survival than with the security and welfare of their people. As a result they pay lip service to ideals of freedom and equality while hanging onto repressive religious or other ideologies as a means of buying legitimacy. Therefore, our voice as Muslims or as Arabs is compromised in the international arena, and our concerns lose credibility. If we are to demand the respect and justice we feel is our due, we must be able to respect those institutions, rulers, and mosques that speak on our behalf and represent us and our religion."

"You forget that these regimes are often sustained and protected by the U.S.!" this man answered in a voice that rose in spite of his attempts to maintain his composure.

I understood his sense of suffering, grievance, and political weakness, but resignation was something I was determined to fight after 9/11. So I continued to argue, "Muslims need to wrestle their religion away from the abuse it has taken at the hands of repressive regimes and the fundamentalist religious authorities that help to keep them in control. If only we could let Islam's true spirit infuse and influence our institutions and actions, then perhaps we could serve our interests and goals more effectively on the world stage."

Indeed, read in its true spirit, freed from political agendas and liberated from its service to the flawed human heart, Islam, I had come to learn, could be a beacon for true enlightenment, progress, development, and security. Moreover, if Islam regained that voice, it would help to disarm those radical groups who abuse the Quran and interpret it in a way that fits their own political agenda and violent designs.

My lunch guest soon tired of the political talk. While we had the same goals for Muslim and Arab states—reform, transparency, and accountability—we disagreed about how much power people in the Arab and Muslim world have over their own destinies. Like many, my lunch companion felt a complete sense of political impotence, which translated into a sense of resignation in which everything is attributed to American design if not conspiracy.

Months after my conversation, I reflected on it with Suzanne and Priscilla. Radicals are able to tap into this sense of American-inflicted injustice and suffering in the Arab and Muslim world, I explained. For instance, that injustice and suffering are evidenced daily on television screens that show Muslim children dying under Israeli occupation while America remains uncritical, lending unconditional support to Israeli policies. The suffering endured by the Iraqis during the American-led war in which close to 100,000 Iraqi civilians have died, according to an estimate by the Johns Hopkins School of Medicine, is also a major source of grievance. While that figure is disputed by some in America, it is wholeheartedly believed by the Muslim world.

CHAPTER NINETEEN

From Here to Eternity

Ranya:

My relationship with Daisy and the imam continues to flourish. At our last meeting, I was excited to discover that they have been working on plans to develop a permanent space that will house our growing Muslim community. I look forward to the day when their vision will become a reality, where Muslim children are offered Sunday school classes, and where we can pray and celebrate holidays together.

When Imam Feisal and his wife Daisy Khan invited me to participate in a three-day spiritual retreat called "Muslim Leaders of Tomorrow," in Garrison, New York, and asked if I would moderate a workshop there entitled "Coalition Building through Interfaith Dialogue," I was truly honored. At last I had the opportunity to dispel any lingering doubts about my authenticity as a Muslim. Daisy and the imam had reached across the country to invite a diverse group of young American Muslims who had a common trait: All had been involved in projects that distinguished them as potential leaders among American Muslims. The objective of the retreat was nothing short of the transformation of the national conversation about Islam. Panel discussions and workshops covered a wide range of topics, including intra-Muslim dialogue, women in Islam, leadership in Islam, and the representation of Islam in the media. The latter panel included representatives from *The Wall Street Journal, New York Newsday,* and *The Charlie Rose Show.*

I set off on Saturday morning with great anticipation. My husband had booked a car service, which arrived promptly at eight o'clock, and my children said their clingy good-byes. (They were used to their father making business trips over some weekends, but this sudden role reversal threw them off balance!)

As I left the city, I could not help but notice how comfortable I was compared with the anxiety I had felt a month earlier as I had handed over a copy of my writing to Daisy and the imam. I was so worried that they might think I had gone too far. I even joked to Priscilla and Suzanne that their disapproval would be the last straw leading to my conversion from Islam. Not only had they approved, but they had invited me to attend this conference.

After reviewing my notes for the workshop, I settled back and took in the beautiful scenery, along the shimmering Hudson River. I felt a spiritual serenity. It was interrupted, however, by my driver and his friend who was acting as his co-navigator on this early morning trip from Manhattan to Garrison, a good fifty miles away. Although they were speaking Urdu, I could guess that we were lost. So I took out the map and directions that had been emailed to me and handed them over in an effort to set us right. As we finally got back onto the proper course, I noticed that the chatter between my driver and his friend had become more animated and intense. Leaning forward, I then saw that the printout I had given them had the name of the retreat and the titles of some of the lectures. In order to relieve them of their curiosity, I asked whether they were Muslims and briefly explained the premise of the retreat.

"Are *you* Muslim?" the young driver asked me.

"Yes, I am," I affirmed.

"Then where is your headscarf?" he challenged defiantly, forgetting the customer-client protocol.

"As a Muslim, I do not choose to wear one," I asserted.

And there you had it, all the tensions within Islam neatly encapsulated in a black town car. It suddenly struck me as absurdly funny that I, an American Muslim of Palestinian heritage, was being driven by a Pakistani Muslim in a car service called Tel Aviv Cars to a Muslim leadership conference in Garrison, New York. This incident enhanced my appreciation for the day that lay ahead of me.

Once I had checked in, I found a seat in the Meditation Hall, where seventy participants had already gathered. After Imam Feisal delivered an inspirational keynote address in which he shared his vision for the conference, we divided into discussion groups. Each group was asked to write down some thoughts to share with the wider group about what was troubling American Muslims today.

There was no shortage of concerns, and as we began to share them, we realized that we faced the same frustrations. One of the most common themes was the deep sense of isolation that American Muslims experienced in their daily lives. They felt alienated from Muslims abroad as well as from those who have dominated Muslim life in America through their influence over mosques and other Muslim organizations. Participants also felt alienated from the larger non-Muslim American community and expressed interest in reaching out through interfaith dialogue.

The Muslims at the conference were primarily upset about the ethnic divisions within the Muslim American community and its lack of effective leadership, communication, and vision. But they expressed many other frustrations as well. They were tired of Muslim stereotypes, tired of being judged and asked to justify their religion. They worried about extremism. They also worried about the direction of Islam in America and the future status of their Muslim children as Americans. Some were very worried about the possibility of another terrorist attack and its consequences on the civil rights of American Muslims.

Fortunately, the tenor of the discussion changed as we were asked to reflect on what excited us about Islam in America today. Most expressed excitement about what they sensed as a unique opportunity to participate and contribute to a dynamic evolution of Islam in America. They welcomed the diversity of ideas, as we American Muslims charted our own course and affirmed our identity. It was not until we broke for lunch and I had the opportunity to meet and exchange ideas with some of the other talented participants that I truly appreciated the potential of their energy and dynamism. It heralded an historic opportunity for Muslim Americans.

After a meal of delicious Moroccan-style couscous with vegetable tomato sauce and cucumber yogurt salad, I headed for my workshop room. There I met my fellow coordinator, Eboo Patel, the founder and executive director of the Interfaith Youth Corps, a Chicago-based organization that brings young people from diverse religious communities together for cooperative community service. I realized that Eboo was the perfect balance to my own interfaith experience. While he represented community efforts, my experience was on the individual level.

Once the workshop began, Eboo described to participants how his program enabled religiously diverse youth to affirm their identities and build friendships through work toward a common community service goal. He showed an inspirational video clip and encouraged us to establish local chapters of the Interfaith Youth Corps. Then I took over and described to the group my own interfaith experiences with Priscilla and Suzanne in my Faith Club.

After I finished speaking, a young woman at the workshop asked, "Why should we spend our time and energy on interfaith projects when there are so many more urgent issues within Islam?"

My answer came easily. "Because until we convince our fellow citizens on a very personal level that being an American Muslim is really just being one of them, then all other efforts will fall upon deaf ears. Our fellow Americans must understand that we, Muslim Americans, share their ideals, their values, their democracy, their God, their streets and neighborhoods. We must help them recognize that we are part of the fabric of the religious heritage of this nation and that we follow in the footsteps of other religious traditions. Until we do that, our children will not be equal American citizens."

Leaving the conference that night, I was full of optimism as I contemplated the opportunity that American Muslims have to affirm our voice and influence our destiny. We are privileged to be potential pioneers of change. Yet we recognize that this can also be a burden, for if we do not succeed, seven million Muslim Americans may continue to feel disenfranchised and their religious legacy may be a burden to their children. As a mother I have had to consider this issue for my own children, though I now recognize that there are also privileges that a Muslim religious identity can afford them. As Muslims, we have access to the full circle: the story of Moses, which is the story of freedom, the story of Jesus, which is the story of love, and the story of Muhammad, which is the story of equality and a universal God.

I look forward to a day when we will speak of the Great American Judeo-Christian-Muslim heritage.

Priscilla:

Although I've found myself talking about religion a lot these days, along with the rest of the world, I'm careful to issue a disclaimer to people. "I'm not a historian," I say when I talk about many of the amazing things I've learned in my Faith Club. "And I'm not a politician, a political scientist, a theologian, or a peace negotiator. My story is just the story of how I met Ranya and Suzanne and how they changed my life and the way I look at things."

Many people seem to want things black and white, but our relationship makes things much more complex. My life is much more complex. I'm not always on solid ground. "Where is my faith?" I ask myself on some days. What happened to my born-again conversion? I don't always seem to be born again. Sometimes I seem to be curled up in the fetal position, hiding.

I bumped into Rabbi Sirkman, and told him just that. I explained that my mother had been deteriorating lately, and so was I. "My faith is sometimes shaky," I admitted to my rabbi. "That's because you're Jewish!" Jeffrey said with a smile. "That's the thing with us Jews. We're all shaky, but we're still here!"

So what can I do to shore up my shaky self? I can enumerate the lessons Suzanne and Ranya have taught me. Even with all the horror in the world—massacres in the Sudan, tsunamis and earthquakes in Asia, hurricanes in the United States, terrorist attacks worldwide, and the war in Iraq—I've seen the good Suzanne and Ranya talked to me about. Along with heartbreaking human suffering, I've seen life-affirming acts of love, courage, and compassion take hold, proving to me so vividly what Suzanne and Ranya taught me when they described the world on September 11th—that there is too much good on earth for me to give up. "The world is imperfect," I tell my children, "but there are millions of perfect moments."

I try to live with humility now. I have submitted, as Ranya would say. I don't claim to have all the answers, but I don't think anyone else does, either. I believe, as Imam Feisal pointed out, that there is no temporal justice. No one but God can judge me or my faith, and I try not to be judgmental of others and their faith.

I often think of an F. Scott Fitzgerald quote: "We have two or three great moving experiences in our lives—experiences so great and moving that it doesn't seem at the time that anyone else has been caught up and pounded and dazzled and astonished and beaten and broken and rescued and illuminated and rewarded and humbled in just that way ever before." For me, my experience in my Faith Club has been one of those moving experiences.

I was trying to will my blood pressure down one day, so I turned on the TV for some mindless entertainment. An actress on a talk show was explaining her decision to raise her children with "good Christian values."

So much for mindless entertainment. "What about *my* values?" I wondered. "What does this woman think about Jewish values?"

I picked up the phone and called Suzanne, told her about the woman's comment. "What do you make of that?" I asked her. "What do people with good Christian values think about Jewish people's values?"

"They're the same!" Suzanne said in her honest, straightforward way. "But I don't think everyone recognizes that. They confuse social values with Christian values. Or they see that our religious practices are different, so they assume our moral values are different, too. We should all be taught early on that our religions boil down to one morality: to love God with all your heart, soul, mind, and strength and to love your neighbor as yourself."

I marveled at how completely Suzanne had answered my question.

"So you're saying that we all share human values?" I asked her.

"I think so," she said. "Even though our social values may be different."

Hateful rhetoric and violence often dominate news headlines, but I don't need to pick up the telephone to call Ranya every time a bomb, literal or figurative, goes off somewhere. I know deep in my heart what is deep in her heart. I know that Ranya will continue to teach me about the world through her eyes and the filter of her family's experience and heritage. My worldview is bigger than I ever thought it could be, thanks to her. What binds us as friends goes beyond borders, politics, or religion. What concerns us is that we treat each other with love, respect, and trust.

Suzanne's and Ranya's words continue to comfort me. When life gets tough, I think of them. When my spirit soars, I thank them for helping me to find my spirit.

My spirit does soar more than it sinks. I switched blood pressure medications, and my heart is beating more regularly now. I feel incredibly grateful for the life I have, and I have faith that I will somehow find a way to make the most out of what God's given me. I will try to live with strength and grace. I will continue to thank God for returning my soul, bruised as it might be, to my body every morning. I will continue to find love even when my heart is breaking, because, at the end of the day, what Suzanne and Ranya have taught me about most is love, a subject I had fancied myself an expert on.

I recently attended the funeral of a dear friend of my mother-in-law's, a woman I admired for her down-to-earth nature and lively spirit. It was held in a small temple in the woods, with light streaming through skylights in the cathedral ceiling. Like my mother-in-law's friend, the proceedings were simple and straightforward. And as the family followed her casket out of the temple, the rabbi read a poem that spoke to me, that described what I would like to leave behind at the end of the day.

Epitaph
by Merritt Malloy

When I die
Give what's left of me away
To children
And old men that want to die.
And if you need to cry,
Cry for your brother
Walking the street beside you.
And when you need me,
Put your arms
Around anyone
And give them
What you need to give to me.

I want to leave you something,
Something better
Than words
Or sounds.

Look for me
In the people I've known
Or loved,
And if you cannot give me away,

At least let me live on in your eyes
And not on your mind.

You can love me most
By letting
Hands touch hands,
By letting
Bodies touch bodies
And by letting go
Of children
That need to be free.

Love doesn't die,
People do.
So, when all that's left of me
Is love,
Give me away.

Suzanne:

My faith returned to me gradually. It wasn't only through the practice of religious ritual, but interestingly through poetry, prayer, and dreams. I've learned to live with doubt, but I also carry hope in my heart. I pray to God every day, thanking him for the tender touch of my children's small hands. I savor the feel of their skin as I wash them in the bath. This gift of motherhood has made my life more fulfilling than anything else could. Even if this life is all there is, I'm grateful for it.

Though I have been changed by my Faith Club experience I still participate in my Episcopal church because I love the community and the intellectual and spiritual stimulation it provides. I guess at this point you could call me an Episcopalian with a Universalist streak. But I know that label just marks one dot on the continuum of my faith journey.

One of the most important things I have learned from my Faith Club is not to judge anyone else's faith because everyone, from my seven-year-old son who insists there's no God to the most erudite priest, is on a journey toward God, and every dot on that journey is sacred.

I still get spiritual nourishment and stimulation from my Faith Club soul mates as we continue to meet to discuss religion in the world and in our own messy lives. I've discovered that everyone's faith is a little bit messy. After the death of Pope John Paul II, the newspapers were full of polls of American Catholics showing that the majority of them disagree with the positions of the Catholic Church on many social and doctrinal issues. Yet they still practice the Catholic faith. Somehow, they live with the contradictions I thought I had escaped in my own departure from Catholicism. I see now that faith is never free of contradiction, never as tidy as a textbook. It waxes and wanes, perplexes and inspires us. It is a gift from God, but like many of those gifts, its value increases according to the work you put into it.

I carry Ranya and Priscilla with me every day now, especially in the quiet times I spend walking on empty New Hampshire country roads. One late winter weekend I was out walking when the temperature surged above fifty degrees. The snow was melting, and water coursed purposefully in an icy stream that zigged and zagged alongside the road. What had been lodged in the ice had broken free and was being carried toward its inevitable destination. The dark, austere trees stood stiffly at attention, waiting to be robed again in the green of spring. The maples were linked by black tubing that hung ready to collect their sap during the real spring thaw that was still to come. I breathed deeply of the wet, pine-filled air and thanked God for the day.

My Faith Club had been on my mind that afternoon. I was wearing the opal necklace my mother had given me, and now as I walked I caressed its oval stone and smooth, silver back. I thought about the journey that had brought that opal, the restorer of my faith, into my hands.

"Thank you, God, for this gift of faith," I prayed. "Help me to gain strength from it as I try to live a life of love inside my home and outside in the world." I thanked God for the experience of seeing life and death through the eyes of two people who were so different from myself. It was a gift, I thought, as valuable as the necklace and everything it represented.

Then as I looked to the summit of the hill where the road disappeared, I pictured Ranya, Priscilla, and me walking the hill together at the end of our own life roads. I knew my friends so well now, and I laughed at my image of the three of us. There was Priscilla feverishly touching every granite stone, pine tree branch, and clump of snow we passed saying, "Thank you, God, for letting me experience this." Then Ranya, draped in the snow white cloth of her Hajj, looking regretfully yet gracefully over her shoulder at all the beauty and love she had to leave behind.

And finally I saw myself reaching the end of the road, taking a deep breath to summon my courage and then jumping with the trust of a child, saying, "Catch me, God! Here I come! I hope you're waiting!" A sketch of the three of us would make a good cartoon, I thought. And someday maybe we'll know what appears in the next frame.

Bibliography

Abdul al Rauf, Imam Feisal, *What's Right with Islam, A New Vision for Muslims and the West,* HarperCollins, 2004.

Ali, Samina, *Madras on Rainy Days: A Novel,* Farrar Straus and Giroux, 2004.

Armstrong, Karen, *Holy War: The Crusades and Their Impact on Today's World,* Anchor Books, 2001.

———, *A History of God,* Alfred A. Knopf, 1993.

———, *Muhammad: A Biography of the Prophet,* HarperCollins, 1993.

———, *The Spiral Staircase,* Alfred A. Knopf, 2004.

Benvenisti, Meron, *Sacred Landscape, The Buried History of the Holy Land Since 1948,* University of California Press, 2000.

Bickerton, Ian, and Carla Klausner, *A Concise History of the Arab-Israeli Conflict,* Prentice Hall, 1997.

Blech, Benjamin, *The Complete Idiot's Guide to Jewish History and Culture,* Alpha Books, 2003.

Bloom, Harold, *Genius: A Mosaic of One Hundred Exemplary Creative Minds,* Warner Books, 2001.

Blumenfeld, Laura, *Revenge: A Story of Hope,* Washington Square Press, 2003.

Brickner, Balfour, *Finding God in the Garden: Backyard Reflections on Life, Love and Compost,* Little, Brown, 2002.

Carey, Rhoane, and Jonathan Shainin, *The Other Israel: Voices of Refusal and Dissent,* The New Press, 2002.

Carroll, James, *Constantine's Sword: The Church and the Jews,* Mariner Books, 2002.

Carson, Claybourne, and Peter Halloran (eds.), *A Knock at Midnight: Inspiration from the Great Sermons of Reverend Martin Luther King, Jr.,* Warner Books, 1998.

Bibliography

Christison, Kathleen, *Perceptions of Palestine*, University of California Press, 1999.

Cleary, Thomas, *The Essential Koran: The Heart of Islam*, HarperCollins, 1993.

Dawood, N. J. (translator), *The Koran*, Penguin Books, 2004.

Ehrman, Bart D., *Misquoting Jesus: The Story Behind Who Changed the Bible and Why*, HarperCollins, 2005.

Emerick, Yahiya, *The Complete Idiot's Guide to Understanding Islam*, Alpha Books, 2002.

Ernst, Carl W., *Following Muhammad: Rethinking Islam in the Modern World*, University of North Carolina Press, 2003.

Feiler, Bruce, *Abraham, A Journey to the Heart of Three Faiths*, HarperCollins, 2002.

———, *Walking the Bible*, HarperCollins, 2001.

Findley, Paul, *Silent No More: Confronting America's False Images of Islam*, Amana Publications, 2001.

Friedman, Thomas, *From Beirut to Jerusalem*, Anchor Books, 1990.

Fromkin, David, *A Peace to End All Peace: The Fall of the Ottoman Empire and the Creation of the Modern Middle East*, Henry Holt, 1989.

Gandhi, Mahatma, *The Message of Jesus Christ*, Bhavan Vidya Bharatiya pocket Gandhi series, 1986.

Gerstein, Mordicai, *The Mountains of Tibet*, HarperTrophy, 1989.

Gilsenan, Michael, *Recognizing Islam: Religion and Society in the Modern Middle East*. I. B. Tauris & Co. Ltd., 2000.

Grieb, A. Katherine, *The Story of Romans: A Narrative Defense of God's Righteousness*, Westminster John Knox Press, 2002.

Halevi, Yossi Klein, *At the Entrance to the Garden of Eden: A Jew's Search for God with Christians and Muslims in the Holy Land*, HarperCollins, 2001.

Hass, Amira, *Drinking the Sea at Gaza: Days and Nights in a Land Under Seige*, Owl Books, 2000.

Heschel, Abraham Joshua, and Susannah Heschel, *Moral Grandeur and Spiritual Audacity: Essays*, Farrar, Straus and Giroux, 1997.

Irving, T. B. (translator), *The Qur'an*, Goodword Press, New Delhi, 1999.

Lamott, Annie, *Traveling Mercies: Some Thoughts on Faith*, Anchor Books, 2000.

Lughod, Ibrahim Abu, and Arnold J. Toynbee, *The Transformation of Palestine, Essays on the Origins and Development of the Arab-Israeli Conflict*, Northwestern University Press, 1987.

Lewis, C. S., *Mere Christianity,* Macmillan, 1993.

Maalouf, Amin, *The Crusades Through Arab Eyes,* Schocken, 1989.

Makiya, Kanan, *The Rock: A Tale of Seventh-Century Jerusalem,* Vintage Books, 2002.

Menocal, Maria Rosa, *Ornament of the World: How Muslims, Jews and Christians Created a Culture of Tolerance in Medieval Spain,* Little, Brown, 2002.

Morris, Benny, *The Birth of the Palestinian Refugee Problem Revisited,* Cambridge University Press, 2004.

Nasr, Seyyed Hossein, *The Heart of Islam: Enduring Values for Humanity,* HarperCollins, 2004.

Neumark, Heidi B., *Breathing Space: A Spiritual Journey in the South Bronx,* Beacon Press, 2003.

Ohlson, Kristin, *Stalking the Divine,* Penguin Group, 2005.

Oz, Amos, *A Tale of Love and Darkness,* Harcourt, 2004.

Pagels, Elaine, *Beyond Belief: The Secret Gospels of Thomas,* Random House, 2003.

————, *The Gnostic Gospels,* Vintage, 1989.

Podwal, Mark, *Jerusalem Sky: Stars, Crosses, and Crescents,* Random House Children's Books, 2005.

Pogrebin, Abigail, *Stars of David: Prominent Jews Talk About Being Jewish,* Broadway Books, 2005.

Prothero, Stephen, *American Jesus,* Farrar, Straus and Giroux, 2003.

Rice, Ben, *Pobby and Dingan,* Knopf Publishing Group, 2000.

Ross, Dennis, *The Missing Peace,* Farrar, Straus and Giroux, 2004.

Sacks, Rabbi Jonathan, *Celebrating Life,* Continuum, 2005.

————, *The Dignity of Difference,* Continuum, 2002.

Said, Edward W., *Out of Place, A Memoir,* Alfred A. Knopf, 1999.

————, *The End of the Peace Process: Oslo and After,* Random House, 2000.

Segev, Tom, *One Palestine Complete,* Henry Holt, 1999.

————, *The Seventh Million: Israelis and the Holocaust,* Henry Holt, 2000.

Shipler, David K., *Arab and Jew: Wounded Spirits in a Promised Land,* Penguin Books, 2002.

Stern, Jessica, *Terror in the Name of God: Why Religious Militants Kill,* Echo, 2003.

Wills, Garry, *What Jesus Meant,* Viking Books, 2006.

Acknowledgments

With gratitude to Elizabeth Kaplan and Leslie Meredith, Martha Levin, Dominick Anfuso, Carisa Hays, Suzanne Donahue, Heidi Metcalfe, Shannon Gallagher, Amanda Walker, Andrew Paulson, Imam Feisal Abdul al Rauf, Rabbi Jeffrey Sirkman, the Reverend Craig Townsend, Richard Cohen, Daisy Khan, the Reverend Louis Kilgore, Mark Lawless, Jane Nishimura, Joanne Praeger, Patricia Van Ness, and Carolyn Welcome.

I thank God for my parents, Hisham and Aida, who continue to teach me about love, and for Sami—my love.

Thank you, Mom and Dad, for loving me unconditionally, and thank you, David, for loving and supporting me every day.

I have been blessed all my life with abundant love from friends and family. The following people were especially supportive during the writing of this book: Betty Bowman, Chaim Cohen, Lu Doyle, Luann Jacobs, Roberta Jaeger, the Leviten Family, Linda Lipsett, Sonia Merrit, Margaret Mikol, Barbara Sadick, Claudia Sussman, Alice Tisch, Meredith Vieira, the Warner Family.

About the Authors

Ranya Idliby is an American of Palestinian descent. Growing up, she spent many years in both Dubai and McLean, Virginia. She graduated from Georgetown University with a bachelor of science from the School of Foreign Service. At the London School of Economics she earned her MS in international relations and continued her postgraduate education as a PhD candidate. She lives in New York City with her husband and two children.

Suzanne Oliver has worked as a writer and editor at *Forbes* and *Financial World* magazines and was the managing editor of *Smartmoney.com*. She was raised in Kansas City, Missouri, and graduated from Texas Christian University. Currently, she lives with her husband and three children in New York City and Jaffrey Center, New Hampshire.

Priscilla Warner grew up in Providence, Rhode Island, where she began her interfaith education at a Hebrew day school and then at a Quaker high school. A graduate of the University of Pennsylvania, she worked as an art director at various advertising agencies in Boston and New York. She lives with her family in a suburb of New York City.

The Faith Club

A Muslim, a Christian, a Jew—
Three Women Search for Understanding

Ranya Idliby, Suzanne Oliver, Priscilla Warner

Reading Group Guide

A Conversation with the Authors

Discussion Questions and Activities

Frequently Asked Questions

How to Start a Faith Club

10 Things You Should Know Before Your First Faith Club Meeting

Faith Club Meeting Icebreakers

The Five-Step Faith Club

More Faith Club Questions

Things to Know About Judaism/Christianity/Islam

Reading Group Guide for
The Faith Club

The following information, reading group guide questions, and author interviews are intended to help you find interesting and rewarding approaches to your reading of *The Faith Club*. We hope these elements enhance your enjoyment and appreciation of the book and inspire you to start your own faith club.

A Conversation with the Authors

All Three:

1. **At the beginning of the process, you are all at very different stages of faith; Ranya, you say on page 93, "it often felt like I had faith but no religion, that Priscilla had religion but no faith, and that Suzanne had both." Do you all feel that you are coming out of this process with both faith and religion?**

RANYA: *Yes! And that is the most surprising and fulfilling part for me—to have found my religion as an American and as a Muslim. I started off with doubt and insecurity about Islam and ended up a more committed and confident Muslim. In the beginning, my problem with religion was twofold. First, as a concerned mother I was alienated and challenged by the dominant voice of Islam, especially after 9/11, when Islam in America seemed to be more of a burden than a privilege. Through the Faith Club I was able to find within the religion of Islam the traditions that support the foundations of my faith, which has always been built on the idea of an equal-opportunity God—a God that does not discriminate among his worshipers on the basis of favored rituals, or give only members of one religion privileged rights to heaven. My second problem with religion was not specific to Islam. I am still saddened to see how religion in our world is more often than not a divisive force, in which rituals are used to define communities and relegate to "other" all those who do not engage in the same practices. It is my hope, as it has been our experience in the Faith Club, that as more people have this dialogue about faith, there will be an increased awareness of how all religions can embrace a universal faith in a universal God.*

PRISCILLA: *I was always proud to be a Jew, but I am even prouder now, after watching Suzanne marvel at the strength it takes to live life without the promise of an afterlife and after reading the Torah, which, as Ranya pointed out to me, was the first holy book for all three religions. I have found my own definition of God, which is the foundation of my faith, and I have acknowledged my humble place in the universe. I have learned that good and evil can coexist. I have accepted the inevitability of my mother's painful deterioration due to Alzheimer's. I pray for patience and compassion as I watch my sister battle several autoimmune diseases. I myself am not afraid to die. And as I experience pain alongside joy, I am grateful for every minute that I'm on this planet.*

SUZANNE: *I began and ended my Faith Club experience with "faith," but my understanding of that faith changed dramatically. I discovered its strength as I talked to Ranya and Priscilla about how I found God in the kind actions of humanity. But I also discovered its weaknesses as I endeavored to define the role of Jesus and to accept that there is truth in more than one religion. Those challenges required that I redefine my faith in a way that validated other religions but didn't negate my belief in Jesus and his resurrection. In this process, my faith was tested, and I felt the fear of living without it. Fortunately, the Episcopal denomination was there to help me along the way. I had been attracted to it because of its liberal attitude toward doctrine, and I found within it one particular priest who helped me define what was elemental in Christianity. This new understanding, which is easily accommodated in the Episcopal faith, enabled me to recognize that there is truth within Judaism and Islam without feeling threatened by that recognition.*

2. **Talk about the writing process: Did you jointly plan events that you would write about? Did you journal individually and then compare your notes? The linking dialogue sections in the book are all verbatim, taken directly from the tapes you made of each session. Were you often surprised by the difference between the recorded conversations and your memories of them?**

PRISCILLA: *The writing we did was honest, heartfelt, and recorded our feelings and growth in real time. Occasionally we would plan to attend a religious service or lecture together, but the book basically unfolded as our lives unfolded.*

I always looked forward to reviewing our taped transcripts. They confirmed my recollection of how fiery and intense our debates were. And when our talks were particularly moving and spiritual, it was thrilling to be able to relive those moments of mutual respect, compassion, and growth. The beauty and universality of the experience was magnified by the existence of the transcripts.

SUZANNE: *Our journal writing began with some broad topics that we wrote about individually: What brought us together? What's your religious background? What kind of God do you believe in? We generally shared our writing at the subsequent meeting, and that provided new avenues for discussion and more writing. Whenever we went anywhere together, we wrote about it. And whenever we experienced conflict, we wrote about it. The transcripts came in especially handy during these times because they enabled me to relive the conversations dispassionately. Freed from the anxiety I may have felt during the conversations, I could hear my Faith Club partners more clearly. And sometimes I could identify the source of my own anxiety. It was like being my own shrink.*

RANYA: *What I still find incredible about the Faith Club was the ease with which our dialogue flowed. The dialogue was addictive, and it became difficult to imagine life without it. There honestly was no shortage of material. Life was our abundant source, overflowing with questions, fears, and aspirations. The taped transcripts were essential to the writing process. They often served as the basis of personal reflections and as inspiration for new journal entries. They were the single most important point of departure and a concrete, tangible record of who we were and who we were becoming. They helped guard and preserve that memory as our ideas developed and became more refined. This was essential for the writing of the book.*

3. **Your children all played an important role in the development of the Faith Club—and of course, they were the inspiration for its initial meeting! What is the most poignant memory of your children during this process? Do you still plan to collaborate on a children's book?**

RANYA: *I have many wonderful memories! But if I have to single out one it would have to be when my husband and I were at Leia's first-grade parent-teacher conference and we were surprised at the work she had produced for a class project. As the only Muslim in her class, she was the one who had challenged me in the first place to embark on this journey—that first holiday season after 9/11—when she asked me whether we celebrated Hanukah or Christmas. A year later, she could still be counted on to challenge my parenting skills. Her teacher had encouraged the students to finish off the phrase "It's okay to————" and then to draw an accompanying picture. My daughter, who had never complained or said a word to us, drew a picture of herself standing apart from two other girls holding hands. The caption read: "It's okay to be Muslim. It makes me feel weird when I am the only Muslim and everyone around me is either Christian or Jewish." The picture is now laminated and prominently displayed on my desk for inspiration (you can see a copy on our website, in our scrapbook). Thankfully, Leia was soon encouraged to give her own "ten-questions" Muslim presentation, where she challenged stereotypes and affirmed her identity. I will never forget her pride and the light in her eyes as she shared with her peers her own empowered, confident American Muslim voice.*

PRISCILLA: *I loved talking to my children about Jesus Christ as I drove through the suburbs in my minivan, coming back from the mall. I truly appreciated Jesus and his message, after Suzanne shared things like the Sermon on the Mount and Ranya shared Gandhi's enormous admiration for Jesus. My children will never view Jesus as a stranger, the way I viewed him before I joined the Faith Club. As for the children's book, we are definitely writing one. Ranya introduced the notion to me, four years ago, that we are all Abraham's children. Now that I know that to be true, I want to share with children all over the world the fact that we are all one family.*

SUZANNE: *My most poignant moment with my children was a minivan moment, too. We were driving to the Bronx Zoo when a theological argument broke out between my daughter, a believer, and my oldest son, a stubborn atheist. I retold the conversation in the book. Try as she might, my daughter was unable to convince my son that God exists. It makes me sad that Thomas doesn't have the same faith my husband and I do. I don't know why it comes naturally to my other two children but not to him. I think that eventually he will find his own Craig Townsend, the priest who helped me out of my religious confusion. In fact, Craig has offered to sit down with Thomas. If only I could get Thomas to agree to sit down with Craig!*

4. **All of you live in a relatively urban, religiously diverse environment— Suzanne and Ranya in New York City, Priscilla just outside it. How do you think the urban setting affected your faith club? Does living in a city make it more or less difficult for each of you to practice your own faiths?**

SUZANNE: *For me, the fact that I live in New York City added urgency to my desire to understand other faiths. Here I know Jews, Muslims, and Hindus. I drive or walk by a mosque and many temples each day. And, unfortunately, our city was the site of the deadliest of the 9/11 attacks. As a New Yorker, I felt an obligation to understand my neighbors and those who consider us to be their enemy. However, now that our nation is at war, I think people across the whole country feel similarly compelled to learn more about Islam and the Middle East.*

I don't think living in an urban environment makes it more or less difficult to practice my faith than it would be elsewhere. What makes it easy is that I am part of a vibrant church community where there is opportunity for meaningful charitable work, spiritual education, and worship every day. Unfortunately, I have time to participate in only a small fraction of it. (Maybe that's because of the complexity of raising my kids in an urban environment!)

PRISCILLA: *After 9/11, I was afraid to live in New York, but didn't want* *to flee the city that I loved. So my passion for New York challenged me to find faith and inner strength. The city, for me, is almost a character in this book. Because of its amazing diversity, I believe New York truly does represent the world, daring me to be brave and inspiring me to find the beauty in life behind all the pain. It is still an obvious terrorist target, but New York is a city worth the struggle it takes to live here. The vibrancy and diversity of every person and experience in New York is as inspiring as any natural wonder on earth. Life is full of many religious moments, whether I'm staring up at a skyscraper, watching crowds of people streaming past me, looking into the eyes of a stranger on a bus, or noticing the raindrops Ranya pointed out to me as they form their concentric circles in puddles on the street. Although I am enormously inspired by the city I love, I believe that I, along with anyone else, can find religion and faith anywhere, whether on the streets of New York, in a suburban synagogue, or, as I did in the book, in an airplane twenty thousand feet above the earth.*

RANYA: *New York is not just an urban setting. It was of course the city that was terrorized on 9/11 in the name of Islam. The only city my children have ever called home was suddenly in the grip of fear and terror invoked in the name of the very religion they were born into. The burden, the guilt, the anxiety, and the challenge this association involved was very much part of the genesis of the Faith Club. I was spiritually desolate, even desperate, in the aftermath of 9/11, but as a mother, apathy was no longer an option. I do not believe that city life affects the way I practice my faith. I like to believe that faith is something we carry within us that can inspire our daily actions and decisions. To have faith is ultimately to believe in our moral capacity as humans to do the right thing.*

5. **What is your favorite aspect of your own religion? Of the other two religions?**

SUZANNE: *My favorite aspect of Christianity is the resurrection of Jesus. I love its demonstration of God's power over death and its suggestion that an afterlife with God is available to all of us. I like the humility of Mus-*

lims before God. Sometimes I want to get too familiar with God, which can be a recipe for disappointment. I think it's important to step back and remember that God is unknowable to us except in glimpses that may be confusing and frightening on their own. In Judaism, I like the fact that the home is the center of much of the prayer and prayer ritual. I think it builds strong faith and strong families, and it supports the idea that we can live our faith everywhere, not just inside a church, temple, or mosque.

RANYA: I love the fact that in Islam there are no stringent conversion rituals or any confirmation rituals required of Muslims. A Muslim is any person who has declared faith in God and who also recognizes Muhammad as the last of a series of Abrahamic prophets that include Moses and Jesus. A simple utterance of this declaration of faith makes you a Muslim. I also appreciate the absence of a clerical hierarchy (this is especially true for Sunni Muslims) that is supposed to act as an intermediary to God. Many verses in the Quran make it the responsibility of the believer to think, read, and apply his or her intellect to reach the proper moral conclusions. Judaism's American experience is certainly an inspiration that I hope one day Islam may be able to emulate, as it provides diversity and flexibility of worship for its followers in the New World by embracing multiple traditions: orthodox, conservative, and reform. In Christianity, I admire the higher ideals that Jesus modeled for humanity. I also think there is a joy and a sense of celebration of life that, although some complain may have gone overboard culturally in the festivities of the holiday traditions, I for one applaud and enjoy.

PRISCILLA: I take enormous pride in the very survival of Judaism, in its sturdiness and endurance, thanks to the strong foundation of the Torah—which, according to our prayer book, is "a tree of life to those who hold fast to it." I love the running debate Jews are constantly having about their religion and the meaning of life. Debate keeps Judaism alive. And it prepared me for the debates I had in the Faith Club! I love the humility of Islam, the act of submission. When I integrated that humility into my life, it made me appreciate all the tiny, beautiful details of the

*world. I accepted my humble place on the planet. And, surprisingly, I dis-
covered that acknowledging my humility, in the vastness of the universe,
made me feel stronger. As for Christianity, I love everything I have
learned about Jesus and the message of his teachings. The Sermon on the
Mount is one of my favorite things to reread over and over again.*

6. **At the end of the book, you provide a guide to how people can begin
   their own faith clubs. What is the single most important piece of advice
   you can give anyone who wants to start their own club? What kept the
   three of you coming back, despite conflicts, arguments, and prejudice?**

PRISCILLA: *Respect one another. If I hadn't felt that Suzanne and Ranya
respected me as a human being, I would never have been able to open up
to them, learn from them, and display the vulnerability and courage
that fueled my spiritual growth. I kept coming back because I kept learning from Ranya and Suzanne about myself, my faith, all religions, and
life itself.*

RANYA: *In order to have a truly meaningful faith club experience, you
must ask yourself the difficult questions, be honest with yourself, and figure out what keeps you within your own religion. Is it because you feel it
is a superior religion? Do you enjoy its cultural traditions? Do you believe
that it is the only way one can truly worship God? What are your ideas
about God, heaven, and prayer? Keep a journal of your thoughts and establish the trust and sincerity that will allow you to have a dialogue with
your faith club partners. Sincerity is very important. From my personal
experience, as long as you feel that your partners are sincere, then you
should be able to weather any conflict. Trust me, you will soon find yourself addicted to the dialogue and to the higher, spiritual connections and
bonds that you will have forged with your faith club partners along the
way.*

SUZANNE: *Read about the religions of your faith club partners. It will
help you understand where they're coming from. Sometimes my outside
reading was able to fill in the gaps in my understanding of Judaism and
Islam and helped me understand the perspectives of Ranya and Priscilla*

*within their own religions. I kept coming back to our meetings because I
was hooked. I loved what I was learning. I was interested in Ranya and
Priscilla. I wanted to understand what made their faith tick, and I
wanted to understand my own faith better, too. I may be in the minority
on this one, but I think that testing the tenets of one's faith in a challenging and safe environment is an exciting thing to do!*

Suzanne:

1. **Suzanne, you are initially presented in the book as the most solid in
both your faith and your religion. However, you are also the only
member of the group who was practicing a different faith (Episcopal)
from the one in which you were raised (Catholicism). How did your
conversion influence your experience in the Faith Club? Do you think
it made you more open to different viewpoints than you would have
been otherwise?**

My "conversion" was not a dramatic one. In fact, I am reluctant to call it a
conversion. I stayed within the religion of Christianity but switched to a denomination whose liberal theology reflected my own. My departure from the
Catholic Church was difficult because it disappointed my parents, but it
didn't reflect a change in my personal beliefs.

So how did this denominational change affect my Faith Club experience? It probably made me a little impatient with Ranya's complaints about
not having a mosque in which she felt comfortable. My husband and I tried
five different church communities before we found St. James'. I didn't understand why Ranya was not similarly shopping for a mosque. It took a while for
me to appreciate how very limited her options were. There simply is not an
equivalent of St. James' in Manhattan's Muslim community.

Did my conversion make me more open to different viewpoints than I
would have been otherwise? I think that by nature I am interested in others'
thoughtful views on faith, and that is one of the reasons I felt more comfortable in the Episcopal Church. It doesn't present itself as being the "only one
Church of Christ that is fully in possession of the truth of the Gospel," as the
Catholic Church states in a Vatican II document. Catholicism considers all

faiths, other than the Catholic and Eastern Orthodox Churches, as capable of reflecting a ray of truth, but still deficient in one way or another. It even considers other Christian churches as not "churches in the proper sense." Within the confines of that theology, I don't think I could have been as open to Judaism and Islam as I was in my Faith Club experience. But other Catholics may not have the same problem I did. The Catholic Church does say that salvation is accessible to those who are not members of the "Church," and it encourages interreligious dialogue. There is a bias, however, in that Catholics should enter the conversation cognizant of the equality of the dignity of the individuals taking part, but not the equality of their different beliefs and practices. As a member of the Episcopal Church, I didn't feel any guilt about my growing appreciation for Islam and Judaism as true religions, equally beloved by God.

2. **As the discussions deepened, you began to struggle with a fundamental tenet—arguably *the* fundamental tenet—of Christianity: Christ's divinity. Have you resolved this question for yourself? Is it important to have moments of doubt about your beliefs?**

Thanks to the doubt that was the result of my Faith Club discussions, I have come to understand Jesus' divinity in a powerful new way. I see Jesus as the form in which God's will—that we love God and our neighbors—and our human destiny—one of suffering and redemption—are revealed. I recognize that the Gospels don't portray Jesus as interpreting God's law or wishes, but as the manifestation of them. I see Jesus' resurrection as distinguishing him from the prophets and supporting the idea that he is one with God.

When the phrase "Son of God" began to make me uncomfortable in my Faith Club experience, I replaced it with the phrase "of the same essence." I am comfortable with that phraseology. In fact, I recently read that the prayers in the Latin Catholic mass used the phrase "con-substantiated with God" when describing Jesus. This means "united in one common substance, nature, or essence." For me it is a more mature definition than the colloquial phrase "Son of God."

I think it is natural to have periods of doubt in one's faith. The surprise for me was that I came out the other end with a more defined faith than I had before. I am no longer frightened so much by the specter of doubt. I see that, as I struggle with my faith, my faith can become stronger. And in those periods of doubt, I am always comforted by the Reverend Craig Townsend's advice to me: "The opposite of faith is not doubt. It's certainty."

Ranya:

1. **Ranya, your upbringing in Dubai and McLean was interwoven with some Christian traditions, but because of your grandparents' and father's experience in Palestine, it was politically antagonistic to Judaism. How did these early influences affect your interactions with Suzanne and Priscilla?**

I certainly grew up more familiar with Christian traditions; however, my family's dispossession from Palestine never translated into a sweeping prejudice against Judaism or Jews. This may be because my father, like many Palestinians, always pointed out that our conflict was political and not religious or personal. So at our first Faith Club meeting, when Priscilla and Suzanne walked through the door, they did so on an equal footing. After all, I had reached out to them after 9/11 out of the despair and alienation I was feeling as an American Muslim. In my mind, it was Islam that for many was the "condemned" religion in America, and I was desperate to defend and reconnect it to the Judeo-Christian tradition.

As time passed, however, their respective Christian and Jewish perspectives did ultimately set us up for different types of conflicts and disagreements. Before my dialogue with Priscilla, everytime I got into a religious or a political conversation with Jewish friends, I automatically knew when to stop or to hold back in order to safeguard the friendship. The big difference with Priscilla was that in the cocoon of the Faith Club, and with our declared mission and objectives, we risked all, and we pushed the envelope to its breaking point. The result was liberating. When Priscilla's Jewish friends expressed disbelief at the truth of my family's painful dispossession, she did not withhold her doubt. When I finally challenged her to reexamine Zionism from a Palestinian perspective and recognize the suffering and victimization of Palestinian Muslims and Christians under a Jewish military occupation, it was not without tears that we were able to cross that bridge. The most gratifying conclusion for that discourse was when Priscilla and I attended Yom Kippur services at her temple. We knew without exchanging a word that we stood shoulder to shoulder and listened united in heart and mind to the prayers of atonement and peace. As for Suzanne, our conflict was not so political, but rather based on what I have in the past felt was a certain Christian prejudice that is quick to condemn Islam and its prophet as a regressive, violent religion spread through the sword. Many Christians can view Christianity with the most liberal of lenses and view Islam only with the most literal of lenses.

2. **On page 198 you say that Suzanne's faith "gave [her] . . . a confidence in [her] . . . religion that I did not have yet. I still felt insecure about Islam as a religion and insecure about my daughter's Muslim identity." Why do you feel this insecurity about Islam? Has the Faith Club helped solidify your confidence in your identity as a Muslim woman?**

If it were not for the insecurity I felt about Islam, I do not know that I would have reached out to Suzanne and Priscilla in the first place. I probably have always felt that insecurity because I belong to a generation that came of age when the loudest and most recognizable Muslim voice is literal, angry, or Wahabist [a reactionary brand of Islam that has striven to "purify" Islam by returning to the beliefs and practices of the first three decades of Muslim rulers]. The reasons for the success and predominance of this movement within Islam have been studied by many. The most persuasive arguments attribute this influence to the power that comes with the petrodollars that fund and support it. Another persuasive argument has to do with the condition of the Muslim state, its political institutions, and its mosques. Religion can be only as enlightened as the hand it finds itself in. The truth is that, historically, Islam has always had a rich history of diversity. For those who are doubtful, I have even found Quranic verses that support the idea that diversity in religion and worship is by God's intended design. The Faith Club has definitely solidified my confidence and identity as a Muslim woman. If ever I felt vulnerable to those who cast doubt on my credentials as a Muslim, I am now completely immune. As Imam Feisal explained to me, in Islam there is no temporal justice. This means that in matters of faith only God can be the judge. Most important, I do not feel that I am a lone voice in the wilderness. I feel that I belong to a vibrant, nascent American Muslim community that shares my ideals and aspirations. I am full of hope and optimism about the potential of Islam in America. I, like many others, dream of a day when our children can truly speak of the Great American Judeo-Christian-Muslim tradition.

Priscilla:

1. **Priscilla, at the beginning of the book you say you weren't "sure whether [you] believed that God really existed." Your journey to faith, then, is arguably the longest. How did your uncertainty contribute to your experience as a member of the Faith Club? Do you think it was harder or easier for you to challenge yourself and your beliefs as a result of your doubt?**

I think it was easy for me to open up to Suzanne and Ranya soon after I met them, to examine and question my beliefs, because I had no other choice. I was desperate to do so. I was in emotional pain and in the midst of a spiritual crisis. September 11th had turned everyone's world upside down, and my world had been shaky to begin with because of my history of panic attacks. My usual ways of coping seemed silly and ineffective. I was praying, but I had no idea why. And once I admitted that to Suzanne and Ranya, I felt liberated. I had nothing to lose. I was open to the theories and ideas they offered to me about faith and religious convictions. I could find out what worked for me and what didn't. I started out lost, so I was desperate to find myself on every level, at every meeting. I wanted to change the way I looked at the world, and in that way, my doubt and uncertainty fueled my spiritual growth.

2. **On page 25 you say that you "wanted [your] . . . learning experience to be a private, personal one." Yet as the Faith Club evolved, you became quite vocal in your defense of Ranya's political views, despite their un-**

popularity with many of your friends. How did your understanding of the "learning experience" change? Do you think that taking a public stand is necessary for the full development of one's faith?

My relationship with Ranya and Suzanne, odd as it may sound, is still private and personal to me, despite the fact that we wrote a book about it, because I carry what I learned deep in my heart. Every time I took a step toward understanding my faith, they were there to support me, challenge me, and illuminate things for me. Their faith rubbed off on me. I am a changed person for knowing them. I began to experience things differently. When I heard people talking about "Muslims" or "Palestinians," to me they were talking about Ranya, and I needed to speak out on her behalf, in her honor. Although I began to speak publicly, it came from a very private place. When I hear cruel, insensitive, or ignorant comments about Islam or Palestinians, those comments are not simply abstract concepts or political rhetoric. They are direct attacks on the beliefs and heritage of my dear friend, who has become like family to me. And when I speak out, I am trying to do justice to Ranya's humanity, her strong moral conscience and courage.

I don't feel that all people need to be public about their beliefs. I admire those who worship quietly and privately, as well as those who feel their personal faith requires them to take a public stand on moral issues. However, I do think it's crucial to be respectful of other people's beliefs at all times.

Discussion Questions

1. How did the book's format (a three-way memoir written in the first person) contribute to the overall feel of the book? At what points did the women write different versions of the same event? (One specific example can be found when Ranya confronts Priscilla about the Israel/Palestinian conflict, pp. 129–143.) How does each woman's individual prejudices and religion color her interpretations of the discussions?

2. How does each woman's role as a mother influence the direction and tone of the Faith Club? Would the club have been different if it included both mothers and women with no children? How did the children play a role in the challenges to each woman's faith?

3. To which woman did you most relate, and why? Was it the one you expected to when you began the book? If you identified with one of the women because you share her religious beliefs, did you agree with her presentation of your faith? What did you disagree with, and why?

4. Much of the first half of the book deals with Suzanne's and Priscilla's struggles to define anti-Semitism and to confront their prejudices about the other's faith. Did you feel that Ranya was unfairly relegated to the role of "mediator" (p. 46), or did she welcome it? "For months, I had to bide my time patiently" (p. 126). Why do you think Ranya waited to bring up her own struggles with Suzanne's and Priscilla's faiths?

5. On page 106, Ranya says, "the more that science unravels about the wonders of life and the universe, the more I am in awe of it." Do you think this combination of science and faith is realistic, or must one ultimately take precedence over the other?

6. Suzanne's first sentence speaks of the "cozy, homogeneous community" at her Episcopal church. What is Priscilla's "comfort zone"? What is Ranya's? How does each woman step out of her individual "cozy and homogeneous" comfort zone, and in what ways do they remain there?

7. On page 147, Priscilla wonders if worrying is "a form of gratefulness."

What do you think she means by this? Does Priscilla's worry ultimately strengthen her faith? How does each woman show gratitude in her life and in her faith?

8. On page 204, Craig Townsend tells Suzanne, "the opposite of faith is not doubt, it's certainty." What does he mean by this? Is doubt necessary for true faith?

9. In Chapter 12, "Intimations of Mortality," the women discuss their differing views about death and the afterlife. Which understanding of death was most comforting to you? Which image of the afterlife was most comforting? Are they from the same religion?

10. When Priscilla confronts Suzanne about her confession that she was uncomfortable being mistaken for a Jew, Ranya says, "She wouldn't want to be a Muslim either." Do you agree? Why or why not? Is Suzanne's discomfort an inevitable result of being a member of the majority, of "not [being] forced to accommodate [herself] to the culture, religion, or even friendship of minorities"?

11. Ranya provides a vivid description of her own method of prayer on page 175: "My prayer is essentially a form of meditation in which I singularly apply my limited human physical capacity to try to connect with that omnipresent universal unknown force: God." (Suzanne's description of her prayer is on page 161; Priscilla's is on page 176.) How is each woman's method of prayer different? How is it similar? How do Suzanne's, Ranya's, and Priscilla's prayer styles reflect the differences and similarities in their childhoods?

Activities

1. Before the meeting, visit the authors' website, www.thefaithclub.com, to explore viewpoints about your own and others' faiths. Use the journaling topics suggested in How to Start a Faith Club; have each member select a topic and bring in questions and reflections to share with the group.

2. During the meeting, serve some of the food that Priscilla, Ranya, and

Suzanne served at many of their Faith Club meetings. For example, you could serve hot chocolate and jasmine tea to your guests. And don't forget Priscilla's favorite—a variety of chocolate bars for a special treat!

3. An important aspect of the authors' Faith Club is their visits to each other's places of worship. Schedule a weekend visit to your local mosque, synagogue, or church. If you can, set up a discussion with the imam, rabbi, or priest.

Frequently Asked Questions

How did the three of you meet?

SUZANNE: *I met Ranya at the school bus stop. Our daughters started kindergarten together in September of 2001.*

RANYA: *At the time I was actively looking for two mothers—one Christian and one Jewish—who would be interested in writing a children's book, a book that could highlight our common religious heritage through biblical stories that unite the Jewish, Christian, and Muslim faiths.*

PRISCILLA: *I was the lucky one. I just answered a telephone call. Suzanne described the children's book project to me, asked me if I'd like to get together with her and Ranya to discuss it, and I drove into the city to meet them for the first time. That phone call changed my life forever.*

Why did you write this book?

RANYA: *For my children and all our children. I start the book with a quote from Rumi—a thirteenth-century Muslim poet and scholar—about burdens being the foundations of ease. And ultimately the book, for me, is about how something that is a burden or a challenge in life can be made into a positive force, a force for change in our world. I, like many Muslims, became acutely sensitive to how our children may be challenged, even burdened, by their religion, especially in America after the terror of 9/11. My most ambitious wish for the book is that it may somehow help to empower Muslims looking for answers and ways to take ownership of their religion. And I hope it will dispel prejudice and fear, so that one day we may be able to speak sincerely of the American Judeo-Christian-Muslim tradition.*

SUZANNE: *I started this book project in order to learn more about Judaism and Islam and to understand how Ranya and Priscilla practice these faiths. Our dialogue was a chance to find common bonds in our religions and to pass these discoveries on to the next generation. The world is getting smaller, and our religions are caught in conflict, so it was important to me to understand these religions better. In the process I was challenged to define what it meant to me to be a moderate Christian in America at a time when fundamentalists control the dialogue about our religion. I want to encourage other Christian Americans to take a similar journey that I hope will lead to mutual respect and understanding within our communities and in the broader world.*

PRISCILLA: *I used to say I wrote the book because I was in a state of panic, but now I realize I was really in a spiritual crisis, which I had confused with an emotional crisis. I had been paralyzed by the attacks of 9/11. I was terrified of terrorism. And talking about religion and how it was affecting the world seemed like a way for me to feel empowered. What I got as a result of all my talking was a definition of my God, my spirituality. I think I was lost, and now I'm found.*

How did you decide what you would discuss at your meetings?

RANYA: *First, our agenda was obvious. We were writing a children's book. Soon, even the children's book tested our religious sensibilities as we grappled with our own prejudices and beliefs. We realized that to be effective communicators for our children, we had a lot to learn as adults. As we pursued the adult dialogue, and we became the Faith Club, our conversations came about organically. Life was our biggest source of material, from aging parents and curious children to cocktail parties and Easter bunnies.*

PRISCILLA: *Things got pretty heated after just a few meetings. We were forced to examine a lot of things I never in a million years thought we'd have to address. And then when life started intervening, our meetings took on a more urgent tone, at least for me. My mother was diagnosed with Alzheimer's and my sister with breast cancer. So I had a lot on my plate, a lot to talk about.*

SUZANNE: *We sought each other's opinions on everything from faith and prayer to death and heaven. We dissected magazine and newspaper articles on religion, trying to understand each others' viewpoints. And we* *wrote, a lot, about what was on our minds. At our meetings we read our writing aloud, and that led to hours of discussion.*

How much outside research and reading did you do?

PRISCILLA: *I would read books that caught my attention because of a story they told, and I would read bits and pieces of historical or religious books because our conversations really required me to be knowledgeable about a lot of issues. Ranya and Suzanne raised the bar for me. And then there were newspaper articles and TV shows that caught my attention because they were covering topics we'd talked about in our faith club.*

SUZANNE: *I started out with simple books about Judaism and Islam, literally with The Complete Idiot's Guide series. Then as I learned more, my reading material became more sophisticated, and it veered toward Christianity as I sought to understand my own religion better. I read books by C. S. Lewis, Karen Armstrong, Elaine Pagels, Augustine, and, of course, I read the Bible. It was the first time I had picked it up on my own to actually read the Gospels outside of church services.*

RANYA: *Many hours. In addition to books that I turned to when I was stuck for answers, I spent a lot of time on the internet visiting Muslim and other sites. Some sites had cyber dialogue, now known as blogs, which helped me keep in touch with what was on people's minds.*

Did you have any rules for your meetings?

RANYA: *Yes: honesty. A tenet we tried to live by. As long as that was true, there was sincerity in our dialogue that helped us overcome conflict.*

SUZANNE: *I would add openness. It was important for us not to keep suspicions or hurt feelings bottled up for too long. It blocked our ability to understand each other. We were required to air what was on our minds, if not immediately then at least in short order.*

RANYA: *And the commitment to keep coming back was very important, even if you felt someone had hurt you or you were unfairly judged, stereotyped, or criticized. Because our biggest moments of truth and* *growth could happen only when there was a certain amount of conflict and tension. When dialogue forces you out of your comfort zone, then you are forced to really examine things in ways you had not thought of before, and as a result you gain a greater understanding of yourself and of others.*

PRISCILLA: *I think it's important for people to be humble. That's what I got out of this experience, a sense of humility. The knowledge that I don't have all the answers, that no one else does either, and that the more ideas we share, the richer our lives are for it.*

What surprised you most about your faith club experience?

PRISCILLA: *I was surprised at how much I stereotyped people, like Suzanne, who went to church regularly and accessed their religion in a very traditional way. I have a lot of friends who go to church, who teach Sunday school, but I never stereotyped them. Maybe because we're friends, and I know their values. But since I didn't know Suzanne, I'm ashamed to say that I looked at her differently. And I think that's an important component of the book—that none of us knew one another well. So any stereotypes or fears we had were very vivid. And sometimes shocking, at least for me. I knew plenty of Christian people, but then I met this woman from Kansas City, who'd gone to school in Texas . . .*

SUZANNE: *I think because I grew up in a Catholic tradition, I equated one's spirituality or religiousness with going to church every Sunday, with the external signs of practicing a religion. Ranya and Priscilla challenged me to think of faith outside of an institutional framework. Then I was very surprised, when I went back to the Gospels, to see how much Jesus opposed the rule-bound way Judaism was practiced in his time.*

RANYA: *I am surprised by the fact that I am now a more confident and committed Muslim. I started out insecure about my qualifications as a Muslim and skeptical about religion in general. I used to say I have faith but no religion. Because of the Faith Club, I now know that Islam, like Judaism and Christianity, has a rich history of plurality and diversity from within. Imam Feisal Abdul al Rauf, whom I met through my Faith*

Club experience, confirmed my legitimacy and credentials as a Muslim when he related a story about the prophet Muhammad in which he was asked, "What does it take to be a Muslim?" Three steps are involved: belief (Islam), faith (Iman), and actions of faith (Ihsan). Only when these elements of faith are fulfilled can you then use rituals and religion as a way to experience and seek proximity to God.

What's the importance for you of sharing this experience with others?

RANYA: *For Muslims it's a calling to pick up the Quran and read it for themselves. I know there are many Muslims out there who are alienated and frustrated by the stereotypes that define their religion and by the institutions that seem to control it. I encourage them to engage in this dialogue, to take control of their religion and to work toward building institutions and communities that will comfort their present and safeguard their children's future. For non-Muslims, I think the book is a call saying, Don't alienate us, don't make us "the other." We are part of you, we are part of the Abrahamic family. Our God is your God. We are part of the fabric of what this society is about.*

SUZANNE: *I would like to shake Christians up a little bit, the way Ranya and Priscilla shook me up! I was very comfortable in my religion, having left the hierarchical and doctrinal Catholic religion for the looser Episcopal religion. But I didn't realize how I could have pressed that religious journey so much farther than I already had. So I want people to question the faith they profess. I want people to question the leaders who are speaking in the name of Christianity. I want moderates to reclaim our understanding and our language regarding Christianity. We should talk loudly about Jesus, faith, baptism, the Bible, and salvation in the liberal way in which we understand them. Otherwise the opponents of evolution, abortion, homosexuality, and universalism will continue to monopolize the Christian dialogue. Finally, I want Christianity to become a force for universality, a force for finding community within all believers of all faiths.*

PRISCILLA: *I entered the relationship, after 9/11, in order to bring my children hope and to bring me hope, and what I want people to get out of the book is a sense of hope, of optimism. People often told us that they were envious of our relationship, of our faith club. I think a lot of people are walking around in spiritual pain. I think people are craving the kind of connection we have with each other. And I think we live in a time when we have no real choice other than to connect with each other. I quote W. H. Auden these days: "We must love one another or die." We've tried other ways of communicating. We've tried not communicating. We've tried using force in order to get our points across. But in our little trio, we've seen what happens when you keep at it, keep forcing the dialogue. If this kind of dialogue could spread, one trio at a time, it could eventually make a huge difference.*

How did three people write one book together?

PRISCILLA: *With a lot of difficulty, conflict, and perseverance! It was particularly challenging when we were in three different geographical locations, or more . . . with Ranya in Greece and Long Island, with me in Martha's Vineyard and New York, with Suzanne in New Hampshire. We wrote a great deal of the book in cyberspace, which is very efficient, but very challenging because there is no nuance in cyberspace, and there is a lot of nuance in our relationship to each other.*

SUZANNE: *Another difficulty arose from the fact that we are different people at the end of the book than at the beginning. Sometimes it was difficult to preserve that naïveté as we edited and shaped the book.*

RANYA: *Collaborations are not easy. They are like marriages, with their ups and downs. But you learn at the end of the day about your partners' strengths and weaknesses. Also, as any writer will tell you, those long, endless hours of editing can be very lonely. It certainly was easier when I was up working at 3:00 a.m. and I heard the email jingle "you've got mail"—knowing that one of my coauthors was also awake.*

Who should read your book?

RANYA: *Everyone! Especially men! Especially the ones that control the world! White male politicians!*

Suzanne: *Anyone who is interested in religion or in the way religion influences our human interactions today.*

Priscilla: *I'd like all kinds of people to read this book—people who know a lot about their religion, people who know very little, people who question whether there is a God, young people, old people. I'd love atheists to read this book. I'd love to see a group of elderly people, people who have an enormous amount of life experience, read and talk. I think that would be such a rich conversation. And young people would bring so much passion and honesty to the table.*

Do you have to be religious to enjoy the book?

Ranya: *I don't think* The Faith Club *is a religious book. I think it's a human book. You can be from anywhere. You can be green, yellow, blue . . . It's about the experience we have day to day living our human lives with all our anxieties, our challenges, our hopes. If you want to call life religious, then so be it. This is a book about life more than it is about religion. The book is about friendship, respect, alienation, fear. It's about our future, about stereotypes, hate, prejudice. In a world where we need to have categories, this book is in the religious one, but I don't think this book can be categorized because I think it encompasses our human experience.*

Priscilla: *I never really thought of myself as a religious person, and never thought I'd ever write a book about religion. But clearly I was in need of this experience, of an examination of my faith, and there are probably a lot of other people like me out there who would enjoy this book.*

Suzanne: The Faith Club *is a book about people challenging themselves and challenging each other about the meaning of life, the meaning of being human today, being American today, of being religious or nonreligious, believing in God or not believing in God. It's about people exploring the opinions they have about other people—opinions we walk around with every day but don't really recognize. It's about understanding the stereotypes and prejudices that have influenced us since childhood and* *recognizing that those attitudes influence the way we view the world today. And that's something that every person—male, female, religious, nonreligious, young or old—can benefit from. Hopefully it will lead readers on their own quest for self-discovery. To help them we've included faith club material in this book.*

RANYA: *I think it's a book for people who choose to question and think about life, and I think the beauty of the book is that we've discovered through our experience that often we don't have the time anymore to stop and smell the roses. This book encourages people to stop for a moment, unravel, turn your world around, and ask big "if" questions. Generally, in our everyday life we don't find ourselves doing that, and I think the Faith Club gives us that opportunity.*

שאלות שנשאלות לעתים קרובות

ש. כיצד נפגשתן שלושתכן?

ת. סוזן: פגשתי את רניה בתחנה של ההסעה לביה"ס. בנותינו התחילו גן חובה ביחד בספטמבר 2001.

רניה: בזמנו חיפשתי אחר שתי אמהות – נוצרייה ויהודייה – שתהיינה מעוניינות לכתוב ספר לילדים. ספר שיוכל להדגיש את המסורת הדתית המשותפת שלנו דרך סיפורי התנ"ך שמאחדים את האמונה היהודית, הנוצרית והמוסלמית.

פריסילה: אני הייתי ברת מזל. אני רק עניתי לצלצול טלפון. סוזן תארה בפני את הפרויקט של ספר הילדים, שאלה אותי אם היית רוצה להפגש אתה ועם רניה לשוחח על כך, ונסעתי לעיר לפגוש אותן בפעם הראשונה. צלצול טלפון זה שינה את חיי לתמיד.

ש. מדוע כתבתן את הספר הזה?

ת. רניה: לילדי ולכל הילדים שלנו. התחלתי את הספר עם ציטוט רומי – משורר מוסלמי מהמאה ה-13 ומלומד – על נטל כבסיס להקלה. ובאופן מוחלט הספר, בשבילי, מתאר איך משהו שהוא נטל או אתגר בחיים יכול להיהפך לכוח חיובי, כוח לשינוי העולם שלנו. אני, כמו מוסלמים רבים, הפכתי לרגישה באופן קיצוני לאופן שבו ילדינו יכולים להיות מאותגרים, אפילו מולחצים בגלל הדת שלהם, במיוחד באמריקה שאחרי הטרור של ה - 11 בספטמבר. השאיפה הגדולה ביותר של הספר היא שהוא יכול להקל על מוסלמים המחפשים תשובות ודרכים ליצג את דמם ולבער דעות קדומות ופחדים, כך שיום אחד נוכל לדבר ברצינות על מסורת יהודית-נוצרית-מוסלמית אמריקנית.

סוזן: התחלתי את הפרויקט של הספר כדי ללמוד יותר על יהדות ואיסלם ולהבין כיצד רניה ופריסילה מקיימות אמונות אלה. הדיאלוג שלנו היה הזדמנות למצוא מכנים משותפים בדתות שלנו ולהעביר את הממצאים האלה לדור הבא. העולם נעשה קטן יותר, והדתות שלנו לכודות בעימות, לכן זה היה לי חשוב להבין את הדתות האלה טוב יותר. בתהליך זה היה לי אתגר להגדיר לעצמי מה המשמעות של היותי נוצרייה מתונה באמריקה בתקופה שבה קיצוניים שולטים בדיון הפומבי בדתות שלנו. אני רוצה לעודד נוצרים אמריקנים לצאת למסע דומה שאני מקווה שיוביל להערכה הדדית ולהבנה בתוך הקהילות שלנו ובעולם הרחב יותר.

פריסילה: אני נהגתי לומר שכתבתי את הספר בגלל שהייתי במצב של חרדה, אבל עכשיו אני מבינה שהייתי באמת במשבר רוחני, שבלבלתי אותו עם משבר רגשי. הייתי משותקת בגלל המתקפה של ה - 11 בספטמבר. נחרדתי מטרור. הדיבור על דת וכיצד היא השפיעה על העולם

נראה לי כדרך להתאושש. מה שקיבלתי כתוצאה מכל הדיבורים שלי היה הגדרה של אלוהים, ושל הרוחניות שלי. אני חושבת שהייתי אבודה, ועכשיו מצאתי את עצמי.

ש. כיצד החלטתן על על מה תדברו בפגישותיכן?

ת. רניה: ראשית, התוכנית שלנו הייתה ברורה. כתבנו ספר ילדים. במהרה, אפילו ספר הילדים העמיד במבחן את הרגישויות הדתיות שלנו, מאחר שהתמודדנו עם הדעות הקדומות והאמונות שלנו. הבנו שכדי לתקשר בצורה יעילה עם ילדינו עלינו ללמוד הרבה כמבוגרות. כשהמשכנו בדיאלוג הבוגר שלנו ונהפכנו למועדון האמונה, השיחות שלנו נבעו באופן טבעי. החיים היו המקור הגדול ביותר לנושאים שלנו, מהורים מזדקנים וילדים סקרנים, למסיבות קוקטייל וארנבונים של פסחא.

פריסילה: העניינים התחממו למדי אחרי מספר פגישות. נאלצנו לבדוק דברים רבים שמעולם לא חשבתי שנצטרך להתייחס אליהם. ואז כאשר החיים החלו להתערב, הפגישות שלנו קיבלו טון דחוף יותר, לפחות מבחינתי. אמא שלי אובחנה כחולת אלצהיימר, ואחותי כחולה בסרטן השד. כך שהיה לי עם מה להתמודד ועל מה לדבר.

סוזן: בדקנו את דעות כל אחת ודעות כולנו על כל דבר החל מאמונה ותפילה עד מוות וגן העדן. הוצאנו מאמרים על דת מכתבי עת ועיתונים, כדי להבין את האחת את נקודת הראות של רעותה. וכתבנו, הרבה, על כל מה שעלה בדעתנו. בפגישות שלנו קראנו את מה שכתבנו בקול רם, וזה הוביל לשעות של שיחה.

ש. עד כמה עשיתן בדיקת מקורות וקריאה?

ת. פריסילה: אני הייתי הבטלנית של הקבוצה כאשר זה הגיע למחקר! הייתי קוראת ספרים שתפסו את תשומת לבי בגלל הסיפור שהם סיפרו, והייתי קוראת קטעים מספרים היסטוריים או דתיים מאחר שהשיחות שלנו באמת דרשו ממני ידע בתחומים רבים. רניה וסוזן העלו את המשוכה בשבילי. ואז היו גם מאמרים בעתון ותוכניות טלוויזיה שתפסו את תשומת לבי, כי הם כיסו נושאים שדיברנו עליהם במועדון האמונה.

סוזן: אני התחלתי עם ספרים בסיסיים על יהדות ואיסלם. באופן מילולי עם הסדרות של "המדריך המלא לאידיוט". ואז כשלמדתי יותר, חומר הקריאה שלי הפך להיות מתוחכם יותר, והוא נטה לכיוון הנצרות כי חיפשתי להבין טוב יותר את הדת שלי. קראתי ספרים של סי.אס. לואיס, קרן ארמסטרונג, אלין פיגלס, אוגוסטינוס, וכמובן, קראתי את הברית החדשה. זו הייתה הפעם הראשונה שנטלתי אותה מיוזמתי לקרוא ממש את האוונגליונים מחוץ לתפילות בכנסיה.

רניה: במשך שעות רבות. בנוסף על הספרים שפניתי אליהם כשנתקעתי בשאלות ללא תשובות, ביליתי הרבה זמן באינטרנט בביקור באתרים מוסלמים ואתרים אחרים. באתרים מסוימים היו

דיאלוגים, בצורה של מה שידוע עתה כבלוגים, שעזרו לי להיות בקשר עם מה שהיה בראשם של אנשים.

ש. האם היו לכם כללים כלשהם לפגישות שלכם?

ת. רניה: כן, כנות. עקרון שניסינו לחיות על פיו. כל עוד שזה היה אמיתי, היתה כנות בדיאלוג שלנו שעזרה לנו להתגבר על עימות.

סוזן: אני הייתי מוסיפה פתיחות. זה היה חשוב לנו לא לכלוא חשדנות או פגיעה ברגשות לזמן רב מדי. זה חסם את היכולת שלנו להבין האחת את האחרת. נדרשנו לאוורר מה שהיה במחשבותינו, אם לא מיד אז לפחות תוך זמן קצר.

רניה: והמחויבות להמשיך ולבוא שוב היתה חשובה מאוד, גם כאשר הרגשת שמישהי פגעה בך או שנשפטת בצורה לא הוגנת, תויגת באופן סטריאוטיפי, או בוקרת. כי הרגע הגדול ביותר של אמת וגדילה יכלה להתרחש כשהיו עימות ומתח במידה מסוימת. כאשר דיאלוג מאלץ אותך לצאת מהאזור הבטוח שלך אז את נאלצת לבחון באמת דברים בדרך שלא היית חושבת עליה קודם וכתוצאה מכך את זוכה בהבנה גדולה יותר של עצמך ושל אחרים.

פריסילה: אני חושבת שזה חשוב שאנשים יהיו ענווים. זה מה שאני קיבלתי מהחוויה הזו, תחושה של ענווה. הידיעה שאין לי את כל התשובות, שגם לאף אחד אחר אין, ושבכל שאנו שותפים ליותר רעיונות, כך חיינו נעשים עשירים יותר.

ש. מה הפתיע אתכן במיוחד בחוויה של מועדון האמונה?

ת. פריסילה: הופתעתי עד כמה תייגתי בצורה סטריאוטיפית אנשים כמו סוזן שהלכו לכנסיה בקביעות והגיעו לאמונה שלהם בצורה מסורתית. יש לי הרבה חברים שהולכים לכנסיה, שמלמדים בבי"ס של יום ראשון, אבל מעולם לא תייגתי אותם בצורה סטריאוטיפית. אולי כי אנחנו חברים, ואני מכירה את הערכים שלהם. אבל מאחר שלא הכרתי את סוזן, אני מתביישת להגיד שהסתכלתי עליה באופן שונה. ואני חושבת שזה מרכיב חשוב בספר – שאף אחת מאתנו לא הכירה האחת את רעותה.

לכן כל אחד מהסטריאוטיפים או הפחדים שהיו לנו היו חיוניים מאוד. ולעיתים מדהימים, לפחות לגבי. הכרתי המון אנשים נוצרים, אבל אז פגשתי את סוזן, אשה זו מקנזס סיטי, שלמדה בקולג' בטקסס...

סוזן: אני חושבת שבגלל שגדלתי במסורת קתולית זיהיתי זהירות רוחניות או דתיות של מישהו עם ללכת לכנסיה כל יום ראשון, עם סימנים חיצוניים של קיום מצוות דת. רניה ופריסילה איתגרו אותי לחשוב על אמונה מחוץ למסגרת מוסדית. אז הייתי מופתעת מאוד כשחזרתי לאונגליונים (ספרי הבשורה) לראות עד כמה ישו התנגד לדרך שבה היהדות בזמנו היתה כפופה לכללים.

רניה: אני מופתעת על ידי העובדה שעכשיו אני יותר בטוחה ומחויבת לאיסלם. התחלתי בחוסר

בטחון ביחס לכישורים שלי כמוסלמית וספקנית ביחס לדת בכלל. נהגתי לומר שיש לי אמונה אבל לא דת. הודות למועדון האמונה אני יודעת עכשיו שהאיסלם, כמו היהדות והנצרות, הוא בעל היסטוריה של ריבוי וגיוון שבא מתוכו. האימם פייסל עבדאל ראוף שאותו פגשתי דרך מועדון האמונה שלי, אישר את הלגיטימיות והאמינות שלי כמוסלמית כשהוא התייחס לסיפור על הנביא מוחמד שבו הוא נשאל "מה דרוש כדי להיות מוסלמי?" שלושה צעדים דרושים לכך: בטחון באל והשלמה (איסלם) אמונה (אימאן) ופעולה של אמונה (היאסאם). רק כאשר מרכיבים אלה קיימים אפשר להשתמש בפולחנים ובדת כדרך לחוות ולחפש קירבה לאל.

ש. מהי החשיבות בשבילכן של שיתוף אחרים בהתנסות הזו?

ת. רניה: בשביל המוסלמים זו קריאה לקחת את הקוראן ולקרוא בו בעצמם. אני יודעת שיש מוסלמים רבים שהם מנוכרים ומתוסכלים על ידי הסטראוטיפים שמגדירים את דתם ועל ידי המוסדות שנראה ששולטים עליה. אני מעודדת אותם להיות מעורבים בדיאלוג הזה, לקחת שליטה על דתם ולעבוד לקראת בנייה של מוסדות וקהילות שיקלו על ההווה שלהם ויגנו על העתיד של ילדיהם. בשביל לא-מוסלמים, אני חושבת שהספר הוא קריאה האומרת: "אל תתנכרו לנו. אל תהפכו אותנו ל"אחר". אנחנו חלק מכם, אנחנו חלק מהמשפחה של אברהם. האל שלנו הוא האל שלכם. אנו חלק מרקמת החברה הזו".

סוזן: אני רוצה לנער קצת את הנוצרים, בדרך שבה רניה ופריסילה ניערו אותי! היה לי נוח מאוד בדת שלי, כשעזבתי את הדת הקתולית הדוקטרינרית וההיררכית לטובת דת אפיסקופלית רופפת יותר. אך לא הבנתי כיצד יכולתי לדחוף את מסע הדת הזה רחוק יותר כל כך ממה שכבר עשיתי. לכן אני רוצה שאנשים יערערו על האמונה שהם מקיימים. אני רוצה שאנשים יערערו על סמכותם של מנהיגים המדברים בשם הנצרות. אני רוצה מנהיגים שיקדמו את ההבנה שלנו ואת השפה שלנו ביחס לנצרות. עלינו לדבר בקול על ישו, אמונה, הטבלה, הברית החדשה, הגאולה בדרך הליברלית שבה אנו מבינים אותם. אחרת המתנגדים לאבולוציה, הפלה, הומוסקסואליות ואוניברסליזם ימשיכו להיות בעלי השליטה הבלעדיים על הדיאלוג הנוצרי. לבסוף, אני רוצה שהנצרות תהפוך לכוח מניע לאוניברסליות, לכוח מניע ליצירת קהילה בקרב כל המאמינים של כל הדתות.

פריסילה: נכנסתי למסגרת הזו, אחרי ה-11 בספטמבר, כדי להביא לילדיי תקווה ולהביא לעצמי תקווה, ומה שאני רוצה שאנשים יקבלו מהספר הוא תחושה של תקווה, של אופטימיות. אנשים תמיד מספרים לנו שהם קינאו במערכת היחסים בינינו, במועדון האמונה שלנו. אני חושבת הרבה על אנשים החיים עכשיו עם סבל רוחני. אני חושבת שאנשים משוועים לסוג הקשר שיש לנו האחת עם האחרת. ואני חושבת שאנחנו חיים בזמן שבו אין לנו ברירה אחרת מאשר להתחבר האחד לשני. אני מצטטת את ו. א. אודן בימים אלה: "אנחנו חייבים לאהוב האחד את השני או למות". ניסינו דרכים אחרות של תקשורת. ניסינו חוסר תקשורת. ניסינו להשתמש בכוח כדי לבטא את דעתנו. אך במשולש הקטן שלנו ראינו מה קורה כאשר את ממשיכה בזאת, ממשיכה לדחוף את

הדיאלוג. אם סוג כזה של דיאלוג יכול היה להתפשט, משולש אחד בכל פעם, זה יכול היה לבסוף להביא לשינוי גדול.

ש. כיצד שלוש נשים כותבות ספר אחד ביחד?

ת. פריסילה: עם קשיים מרובים, עימותים והתמדה! זה היה מאתגר במיוחד כאשר אנחנו היינו בשלושה מקומות שונים, או יותר... עם רניה ביון ובלונג איילנד, אתי במרתה'ס ויניארד וניו-יורק, עם סוזן בניו-המשיר.... כתבנו חלק ניכר מהספר באמצעות התכתבות אלקטרונית, שזה יעיל מאוד, אך מאוד מאתגר גם כן. כי אין ניואנסים בהתכתבות הזו, ויש הרבה מאוד ניואנסים ביחסים שבינינו.

סוזן: קושי אחר עלה מהעובדה שאנו נשים שונות בסוף הספר בהשוואה לתחילתו. לעתים זה היה קשה לשמור את התמימות הזו, כשערכנו ועיצבנו את הספר.

רניה: שיתופי פעולה אינם קלים. הם כמו נישואים עם עליות ומורדות. אבל את לומדת בסופו של דבר על הכוח והחולשה של השותפה שלך. כמו כן, כמו שכל סופרת תספר לך, כל אותן שעות ללא סוף של עריכה יכולות להיות בודדות מאוד. זה לבטח הפך את זה לקל יותר כשהייתי קמה ב-3:00 בבוקר לעבוד ושמעתי את הצלצול של האי-מייל "יש לך מייל" בידיעה שאחת מהמחברות-שותפות שלי היתה ערה גם כן.

ש. מי צריך לקרוא את הספר שלכן?

ת. רניה: כולם! במיוחד גברים! במיוחד אלה ששולטים בעולם! גברים לבנים פוליטיקאים!
סוזן: כל אחד שמתעניין בדת או בדרך שבה הדת משפיעה על היחסים האנושיים בימינו.
פריסילה: אני הייתי רוצה שאנשים הבאים מסביבות שונות יקראו את הספר – אנשים היודעים הרבה על דת, אנשים היודעים מעט מאוד, אנשים שאינם בטוחים אם יש אלוהים, אנשים צעירים, ואנשים זקנים. הייתי שמחה שאתאיסטים יקראו את הספר. הייתי אוהבת לראות קבוצה של אנשים זקנים, אנשים שיש להם ניסיון חיים רב מאוד, קוראים ומדברים. אני חושבת שזו תהיה שיחה עשירה כל כך. ואנשים צעירים יביאו כל כך הרבה תשוקה וכנות לדיון.

ש. האם צריכים להיות דתיים כדי ליהנות מהספר?

ת. רניה: אני לא חושבת שמועדון *האמונה* הוא ספר דתי. אני חושבת שהוא ספר אנושי. את יכולה להיות מכל מקום. את יכולה להיות ירוקה, צהובה, כחולה... זה על החוויה שיש לנו ביום יום, חיים את חיינו האנושיים עם כל החרדות שלנו, האתגרים שלנו, התקוות שלנו. אם את רוצה לקרוא לחיים דת, אז שיהיה כך. זהו ספר על החיים יותר מאשר על דת. הספר הוא על ידידות, כבוד, ניכור, חרדה. הוא על העתיד שלנו, על סטראוטיפים, שנאה, דעה קדומה. בעולם שבו אנו זקוקים

למיונים ודרוגים, הספר הזה הוא ספר דתי, אך אני לא חושבת שספר זה יכול להיות מקוטלג רק כך, כי אני חושבת שהוא מקיף את החוויה האנושית שלנו.

פריסילה: מעולם לא חשבתי על עצמי כאדם דתי באמת, ומעולם לא חשבתי שאכתוב ספר על דת. אבל ברור שחשתי בצורך של חוויה כזו, של בחינה של אמונתי, ויש בוודאי הרבה אנשים אחרים כמוני אי שם שייהנו מספר זה.

סוזן: *מועדון האמונה* הוא ספר על אנשים המאתגרים את עצמם ואת זולתם על משמעות החיים, המשמעות של להיות אדם כיום, להיות אמריקני היום, להיות דתי או לא דתי, מאמין באלוהים או לא מאמין באלוהים. זה על אנשים הבודקים את הדעות שיש להם על אנשים אחרים, דעות שאנו מסתובבים אתן בכל יום אבל לא ממש מזהים אותן. זה על הבנת הסטראוטיפים והדעות הקדומות שהשפיעו עלינו מאז הילדות. ההכרה בכך שגישות אלה משפיעות על הדרך שבה אנו רואים את העולם כיום. וזה משהו שכל אדם – גבר, אשה, דתי, לא דתי, צעיר וזקן – יכול לצאת נשכר ממנו. בתקווה שזה יוביל קוראים לחיפוש משלהם אחר גילוי עצמי. כדי לעזור אנו מציעות להם חומר קריאה נוסף של *מועדון האמונה* בגב הספר.

רניה: אני חושבת שזה ספר לאנשים שבוחרים לחיות בתוך שאלות ומחשבות על החיים, ואני חושבת שהיופי של הספר הוא שאנו מגלים דרך החוויה שלנו שלעתים קרובות אין לנו כבר זמן לעצור, לעשות הפסקה, ולחשוב לרגע. הספר הזה מעודד אנשים לעצור לרגע, להפתח, להביט מחדש בעולמם ולשאול שאלות של "אם" גדול. בדרך כלל, בחיי היום יום שלנו איננו מוצאים את עצמנו עושים זאת, ואני חושבת שמועדון *האמונה* נותן לנו את ההזדמנות הזו.

أسئلة متكررة

س. كيف التقيتم ثلاثتكم؟

ج. **سوزان**: التقيت برانية عند موقف باص المدرسة. فابنتانا كانتا في الروضة معا في أيلول/سبتمبر سنة 2001.

رانية: كان ذلك في الوقت الذي كنت أبحث فيه جاهدة عن والدتين – مسيحية ويهودية – تكونان مهتمتين بتأليف كتاب للأطفال. كتاب بمقدوره أن يلقي الضوء على تراثنا الديني المشترك من خلال القصص المذكورة في الكتب المقدسة والتي توحد بين الديانات الثلاث اليهودية والمسيحية والإسلام.

بريسيلا: أما أنا فقد كنت المحظوظة. فلم يكن عليّ إلا الرد على جرس الهاتف. وصفت لي سوزان مشروع كتاب الأطفال وسألتني إذا ما كنت أرغب في مقابلتها ورانية لمناقشته. وهكذا ركبت سيارتي وذهبت إلى المدينة للالتقاء بهن للمرة الأولى. وهكذا غيرت تلك المكالمة الهاتفية حياتي للأبد.

س. لماذا ألّفتم الكتاب؟

ج. **رانية**: ألفته من أجل أولادي ومن أجل أولادنا جميعا. فأنا أستهل الكتاب بمقولة لجلال الدين الرومي – وهو شاعر وعالم مسلم من القرن الثالث عشر – عن كيف يمكن للأعباء أن تكون أساس الطمأنينة. وبشكل أساسي، فالكتاب بالنسبة لي هو كيف يمكن لشيء يعد عبئا أن تحد أو يُحَول إلى قوة إيجابية، قوة تدفع نحو التغيير في عالمنا. فأنا، وكغيري الكثير من المسلمين، أصبحت مدركة بشكل كبير للتحديات التي قد تواجه أبناءنا، حتى أن دينهم غدا عبئا عليهم خصوصا في الولايات المتحدة الأمريكية بعد الهجمات الإرهابية في الحادي عشر من أيلول/سبتمبر. غاية أمنيتي للكتاب هو أن يساعد ما على البحث عن أجوبة ووسائل ليتفهموا دينهم، لكي نسقط الخوف والإجحاف حتى نستطيع في يوم ما التكلم بإخلاص عن المعتقد اليهودي-المسيحي-الإسلامي.

سوزان: بدأت مشروع الكتاب هذا لأتعلم المزيد عن اليهودية والإسلام ولكي أدرك كيف تمارس كل من رانية وبريسيلا معتقداتهما. وكان حوارنا فرصة للعثور على روابط مشتركة بين أديانا ولتمرير هذه الاكتشافات إلى الجيل التالي. فعالمنا الذي نعيش فيه آخذ بالصغر، ودياناتنا عالقة في الصراعات، ولهذا فقد كان ضروريا بالنسبة لي أن أفهم هذه الأديان بشكل أفضل. وقد واجهني تحد خلال هذه العملية لأن أعرّف ما الذي يعنيه بالنسبة لي أن أكون مسيحية معتدلة في الولايات المتحدة الأمريكية في وقت يتحكم فيه الأصوليون بالخطاب حول ديننا. فأنا أريد أن أشجع الأمريكيين المسيحيين الآخرين للخوض في تجربة مماثلة والتي أرجو أن تقود إلى احترام وتفاهم متبادل في مجتمعاتنا وفي العالم.

بريسيلا: كنت أقول في الماضي بأنني ألفت الكتاب لأنني كنت في حالة هلع، ولكني أدرك الآن بأني كنت في أزمة روحانية أخطأت في تقديرها على أنها أزمة وجدانية. لقد تركتني هجمات الحادي عشر من أيلول/سبتمبر عاجزة، حيث أنني كنت مذعورة من الإرهاب. وبدا لي بأن الحديث عن الدين وكيف أنه يؤثر على العالم

وسيلة تجعلني أشعر بالقوة. وكان ما جنيته من كل أحاديثي هو تحديد لهوية إلهي، وروحانيتي. أعتقد بأني كنت ضائعة، ولكني وجدت نفسي الآن.

س. كيف كنتم تختارون المواضيع التي كنتم تناقشونها في اجتماعاتكم؟

ج. **رانية:** في البداية كانت أجندتنا واضحة، وهي تأليف كتاب للأطفال. ولكن حتى كتاب الأطفال هذا سرعان ما اختبر حساسياتنا الدينية كلما كنا نتشبث بآرائنا المسبقة ومعتقداتنا. فلقد أدركنا بأنه لا بد لنا كبالغين من أن نتعلم الكثير كي نصبح متواصلين فاعلين مع أولادنا. وبعد أن واصلنا حوارنا، وأصبحنا نشكل نادي الإيمان، أخذت محادثاتنا تأتي بطريقة طبيعية. وكانت الحياة مصدرنا الأكبر للأشياء التي نتحدث عنها، من الآباء المتقدمين في العمر والأطفال الفضوليين إلى حفلات الكوكتيل وأرانب عيد الفصح.

بريسيلا: أصبحت الأمور محتدة جدا بعد عدة اجتماعات فقط. فقد اُجبرنا على الخوض في الكثير من الأمور التي لم أفكر أبدا ولا في أي يوم من الأيام بأننا سنضطر إلى التصدي إليها. وعندما بدأت الحياة بالتدخل وفرض نفسها، اتسمت اجتماعاتنا بنبرة أكثر إلحاحا، وذلك بالنسبة لي على الأقل. فقد أصيبت والدتي بمرض الزهايمر، وأختي بسرطان الثدي. وهكذا كان لدي الكثير لأتحدث عنه.

سوزان: لقد سعينا لمعرفة رأي كل منا حول كل شيء بداية بالإيمان والصلاة إلى الموت والجنة. وناقشنا مقالات عن الدين من الصحف والمجلات محاولين فهم وجهة نظر كل منا. وكتبنا الكثير عما كان يدور في خواطرنا. وفي اجتماعاتنا كنا نقرأ ما كتبنا بصوت عال وهو ما كان يقود إلى ساعات من النقاش.

س. كم حجم البحث والقراءة التي قمتم بها خارج اجتماعاتكم؟

ج. **بريسيلا:** أنا كنت المتكاسلة في المجموعة عندما كان الأمر يتعلق بالبحث! كنت أقرأ الكتب التي تجلب انتباهي بسبب القصص التي كانت ترويها رانية وسوزان، وكنت أقرأ مقتطفات من كتب تاريخية أو دينية لأن حواراتنا كانت تتطلب بالفعل أن يكون لدي إلمام حول العديد من القضايا. لقد قامت رانية وسوزان بوضع معايير جديدة لي. ومن ثم كانت هناك مقالات صحفية وبرامج تلفزيونية جلبت انتباهي حيث أنها كانت تعرض لمواضيع كنا قد تحدثنا عنها في نادي الإيمان الخاص بنا.

سوزان: بدأت بقراءة كتب بسيطة حول اليهودية والإسلام، وبالتحديد سلسلة الدليل الوافي للمبتدئين. وبعد أن ازددت في العلم، أخذت بقراءة كتب أكثر تعقيدا، وتوجهت نحو المسيحية حيث سعيت إلى فهم ديانتي نفسها بصورة أفضل. قرأت كتبا ألفها سي أس لويس وكارين آرمنسترونغ وإلين بيغلز وأوغستن، كما وقرأت الإنجيل. وكانت تلك المرة الأولى التي أحمله من تلقاء نفسي لأقرأه خارج صلوات الكنيسة.

رانية: لقد أمضيت ساعات كثيرة في القراءة. فإضافة لقراءة الكتب التي لجأت إليها بحثا عن أجوبة، أمضيت الكثير من الوقت بزيارة المواقع الإسلامية وغيرها على شبكة الإنترنت. وكان لدى بعض هذه المواقع مساحة للحوار تُسمى المدونات، وقد ساعدتني هذه في البقاء على اتصال مع ما كان يدور في أذهان الناس.

س. هل كانت لديكم أي ضوابط تحكم اجتماعاتكم؟

ج. رانية: نعم، الصدق. وهو مبدأ اجتهدنا في أن نتمسك به. وكلما كان الأمر على تلك الحال من الصدق، كان هناك إخلاص في حوارنا ساعدنا في التغلب على الخلاف.

سوزان: وأنا أُضيف مبدأ الانفتاح. فقد كان مهما بالنسبة لنا أن نكتم مخاوفنا أو مشاعرنا المؤلمة لفترة طويلة. فقد كان من الممكن أن يعيق ذلك قدرة كل منا على فهم الآخر. وهكذا كان علينا البوح بما كان يجول في خواطرنا مباشرة أو خلال فترة قصيرة على الأقل.

رانية: لقد كان الالتزام بالمتابعة وحضور الاجتماعات باستمرار في غاية الأهمية، حتى وإن تعرض أحدنا لإساءة أو حكم غير منصف أو الانتقاد أو التنميط. لأن لحظاتنا الصادقة وتطورنا ما كان ليتحقق إلّا بوجود قدر معين من النزاع والتوتر. فعندما يجبرك الحوار على الخروج من صومعتك، تصبح مجبرا لأن تبحث الأمور بطريقة لم تفكر بها مسبقا وكنتيجة لذلك فإنك تكتسب قدرا أكبر من الفهم لنفسك وللآخرين.

بريسيلا: أعتقد بأنه من المهم أن يكون الناس متواضعين. وهذا ما تعلمته من هذه التجربة، إحساس بالتواضع، والإدراك بأني لا أملك إجابات لكل شيء وبأنه لا يوجد مَن يملكها أيضا وبأنه كلما تشاركنا أكثر بالأفكار كلما ازدادت حياتنا غنى.

س. ما أكثر شيء أثار اندهاشكم خلال تجربتكم في نادي الإيمان؟

ج. بريسيلا: لقد تفاجئت بالقدر الذي كانت عليه الصورة النمطية التي رسمتها لسوزان وآخرين مثلها يذهبون للكنيسة بانتظام ويمارسون شعائرهم الدينية بالطريقة المعتادة. فأنا عندي الكثير من الأصدقاء مثلهم ممن يذهبون إلى الكنيسة ويُدرِّسون في مدارس الأحد الدينية، ولكني لم أصنفهم بشكل نمطي أبدا. ربما لأننا أصدقاء ولأنني أعرف قيمهم. **وأنا أشعر بالخجل لأن سابق عدم معرفتي الشخصية بسوزان جعلتني أنظر إليها بطريقة مختلفة.** وأعتقد أن هذا عنصر مهم في الكتاب - وهو أنه لم يكن أي منا يعرف الآخر. وهكذا فإن أي صور نمطية أو مخاوف كنا نمتلكها كانت جلية للغاية. وفي بعض الأحيان كانت فظيعة، بالنسبة لي على الأقل، حيث كنت أعرف الكثير من الأشخاص المسيحيين، ثم إني قابلت هذه المرأة القادمة من كنساس سيتي والتي ذهبت إلى جامعة في تكساس...

سوزان: أعتقد بأن ترعرعي على التراث الكاثوليكي جعلني أربط ما بين روحانية شخص ما أو تدينه بذهابه إلى الكنيسة كل يوم أحد، أي بالدلالات الخارجية على ممارسته لدينه. وقد استوقفتني رانية وبريسيلا لأن أفكر في الإيمان خارج هذا الإطار المؤسسي. ومن ثم تفاجئت جدا حينما رجعت إلى الإنجيل لأجد أن المسيح عارض بشدة الطريقة المُقيَّدة بالأحكام التي كانت اليهودية تُمارس فيها في وقته.

رانية: لقد تفاجئت بحقيقة أني أصبحت مسلمة أكثر إيمانا والتزاما الآن. ففي البداية كنت غير واثقة من أهليتي كشخص مسلم وكنت مشككة في الدين عموما. كنت أقول أن لدي إيمان لا ديانة. وبسبب نادي الإيمان، فأنا أعلم الآن في داخلي بأن الإسلام، كالمسيحية واليهودية، يمتلك تاريخا زاخرا بالتعددية والتنوع. وقد أكد الإمام فيصل عبد الرؤوف والذي التقيته من خلال تجربتي في نادي الإيمان على أهليتي وثبوت أوراق اعتمادي كمسلمة حيث روى لي قصة عن أن النبي محمد سُئل، «مالذي يحتاج المرء أن يفعله لأن يكون مسلما؟» فكانت هناك

ثلاث خطوات معنية بهذا وهي المُعتقد (الإسلام)، والإيمان، وما يصدر عنه من تصرفات (الإحسان). وعندما تتحقق عناصر الإيمان هذه فقط يُمكن للمرء حينها استخدام الشعائر والدين كوسيلة للتقرب لله.

س. ما هي أهمية إشراك الآخرين بهذه التجربة بالنسبة لكم؟

ج. رانية: بالنسبة للمسلمين، هي دعوة لأن يقرؤوا القرآن بأنفسهم. أنا أعلم بأن هناك الكثير من المسلمين في العالم محبطين ويشعرون بالإقصاء بسبب الصور النمطية التي تضع تعريفا لدينهم وبسبب المؤسسات التي تبدو على أنها تتحكم به. فأنا أشد على أيديهم للانخراط في هذا الحوار حتى يتولوا زمام أمور دينهم ويعملوا من أجل بناء مؤسسات ومجتمعات تعزز حاضرهم وتصون مستقبل أبنائهم. أما بالنسبة لغير المسلمين، أعتقد بأن الكتاب يمثل دعوة لهم بألا يقصونا، وألا يجعلونا الطرف «الآخر.» فنحن جزء منكم، وجزء من العائلة الإبراهيمية. وإلهنا هو إلهكم. ونحن جزء من النسيج الذي يمثله هذا المجتمع.

سوزان: أريد أن أهزّ المسيحيين بعض الشيء كما فعلت بي رانية وبريسيلا! فقد كنت مرتاحة جدا في ديني بعد أن تركت الطائفة الكاثوليكية العقائدية الكهنوتية من أجل الدخول في الكنيسة الأسقفية الأكثر تساهلا. ولكني لم أكن أدرك أنه كان بإمكاني مواصلة رحلة البحث الدينية هذه إلى أبعد مما كنت قد وصلت إليه. ولهذا فأنا أريد الناس أن يطرحوا الأسئلة حول إيمانهم الذي يمارسونه. أريدهم أن يسائلوا قادتهم الذين يتحدثون باسم المسيحية. أريد من المعتدلين أن يصوّبوا فهمنا والطريقة التي نتحدث بها بخصوص المسيحية. فينبغي لنا التكلم بصوت عال عن المسيح والإيمان والمعمودية والإنجيل والخلاص بالطريقة المتحررة التي نفهمهم بها. وإلّا فإن المعارضين لنظرية التطور والإجهاض والمثلية الجنسية وشمولية الأديان سيواصلون احتكار الحوار المسيحي. وفي النهاية، أريد أن تصبح المسيحية قوة دافعة باتجاه الشمولية العالمية، قوة دافعة باتجاه إيجاد ألفة ومودة عند جميع المؤمنين من مختلف الأديان.

بريسيلا: دخلت في هذه العلاقة بعد أحداث الحادي عشر من أيلول/سبتمبر لكي أمنح الأمل لنفسي ولأولادي. فأنا أريد للناس أن يخرجوا من قراءة هذا الكتاب بشعور بالأمل وشعور بالتفاؤل. لقد قال لنا الناس مرارا بأنهم يحسدوننا على علاقتنا وعلى نادي الإيمان الخاص بنا. أعتقد أن لدى الكثير من الناس ألم روحي. وأعتقد أن الناس يتوقون لأن يكون لديهم الصلة نفسها التي تربط كل منا بالآخر. كما وأعتقد بأننا نحيا في وقت لا يعطينا خيارا حقيقيا آخر غير أن يتواصل كل منا مع الآخر. وأقتبس في هذه الأيام مقولة إل. و. هـ. أودين: "يجب أن يحب كل منا الآخر وإلا سنموت." فلقد جربنا في الماضي عدة طرق للتواصل، كما جربنا ألا نتواصل. وجربنا اللجوء إلى القوة من أجل إيصال أفكارنا. ولكن رأينا ثلاثتنا ماذا يحصل عندما تصر على الحوار. وإذا انتشر هذا النوع من الحوار، ثلاثة أشخاص في كل مرة، فإن باستطاعته إحداث اختلاف كبير في النهاية.

س. كيف تمكن ثلاثة أشخاص من تأليف كتاب واحد معا؟

ج. بريسيلا: بصعوبة كبيرة! وتضاربات ومثابرة! وكان ذلك تحديا كبيرا على الأخص عندما كان كل منا في مكان مختلف أو أكثر... حيث كانت رانية في اليونان وفي لونغ أيلاند، وأنا في مارثاز فاينيارد وفي نيويورك، وسوزان في نيوهامشير... فقد كتبنا جزءا كبيرا من الكتاب عبر شبكة الإنترنت، وهذا كان فعالا بالتأكيد، ولكنه كان

يشكل تحديا كبيرا أيضا لأن الأحاسيس والمشاعر العميقة ليس من السهل التعبير عنها عبر الإنترنت ولقد كان كل منا يكن الكثير منها نحو الآخر.

سوزان: وثمة صعوبة أخرى نتجت عن حقيقة أننا أناس مختلفين في نهاية الكتاب أكثر مما كنا عليه في بدايته. فكان من الصعب في بعض الأحيان الاحتفاظ بهذه البساطة أثناء تحريرنا للكتاب ووضعه بصورته النهائية.

رانية: الاشتراك في تأليف عمل واحد ليس أمر سهلا، فهو كالزواج بلحظاته السعيدة والمريرة. ولكن المرء يعلم في نهاية المطاف نقاط الضعف والقوة لدى شريكه. وكذلك، وبشهادة أي مؤلف، فإن ساعات التحرير الطويلة قد تكون موحشة. **وبالتأكيد قد خفف من هذه الوحشة كثيرا عندما كنت مستيقظة ومستغرقة في العمل حتى الثالثة صباحا أن أسمع نغمة البريد الإلكترونية تخبرني «لديك رسالة في بريدك»** أعرف من خلالها أن إحدى شريكاتي في التأليف ما زالت مستيقظة أيضا.

س. من عليه أن يقرأ الكتاب؟

ج. **رانية:** الجميع! وخصوصا الرجال! وخاصة أولئك الذين يتحكمون في العالم! رجال السياسة البيض!

سوزان: أي شخص مهتم بالأديان أو بالطريقة التي تؤثر الأديان فيها على تعاملات البشر في يومنا هذا.

بريسيلا: أود أن يقرأه جميع الناس – الذين يعرفون الكثير عن دينهم، والذين يعرفون القليل، والذين يشككون بوجود الله، والشباب، وكبار السن. وأود أن يقرأه الملحدون. كما وأود رؤية مجموعة من كبار السن والذين يملكون قدرا كبيرا من خبرات الحياة يقرؤون هذا الكتاب ويتحدثون بما فيه. وأعتقد أن حديثا كذلك سيكون حوارا غنيا. كما وستضفي قراءة الشباب له الكثير من الرغبة والصدق.

س. هل يتوجب على القارئ أن يكون متدينا كي يستمتع بقراءة الكتاب؟

ج. **رانية:** لا أعتقد أن نادي الإيمان كتاب ديني، وإنما كتاب إنساني. فبغض النظر عن أصلك وعن لون بشرتك... فهو يتحدث عن تجربتنا في حياتنا اليومية بكبر بما فيها من هموم وتحديات وآمال. فإذا أردت أن تدعو الحياة بالدينية، فهو إذن كذلك. فهذا كتاب عن الحياة أكثر منه عن الدين. فهو عن الصداقة والاحترام والعزلة والخوف. وهو عن مستقبلنا وعن الصور النمطية وعن الكراهية وعن الإجحاف. ففي عالمنا الحاضر حيث نحتاج لوجود التصنيفات، أقول أن هذا الكتاب هو كتاب ديني، ولكني لا أعتقد أن هذا الكتاب يمكن تصنيفه لأنه يشتمل على تجربتنا الإنسانية.

بريسيلا: أنا في الحقيقة لم أكن أعتبر نفسي إنسانة متدينة أبدا، ولم أكن أظن أنني سأكتب كتابا عن الدين أبدا. ولكن من الواضح أني كنت بحاجة لهذه التجربة، لامتحان يختبر إيماني، وعلى الأغلب هناك الكثير من الناس مثلي ممن سيستمتعون بقراءة الكتاب.

سوزان: كتاب نادي الإيمان هو كتاب يدور حول أشخاص يتحدون أنفسهم ويتحدى كل منهم الآخر حول معنى الحياة، ومعنى أن يكون الإنسان إنسانا في وقتنا هذا، ومعنى أن يكون الشخص أمريكيا في الوقت

الحاضر، ومعنى أن يكون الشخص متدينا أم غير متدين، ومعنى الإيمان بالله وعدم الإيمان به. وهو عن استكشاف الناس لآرائهم التي يحملونها حيال أناس آخرين – آراء نحملها معنا كل يوم ولكننا في الحقيقة نجهلها. وهو عن فهم الصور النمطية والآراء المسبقة التي أثرت علينا منذ طفولتنا، وعن إدراك أن هذه التوجهات تؤثر على الطريقة التي نرى العالم بها اليوم. وهذا شيء يستطيع كل فرد – ذكرا كان أم أنثى، متدينا أم غير متدين، شابا أم مسنا – أن يستفيد منه. والأمل بأن يقود هذا الكتاب قارئيه إلى بحثهم الخاص لاكتشاف أنفسهم. ولمساعدتهم، فقد ألحقنا بهذا الكتاب إرشادات من نادي الإيمان.

رانية: أعتقد أنه كتاب لأولئك الذين يختارون العيش من خلال التساؤل والتفكر في الحياة، فأنا أرى أن جمال الكتاب يكمن في أننا اكتشفنا من خلال تجربتنا بأننا في الغالب لا نملك الوقت من أجل الوقوف للحظة لنستنشق عبير الزهور. فهذا الكتاب يشجع الناس على التوقف لبرهة والنظر فيما حولهم، وطرح أسئلة كبيرة تبدأ بـ«إذا». فنحن لا نفعل ذلك في حياتنا اليومية، ولكني أعتقد بأن كتاب نادي الإيمان يمنحنا هذه الفرصة.

How to Start a Faith Club

As we shared our experience with others, many people were interested in starting faith clubs of their own but were unsure how to begin. To get you going we've provided a Five-Step Faith Club outline, additional faith club questions, and a primer on the three Abrahamic religions. Once you get your club going, tell us about your conversations by emailing us at

thefaithclub@thefaithclub.com

We'd love to hear from you.

Where can you find people to join your club? You can use our website (www.thefaithclub.com) or form a group with the help of your local church, temple, mosque, or community center. Don't worry; any mix of people and religions should work. The most important thing is that you initiate a conversation that will expose you to a variety of faiths.

And don't underestimate the value of an inner dialogue. If you're too busy to get together with others, you can still use the template below for your own personal study and reflection. The aim is to open your mind and heart to other faiths, ideas, religious practices, and prayers. That is how, ultimately, you will learn what is sacred to you.

Our experience is just one way of exploring your faith. In fact, the format for our meetings came about organically, springing from our own life experiences. Only when we were challenged and felt we needed more information did we do outside reading or research. For our conversations we drew upon everything from newspaper articles to television programs, Holy Scripture to popular movies. We read from a variety of sources, picking and choosing paragraphs and chapters.

How to Start a Faith Club

The following is only a suggested format for your faith club. Feel free to change it to make it your own. Keep a journal, and share your thoughts honestly. Use our website to update discussion topics and keep the conversation going. Most important, bring your own life experiences and honest reflections to each meeting. That is what will add depth and meaning to your Faith Club experience.

10 Things You Should Know Before Your First Faith Club Meeting

1. **You've got stereotypes.** Even if you think you're the most open-minded human on the planet, chances are you've got some negative opinions related to religion. Whether you're suspicious of doubters or believers, evangelicals or Episcopalians, Muslims, Jews, or Sikhs, you're probably entering your first faith club conversation with some prejudice that you will have to overcome in order to truly understand the faith of those you meet.

2. **You are vulnerable.** When you open yourself to new ideas, you may feel vulnerable. Don't mistake this for weakness. Accept it. It will lead to new understanding.

3. **You can be a peacemaker.** If heated words are flying among your faith club members, try to maintain a cool head and help each person see the other's point of view.

4. **There isn't always a "right" answer.** Although we usually wish there were, and some people might think they have it!

5. **Your first reaction is your worst reaction.** If you feel threatened by something another faith club member says, your first impulse will not be a thoughtful one. Before you attack, shut down, or cut the person off, reevaluate the comment and your response.

6. **Secrets corrupt.** If you've got a complaint, share it with your whole faith club, not with just one or two confidantes. You've got to be one for all and all for one.

7. **Every opinion must be respected.** That doesn't mean you shouldn't politely try to change the opinion if you disagree with it.

8. **No one else can do your homework.** If a faith club member is unable to answer your questions about a religious issue, do your own research and share your findings with the group.

9. **Invitations are expected.** The faith you share with other faith club members will have greater meaning if you invite them to participate in a special service or religious tradition.

10. **Get help.** If your faith club experience leaves you confused about your own religion, find a cleric who can help you explore the issues that are frustrating you.

10 דברים שעליכם לדעת לפני הפגישה הראשונה במועדון האמונה

1. יש לכם סטריאוטיפים. אפילו אם אתם חושבים שאתם האנשים הפתוחים ביותר עלי אדמות, מרבית הסיכויים שיש לכם כמה דעות שליליות ביחס לדת מסוימת. אם אתם קצת חשדנים ביחס ללא מאמינים או למאמינים, לאוונגליסטים, אפיסקופלים, מוסלמים, יהודים, או סיקים, קרוב לוודאי שאתם מגיעים לשיחה הראשונה במועדון האמונה שלכם עם דעות קדומות שתצטרכו להתגבר עליהם כדי להבין באמת את האמונות של אלה שאתם פוגשים.

2. אתם פגיעים. כשאתם נפתחים לדעות חדשות, אתם יכולים לחוש פגיעים. אל תבלבלו זאת בחולשה. קבלו זאת ותגיעו לתובנות חדשות.

3. אתם יכולים להיות משכיני שלום. אם ביטויים חריפים מוחלפים בין חברי מועדון האמונה שלכם, נסו לשמור על ראש צלול ולסייע לכל אדם לראות את נקודת המבט של האחר/ת.

4. אין תמיד תשובה "נכונה". למרות שתמיד אנו רוצים שתהיה, ויש אנשים שחושבים שהיא בידם.

5. התגובה הראשונה שלכם היא התגובה הגרועה ביותר שלכם. אם אתם חשים מאוימים על ידי מה שאמר מישהו אחר במועדון האמונה, התגובה הראשונה שלכם לא תהיה שקולה. לפני שאתם תוקפים, משתיקים, או קוטעים מישהו, נסו להעריך מחדש את מה שנאמר ואת תגובתכם.

6. סודות מקלקלים יחסים. אם יש לכם בעיה, שתפו בה את כל חברי מועדון האמונה שלכם, ולא רק איש סוד אחד או שניים. זכרו: אחד בשביל כולם וכולם בשביל אחד.

7. כל דעה יש לכבד. אין זה אומר שאינכם יכולים לנסות באופן מנומס לנסות לשנות את הדעה אם אתם חולקים עליה.

8. אף אחד אחר אינו יכול להכין את שיעורי הבית שלכם. אם חבר במועדון האמונה אינו מסוגל לענות לשאלותיכם על שאלה דתית כלשהי, עשו את הבדיקה שלכם ושתפו את הקבוצה בממצאיכם.

9. הזמנות רצויות. האמונה שבה אתם משתפים חברים אחרים במועדון תקבל משמעות ברורה יותר אם תזמינו אותם להשתתף בטקס מסוים או במנהג דתי.

10. בקשו עזרה. אם מה שקורה במועדון האמונה מותיר אתכם מבולבלים ביחס לדת שלכם, מצאו איש דת שיוכל לעזור לכם לחשוף את מה שמתסכל אתכם.

عشرة أمور ينبغي لك أن تعلمها قبل حضور اجتماعك الأول في نادي الإيمان:

1. أنت لديك صور نمطية.

حتى وإن كنت تظن بأنك أكثر إنسان منفتح على وجه الأرض، إلا أنه يوجد احتمال بأن لديك آراء سلبية تتعلق بالدين. فإذا كنت مرتابا من المشككين أو المؤمنين، أو المسيحيين الجدد أو الإنجيليين، أو المسلمين، أو اليهود، أو السيخ، فإنك على الأرجح ستشارك في أول حوار لك في نادي الإيمان ولديك أحكام مسبقة ينبغي عليك التخلص منها حتى تتفهم حقا دين أولئك الذين تقابلهم.

2. أنت لست محصناً.

حينما تنفتح على أفكار جديدة قد تشعر بأنك لست محصناً. لا تنظر إلى هذا على أنه ضعف. سلّم به، فهو سيقودك إلى إدراك جديد.

3. بمقدورك أن تكون صانع سلام.

فإذا تبادل أعضاء نادي الإيمان الكلام اللاذع فيما بينهم، حاول الحفاظ على هدوئك وساعد كل شخص منهم على فهم وجهة نظر الآخر.

4. لا توجد هناك إجابة «صائبة» دائما.

بالرغم من أننا نتمنى عادة لو كانت هنالك واحدة، وأن بعض الناس قد يظنون أنهم يمتلكونها!

5. ردة فعلك الأولى هي أسوء ردة فعل لك.

إذا كنت تشعر بأنك مهدد بسبب شيء يقوله عضو آخر في نادي الإيمان، فإن اندفاعك الأول لن يكون مدروسا. فقبل أن تهاجم المتحدث أو تقاطعه، قم بإعادة التفكير فيما قاله وفي رد فعلك عليه.

6. الأسرار مُفسدة.

إذا كانت لديك شكوى، قم بعرضها أمام كل أعضاء نادي الإيمان، ولا تعرضها على شخص أو شخصين ممن تأتمنهم فقط. فلا بد أن تكون للكل وأن يكون الكل لك.

7. ينبغي احترام جميع الآراء.

وهذا لا يعني أنه لا ينبغي لك أن تحاول بأدب تغيير رأي لا تتفق معه.

8. لن يقوم أحد بأداء واجباتك نيابة عنك.

إذا لم يستطع عضو في نادي الإيمان الإجابة عن أسئلتك حول مسألة دينية فقم بالبحث بنفسك واعرض نتائجك على المجموعة.

9. الدعوات مأمولة.

سيكون للإيمان الذي تتشارك به مع أعضاء نادي الإيمان الآخرين معنى أعظم إذا دعوتهم للمشاركة في طقس أو تقليد ديني خاص.

10. اطلب المساعدة.

إذا تركتك التجربة في نادي الإيمان في حيرة حول ديانتك، اقصد رجل دين ممن يستطيع مساعدتك في تحري المسائل التي تضايقك.

Faith Club Meeting Icebreakers

How do you start talking to strangers about God, religion, faith, death, prejudice, and eternity? Very slowly. It's not like discussing the weather. You can disagree about tomorrow's forecast, and no one will suffer. But if you imply to someone that her religious practices are devoid of reason, her faith has no validity, or her religion misinterprets scripture, you are threatening the very core of her identity. Don't expect to see her at meeting number two.

So, play it safe instead. Use some of our icebreakers to get to know one another. Faith club members will each reveal a little about themselves, and in the process you'll learn to trust and respect one another. You'll find commonalities that may surprise you and discover differences that you may need to keep in mind as you ease into more intimate and divisive conversation topics. You can try out a few icebreakers at your first meeting or start each meeting with a new one. It's up to you.

If you have a new icebreaker idea, let us know by emailing us at thefaithclub@thefaithclub.com

The Interview. Divide into pairs. Each person gets five minutes to interview another person about her background, including where she is from, what she studied, how religion was practiced in her family, etc. (If you're a small group, take turns interviewing each other.) After ten minutes, the members introduce their partner to the rest of the club. See how accurately people perceive one another based on a first impression.

Find a Partner. Each member takes a name tag and writes down two or three adjectives describing him- or herself. Everybody compares tags, then chooses someone with opposite adjectives and talks to that person for five minutes. Can they come up with two or three adjectives that describe both of them?

They Just Don't Get It. If you are a large faith club, break into groups of three or four people of the same religion. Make a list of five things you'd like people to understand about your religion. If you're a small group, each member can make his or her own list.

Dream Weaver. Share a dream that you think may have had some religious significance. Let the other members of your faith club try to analyze its meaning.

The Lie Detector. Each person takes an index card and writes down three statements about his or her faith. Two are true and one is a lie. Read them aloud, and members try to guess which statement is a lie.

The Quotation Game. Each member brings in an inspirational quotation. Write the quotes on index cards. Shuffle the cards and see if members can guess who brought in each quote. Don't guess your own!

Do You Believe in Miracles? Share a miracle you've heard about in your life. Do you believe it? Do others believe it?

Are You Talking to Me? Write down a sentence that you hope no one ever utters in the confines of your faith club. Take a deep breath, read your sentence aloud, and see what happens to the temperature in the room.

R-E-S-P-E-C-T. Lay your cards on the table. What is the most important thing you want people to respect about you and your religion? Write that point down. Then belt it out!

I Have a Dream. Answer these two questions: Why did you join a faith club? What do you hope to get out of this experience?

The Five-Step Faith Club

1. EXAMINE YOUR RELIGION

Journal Assignment:

What religion are you and why? How does your religious background influence your life and your beliefs?

Club Conversation:

Check out the icebreaker exercises on www.thefaithclub.com. They'll help you relax and have fun as you get to know one another. Share your journal writing. Tell the group something you like about your religion and something you dislike about it.

Personal Reflection:

How do your beliefs compare with those of other faith club members? How are they different? What surprised you about the way your faith club colleagues think about their faith? What issues do you think might arise in your faith club?

Further Reading:

Armstrong, Karen, *Muhammad: A Biography of the Prophet,* Alfred A. Knopf, 1993.

Feiler, Bruce, *Abraham, A Journey to the Heart of Three Faiths,* HarperCollins, 2002.

Lewis, C. S., *Mere Christianity,* Macmillan, 1993.

2. PUT YOUR STEREOTYPES ON THE TABLE

Journal Assignment:

Admit it. You've got stereotypes that relate to religion. We all do. Here's your chance to fess up and learn from your mistakes. What stereotypes do you hold of Muslims, Christians, Jews, or anyone of any religion? Do you stereotype members of your own religion?

Club Conversation:

Share your journal writing. What are the sources of your religious stereo-types? How do fundamentalists affect our stereotypes of religious people? How do stereotypes affect your interactions with others?

Personal Reflection:

What misconceptions did you have regarding religion, and how have your views changed? How can you transcend stereotypes in your personal inter-actions and in the way you interpret the world around you?

Further Reading:

Menocal, Maria Rosa, *Ornament of the World: How Muslims, Jews and Chris-tians Created a Culture of Tolerance in Medieval Spain,* Little, Brown, 2002.

Pogrebin, Abigail, *Stars of David: Prominent Jews Talk About Being Jewish,* Broadway Books, 2005.

Prothero, Stephen, *American Jesus,* Farrar, Straus and Giroux, 2003.

3. DEFINE YOUR GOD

Journal Assignment:

Do you believe God exists? What is God? Write a few paragraphs about a time when you acutely felt God's presence in your life. What about his ab-sence? How have these experiences influenced your faith?

Club Conversation:

Share your journal writing. Why do people believe in God? How do you feel about people who don't believe in God? If God exists, why do evil, pain, and suffering also exist? What is heaven?

Personal Reflection:

What is universal about the way members of your faith club experience God? What is unique? Have their views changed what you believe about God?

Further Reading:

Armstrong, Karen, *The History of God,* Alfred A. Knopf, 1993.

———, *The Spiral Staircase,* Alfred A. Knopf, 2004.

Brickner, Balfour, *Finding God in the Garden,* Little, Brown, 2002.

4. EXPLORE PRAYER AND HOLY TEXT

Journal Assignment:

Do you pray? Write about a prayer experience that has been meaningful to you. What prayers, Holy Scripture, or other writing is inspirational to you? Bring it to share with your faith club.

Club Conversation:

What is prayer? Is it useful? What role do prayer rituals and Holy Scripture play in religion? Is Holy Scripture the literal word of God? What questions do you have about the prayers, scriptures, and rituals of other faiths?

Personal Reflection:

How can you use what you've learned in your faith club to supplement your own prayer? How do different interpretations of scripture affect people's faith?

Further Reading:

Cleary, Thomas, *The Essential Koran: The Heart of Islam,* HarperCollins, 1993.

Ehrman, Bart D., *Misquoting Jesus: The Story Behind Who Changed the Bible and Why,* HarperCollins, 2005.

Sacks, Rabbi Jonathan, *Celebrating Life,* Continuum, 2004.

5. THINK ABOUT RELIGION ON THE WORLD STAGE

Journal Assignment:

Religion drives politicians, activists, governments, and individuals to do good and sometimes to do what others believe is intrusive, inconsiderate, or immoral. Write your own Op-Ed piece about the use and/or abuse of religion on the world stage.

Club Conversation:

Do you think your religion is manipulated, misunderstood, or under attack? How does religion affect the lens through which we view the world? How does religion contribute to world conflict? Does it ever foster peace?

Personal Reflection:

Pretend you are of a religion other than your own. Now read the newspaper or listen to the news. How is your perception of current events different? How can those within your religion promote peace and unity among all religions?

Further Reading:

Blumenfeld, Laura, *Revenge: A Story of Hope*, Washington Square Press, 2003.

Ernst, Carl W., *Following Muhammad: Rethinking Islam in the Modern World*, University of North Carolina Press, 2003.

Wills, Garry, *What Jesus Meant*, Viking, 2006.

More Faith Club Questions

This list of sample questions is based upon our own faith club experience. Use them as a blueprint for more expanded meetings and reflections or as a reading guide to our book. If a particular set of questions seems intimidating at first, choose something easier. We all have issues we can discuss without much emotion. Then there are those issues that can set our rooms on fire.

What if it takes a while for you and your faith club colleagues to be able to talk honestly? What if you can't resolve an issue? What if someone is dominating the conversation? What if someone can't see another person's viewpoint as legitimate? What if feelings get hurt, egos bruised, and tears flow?

Congratulations. Your faith club is a success.

Life will intervene. Things will happen to you or your loved ones, and you'll talk about them within your faith club. World events, good and bad, will stimulate conversation. Give ideas time to brew, but don't let disagreements fester.

A faith club is more than a book club, but that doesn't mean you shouldn't read as much as you can. Newspapers, magazines, and spiritual memoirs are rich with faith club material. We've included a bibliography of our own; however, every club's reading list will be different.

Your faith club discussions may lead you to uncomfortable places—provocative, isolating, and confusing places. That's the whole point. But wherever your talks lead you, just come back to the one safe place in a world wracked with confusion. Come back to your faith club. We'd love to see people's hearts and minds opening all over the world, in faith clubs, one trio at a time.

Who Are You?

What religion are you and why?

How do you practice your religion?

What are some of the personal and educational experiences that have defined your faith, religion, and relationship to God?

What do you hope to learn or accomplish through your faith club?

The Abrahamic Family

Are Christianity, Judaism, and Islam all branches of one religion?

How did Christianity spring from Judaism?

How does Islam relate to Judaism and Christianity?

Are Muslims the banished descendants of Ishmael?

Should the Judeo-Christian tradition be renamed the Judeo-Christian-Muslim tradition?

Who are the Chosen People?

Stereotypes

What stereotypes do you hold of religious people? Of nonreligious people?

What is your stereotype of a Jew? A Christian? A Muslim? Of any other religions?

Would it be uncomfortable for you to be mistaken for a Jew? A Christian? A Muslim?

Is Islam under attack right now? Is Judaism? Christianity?

Are there such things as Christian values? Jewish values? Muslim values?

When have you felt that people stereotyped you based on your religion or faith?

Holy Messengers

What was the message of Moses?

What was the message of Jesus?

What was the message of Muhammad?

What do Jews and Muslims believe about Jesus?

How has the Christian West interpreted Muhammad?

Why was Jesus crucified?

What was the Jews' role in the death of Jesus?

Is the crucifixion story anti-Semitic?

Are Jews too sensitive, too quick to cry "persecution"?

What is the message of Jesus' resurrection?

What is "The Rapture"?

Should Jews learn to appreciate Jesus in a new light?

Should Christians learn to appreciate Muhammad in a new light?

Could You Convert?

Are all religions equal?

Could you convert to a different religion? Which one?

If not, what keeps you within your religion?

How would you feel if your child converted?

Is conversion betrayal?

Have you attended services of another faith? Describe that experience.

God

Do you believe in God?

Where do you find God?

Where is God when evil or disaster strikes?

What is the difference between God's will and Fate?

How does God help us cope with loss and pain?

Where is God when life is unfair?

What does it mean to "submit" in Islam?

How do the Jewish, Christian, and Muslim conceptions of God differ?

How are they similar?

Do all religions address the same God?

The Holy Land

What is the Holy Land, and who has claim to it?

What is the Promised Land?

What is the difference between anti-Zionism and anti-Semitism?

How does the Holocaust experience affect Judaism today?

Do non-Jews underestimate the significance of the Holocaust?

Does criticizing Israel make Jews traitors to their religion?

How did the creation of Israel affect Palestinians?

Are Palestinians victims today?

Does giving money to Israel support the mistreatment of Palestinians?

What moral obligations do Jews have regarding Israel and the Palestinians?

Is there such a thing as "Zionist mythology"?

Intimations of Mortality

What happens to us after we die?

Does heaven exist?

Who gets to go to heaven?

Why do people believe in an afterlife?

What have others taught you about death?

Is our eternity found only in our children and grandchildren?

Prayer

How do you pray?

Why do you pray?

Where do you pray?

What do you expect from God when you pray?

Does it matter to God how you pray?

What is the importance of prayer rituals and communal prayer at houses of worship? Does God answer our prayers?

Holidays

How do Americans celebrate religious holidays? How are they celebrated in the Holy Land? What about the rest of the world?

In our desire to be politically correct regarding religion, are we creating resentment and anxiety?

Should Christians alter their holiday traditions to accommodate America's increasing religious diversity or those who feel sidelined by big holidays such as Christmas?

Is it okay to participate in a religious holiday of a religion other than your own?

Is there a difference between cultural and religious participation in a holiday?

What kind of holiday greeting cards should people send?

How should religious holidays be celebrated in schools?

Keep Going . . .

Is there a difference between faith and religion?

What do you think is the biggest misperception people have about your religion?

What was your biggest misconception about other religions?

Is it possible to separate religion from politics?

How has your faith club experience influenced your beliefs?

Is your faith stronger or weaker than when you joined your faith club?

Things to Know About Judaism

What We Call God

Jews say God's name as Adonai, but that is really not God's name. At Mount Sinai, where the Israelites met God, they knew how to pronounce God's name, Y-H-V-H. But over the centuries, Jews lost the pronunciation key. The High Priest in the Holy Temple of Jerusalem would once a year, on Yom Kippur, enter the sanctuary and say God's name. It is said that at that moment, all Israel, without even hearing it, but simply knowing it was being said aloud, would bow low in awe. But since Jews no longer have a Temple, they do not know how to say God's name. So they use names that describe God.

El Elyon (God Most High). Genesis 14:18–20

Shapat (the Judge). Genesis 18:25

El Olam (the Eternal God). Genesis 21:33

Jahweh—Jirah (the Lord Will Provide). Genesis 22:14

El Elohe—Yisra'el (God, the God of Israel). Genesis 33:20

El Shaddai (God Almighty). Genesis 49:25

As for God's original name, by understanding that it had no vowels, Y-H-V-H, the closest Jews can come to saying it is to listen to the sound of their own breathing. As they take in a breath, they are breathing in the name of God, who breathed into everyone the "breath of life" [Genesis 2].

Holy Book

The Jewish holy book, or Bible, is called the **Tanach.** The first five books of Tanach are called **Torah.** Niviem, or **Prophets,** is the second part of Tanach, and includes the stories of Joshua, Isaiah, and Jonah. Kituvim, or **Writings,** is the last part of Tanach, and includes Psalms and Proverbs.

The Torah is the most important object in any synagogue. It is handwritten on long scrolls of parchment, covered in a velvet case, and kept in a special cabinet, called the *ark*. When the ark is opened, the whole congregation must rise in respect for the Torah. Jews begin reading the Torah on a holiday called **Simchat Torah,** and read a section each week. By the end of the year, they will have read the whole Torah.

Worship and Prayer

Jewish religious services take place in a synagogue. At the front of the synagogue is the **bimah,** or platform, where the ark stands, with the Torah inside. A lamp, called **the eternal light,** always burns above the ark.

The **rabbi** is the spiritual leader of the synagogue, a teacher of the Jewish faith who has studied Jewish history, law, and the Bible for many years. The rabbi helps the congregation to study and understand Torah. Also, when a Jewish person seeks comfort, advice, or information about Judaism, he or she goes to the rabbi for help. In some congregations, the rabbi must be a man. Other congregations have women as rabbis.

Rituals

All Jews believe in one God and in the Bible. Since the 1800s, Judaism has branched out into three large groups: **Orthodox, Conservative,** and **Reform Judaism.** Orthodox Jews practice very traditional Judaism, as it has been handed down for more than two thousand years. They believe that the Torah was given directly to Moses. They follow the kosher laws of the Torah, which forbid them from eating shellfish or pork. Orthodox men pray daily, separate from women.

Reform Jews have adapted Judaism for the modern world. Most do not follow kosher food laws. Men do not always wear **yarmulkes,** or skullcaps, on their heads, which Orthodox men always wear, especially in the synagogue. Reform Jews sometimes wear prayer shawls called **tallit;** Orthodox men always wear tallit in synagogues. Reform Jews hold prayer services in other languages as well as in Hebrew. Orthodox services are always in Hebrew. Conservative Jews are more traditional than Reform Jews, but not as traditional as Orthodox Jews. Many Jewish homes have a **mezuzah** hanging on the doorpost of the house. A mezuzah is a small box; inside is a tiny scroll with a special prayer written on it and passages of the Torah. Some Jews kiss their hands and touch the mezuzah as a sign of respect when they enter or leave a home. The Torah and Jewish prayer books are written in Hebrew, an ancient language with a unique alphabet. Jewish children go to religious school not only to learn prayers, customs, and history, but also to learn how to read Hebrew. When a Jewish boy turns thirteen, he is called up to the bimah of the synagogue to read the Torah to the congregation for the first time in his life. This ceremony is called a **bar mitzvah,** and a big celebration follows the service. Non-Orthodox Jewish girls are also called to the Torah to read for the first time, and that ceremony is called a **bat mitzvah.** At weddings, the Jewish bride and groom sign a wedding contract, called a **ketubah,** before the ceremony, which is held under a canopy called a **chuppah.** After the bride and groom exchange rings, and the rabbi blesses the couple, the groom breaks a wineglass under his foot, to symbolize the destruction of the Holy Temple in Jerusalem and remind Jews that along with great joy, great sorrow also exists in the world.

Holidays

Jewish people have their own calendar, and Jewish months last from one new moon to the next. So holidays fall on different days of the English calendar every year. But one day of prayer, Shabbat, occurs every Friday night and Saturday. According to the Jewish story of Creation, God created the world in six days, and then rested on the seventh day. So the Sabbath, or **Shabbat,** is the seventh day of the week and a special day of rest for all Jews. It begins on Friday night, and can be observed at home or in the synagogue. At either place, Jews light two Shabbat candles and say a special prayer. Two other prayers are recited over a glass of wine and a special bread called **challah.** More observant Jews do not work, travel, or carry money on the Sabbath. On Saturday evening, at the end of Shabbat, a single candle is lit and a special spice box is raised in the synagogue, filling the bimah with a beautiful scent.

In Persia many years ago, a Jewish queen named Esther saved her people from annihilation. The story is written in a text called the Megillah. The story is read every year on a holiday called **Purim,** which falls in February or March. Children reenact the story and dress up as kings, queens, and Haman, the evil prime minister who threatened the Jews' existence. Jews eat special cookies called **hamantaschen,** which are shaped like the triangular hat the evil Haman wore.

On **Passover,** in March or April, Jews celebrate the Israelites' escape from slavery in Egypt. The holiday lasts for eight days, beginning with a dinner called a **seder,** where Jews retell the story of their exodus, or escape. Jews eat flat bread called matzoh to remind them that when the Israelites fled Egypt, they did so quickly, before the bread they were baking had time to rise.

In September, Jews celebrate **Rosh Hashanah,** the Jewish New Year. At the prayer service in the synagogue, someone blows the **shofar,** or ram's horn, to remind people to reflect on all the things they did the year before. Jews eat sliced apples dipped in honey, to wish everyone a sweet New Year. **Yom Kippur,** the Day of Atonement, is the holiest day of the year for Jews, who pray to God to forgive them for the sins they committed over the last year. Adults fast, going without food or drink from sundown the evening before to sundown the day of Yom Kippur. The shofar is blown again at the end of the holiday. In October, Jews celebrate the harvest festival called **Succot.** They build a simple wooden shelter in their yards, decorated with fruit and branches, to remind them of the homes their ancestors made as they wandered in the desert.

Hanukah is usually celebrated in December. This holiday commemorates the defeat of a mighty army by a small band of Jews who drove their enemies out of ancient Jerusalem. These courageous Jews reopened the Holy Temple, but found only enough oil to light the Temple lamp for one night. And then a miracle occurred. The oil lasted for eight full days, until more oil could be brought to the Temple. Jews today light a **menorah,** a candlestick with eight branches, representing the eight days, and a center branch for the candle that lights all the others. On the first night of Hanukah, one candle is lit. On the second night, two candles are lit, and by the eighth night the whole menorah is ablaze.

Judaism Around the World

As we write this, there are around 13 million Jews in the world. More Jews live in the United States than in any other country. Israel is close behind, and may soon overtake the United States in its number of Jews. France, Canada, the United Kingdom, Russia, and the former Soviet republics also have large Jewish populations. Jews have scattered all over the world, to India, Brazil, Argentina, and South America, usually to flee persecution. The worst example of anti-Semitism, or discrimination against Jews, occurred during the Holocaust, when Nazis killed 6 million Jews. Many books and movies have shown the world the horror of the Holocaust.

Things to Know About Christianity

What We Call God

Christians have three names for God. Each name refers to one of the three persons of the **Holy Trinity.** The first is **God the Father,** which refers to the all-powerful Creator. The second is **God the Son,** who is Jesus, who is both God and man. He is one person in whom both the divine and human natures are consistently present. The third Christian name for God is the **Holy Spirit.** This is the term Christians use when referring to the manifestations of God's power on earth, as in the miracles at Jesus' baptism and Pentecost.

Holy Book

The Christian Bible is divided into two sections: the **Old Testament,** which is almost the same as the Jewish Tanach, and the **New Testament.** "Testament" means promise. Christianity, whose roots lie in the Jewish tradition, interprets Jesus' coming as the fulfillment of promises made in the Old Testament. The New Testament consists of the Gospels, which retell the life, death, and resurrection of Jesus; letters and other writings of the early Christian evangelists; and the Book of Revelation, which is about the end of time. There are many different translations of the Bible. We recommend the **Revised Standard Version.**

Worship and Prayer

Christians generally attend worship services at church on Sundays. The services usually include readings from the Bible and a related sermon given by the priest or minister who leads the service. The most important service for most Christians is mass, which includes the celebration of **Holy Communion.** This is a remembrance of the last meal Jesus celebrated with his disciples before his death. Like Jesus did, the priest who leads the service blesses bread and wine and gives each person a piece.

When Christians pray, they sometimes kneel with their eyes closed and hands folded. They often begin and end their prayers by making a sign of the cross on their bodies by touching their head, chest, and both shoulders. This symbolizes the cross on which Jesus died. One very special prayer for Christians is known as the **Lord's Prayer.** According to the Bible, Jesus taught this prayer to his followers. It goes like this: "Our Father who art in heaven, hallowed be thy name. Thy kingdom come, thy will be done, on earth as it is in heaven. Give us this day our daily bread and forgive us our trespasses as we forgive those who trespass against us. And lead us not into temptation, but deliver us from evil."

Rituals

The most holy Christian ceremonies are called **sacraments.** These include **baptism** and the **Eucharist** (Holy Communion). Most churches baptize infants at the baptismal font in the church. The priest pours holy water over the baby's head and anoints the baby with oil. This is a sign of purification and inclusion in the living "Body of Jesus Christ." In some Protestant churches, adults are baptized by immersion into water. In Jesus' time people were baptized in rivers. According to the New Testament, Jesus was baptized by a man named John the Baptist. During the baptism the Holy Spirit appeared in the form of a dove and said, "This is my beloved Son."

Holy Communion is the blessing by a priest of bread and wine, symbolizing Jesus' body and blood. The ritual commemorates Jesus' last meal with his disciples, when he shared bread and wine, saying "This is my body and blood." In this way Jesus promised to be with his disciples until the end of time. Another ritual is **confirmation.** In western Christian churches, children study their religion in order to prepare for confirmation. The ceremony includes an anointing with oil and laying on of hands by a bishop, an important regional church leader.

Holidays

The **Easter** season, which is in the spring, is the most important time in the Christian calendar. It is the time when people celebrate the death and resurrection of Jesus. The forty days before Easter are known as **Lent,** which begins with **Ash Wednesday.** On this day many Christians go to church, where a priest puts a cross of ash on their foreheads. The ash is a reminder that people are no more than dust in comparison with God and that we depend upon God's grace for our salvation. Lent is a time of fasting and giving up luxuries in preparation for Easter. The day before Lent is known as **Shrove Tuesday** or **Mardi Gras.** In many places, people celebrate this day with carnivals and special meals that they will not enjoy during Lent. The week before Easter is known as **Holy Week.** It begins with **Palm Sunday,** which commemorates the day Jesus arrived in Jerusalem and was greeted by crowds waving palms. In many churches palms are distributed to worshipers on this day. **Holy Thursday** is a remembrance of the Last Supper, the Passover meal Jesus celebrated with his disciples the night before he died. **Good Friday** commemorates Jesus' death on the cross. And **Easter,** the most important Christian holiday, celebrates Jesus' resurrection from his tomb three days after his death. On Easter, Christians decorate eggs as a symbol of new life.

The Christian **Christmas** season celebrates the birth of Jesus. The four weeks before Christmas, which is on December 25, are known as **Advent.** This is a time of special prayer in preparation for Christmas. Children often have Advent calendars that mark the days until the big holiday. Advent wreaths have four candles, one for each of the four Sundays preceding Christmas. Many churches have Christmas pageants in which children dress up and act out the Christmas story. According to the Bible, Jesus' parents (Mary and Joseph) traveled to Bethlehem for a census but were unable to find a room there. So they slept in a stable, where Jesus was born and laid in a manger. Many churches have crèches or nativity scenes that picture Jesus, Mary, and Joseph in the stable with animals and shepherds looking on. **Epiphany,** which is on January 6, ends the Christmas season. On this day Christians remember the visit of the three kings who brought the baby Jesus gifts of gold, frankincense, and myrrh. Their visit shows that Jesus came as a savior for the whole world, not just for the Jews.

Christianity Around the World

There are close to 2 billion Christians in the world. About half of these belong to the Roman Catholic Church, whose leader is the pope. Catholics believe that the pope is a direct successor of Jesus' disciple Peter, whom they consider the first pope. They believe the pope is God's representative on earth and is infallible when speaking about church doctrine. The pope's headquarters is in Rome. The majority of Roman Catholics live in Europe and the Americas. In 1054 the Eastern Church, also known as the Orthodox Church, split from the Roman Catholic Church. Today there are about 215 million members of the Orthodox Church, most of whom reside in Eastern Europe and Russia. The remaining Christians belong to Protestant denominations that have split from the Roman Catholic Church. Examples of these include the Baptist, Episcopal, Lutheran, and Presbyterian Churches.

Things to Know About Islam

What We Call God

Allah is the Arabic word for God. It is used by Arab Christians as well as Muslims. For Muslims, God was not created and there is no other being like him. Muslims believe that one of God's most important qualities is his "Oneness." According to Muslims, if God is One, then there cannot be different or rival Gods, such as a God for the Jews, a God for the Christians, and a God for the polytheists. God is believed to have 99 beautiful names. These are descriptive adjectives given throughout the Quran, including All Powerful Creator of the Cosmos, The Compassionate, The Merciful, The Guardian, The Loving, The Patient, and The Ever Forgiving. Muslims traditionally repeat these descriptive names with the help of a rosary known as a **misbah.** This rosary has 100 beads. Ninety-nine represent God's qualities, while one larger bead symbolizes God.

Holy Book

The Muslim holy book is called the **Quran.** It is believed to be the word of God, revealed to the prophet Muhammad through the Angel Gabriel over a period of twenty-two years. Initially written on any available materials, it was compiled in its final form after the death of the prophet Muhammad in 632 A.D. It is divided into 114 chapters (**suras**) consisting of verses (**ayat**). All chapters except for chapter nine start with "in the name of God the merciful and the compassionate." Muslims learn the Quran in its original language, Arabic, because its recitation as the word of God is a ritual that allows Muslims to experience God symbolically, as a community of the faithful. This is comparable to the symbolic Christian experience of God found in the taking of the Eucharist, which defines the Christian community. Islam prohibits pictorial depictions of God as a way to discourage idol worship. As a result, the art of writing (calligraphy) is used to decorate the Quran and mosques. Muslims look to the Quran along with the **Hadith** (a collection of teachings thought to derive from the prophet and his companions) for guidance in many aspects of life. Muslim law, known as **Shari'a,** is based upon the Quran and the Hadith.

Worship and Prayer

Muslims gather at their mosque on Fridays at noon for communal prayer. The Imam leads the prayer and addresses the congregation from a stepped platform called a **minbar.** He never preaches from the top step, which is symbolically reserved for the prophet Muhammad. Mosques are built with a special tower called a minaret, where a person known as the **muezzin** calls the people to prayer five times a day. When Muslims pray they face toward Mecca, the birthplace of the prophet Muhammad. The direction is marked by an alcove known as the **mihrab,** which serves as a focal point for the prayer hall. The prayer hall has no seats because prayer involves standing, kneeling, and prostrating. All prayers end with the same call for peace for the prophet Muhammad, his followers, and the descendants of Abraham. In some mosques there are separate balconies for women, although in the most important mosque in Mecca, Masjid al-Haram, women and men pray in the same hall and are not segregated. Before praying, Muslims clean themselves by washing their face, mouth, nostrils, hands, lower arms, and feet. For hygienic reasons worshipers are required to remove their shoes before entering a mosque, and many Muslims use a prayer mat, some with an attached compass to indicate the direction of Mecca. Mosques are usually domed structures with pillars and arches decorated with calligraphy and abstract geometric designs. The interiors are kept simple so as not to distract worshipers. The Blue Mosque in Istanbul and the Great Mosque of Córdoba in Spain are famous for their architecture. The Dome of the Rock and Masjid al-Aqsa in Jerusalem are among the most important mosques for Muslims. The Noble Sanctuary, as the holy area in Jerusalem is named, marks the place of the prophet Muhammad's night journey and ascension to heaven. Muslims believe humanity will assemble there on the Day of Judgment.

Rituals

The most important rituals in Islam are collectively known as the Five Pillars of Islam. **Shahada** is the first and most important ritual. It is a simple declaration, "There is no god, but God, and Muhammad is the messenger of God." These words are a profession of faith and provide the basis for conversion. A person who sincerely recites the Shahada is considered a Muslim; no other ritual is needed.

Salat is prayer performed five times a day at specific times facing toward Mecca. The call by the muezzin from the minaret lets people know it is time for prayer. All prayers end with ritual salutations and calls for peace for the prophet Muhammad, his followers, and the descendants of Abraham, which include Moses and Jesus. Friday is the day that Muslims pray communally in a mosque. As a result, weekends in Muslim countries are either Thursday and Friday or Friday and Saturday.

Zaka is the giving of money to help the less fortunate. Muslims who are financially able are expected to give 2.5% of their net worth for social welfare.

Sawm is the practice of fasting during the month of Ramadan. Muslims will not eat or drink from dawn until dusk during this holy time. The idea behind such a fast is to teach people to empathize with those less fortunate who are often hungry and thirsty. Only healthy and mature Muslims are required to fast. Although Ramadan is a time for reflection and discipline, it has also become a time of special gatherings of family and friends with delicious meals followed by traditional desserts. Muslims may decorate their homes with the crescent moon shape and star, which have come to symbolize Islam. Socializing often extends late into the night, ending with a late or early predawn meal called **suhur.**

Hajj is the pilgrimage to Mecca required at least once in the lifetime of a Muslim. Muslims perform specific rituals and prayers around the **Ka'aba,** a black cubic structure believed to be God's first house on earth, rebuilt by Abraham and Ishmael, and where Abraham nearly sacrificed his son Ishmael. Around two million Muslims perform the annual pilgrimage. Pilgrims wear seamless white clothes so that no stitch or fabric can distinguish one worshiper from the other. This is a sign of the equality of all under God.

Holidays

Muslim holidays fall according to the Islamic calendar, which has 12 months each lasting from one new moon to the next. The Islamic year begins on the day of **Hijra,** which recalls Muhammad's migration from Mecca to Medina in the year 622 A.D. The year 2006 A.D. corresponds to the year 1427 A.H. (after Hijra) of the Islamic calendar.

Ashura is celebrated on the tenth day of the first Muslim month. For many Muslims this day commemorates wonderful events like the coming to rest of Noah's ark, the birth of the prophet Abraham, and the building of the **Ka'aba.** For Shia Muslims, however, it is a day of special sorrow commemorating the martyrdom of Muhammad's grandson Hussain in the battle of Kerbala in Islam's first century. It is commemorated in Shia communities with the reenactment of these events and is a time for mourning.

Milad al Nabi is the prophet's birthday. It occurs on the 12th day of the third Islamic month. It is celebrated in some Muslim countries with great festivities.

Laylat Al Miraj is celebrated on the 27th day of the seventh month, and it commemorates the journey of the prophet from Mecca to Jerusalem and his ascension to the seven heavens.

Laylt al Baraa falls on the 15th day of the eighth month. It is a night when forgiveness is granted to those who repent. It is also a time when people forgive and settle disputes. Many Muslims spend the night in prayer.

Ramadan is the 9th and holiest month of the Islamic calendar. Mature and healthy Muslims fast from dawn to dusk so that they can empathize with the struggles of the poor who often go hungry and thirsty. Although Ramadan is a month of reflection and self-discipline in which people earn the blessing of God and his forgiveness, it is also a time when family and friends gather for special meals and late nights of socializing.

Laylt Al Qadr commemorates the first revelation to the prophet and is usually on the 27th day of the 9th month, known as the month of Ramadan. It is said to be equal to one thousand months, and on this night the prayers of the sincere Muslim are said to be answered. Most Muslims go for special night prayers at their mosques.

Eid al Iftar is the feast that celebrates the end of the month of Ramadan. Elaborate dishes are prepared as family and friends gather around the table to celebrate. The traditional greeting is "Eid Mubarak," which translates to Blessed Eid. Children are dressed in their best clothes, often bought for the occasion, and gift giving and merrymaking are widespread.

Hajj, the required pilgrimage to Mecca, falls in the 12th Islamic month. The 9th day of the Hajj is known as the day of Arafat, when fasting pilgrims stand before God on Mount Arafat and Muslims around the world gather at local mosques for prayer in spiritual solidarity with the pilgrims.

Eid al Adha commemorates Abraham's willingness to sacrifice his son Ishmael to God and God's mercy in substituting a lamb for Ishmael. This feast coincides with the end of Hajj. Traditionally, Muslims will sacrifice a sheep and distribute its meat to the poor. They then celebrate with their own family and friends.

Islam Around the World

With 1.6 billion followers, Islam is the world's second largest religion. About one in five people in the world is Muslim. The largest population of Muslims is found in Asia, with Indonesia being the most populous Muslim country. Africa constitutes approximately 27 percent of world Muslims, and Arab lands represent 18 percent. Islam is the fastest-growing religion in Europe and North America, and there are nearly six million Muslims in the United States. Approximately 90 percent of Muslims practice **Sunni Islam.** Another variety, **Shia Islam,** is dominant in Iran and is popular in southern Iraq, Lebanon, and Bahrain. The division between Sunni and Shia occurred during a dispute over who would succeed Muhammad after his death. Shias wanted Muhammad's nearest relative while Sunnis wanted to choose the best-qualified man. Little else separates them except that the Shias exalt their **imams,** a succession of leaders whom they regard as a line of inspired teachers. **Sufism** is a mystical branch of Islam that promotes the use of music, chanting, dancing, and breathing exercises to reach a mystical state.

דברים שצריך לדעת על יהדות

מה שאנו מכנים אלוהים

אל עליון, בראשית י"ד: 20 – 18

שופט, בראשית י"ח: 25

אל עולם, בראשית כא: 33

יהווה – יִרְאֶה, בראשית כ"ב: 14

אל אלוהי ישראל, בראשית ל"ג: 20

אל שדי, בראשית מ"ט: 25

כתבי הקודש

הספר הקדוש היהודי נקרא התנ"ך. חמישה הספרים הראשונים של התנ"ך נקראים תורה. נביאים, הוא החלק השני של התנ"ך, והוא כולל את הספרים יהושע, ישעיה, ויונה. כתובים, הוא החלק האחרון של התנ"ך, והוא כולל את תהילים ומשלי.

התורה היא הדבר החשוב ביותר בכל בית כנסת. היא כתובה ביד על מגילת קלף ארוכה, מכוסה בכיסוי קטיפה ומוחזקת בתא מיוחד, המכונה ארון הקודש.

כשארון הקודש נפתח, כל קהל המתפללים צריך לקום לכבוד התורה. יהודים מתחילים את הקריאה בתורה בחג שנקרא שמחת תורה, וקוראים חלק בכל שבוע. בסוף השנה, צריך להשלים את קריאת כל התורה.

פולחן ותפילה

הטכסים היהודיים הדתיים מתנהלים בבית הכנסת. בקידמת בית הכנסת יש בימה, שעליה עומד הארון, כשספר התורה בתוכו. מנורה, הנקראת אש התמיד, בוערת תמיד מעל הארון.

הרב הוא המנהיג הרוחני, מורה האמונה היהודית, מישהו שלמד היסטוריה יהודית ותורה במשך שנים רבות. הרבי עוזר לקהילה ללמוד ולהבין את התורה. כמו כן, כאשר יהודי מחפש נחמה, עצה, או מידע על יהדות, הוא הולך לקבל עזרה מהרב. בכמה קהילות הרב חייב להיות גבר. בקהילות אחרות יש רבנים נשים.

מצוות

כל היהודים מאמינים באל אחד ובתורה. מאז 1800, היהדות בארצות הברית הסתעפה לשלוש קבוצות גדולות: אורתודוכסית, קונסרבטיבית ויהדות רפורמית. יהודים אורתודוכסים מקיימים

יהדות מסורתית מאוד, כפי שהיא נשמרה מעל לאלפיים שנה. הם מאמינים שהתורה נמסרה ישירות למשה. הם מצייתים לחוקי הכשרות של התורה, שאוסרים עליהם לאכול פירות ים ובשר חזיר. גברים אורתודוכסים מתפללים כל יום, בנפרד מנשים.

יהודים רפורמים התאימו את היהדות לעולם המודרני. רובם אינם מצייתים לחוקי הכשרות. גברים אינם חובשים בדרך כלל כיפה לראשם, כמו גברים אורתודוכסים. יהודים רפורמים לעתים עוטים טלית; גברים אורתודוכסים תמיד עוטים טלית בבית הכנסת. יהודים רפורמים מקיימים טכסי תפילה בשפות אחרות בנוסף לעברית. טכסים אורתודוכסים מתנהלים תמיד בעברית. יהודים קונסרבטיבים הם יותר מסורתיים מהיהודים הרפורמים, אך לא מסורתיים כמו היהודים האורתודוכסים.

בבתים יהודים רבים יש מזוזה התלויה בכניסה לבית. מזוזה היא תיבה קטנה. בתוך התיבה יש מגילה זעירה עם תפילה מיוחדת הכתובה עליה, וקטעים מתוך התורה. יש יהודים הנוגעים בידם במזוזה ומנשקים את ידם כסימן של כבוד, כאשר הם נכנסים או יוצאים מהבית. התורה וספר התפילות היהודי כתובים בעברית, שהיא שפה עתיקה עם אלפבית מיוחד. ילדים יהודים הולכים לבתי ספר דתיים לא רק כדי ללמוד תפילות, מנהגים והיסטוריה, אלא גם כדי ללמוד לקרוא עברית. כאשר ילד יהודי מגיע לגיל 13, הוא נקרא לעלות לבימה של בית הכנסת לקרוא את התורה לקהילה בפעם הראשונה בחייו. טכס זה נקרא בר מצווה, וחגיגה גדולה נערכת לאחר הטכס. ילדות יהודיות שאינן אורתודוכסיות נקראות אף הן לעלות לתורה לקרוא בה בפעם הראשונה, והטכס נקרא בת מצווה. בנישואים, הכלה והחתן היהודיים חותמים על הסכם נישואין הנקרא כתובה, לפני הטכס, שנערך מתחת לחופה. אחרי שהכלה והחתן מחליפים טבעות, והרבי מברך את הזוג, החתן שובר כוס מתחת לרגלו, לסמל את חורבן המקדש בירושלים ולהזכיר ליהודים שלצד השמחה הגדולה, קיים גם צער גדול בעולם.

חגים

ליהודים לוח שנה משלהם, וחודשים יהודיים נמשכים ממולד ירח אחד למישנהו. לכן יהודים יחוגו חגים בימים שונים בלוח השנה הלועזי בכל שנה. אך יום אחד של תפילה, שבת, מתרחש בכל יום שישי בלילה ובשבת. לפי הסיפור היהודי של הבריאה, אלוהים ברא את העולם בשישה ימים, ואז הוא נח ביום השביעי. לכן שבת הוא היום השביעי בשבוע ויום מיוחד מכל שאר הימים לכל היהודים. הוא מתחיל ביום שישי בלילה, ונחוג בבית או בבית הכנסת. בבית או בבית הכנסת, יהודים מדליקים נרות שבת ומתפללים תפילה מיוחדת. שתי תפילות נוספות נערכות על כוס יין ועל לחם מיוחד הנקרא חלה. יהודים המחמירים בשמירת השבת אינם עובדים, נוסעים, או נושאים כסף בשבת. במוצאי שבת מדליקים נר יחיד וקופסה בשמים מיוחדת מורמת וממלאת את הבימה בריח נהדר.

לפי הסיפור התנכי היתה בפרס לפני שנים רבות מלכה יהודיה בשם אסתר, שהצילה את עמה

מהשמדה. סיפורה של אסתר מופיע בטקסט הידוע כמגילה. הסיפור נקרא בכל שנה בחג הנקרא פורים בפברואר או במרס. ילדים ממחיזים את הסיפור ומתחפשים כמלכים, מלכות והמן, ראש הממשלה הרשע שאיים על עצם קיומם של היהודים. יהודים אוכלים עוגיות מיוחדות הנקראות אוזני המן, שמעוצבות בצורה של כובע משולש שהמן הרשע חבש.

בפסח, במרס או באפריל, יהודים חוגגים את יציאת העברים מעבדות במצרים. החג נמשך שמונה ימים, מתחיל בארוחה הנקראת סדר, שבה מספרים היהודים מחדש את סיפור יציאת מצרים. בפסח אוכלים לחם שטוח הנקרא מצה בכדי להזכר בכך שכאשר העברים יצאו ממצרים, הם עשו זאת מהר כל כך, לפני שהלחם שאפו הספיק לתפוח.

בספטמבר, יהודים חוגגים את ראש השנה, תחילת השנה היהודית החדשה. בתפילה בבית הכנסת, מישהו תוקע בשופר, בכדי להזכיר לאנשים לעשות את חשבון הנפש לגבי השנה החולפת. יהודים אוכלים פלחים של תפוחי עץ טבולים בדבש, כדי שתהיה לכולם שנה חדשה מתוקה. יום כיפור, יום צום, הוא היום הקדוש ביותר בכל השנה ליהודים, המתפללים לאלוהים שיסלח להם על חטאים שהם ביצעו במהלך השנה הקודמת. מבוגרים צמים, ללא אוכל או שתייה, מזריחה עד שקיעה. תוקעים בשופר בסוף החג.

באוקטובר, יהודים חוגגים את חג האסיף הנקרא סוכות. הם בונים סוכה פשוטה בחצר, מקושטת בפירות ובענפים, להזכיר לעצמם את הבתים שאבותיהם בנו בשעה שהם נדדו במדבר. חנוכה נחוג בדרך כלל בדצמבר. חג זה מציין את התבוסה של צבא אדיר בידי קבוצה קטנה של יהודים, שהצליחו לסלק את אויביהם מירושלים העתיקה. יהודים אמיצים אלה פתחו מחדש את בית המקדש, אך מצאו שמן שהספיק להדליק את מנורת המקדש רק ללילה אחד. ואז קרה נס. השמן הספיק לשמונה ימים מלאים, עד ששמן נוסף הובא לבית המקדש. יהודים היום מדליקים חנוכיה עם שמונה קנים, המיצגת את שמונה הימים, ובאמצע כן לשמש, הנר המדליק את כל שאר הנרות. בלילה הראשון של חנוכה, נר אחד מודלק. בלילה השני, שני נרות מודלקים, ובלילה השמיני כל החנוכיה מוארת.

יהדות מסביב לעולם

כשאנו כותבים זאת, יש בערך 13 מיליון יהודים בעולם. יותר יהודים חיים בארה"ב מאשר בכל מדינה אחרת. ישראל באה מיד אחרי ארה"ב, ויכולה בקרוב לעבור אותה במספר היהודים שבה. בצרפת, קנדה, בריטניה, רוסיה ובחבר המדינות יש גם אוכלוסיות יהודיות גדולות. יהודים התפזרו בכל העולם, בהודו, ברזיל, ארגנטינה ודרום אמריקה, בדרך כלל כדי לברוח מרדיפות. הדוגמה הנוראה ביותר של אנטישמיות, או אפליה כנגד יהודים, התרחשה במהלך השואה, כאשר הנאצים רצחו 6 מיליון יהודים. הרבה ספרים וסרטים הראו לעולם את זוועת השואה.

דברים שצריך לדעת על הנצרות

מה שאנו מכנים אלוהים

לנוצרים יש שלושה שמות לאלוהים. כל שם מתייחס לאחד מתוך שלוש ישויות של השילוש הקדוש. הראשון הוא אלוהים האב, שמתייחס לבורא הכל יכול. השני הוא אלוהים הבן, שהוא ישו, אלוהים ואדם ביחד. הוא אדם אחד שבו מגולמות ביחד התכונות האלוהיות והאנושיות. השם הנוצרי השלישי לאלוהים הוא רוח הקודש. זה המונח שנוצרים משתמשים בו כאשר הם מתייחסים לגילויים של כוח אלוהים בעולם כמו בניסים, בהטבלה של ישו, ובשבועות.

כתבי הקודש

התנ"ך של הנוצרים מחולק לשני חלקים: הברית הישנה, שהוא כמעט כמו התנ"ך היהודי, והברית החדשה. ברית משמע הבטחה. הנצרות, ששורשיה הם במסורת היהודית, מפרשת את בואו של ישו כהגשמה של ההבטחה שניתנה בברית הישנה. הברית החדשה מושתתת על האונגליונים, המספרים על חייו, מותו, ותחייתו מחדש של ישו; מכתבים וכתבים אחרים של שליחים נוצרים מוקדמים וספר חזון יוחנן, המנבא את אחרית הימים. יש תרגומים רבים ושונים של התנ"ך. אנו ממליצים על הגירסה התקנית (הנהוגה אצל הפרוטסטנטים).

פולחן ותפילה

באופן כללי נוצרים משתתפים בפולחן דתי בכנסיה בימי ראשון. הפולחן כולל בדרך כלל קריאה מהתנ"ך ודרשה שמתייחסת אליה, שניתנת על ידי הכומר או איש דת שמוביל את הטקס. הפולחן החשוב ביותר למרבית הנוצרים הוא המיסה שכוללת את אכילת לחם הקודש. זוהי תזכורת לארוחה האחרונה שישו חגג עם מאמיניו לפני מותו. כפי שישו עשה, הכומר שמוביל את הפולחן מברך על הלחם ונותן לכל אחד פרוסה.

כאשר נוצרים מתפללים הם לפעמים כורעים ברך כשעיניהם עצומות וידיהם שלובות. הם תמיד מתחילים ומסיימים את תפילותיהם על ידי עשיית סימן של צלב על גופם על ידי נגיעה בראשם, חזם, ושתי כתפיהם. זה מסמל את הצלב שעליו ישו מת. תפילה אחת המיוחדת לנוצרים ידועה כתפילת האדון [הידועה גם כ"אבינו שבשמים"]. על פי הברית החדשה, ישו הורה תפילה זו לתלמידיו.

הנה נוסח התפילה:

אבינו שבשמים, יתקדש שמך, תבוא מלכותך ייעשה רצונך כאשר בשמים גם בארץ. את לחם חוקנו תן לנו היום, ומחל לנו על חובותינו כאשר מחלנו גם אנחנו לחייבינו. ואל תביאנו לידי ניסיון, כי אם תחלצנו מן הרע.

מצוות

הטכסים הנוצרים הקדושים ביותר נקראים סקרמנטים. אלה כוללים את הטבילה ואכילת לחם הקודש. רוב הכנסיות מטבילות תינוקות בברכת ההטבלה בכנסיה. הכומר זולף מים קדושים על ראש הילד ומושח את ראש התינוק בשמן. זהו סמל לטהרה והכניסה של החיים ל "גוף של ישו הנוצרי". בכמה כנסיות פרוטסטנטיות בוגרים מוטבלים על ידי טבילה במים. בתקופה ישו אנשים הוטבלו בנהרות. על פי הברית החדשה, ישו הוטבל על ידי אדם שנקרא יוחנן המטביל. במשך ההטבלה רוח הקודש הופיעה בצורה של יונה ואמרה: "זהו בני האהוב".

אכילת לחם הקודש מקבלת תוקף בזכות הברכה של הכומר על הלחם והיין, המסמלים את הגוף והדם של ישו. הפולחן מציין את הארוחה האחרונה של ישו עם שליחיו שבה הוא חלק אתם את הלחם והיין, באומרו: "אכלו את הלחם כי זה בשרי, שתו את היין כי זה דמי". בדרך זו ישו הבטיח להיות עם מאמיניו עד קץ הימים. פולחן אחר הוא וידוי. בכנסיות נוצריות מערביות, ילדים לומדים את דתם כדי להכין את עצמם לוידוי. הטכס כולל משיחה בשמן והנחת הידיים של בישוף, שהוא מנהיג כנסיה אזורי חשוב.

חגים

עונת הפסחא, שהיא באביב, היא התקופה החשובה ביותר בלוח השנה הנוצרי. בעונה זו אנשים חוגגים את אירועי מותו ותחייתו של ישו. ארבעים הימים לפני הפסחא ידועים כ**תענית (לנט)**, המתחילה ביום רביעי של האפר. ביום זה נוצרים רבים הולכים לכנסיה שבה הכומר שם צלב של אפר על מצחם. האפר הוא תזכורת שהאנשים אינם אלא אפר בהשוואה לאלוהים ושאנו תלויים בחסד האלוהי לגאולתנו. לנט (תענית) הוא הזמן של צום וויתור על מותרות בהכנה לפסחא. היום לפני הלנט ידוע כיום שלישי השמן (מרדי גרא). במקומות רבים, אנשים חוגגים יום זה בקרניבלים ובארוחות מיוחדות שהם לא יהנו מהן במהלך התענית. השבוע שלפני הפסחא ידוע כשבוע קדוש. הוא מתחיל עם יום ראשון של הדקלים שמציין את היום שבו ישו הגיע לירושלים ובורך על ידי ההמון שנופף לו בדקלים. בכנסיות רבות ניתנים למתפללים דקלים ביום זה. יום חמישי הקדוש הוא זיכרון לארוחה האחרונה, ארוחת הפסח (הסדר) של ישו, שאותה הוא חגג עם מאמיניו בלילה שלפני מותו. יום שישי הטוב מציין את מותו של ישו על הצלב. ופסחא, החג הנוצרי החשוב ביותר, מציין את התחייה מחדש של ישו ועלייתו מקברו שלושה ימים לאחר מותו. בפסחא הנוצרים מקשטים ביצים כסמל לחיים חדשים.

העונה של חג המולד הנוצרי חוגגת את הולדתו של ישו. ארבעת השבועות לפני כריסמס, שזה ה-25 בדצמבר, ידועים כביאת הגואל. זו התקופה של תפילות מיוחדות בהכנה לחג המולד. ילדים מחזיקים בלוחות שנה מיוחדים של ביאת הגואל המציינים את הימים עד החג הגדול. זרים של ביאת הגואל מחזיקים בארבעה נרות, אחד לכל אחד מארבעת ימי הראשון שקודמים לחג המולד. בכנסיות רבות יש מופעים, שבהם ילדים מתחפשים ומשחקים את הסיפור של הולדת ישו. על

פי הברית החדשה, הוריו של ישו (מריה ויוסף) נסעו לבית לחם למפקד אוכלוסין אך לא מצאו שם מקום ללון. לכן הם ישנו באורווה שבה ישו נולד והונח באבוס. בכנסיות רבות יש תצוגות או תמונות של לידת התינוק המראות את ישו, מריה ויוסף באורווה עם חיות ורועים המתבוננים בהם. חג ההתגלות (האפיפני), שחל ב-6 בינואר, מסיים את עונת המולד. ביום זה הנוצרים זוכרים את הביקור של שלושת המלכים, שהביאו לישו התינוק מתנות של זהב, מור ולבונה. הביקור שלהם מראה שישו בא כגואל לעולם כולו, לא רק ליהודים.

נצרות מסביב לעולם

יש קרוב לשני מיליארד נוצרים בעולם. כמחציתם שייכים לכנסיה הקתולית, שמנהיגה הוא האפיפיור. הקתולים מאמינים שהאפיפיור הוא היורש הישיר של פטרוס, שליח ישו, הנחשב על ידם כאפיפיור הראשון. הם מאמינים שהאפיפיור הוא הנציג של אלוהים עלי אדמות והוא אינו מסוגל לטעות כאשר מדובר בדוקטרינה של הכנסיה. המטה של האפיפיור הוא ברומא. רוב הקתולים חיים היום באירופה ובאמריקות. ב-1054 הכנסיה המזרחית, הידועה גם ככנסיה האורתודוכסית, התפלגה מהכנסיה הקתולית. כיום יש בערך 215 מיליון חברים בכנסיה האורותודוקסית, ומרביתם חיים במזרח אירופה וברוסיה. שאר הנוצרים משתייכים לחלקים פרוטסטנטיים, שהתפצלו מהכנסיה הקתולית. דוגמאות להם כוללות את הכנסיות הבפטיסטיות, האפיסקופליות, הלותרניות, והפרסבטריאניות.

דברים שצריך לדעת על האיסלם

מה שאנו מכנים אלוהים

אללה היא המילה הערבית לאלוהים. משתמשים בה ערבים נוצרים ומוסלמים כאחד. למוסלמים, אלוהים לא נוצר ואין ישות אחרת כמוהו. המוסלמים מאמינים שאחת המעלות החשובות ביותר של אלוהים היא יחדיותו. על פי המוסלמים אם אלוהים הוא אחד, אז לא יכולים להיות אלים אחרים או מתחרים, כגון אלוהים ליהודים, אלוהים לנוצרים ואלוהים למאמינים בריבוי אלים (פוליתאיזם). הם מאמינים שלאלוהים יש 99 כינויים. אלה הם שמות תואר שניתנו לאורך הקוראן, כולל בורא כל יכול של כדור הארץ, הרחמן, הרחום, השומר, האוהב, הסובלני והסולח תמיד. מוסלמים באופן מסורתי חוזרים על כינויים אלה בעזרת מחרוזת הידועה כמחרוזת תפילה. מחרוזת זו היא בעלת 100 חרוזים. תשעים ותשעה מציגים את המעלות של אלוהים והחרוז הגדול ביותר מייצג את אלוהים.

כתבי הקודש

הספר הקדוש של המוסלמים נקרא קוראן. הם מאמינים שהוא דבר האלוהים, שהתגלה לנביא מוחמד באמצעות המלאך גבריאל [ג'בריל] במשך תקופה של 22 שנה. לאחר שנכתב בצורה ארעית, הוא הושלם בצורתו הסופית לאחר מותו של הנביא מוחמד ב-632 לספירה. הוא מחולק ל-114 פרקים (סורות) המורכבים מחרוזים (איט). כל הפרקים, להוציא פרק תשע, מתחילים ב"בשם אללה הרחמן והרחום". מוסלמים לומדים את הקוראן בשפתו המקורית, ערבית, משום ששינוים שלו כדברי אלוהים הוא פולחן שמאפשר למוסלמים לחוות את אלוהים באופן סמלי, כקהילה של מאמינים. זה מקביל לחוויה הסמלית הנוצרית שבאכילת לחם הקודש, שמגדירה את הקהילה הנוצרית. האיסלם אוסר על תאור חזותי של אלוהים כדי להאבק בעבודת אלילים. כתוצאה מכך, משתמשים באמנות הכתיבה (הקליגרפיה) בעיטור הקוראן והמסגדים. מוסלמים מעיינים בקוראן ביחד עם החדית' (אוסף של הלכות שמיוחסות לנביא ומלוויו) בכדי שידריכו אותם בהיבטים שונים של החיים. החוק המוסלמי, הידוע כשריעה, מבוסס על הקוראן והחדית'.

פולחן ותפילה

המוסלמים מתאספים במסגד ביום שישי בצהריים לתפילה בציבור. האימאם מנהל את התפילה ופונה לקהל המתפללים מעל דוכן עם מדרגות הנקרא מינבר. הוא לעולם אינו נושא דרשה מהמדרגה הגבוהה ביותר, שבאופן סמלי נשמרת לנביא מוחמד. מסגדים בנויים עם מגדל מיוחד הנקרא צריח, שממנו אדם הידוע כמואזין קורא לאנשים לתפילה חמש פעמים ביום. כשמוסלמים מתפללים הם מפנים את פניהם לכיוון מכה, מקום הולדתו של הנביא מוחמד. הכיוון מצויין עלי ידי גומחה הידועה כמיחראב, שמתפקדת כנקודת מיקוד לאולם התפילה. באולם התפילה אין כסאות מאחר שהתפילה כרוכה בעמידה, כריעה ברך והשתטחות. כל התפילות מסתיימות באותה קריאה לשלום לנביא מוחמד, ממשיכיו וצאצאי אברהם. במסגדים אחדים יש מרפסות נפרדות לנשים, למרות שבמסגד החשוב ביותר במכה, מאג'ד אל אהראם, נשים וגברים מתפללים באותו **אולם ואינם נפרדים**. לפני התפילה, מוסלמים מטהרים את עצמם על ידי רחיצת פנים, פה, נחיריים, ידים, בחלק התחתון של הזרועות והרגליים. מטעמי ניקיון המתפללים נדרשים לחלוץ את נעליהם לפני כניסתם למסגד, ומוסלמים רבים משתמשים בשטיחונים, חלקם עם מצפנים המוצמדים אליהם כדי לציין את הכיוון למכה. מסגדים הם בדרך כלל מבנה בעל כיפה עם עמודים וקשתות, המעוטרים בקליגרפיה ובצורות גאומטריות מופשטות. עיצוב הפנים נשאר פשוט כדי לא להסיח את דעת המתפללים. המסגד הכחול באיסטנבול והמסגד הגדול בקורדובה בספרד מפורסמים באדריכלות שלהם. כיפת הסלע ומסגד אל-אקצא בירושלים הם בין המסגדים החשובים ביותר למוסלמים. הר הבית, כפי שנקרא האזור הקדוש בירושלים, מציין את המקום של מסע הלילה של הנביא מוחמד ועלייתו לשמיים. מוסלמים מאמינים שהאנושות תתכנס שם ביום הדין.

מצוות

המצוות החשובות ביותר באיסלם ידועות באופן כללי כחמשת היסודות של האיסלם. א- **שהאדה** היא המצווה הראשונה והחשובה ביותר. היא הצהרה פשוטה "אין אלוהים בלעדי אללה, ומוחמד הוא שליחו של אללה". מלים אלה הן הצהרה של אמונה המספקת את הבסיס להמרת הדת. אדם החוזר ברצינות על הא-שהאדה נחשב למוסלמי ואין צורך במצווה אחרת.

הצלאה היא התפילה המתבצעת חמש פעמים ביום בזמנים מדויקים תוך פנייה למכה. הקריאה של המואזין מהצריח מאפשרת לאנשים לדעת שזהו הזמן להתפלל. כל התפילות מסתיימות בברכות טכסיות וקריאות לשלום לנביא מוחמד, למאמיניו ולצאצאים של אברהם **שכוללים את משה וישו.** יום שישי הוא היום שהמוסלמים מתפללים בציבור במסגד. כתוצאה מכך, סופי שבוע בארצות מוסלמיות הם או יום חמישי ושישי או שישי ושבת.

זכאה היא תרומת כסף כדי לעזור לנזקקים. מוסלמים בעלי יכולת כספית אמורים לתת %2.5 מנכסיהם לצדקה חברתית.

צום הוא התענית במשך חודש הרמדאן. מוסלמים אינם אוכלים או שותים מזריחה עד שקיעה במשך חודש קדוש זה. הרעיון מאחורי צום זה הוא ללמד את האנשים להזדהות עם הנזקקים שתמיד רעבים וצמאים. רק מוסלמים בריאים ובוגרים נדרשים לצום. רמדאן הוא גם זמן להתבוננות פנימית ומשמעת, הוא הפך גם זמן לכינוסים מיוחדים של משפחה וחברים עם ארוחות טעימות ועם קינוחים מסורתיים. מוסלמים יכולים לקשט את בתיהם עם זרים בצורת ירח וכוכב שהפכו לסמלי האיסלם. פגישות חברתיות מתארכות בדרך כלל עד מאוחר בלילה ומסתיימות בארוחה מאוחרת או מוקדמת לפני הזריחה שנקראת סוהור.

חג' הוא העלייה לרגל למכה הנדרשת לפחות פעם אחת בחייו של כל מוסלמי. מוסלמים מקיימים מצוות מסוימות ותפילות מסביב לכעבה, אבן שחורה בצורת קובייה שמאמינים שהיא הבית הראשון לאלוהים שנבנה בידי אברהם וישמעאל, ושבו אברהם כמעט והקריב את בנו ישמעאל. בסביבות שני מיליון מוסלמים מקיימים את העלייה השנתית לרגל. עולי רגל לובשים בגדים לבנים שלא נגעו בהם חוט ומחט כך ששום תפר או אריג לא יבחין בין מאמין אחד למישנהו. זהו סימן לשיוויון של כולם בפני האלוהים.

חגים

החגים המוסלמים חלים על פי לוח השנה האסלמי שיש בו 12 חודשים הנמשכים ממולד ירח אחד למשנהו. השנה האסלמית מתחילה ביום של ההיג'רה, שמציין את ההגירה של מוחמד ממכה למדינה בשנת 622 לספירה. שנת 2007 לספירה מקבילה לשנה 1427 (אחרי ההיג'רה) בלוח השנה האסלמי.

עשוראא (عشوراء), נחוג ביום העשירי בחודש המוסלמי הראשון [המחרם]. למוסלמים רבים יום

זה מציין את האירועים הנהדרים כמו תיבת נוח שהגיעה אל המנוחה, לידתו של הנביא אברהם, ובניין הכעבה. למוסלמים שיעים, לעומת זאת, זה יום מיוחד של צער המציין את מות הקדושים של חוסיין, נכדו של מוחמד, בקרב בכרבלה במאה האסלמית הראשונה. יום זה מציין בקהילות השיעיות בהמחזה של אירועים אלה והוא יום אבל.

אל-מוולאד א-נבווי (المولد النبويّ), הוא יום הולדת של הנביא. זה מתרחש ביום ה-12 של החודש האיסלמי השלישי. הוא נחוג בארצות מוסלמיות מסוימות בפסטיבלים גדולים.

לילת אל-מעראג' (الإسراء والمعراج), נחוג ביום ה-27 של החודש השביעי והוא מציין את הנסיעה של הנביא ממכה לירושלים ועלייתו לרקיע השביעי.

לילת אל- בארא (ליל תשובה) מתרחש ביום ה-51 של החודש השמיני. זהו לילה שבו מועָנקת מחילה לאלה שמכים על חטא. הוא גם זמן שבו אנשים סולחים ומיישבים מחלוקות. מוסלמים רבים מבלים את הלילה בתפילה.

רמדאן (رمضان). הוא החודש התשיעי והקדוש ביותר בלוח השנה האסלמי. מוסלמים בוגרים ובריאים צמים משחר עד ערבית כדי שיוכלו להזדהות עם המאבקים של העניים שתמיד הולכים רעבים וצמאים. למרות שהרמדאן הוא חודש של התבוננות פנימית ומשמעת עצמית לקבלת ברכת האל ומחילתו, הוא גם זמן שבו משפחה וחברים נפגשים לארוחות מיוחדות ולחיי חברה עד מאוחר בלילה.

לילת אל קדר (ליל הגורל/הגזירה) מציין את ההתגלות הראשונה לנביא והוא תמיד ביום ה-27 של החודש ה-9, הידוע כחודש של הרמדאן. נאמר שהוא שווה ערך לאלף חודשים ובלילה זה התפילות של המוסלמים האדוקים אמורות להיענות. רוב המוסלמים הולכים ללילה של תפילה מיוחדת במסגדים שלהם.

עיד אל-פיטר (חג הפסקת הצום, החג הקטן) הוא החג לציון הסיום של חודש הרמדאן. מנות גדושות מוכנות כי חברים ובני משפחה נאספים מסביב לשולחן כדי לחגוג. הברכה המסורתית היא "עיד מובאראק" שפרושה החג המבורך. ילדים לבושים במיטב בגדיהם שנרכשים במיוחד לכבוד האירוע ומקובל לתת מתנות ולקיים שמחות.

חג' הוא מצוות עלייה לרגל למכה שנופל בחודש ה-12 המוסלמי. היום ה-9 של החג' ידוע כיום של ערפאת שבו העולים לרגל הצמים עומדים בפני האל על הר עראפת ומוסלמים מסביב לעולם מתאספים במסגד המקומי לתפילה מתוך הזדהות רוחנית עם עולי הרגל.

עיד אל אד'חא (חג הקורבן, החג הגדול) מציין את הנכונות של אברהם להקריב את בנו ישמעאל לאל והרחמים של האל בהחלפת ישמעאל טזה. חג זה משתלב עם הסיום של החג'. באופן מסורתי, מוסלמים מקריבים כבשה ותורמים אותה לעניים. אז הם חוגגים עם בני משפחה וחברים.

איסלם מסביב לעולם

עם 6.1 מיליארד מאמינים, האיסלם הוא הדת השנייה בגודלה בעולם. בערך אחד מתוך חמישה אנשים בעולם הוא מוסלמי. האוכלוסייה הגדולה ביותר של מוסלמים נמצאת באסיה, ביחד עם אינדונזיה שהיא המדינה האיסלמית המאוכלסת ביותר. אפריקה מרכיבה 27% לערך של מוסלמים בעולם, וארצות ערב מיצגות 18%. איסלם הוא הדת הגדלה בצורה המהירה ביותר באירופה ובצפון אמריקה, ויש קרוב לשישה מיליון מוסלמים בארה"ב. בערך 90% מוסלמים מאמינים באיסלם סוני. פלג אחר, **איסלם שיעי**, שולט באירן ופופולארי בדרום עירק, לבנון, ובחריין. החלוקה בין סונים ושיעים נוצר במשך המאבק על היורש של מוחמד לאחר מותו. השיעים רצו בשאר הבשר הקרוב ביותר למוחמד, בעוד הסונים רצו לבחור באיש המעולה ביותר. חוץ מזה אין כמעט הבדל ביניהם מלבד העובדה שהשיעים מאמינים באימאמים שלהם, רצף של מנהיגים שהם מתייחסים אליהם כשורה של מורים רוחניים. **סופיזם** הוא ענף מיסטי של האיסלם שמעודד את השימוש במוסיקה, שירה, מחול ותרגילי נשימה כדי להגיע למצב מיסטי.

أمور يجب معرفتها عن اليهودية:

من نسميه الله.

تعبر التوراة عن أسماء الله المتعددة عن طريق وصف أفعاله من خلال قصص توراتية محددة.

إيل عليون (الله العلي) سفر التكوين 14: 18-20

شابت (ديّان كل الأرض) سفر التكوين 18: 25

إيل عولام (الإله السرمدي) سفر التكوين 21: 33

يهوه - يراه (الرب يرى) سفر التكوين 22: 14

إيل إلوه - يسرائيل (الله القدير - إله إسرائيل) سفر التكوين 33: 20

إيل شداي (القدير) سفر التكوين 49: 25

الكتاب المقدس.

يسمى الكتاب المقدس اليهودي التناخ. وتسمى الأسفار الخمسة الأولى من التناخ التوراة. ويشكل نيفيئيم، أو الأنبياء القسم الثاني من الكتاب المقدس ويتضمن قصص يشوع، وأشعياء، ويونس. أما القسم الثالث، كيتوفيم أو الكتابات، فهو القسم الأخير من التناخ ويحتوى على المزامير والأمثال.

وتعد التوراة الغرض الأهم في أي كنيس. وهي مخطوطة باليد على لفائف طويلة من ورق البرشمان تكون مغلفة بحافظة مخملية وموضوعة في خزانة خاصة تسمى التابوت. وعندما يفتح التابوت يتوجب على جموع المصلين الوقوف احتراما للتوراة.

يبدأ اليهود بقراءة التوراة في عيد يسمى بهجة التوراة، ويقرأون قسما منها في كل أسبوع. ومع نهاية العام، يكونون قد انتهوا من قراءتها بالكامل.

العبادة والصلاة.

تقام الصلوات الدينية اليهودية في الكنيس. ويوجد في مقدمة الكنيس البيما أو المنصة، ويوضع عليها التابوت وبداخله التوراة. وهناك مصباح يسمى النور الأزلي وهو مُوقد دائماً فوق التابوت.

والحاخام هو القائد الروحي، ومعلم الدين اليهودي الذي يكون قد أمضى سنوات عديدة في دراسة التاريخ اليهودي والشريعة والكتاب المقدس. ويساعد الحاخام جموع المصلين على فهم ودراسة التوراة. وهو من يقصده من يدين باليهودية بحثا عن المواساة أو المشورة أو المعلومات عن العقيدة اليهودية. ولدى بعض الطوائف، يتوجب على الحاخام أن يكون من الرجال. أما في بعض الطوائف الأخرى فهناك نساء يتولين منصب الحاخام.

الشعائر الدينية.

يؤمن جميع اليهود بإله واحد، وبالكتاب المقدس. تفرعت اليهودية منذ القرن التاسع عشر إلى ثلاث جماعات كبيرة: اليهودية الأورثوذكسية، واليهودية المحافظة، واليهودية الإصلاحية. يمارس اليهود الأورثوذكس اليهودية التقليدية كما تم توارثها خلال أكثر من ألفي سنة مضت. وهم يؤمنون بأن التوراة أعطيت مباشرة إلى موسى. وهم ينصاعون للقوانين الشرعية في التوراة المتعلقة بالمأكل والتي تحرم عليهم أكل الأسماك الصدفية ولحم الخنزير. ويصلي الرجال من اليهود الأورثوذكس يوميا بمعزل عن النساء.

أما اليهود الإصلاحيون فقد قاموا بأقلمة اليهودية مع معطيات العالم المعاصر. وهم في معظمهم لا يتبعون قوانين الطعام الحلال (الكوشر) الشرعية. ولا يضع الرجال منهم اليرملك أو طاقية الصلاة على رؤوسهم والتي يلبسها دائما الرجال من اليهود الأورثوذكس وخاصة في الكنيس. وفي بعض الأحيان يرتدي اليهود الإصلاحيون شال الصلاة ويسمى الطاليت، بينما يرتديه اليهود الأورثوذكس الرجال دائما في الكنيس. ويقيم اليهود الإصلاحيون الصلوات باللغة العبرية وبلغات أخرى أيضا، بينما يقيم اليهود الأورثوذكس صلواتهم بالعبرية دائما. أما اليهود المحافظون فهم أكثر تمسكا بالتقاليد من اليهود الإصلاحيين ولكن ليس للدرجة نفسها كاليهود الأورثوذكس.

وكثير من العائلات اليهودية تعلق المزوزا على أبواب منازلها. والمزوزا عبارة عن علبة صغيرة تحتوي على لفيفة صغيرة جدا مكتوب عليها دعاء خاص بالإضافة إلى مقاطع من التوراة. ويقوم بعض اليهود عند دخولهم البيت أو خروجهم منه بلمس المزوزا ثم يقبلون أيديهم كتعبير عن الاحترام. وتكتب التوراة وكتب الصلوات اليهودية باللغة العبرية وهي لغة قديمة ذات حروف هجائية فريدة. فأطفال اليهود لا يذهبون إلى المدارس الدينية لتعلم الصلوات والعادات والتاريخ وحسب، وإنما لتعلم قراءة العبرية أيضا. وعندما يبلغ الصبي اليهودي الثالثة عشر من العمر، يدعى حينها للصعود على منبر الكنيس لقراءة التوراة على جمع المصلين للمرة الأولى في حياته. ويسمى هذا الطقس بار متسفيه، ويقام احتفال كبير بعد الفراغ من الصلاة. كما وتدعى فتيات اليهود من غير الأورثوذكس لقراءة التوراة للمرة الأولى ويسمى هذا الطقس بات متسفيه. وفي الأعراس، يوقّع العريس والعروس اليهوديان عقد زواج يسمى كيتوباه قبل الاحتفال والذي يُعقد تحت مظلة من القماش تسمى خوباه. وبعد أن يعطي كل من العريس والعروس خاتمه للآخر، وبعد أن يبارك الحاخام الزوجين، يقوم العريس بكسر كأس نبيذ تحت قدمه ليرمز بذلك لهدم الهيكل المقدس في القدس ولتذكير اليهود بأن العالم فيه السعادة الغامرة والأسى العميق.

الأعياد.

لليهود تقويمهم الخاص بهم. ويمتد الشهر اليهودي من ظهور الهلال إلى ظهور هلال الشهر الذي يليه. وبهذا تقع الأعياد في أيام مختلفة من التقويم الميلادي كل عام. ولكن يوم صلاة واحد، وهو شبات، يصادف كل مساء جمعة وسبت. فبالاستناد إلى رواية الخلق اليهودية، خلق الله العالم في ستة أيام واستراح في اليوم السابع. وعليه فإن السبت هو اليوم السابع في الأسبوع وهو يوم راحة لجميع اليهود. ويبدأ يوم السبت من ليل الجمعة، وتتسنى إقامة طقوسه في البيت أو الكنيس. وفي كلتا الحالتين، يضيء اليهود شمعتي السبت ويؤدون صلاة خاصة. كما وتؤدى صلاتان أخرتان يتم خلالهما شرب كأس من النبيذ وتناول خبز من نوع معين يسمى هالا. وأما بالنسبة

لليهود الأكثر مراعاة لطقوس السبت، فإنهم لا يعملون ولا يسافرون ولا يحملون النقود في هذا اليوم. وفي مساء السبت، وبعد انقضاء اليوم، تضاء شمعة واحدة ليوضع فوقها مشعل للطيب يملأ منبر الكنيس برائحة جميلة.

وفي التاريخ القديم لبلاد فارس، أنقذت ملكة يهودية تدعى إستير شعبها من الإبادة في قصة مكتوبة بنص يطلق عليه مجيله. وتقرأ هذه القصة كل عام في عيد يسمى بوريم، ويكون في شهر شباط/فبراير أو شهر آذار/مارس. ويقوم الأطفال بتجسيد القصة، حيث يلبسون كالملوك والملكات وكهمان، وهو رئيس الوزراء الشرير الذي هدد وجود اليهود. ويتناول اليهود في هذا العيد كعكا خاصا يسمى هامانتاشن، ويتم تحضيره على شكل القبعة المثلثة التي كان يلبسها هامان الشرير.

أما في عيد الفصح الذي يكون في شهر آذار/مارس أو شهر نيسان/إبريل، فيحتفل اليهود بخلاص بني إسرائيل من العبودية في مصر. ويستمر هذا العيد لثمانية أيام ويبدأ بتناول عشاء يطلق عليه سيدر، ويقوم اليهود بسرد قصة خروجهم الجماعي أو خلاصهم. يأكل اليهود في هذا العيد خبزا رقيقا غير مختمر يسمى ماتسا ليذكرهم بحقيقة أن بني إسرائيل وعند خروبهم من مصر قاموا بذلك علي عجل قبل أن يتسنى للخبز الذي كانوا يخبزونه أن يختمر.

أما في شهر أيلول/سبتمبر، فيحتفل اليهود بعيد روش هاشانا، وهو رأس السنة اليهودية. عند الصلاة في الكنيس، يقوم شخص بالنفخ في بوق مصنوع من قرن كبش، شوفار، ليذكر الناس بأن عليهم التفكر بكل ما عملوه في السنة المنصرمة. ويأكل اليهود في هذا العيد قطع التفاح المغموسة بالعسل وذلك للتيمن بأن تكون السنة الجديدة سنة حلوة. أما يوم كيبور، يوم الغفران، فهو أكثر أيام السنة قداسة عند اليهود. يقومون فيه بالصلاة لله ليغفر لهم ما اقترفوه من ذنوب على مر العام الفائت. ويصوم البالغون في هذا اليوم، حيث لا يتناولون الطعام ولا الشراب من شروق الشمس حتى غروبها. ويُنفخ في الشوفار عند نهاية العيد. وفي شهر تشرين الأول/أكتوبر، يحتفل اليهود بعيد الحصاد الذي يسمى سوكوت. ويقومون في هذا العيد ببناء مآوٍ خشبية بسيطة في باحات منازلهم تزينها الفواكه والأغصان، وذلك لتذكيرهم بالمنازل التي صنعها أجدادهم خلال هيامهم في الصحراء.

أما حانوكا، فيتم الاحتفال به عادة في شهر كانون الأول/ديسمبر. ويُحتفل في هذا العيد بذكرى هزيمة جيش الأعداء الجرار وإخراجهم من القدس على يد عصبة من اليهود. وأعاد هؤلاء اليهود الشجعان افتتاح الهيكل المقدس، ولكنهم وجدوا من الزيت ما يكفي لإضاءة مشعل الهيكل لليلة واحدة فقط. وهنا حدثت معجزة، حيث دام الزيت مدة ثمانية أيام إلى أن تم إحضار المزيد من الزيت إلى الهيكل. وفي أيامنا هذه يضئ اليهود شمعدانا به ثمان شموع تمثل الأيام الثمانية، وبه أيضا حامل لشمعة تتوسطهم تستخدم في إضاءة الشموع الأخرى. وفي الليلة الأولى من عيد حانوكا تضاء شمعة واحدة. وفي الليلة الثانية تضاء شمعتان. ومع حلول اليوم الثامن يكون الشمعدان مضاء بالكامل.

اليهودية حول العالم.

يبلغ عدد اليهود في العالم ـ في وقت كتابة هذه الصفحات ـ حوالي 13 مليون نسمة. ويفوق عدد من يعيش منهم في الولايات المتحدة الأمريكية عدد اليهود في أي دولة أخرى. ويأتي عددهم في إسرائيل في المرتبة الثانية مقاربا لعدد من يعيش منهم في الولايات المتحدة الأمريكية. وربما يتفوق عددهم في إسرائيل على مثيله في الولايات المتحدة قريبا. وهناك أيضا جاليات يهودية كبيرة في كل من فرنسا وكندا والمملكة المتحدة وروسيا وجمهوريات

الاتحاد السوفيتي السابق. وقد ارتحل اليهود إلى جميع أنحاء العالم، إلى الهند والبرازيل والأرجنتين وأمريكا الجنوبية وكان ذلك غالبا للفرار من الاضطهاد. وكان أسوء مثال على معاداة السامية، أو التمييز العنصري ضد اليهود، قد حصل في الهولوكوست حينما قتل النازيون أكثر من ستة ملايين يهودي. وقد أظهرت العديد من الكتب والأفلام للعالم الرعب الذي صاحب الهولوكست.

أمور يجب معرفتها عن المسيحية:

من نسميه الله.

يوجد لدى المسيحيين ثلاثة أسماء لله. وكل اسم من هذه الأسماء يشير إلى الأقانيم الثلاثة للثالوث المقدس. والاسم الأول هو الله الأب والذي يدل على الخالق العظيم. والاسم الثاني هو الله الابن أي يسوع المسيح وهو إله وبشر في آن واحد. وهو أقنوما واحدا تتجسد فيه الطبيعتان اللاهوتية والبشرية دامًا. أما الاسم الثالث لله في المسيحية فهو الروح القدس. وهذا هو المصطلح الذي يستخدمه المسيحيون عند الإشارة إلى تجلي قدرة الله على الأرض كما في المعجزات عند تعميد المسيح وعيد العنصرة.

الكتاب المقدس.

ينقسم الإنجيل المسيحي إلى قسمين: العهد القديم، وهو تقريبا التناخ اليهودي نفسه، والعهد الجديد. والعهد يعني الوعد. وتفسر المسيحية والتي تكمن جذورها في الناموس اليهودي خروج المسيح على أنه تحقيق لما وعد به العهد القديم. ويتألف العهد الجديد من الإنجيل والذي يروي حياة يسوع المسيح وموته وقيامته؛ والرسالات والكتابات الأخرى لكتّاب الإنجيل الأربعة الأوائل؛ وسفر الرؤيا والذي يتحدث عن نهاية العالم. وهناك العديد من الترجمات المختلفة للإنجيل. ونحن نوصي بالنسخة القياسية المنقحة.

العبادة والصلاة.

يذهب المسيحيون عموما إلى الكنائس يوم الأحد لأداء الصلاة. وعادة ما تتضمن هذه الصلوات قراءات من الإنجيل وخطبة لها علاقة مما مت قراءته يلقيها الكاهن أو القس الذي يقود الصلاة. والقداس الأهم بالنسبة لأغلبية المسيحيين هو قداس يحتفل فيه بتناول القربان. وهو إحياء لذكرى العشاء الأخير الذي تناوله المسيح مع تلاميذه قبل وفاته. وتماما كما فعل المسيح، يقوم الكاهن الذي يقود الصلاة مباركة الخبز والنبيذ ويعطي كل شخص من الحاضرين كسرة من الخبز.

وعندما يصلي المسيحيون فإنهم في بعض الأحيان يجثون على ركبهم ويغمضون أعينهم ويشبكون أيديهم. وغالبا ما يبدءون صلاتهم وينهونها بالإماء بإشارة الصليب على أجسادهم وذلك بلمس رؤوسهم ثم صدورهم ثم كلتا الكتفين. وهذا يرمز إلى الصليب الذي مات عليه المسيح. وهناك صلاة لها خصوصيتها الكبيرة لدى المسيحيين تعرف بالصلاة الربية. وحسب الإنجيل، قام يسوع المسيح بتعليم هذه الصلاة لأتباعه. وهي كالآتي: «أبانا الذي في السماوات، ليتقدّس اسمك. ليأتِ ملكوتك، لتكن مشيئتك كما في السماء كذلك على الأرض. أعطنا خبزنا كفاف يومنا واغفر لنا خطايانا كما نغفر نحن لمن يسئ إلينا. ولا تُدخلنا في التجارب، لكنّ نجّنا من الشرّير».

الشعائر الدينية.

يطلق على أقدس الاحتفالات المسيحية اسم الأسرار المقدسة وهي تشمل:

How to Start a Faith Club

المعمودية والقربان المقدس (تناول القربان). تقوم معظم الكنائس المسيحية بتعميد الرُّضع في حوض المعمودية في الكنيسة حيث يقوم الكاهن بصب الماء المقدس على رأس الطفل ويمسح رأس الرضيع بالزيت. وترمز هذه العملية إلى الطهارة وإلى الانضمام إلى «جسد يسوع المسيح» الحي. وفي بعض الكنائس البروتستانتية يتم تعميد البالغين بتغطيسهم في الماء. وفي عهد يسوع المسيح، كان الناس يُعمَّدون في الأنهر، واستنادا إلى العهد الجديد فإن المسيح تم تعميده من قبل رجل يدعى يوحنا المعمدان. وفي أثناء التعميد تجلى الروح القدس على هيئة حمامة وقال: "هذا هو ابني الحبيب."

تناول القربان وهو مباركة الكاهن للخبز والنبيذ واللذين يرمزان إلى جسد المسيح ودمه. ويحي هذا الطقس الديني ذكرى العشاء الأخير الذي جمع المسيح بتلاميذه حيث تقاسم الخبز والنبيذ معهم قائلا «هذا جسدي ودمي.» وبهذا وعد المسيح بأن يبقى مع تلاميذه حتى آخر الزمان. وهناك طقس ديني آخر يسمى التثبيت. ففي الكنائس المسيحية الغربية، يدرس الأطفال ديانتهم للاستعداد للتثبيت. ويتضمن هذا الطقس دهن الأيادي بالزيت وبسطها من قبل الأسقف والذي يعد قائدا إقليميا هاما للكنسية.

الأعياد.

موسم عيد الفصح، ويأتي في الربيع، وهو أهم وقت في التقويم المسيحي. ففي هذا الوقت يحتفلون بموت المسيح وقيامته. وتُعرف الأيام الأربعين التي تسبق عيد الفصح بالصوم الأربعيني والذي يبدأ بأربعاء الرماد. وفي هذا اليوم يذهب المسيحيون إلى الكنيسة حيث يضع الكاهن صليبا من الرماد على جباههم. والرماد هو تذكرة بأن البشر ليسوا أكثر من رماد مقارنة بالله، وبأننا نعتمد على رحمة الله في خلاصنا. والصوم الأربعيني هو وقت صيام ووقت يتم التخلي فيه عن الكماليات للتحضير لعيد الفصح. ويُعرف اليوم الذي يسبق الصوم الأربعيني بثلاثاء المرافع. وفي العديد من الأماكن، يحتفل الناس في هذا اليوم بإقامة المهرجانات وتناول وجبات معينة لن يكون بمقدورهم تناولها خلال فترة الصوم. أما الأسبوع الذي يسبق عيد الفصح فيسمى أسبوع الآلام. ويبدأ هذا الأسبوع بأحد الشعانين والذي يحيي ذكرى اليوم الذي وصل فيه المسيح إلى القدس حيث خرج الناس لتحيته ملوحين بسعف النخل. وفي بعض الكنائس، يُوزّع سعف النخل على المتعبدين في هذا اليوم. أما خميس الفصح فهو إحياء لذكرى العشاء الأخير، وهي وليمة الفصح التي تناولها المسيح وتلاميذه في الليلة التي سبقت وفاته. أما جمعة الآلام فتحيي ذكرى موت المسيح على الصليب. وعيد الفصح، العيد الأهم عند المسيحيين، فيحيي ذكرى قيامة المسيح من قبره بعد ثلاثة أيام من موته. وفي عيد الفصح يُزيّن المسيحيون البيض كرمز على تجدد الحياة.

أما عيد الميلاد المسيحي فيحتفل بذكرى مولد المسيح. وتُعرف الأسابيع الأربعة التي تسبق يوم الميلاد، والذي يوافق 25 كانون الأول/ديسمبر، بأيام الأحد الأربعة السابقة للميلاد. وهذا وقت لأداء صلوات ذات طابع خاص تحضيرا لعيد الميلاد. وغالبا ما يضع الأطفال تقويما بأيام الأحد الأربعة هذه ليحسبوا الأيام المتبقية لحلول هذا العيد الكبير. وهناك أكاليل أيام الأحد الأربعة السابقة لعيد الميلاد يوضع عليها أربع شموع، شمعة لكل يوم أحد من الأيام الأربعة هذه التي تسبق عيد الميلاد. وتقيم العديد من الكنائس احتفالات لعيد الميلاد يرتدي فيها الأطفال ملابس لتمثيل قصة عيد الميلاد. وحسب ما يرويه الإنجيل، فإن مريم ويوسف النجار سافرا إلى بيت لحم لإجراء تعداد سكاني ولكنهما لم يجدا غرفة ينزلان بها. وهكذا فقد باتوا الليلة في اسطبل حيث وُلد المسيح ووُضع

في مذود. ولدى العديد من الكنائس لوحات تجسد واقعة ميلاد المسيح وتُظهر المسيح ومريم ويوسف في الاسطبل والحيوانات والرعاة ينظرون إليه. أما عيد الغطاس، وهو اليوم السادس من كانون الثاني/يناير، فهو نهاية موسم عيد الميلاد. وفي هذا اليوم يستذكر المسيحيون زيارة الملوك الثلاثة الذين أحضروا للمسيح وهو رضيع هدايا من الذهب، والبخور، والمر. وزيارتهم هذه تُظهر بأن المسيح جاء مخلصا للعالم بأسره وليس لليهود فحسب.

المسيحية حول العالم.

هناك ما يقرب 2 مليار مسيحي في العالم. ينتمي نصفهم تقريبا إلى الكنيسة الكاثوليكية والتي يرأسها البابا. يؤمن الكاثوليك بأن البابا هو الوريث المباشر لتلميذ المسيح بطرس والذي يعتبرونه البابا الأول. كما ويؤمنون بأن البابا هو ممثل الله على الأرض وهو معصوم من الخطأ عندما يتحدث في عقيدة الكنيسة. ويقع مقر البابا في روما. ويعيش معظم أتباع الكنيسة الكاثوليكية في أوروبا والقارة الأمريكية. وفي عام 1054 قامت الكنيسة الشرقية ـ والتي تُعرف كذلك بالكنيسة الأورثوذكسية ـ بالانشقاق عن الكنيسة الكاثوليكية. وفي يومنا هذا، هناك 215 مليون تابع للكنيسة الأورثوذكسية تقريبا، يعيش معظمهم في أوروبا الشرقية وروسيا. أما من تبقى من المسيحيين فينتمون إلى الطوائف البروتستانتية التي انشقت عن الكنيسة الكاثوليكية. ومن الأمثلة على هذه الطوائف هناك الكنيسة المعمدانية، والكنيسة الأسقفية، والكنيسة اللوثرية، والكنيسة الكهنوتية.

أمور يجب معرفتها عن الإسلام:

من نسميه الله.

لفظ الجلالة الله هي الكلمة العربية التي تقابل كلمة "God". ويستخدمها كل من العرب المسلمين والمسيحيين على حد سواء. يؤمن المسلمون بأن الله لم يُخلق وهو ليس كمثله شيء. ويؤمن المسلمون كذلك بأن أحد أهم صفات الله هي «وحدانيته». فإن كان الله واحدا ، فمن وجهة نظر المسلمين يستحيل أن يكون هناك آلهة مختلفة أو أنداد، كإله لليهود، وإله للمسيحيين، وإله للمشركين. ويُعتقد بأن لله 99 من الأسماء الحسنى. وهي صفات مذكورة في القرآن ومنها الجبار والخالق والرؤوف والرحيم والمهيمن والودود والصبور والغفار. ومن عادة المسلمين ذكر هذه الأسماء الوصفية باستخدام المسبحة. ولهذه المسبحة مائة خرزة. تمثل تسعة وتسعون منها صفات الله بينما ترمز الخرزة الكبيرة المتبقية إلى الله.

الكتاب المقدس

يُسمى الكتاب المقدس لدى المسلمين القرآن. وهم يؤمنون بأنه كلام الله الذي أوحاه إلى النبي محمد بواسطة الملاك جبريل على مر 22 سنة. كُتب القرآن في بداية الأمر على ما كان متوفرا من المواد، وتم جمعه بشكله النهائي بعد وفاة النبي محمد في سنة 632 للميلاد. ويتكون القرآن من 114 سورة يتألف كل منها من آيات. وتبدأ جميع السور عدا السورة التاسعة بـ "بسم الله الرحمن الرحيم." ويتعلم المسلمون القرآن بلغته الأصلية، وهي اللغة العربية، لأن تلاوته على أنه كلام الله يعد شعيرة تمكّن المسلمين من معرفة الله بشكل رمزي كمجتمع مؤمن. وهذا يمكن تشبيهه بمعرفة المسيحيين الرمزية لله والمتضمَنة في تناول القربان المقدس، والتي يُعرف بها المجتمع المسيحي. وينظر المسلمون إلى القرآن والحديث (مجموعة تعاليم يُعتقد بأنها مستمدة من النبي وأصحابه) كمصدر يسترشدون به في العديد من جوانب الحياة. والقانون الإسلامي المعروف بالشريعة مؤسس في معظمه على القرآن والحديث.

العبادة والصلاة.

يجتمع المسلمون في المساجد يوم الجمعة وقت الظهر لأداء صلاة جماعية. ويؤم الإمام جموع المصلين ويخطب فيهم من على منصة ذات درجات تسمى المنبر. والإمام لا يخطب أبدا في الناس من على الدرجة الأخيرة من الأعلى والتي يُحتفظ بها بشكل رمزي للنبي محمد. يُبنى للمساجد برج خاص يسمى المئذنة حيث يقوم شخص يُعرف بالمؤذن بدعوة الناس إلى الصلاة منها خمس مرات في اليوم. وحين يصلي المسلمون يتوجهون نحو مكة، مسقط رأس النبي محمد. ويُشار إلى هذا الاتجاه بواسطة فجوة في جدار المسجد من الداخل تسمى المحراب والذي يشكل النقطة المركزية لقاعة الصلاة. ولا تحتوي قاعة الصلاة على مقاعد لأن الصلاة تشتمل على الوقوف والركوع والسجود. وتنتهي جميع الصلوات بالصلاة على النبي محمد وتابعيه وعلى آل إبراهيم. وتوجد في بعض المساجد شرفات منفصلة للنساء إلا أنه وفي أقدس مساجد المسلمين وهو المسجد الحرام بمكة، تصلي النساء والرجال في نفس القاعة.

ويقوم المسلمون بتطهير أنفسهم قبل أداء الصلاة وذلك بغسل وجوههم وأفواههم وأنوفهم وأيديهم حتى المرافق وأرجلهم حتى الكعبين. وللمحافظة على نظافة المكان، يُطلب من المصلين خلع أحذيتهم قبل الدخول إلى المسجد، كما ويستخدم الكثير من المسلمين سجاجيد للصلاة، وبعض أنواع هذه السجاجيد مثبت عليها بوصلة تشير إلى اتجاه القبلة. والمساجد في العادة مبان ذات قباب وأعمدة وأقواس تزخرفها الخطوط والأشكال الهندسية التجريدية. وتُبقى المساجد بسيطة من الداخل حتى لا تشتت انتباه المصلين. ويشتهر كل من الجامع الأزرق في اسطنبول والمسجد الجامع بقرطبة في إسبانيا بطرازهما المعماري. ومن بين أهم المساجد لدى المسلمين مسجد قبة الصخرة والمسجد الأقصى بمدينة القدس. وتُعرف ساحتهما بالحرم القدسي الشريف والذي يرتبط لدى المسلمين بذكرى إسراء النبي محمد ومعراجه. ويعتقد المسلمون أيضا بأن حشر البشر يوم القيامة سوف يتم في هذا المكان.

الشعائر الدينية

تشكل الشعائر الدينية الأهم في الإسلام مجتمعة ما يعرف بأركان الإسلام الخمس. الشهادة هي أول وأهم شعيرة. وهي تصريح بسيط بأن «لا إله إلا الله وأن محمدا رسول الله.» وتعد هذه الكلمات مجاهرة بالإيمان وتشكل الأساس لاعتناق الإسلام. فالشخص الذي يلقي الشهادة بإخلاص يُعتبر مسلما من غير الحاجة لشعيرة أخرى.

الصلاة ، وهي تُؤدى خمس مرات في اليوم في أوقات محددة يستقبل المصلون فيها وجهة مكة. ويعلم الناس بحلول وقت الصلاة من أذان المؤذن الذي يعتلي المئذنة. وتنتهي جميع الصلوات بأداء التحية والصلاة على النبي محمد وتابعيه وعلى آل إبراهيم ومن بينهم موسى وعيسى. ويوم الجمعة هو اليوم الذي يصلي فيه المسلمون جماعة في المسجد. وكنتيجة لذلك، فإن عطلة نهاية الأسبوع في البلاد الإسلامية تكون إما الخميس والجمعة أو الجمعة والسبت.

الزكاة ، وهي دفع الأموال لمساعدة الفقراء. فيُفترض أن يدفع المسلمون القادرون ماديا ما مقداره 2.5 بالمائة من مجموع رؤوس أموالهم لتُصرف في أوجهها الشرعية.

الصوم ، وهو صوم شهر رمضان. فالمسلمون يمتنعون عن الطعام والشراب من الفجر حتى الغسق طوال هذا الشهر المبارك. والقصد من وراء هذا الصوم هو جعل الناس يحسون بما يحس به الفقراء منهم والذين يكونون في الغالب جوعى وعطشى. والمسلمون البالغون والأصحاء فقط هم من يُفترض منهم الصوم. ومع أن شهر رمضان هو وقت للتفكر وتهذيب النفس، إلا أنه أصبح وقتا لتجمع العائلة والأصدقاء وتناول الأطباق الشهية والحلويات التقليدية. وقد يزين المسلمون منازلهم بواسطة أشكال على هيئة هلال ونجمة وهو الشكل الذي أصبح يرمز إلى الإسلام. وغالبا ما تمتد جلسات العائلة والأصدقاء إلى وقت متأخر من الليل حيث تنتهي بتناول وجبة قبل طلوع الفجر تُسمى السحور.

الحج ، وهو الحج إلى مكة، ويُفترض أداؤه مرة واحدة على الأقل في حياة المسلم. ويؤدي المسلمون شعائر وصلوات معينة حول الكعبة وهي حجر أسود ذو شكل مكعب يُعتقد بأنها أول بيت لله على الأرض أعاد إبراهيم وإسماعيل بناءه، وهي البقعة التي كاد أن يضحي إبراهيم بولده إسماعيل. ويقوم حوالي مليونا مسلم

بتأدية الحج كل عام. ويلبس الحجاج ملابس بيضاء غير مخيطة وذلك حتى لا يكون هناك تطريز أو قماش يميز عابدا عن آخر. وهذه علامة على المساواة أمام الله.

الأعياد

تقع أعياد المسلمين استنادا إلى التقويم الهجري والذي يتكون من 12 شهرا يبدأ كل منها بظهور الهلال وينتهي بظهور هلال الشهر الذي يليه. تبدأ السنة الهجرية في يوم الهجرة، والذي يعيد للأذهان هجرة محمد من مكة إلى المدينة في سنة 622 للميلاد. فسنة 2006 للميلاد توافق سنة 1427 للهجرة في التقويم الهجري.

يوم عاشوراء ويحتفل به في اليوم العاشر من الشهر الهجري الأول. وبالنسبة للكثير من المسلمين، يذكرهم هذا اليوم بأحداث مهمة كاستقرار سفينة نوح وميلاد النبي إبراهيم وبناء الكعبة. أما بالنسبة للمسلمين الشيعة، فهو يوم يحمل أسى حيث يحيي ذكرى استشهاد الحسين حفيد النبي محمد في معركة كربلاء التي وقعت في القرن الهجري الأول. ويتم إحياء هذه الذكرى في المجتمعات الشيعية بإعادة تجسيد هذه الأحداث، ويعد هذا اليوم وقتا للحداد والحزن.

المولد النبوي وهو يوم ميلاد النبي، ويصادف يوم الثاني عشر من الشهر الثالث في التقويم الهجري. ويتم الاحتفال به في بعض البلدان الإسلامية بإقامة مهرجانات كبيرة.

ليلة المعراج ويكون الاحتفال بها في اليوم السابع والعشرين من الشهر السابع وهي تحيي ذكرى رحلة النبي من مكة إلى القدس وعروجه إلى السموات السبع.

ليلة البراءة وتصادف يوم الخامس عشر من الشهر الثامن. وفي هذه الليلة تحلّ المغفرة على التائبين. وهي مناسبة للناس ليصفحوا عن بعضهم ويسوّوا خلافاتهم. ويقضي الكثير من المسلمين الليلة في الصلاة.

رمضان وهو الشهر التاسع والأكثر قداسة في التقويم الهجري. يصوم البالغون والأصحاء من المسلمين من الفجر حتى الغسق كي يحسوا بما يعانيه الفقراء والذين يغدون في الغالب جوعى وعطشى. ومع أن شهر رمضان هو وقت للتفكر وتهذيب النفس يكسب فيه الناس رضوانا ومغفرة من الله، إلا أنه أصبح كذلك وقتا تجتمع فيه العائلة والأصدقاء لتناول أطباق معينة والتسامر لوقت متأخر في الليل.

ليلة القدر وهي الليلة الأولى التي نزل بها الوحي على النبي، وعادة ما تصادف يوم السابع والعشرين من الشهر التاسع، والذي يعرف بشهر رمضان. ويُقال بأنها تساوي ألف شهر، وبأن صلوات وأدعية المسلمين المخلصين مستجابة فيها. ويذهب معظم المسلمين إلى المساجد لإقامة هذه الليلة بالصلاة.

عيد الفطر وهو العيد الذي يُحتفل به بنهاية شهر رمضان. ويتم فيه تحضير العديد من المأكولات بينما تجتمع العائلة والأصدقاء على مائدة الطعام للاحتفال بهذه المناسبة. والتحية المستخدمة في هذه المناسبة هي "عيد مبارك". ويلبس الأطفال أجمل ثيابهم والتي غالبا ما تُشترى لأجل هذه المناسبة، ويتبادل الناس الهدايا ويعمّ الشعور بالسرور.

الحج وهو الحج المفروض إلى مكة ويكون موسمه في الشهر الثاني عشر. يُعرف اليوم التاسع من الحج بيوم عرفات حيث يقف الحجاج الصائمون أمام الله على جبل عرفات، ويقوم المسلمون في جميع أنحاء العالم بالذهاب إلى مساجدهم من أجل الصلاة والتضامن الروحاني مع الحجاج.

عيد الأضحى وهو يحتفل بذكرى استعداد إبراهيم للتضحية بابنه إسماعيل من أجل الله وبذكرى رحمة

الله في افتداء إسماعيل بكبش. ويصادف هذا العيد نهاية الحج. وكتقليد يقوم المسلمون بالتضحية بذبح ضحية من الماعز أو الضأن ويوزعون ثلث لحمها على الفقراء، ومن ثم يحتفلون بالمناسبة مع عائلاتهم وأصدقائهم.

الإسلام حول العالم

يحتل الإسلام المرتبة الثانية في العالم من ناحية عدد الذين يدينون به فهناك 6.1 مليار مسلم في العالم. وهناك تقريبا شخص مسلم من كل خمسة في العالم. تتواجد الشريحة الأكبر من المسلمين في قارة آسيا حيث تقع إندونيسيا والتي تعد أكبر دولة مسلمة. وتشكل قارة أفريقيا ما مقداره 72 بالمائة تقريبا من مسلمي العالم، بينما يمثل العرب 81 بالمائة. والإسلام هو الدين الأسرع انتشارا في أوروبا وأمريكا الشمالية، وهناك ما يقرب من ستة ملايين مسلم يعيشون في الولايات المتحدة.

يمارس ما نسبته 09 بالمائة من مسلمي العالم تقريبا المذهب السني. أما المذهب الشيعي فيسود في إيران وينتشر في مناطق جنوب العراق ولبنان والبحرين. وقع الشرخ بين السنة والشيعة بسبب خلاف حول من سيخلف النبي محمدا بعد وفاته. فقد أراد الشيعة أن يخلفه أقرب الناس إليه، بينما أراد السنة اختيار الرجل ذي المؤهلات الأنسب. وما عدا ذلك فهناك الشيء القليل الذي يباعد بينهم باستثناء تمجيد الشيعة لأئمتهم، وهم سلسلة متوالية من القادة الذين ينظرون إليهم كسلالة من المعلمين المستلهمين.

أما الصوفية فهي مذهب إسلامي ينطوي على جوانب غامضة يستخدم الموسيقى والترانيم والرقص وتمارين التنفس من أجل الوصول إلى حالة روحانية.